MW01053103

"*The Woman* reveals the profoun
mystery of salvation. It also reve
of Venerable Fulton Sheen. But
strates, and imitates, the missionary hearts of the Blessed Virgin
Mary and of Archbishop Sheen. In this book, their hearts, formed
for the salvation of souls, speak to ours. *The Woman* is a wonderful
resource for Mariology in the era of the New Evangelization."

   - Most Rev. James D. Conley
     Bishop of the Diocese of Lincoln, Nebraska

"We tend to think of Archbishop Sheen as the appealing television preacher, the best-selling writer, the Catholic celebrity with
ecumenical appeal. Of his greatness there is no question. But we
have overlooked the amazing depth of his spiritual and theological
insight. Peter Howard takes us there in a way that will come as a
surprise to many: through Sheen's writings on the figure in whom
all the Church's sublime mystics converge: the Mother of God."

   - Dale Ahlquist
     President and Founder of the American Chesterton Society

"*The Woman* is an extraordinary work that more fully opened my
eyes to the gift that Fulton Sheen is to the Church and to the depth
of insight available to us through reflection on Mary's participation in our redemption. Dr. Howard has provided both a scholarly
and accessible treatment that will draw the reader's heart ever more
deeply into the heart of the Church.

   - Dan Burke
     *President and Founder of the Avila Institute for Spiritual
     Formation and Executive Director of EWTN's National
     Catholic Register*

The Woman

THE MYSTERY OF MARY AS MEDIATRIX
IN THE TEACHING OF FULTON J. SHEEN

"He told me that I had written and spoken well of the Lord Jesus, and that I was a loyal son of the Church." (Pope St. John Paul II embracing Archbishop Fulton Sheen, 2 October 1979, two months before Sheen's death, St. Patrick's Cathedral, New York.)

The Woman

THE MYSTERY OF MARY AS MEDIATRIX
IN THE TEACHING OF FULTON J. SHEEN

PETER J. HOWARD, S.T.D.

LEONINE PUBLISHERS
PHOENIX, ARIZONA

NIHIL OBSTAT
Mr. David Uebbing, M.A.
Censor Librorum

IMPRIMATUR
✠ Most Reverend Samuel J. Aquila, S.T.L.
Archbishop of Denver
Denver, Colorado USA
November 13, 2014

The Imprimatur ("Permission to Publish") is a declaration that a book is considered to be free of doctrinal or moral error. It does not imply that those who have granted the Imprimatur agree with the contents, opinions or statements expressed by the author.

The Scripture citations used in this work are taken from *The Holy Bible: Revised Standard Version*, Catholic Edition (San Francisco: Ignatius Press, publ. May, 1994; copyright © 1966).

Photographs courtesy of The Archbishop Fulton J. Sheen Archives, Catholic Diocese of Rochester, Rochester, New York. Used with permission.

Cover image, "The Annunciation," by Girolamo Lucenti da Correggio, c. 1615, State Hermitage Museum, Saint Petersburg, Russia.

Published by Leonine Publishers LLC
Phoenix, Arizona
USA

ISBN-13: 978-1-942190-06-6
Library of Congress Control Number: 2014956406

Printed in the United States of America
10 9 8 7 6 5 4 3 2 1

Visit us online at www.leoninepublishers.com
For more information: info@leoninepublishers.com

ACKNOWLEDGMENTS

I am indebted to many whose material and spiritual assistance have greatly contributed to the successful completion of this work. First, I wish to thank my beloved wife, Chantal. Pursuing a doctorate with a growing family posed many challenges for her—my annual trips to Rome for almost two months at a time as well as the many nights and weekends she sacrificed so that I could work uninterruptedly on my dissertation. Throughout these challenges she always was understanding and never ceased to encourage me to do what was necessary to successfully complete this dissertation.

I also wish to extend a special word of gratitude to Monsignor Arthur Calkins, whose generous assistance, encouragement and prayers throughout my licentiate and doctorate studies in Rome were of inestimable value. During those years, he selflessly shared his extensive personal library of scholarly work compiling the Marian papal magisterium of the past three centuries. This material provided important historical and theological context to both my licentiate and doctorate theses, and for this I am most grateful. His personal dedication and commitment to living as a true servant of Mary is a great inspiration to me.

This work would not have been possible without the equally generous assistance of Sr. Connie Derby, RSM, director of the Fulton Sheen Archives in Rochester, New York. Sr. Connie went out of her way to help accommodate my needs in gaining access to Fulton Sheen's unpublished works located in the Sheen Archives. In addition, I wish to thank my brother, Bill, who generously gave of his time and editorial finesse, which greatly enhanced my work. Also, I give thanks to Dr. Michael Woodward, director of the

Cardinal Stafford Library in Denver, who was willing to assist me with my research whenever I called upon him.

There have been many who have faithfully supported this work through their prayers whom I wish to acknowledge, beginning with my parents and family. Fulton Sheen always sought the prayers of the suffering because he knew how powerful such prayers are as they are united to the Cross. In that light, I especially thank my loving and generous parents who selflessly offered up many prayers united with sacrifices for the successful completion of this work. I have no doubt that my devotion to Our Blessed Mother would not be what it is today without the example and efforts of my mother, who introduced Mary into my life, and my father's patient offering of his sufferings for the light of faith to take root in all of his children (which it indeed has). I especially dedicate this work to my father whom our heavenly Father called home not too long ago.

Lastly, I am most grateful for the direction of Father Robert Christian, O.P., throughout my doctoral studies. His openness, encouragement and patience to work with me under exceptional circumstances made this study possible. In addition, his high academic standards and expectations challenged me to greater intellectual heights from which I have benefited immensely and for which I am grateful.

I pray that Our Blessed Mother, Mary Immaculate, and her servant Fulton Sheen are pleased with this work. I entrust it entirely to her maternal care with the hope that she will use it to deepen the understanding of its readers concerning her central role as Mediatrix in salvation history. Like Fulton Sheen, may this knowledge move our hearts to a more perfect and true devotion to the Mother of Jesus Christ and His Mystical Body that leads to a more perfect knowledge of and love for the Most Holy Trinity.

21 November 2014
Presentation of the Blessed Virgin Mary

Peter Howard

CONTENTS

CHAPTER II
THE RELEVANCE OF VENERABLE FULTON J. SHEEN AND HIS THEOLOGICAL APPROACH TO MARY'S MEDIATION

CHAPTER III
Mary's Mediation in the Mystery
of the Incarnation

CHAPTER IV

MARY AS MATERNAL MEDIATRIX IN THE MYSTICAL PROLONGATION OF THE INCARNATION

APPENDIX
"Status Quaestionis" of the Church's Teaching on Mary's Mediation

ABBREVIATIONS

AAS   *Acta Apostolicæ Sedis (1909 –).*

Acta   *Acta Synodalia Sacrosancti Concilii Oecu-*
                menici Vaticani Secundi (Typis Polyglottis
                Vaticanis, 1971).

ASS   *Acta Sanctæ Sedis (1865-1908).*

CCC   *Catechism of the Catholic Church: Second*
                Edition (United States Catholic Conference,
                Inc.—Libreria Editrice Vaticana, 1997).

Daybook   *George H. Tavard, Council Daybook, Session*
                3 (Washington D.C.: National Catholic Wel-
                fare Conference, 1965).

Flannery   *Austin Flannery, O.P., ed., Vatican Council*
                II: The Conciliar and Post Conciliar Docu-
                ments (Collegeville, Minn.: Liturgical Press,
                1975).

LG   *Dogmatic Constitution on the Church,*
                Lumen Gentium.

MC   *Marialis Cultus.*

MD	*Mulieris Dignitatem.*
OL	*Our Lady: Papal Teachings, trans. Daughters of St. Paul (Boston: St. Paul Editions, 1961).*
OR	*L'Osservatore Romano, daily Italian edition.*
ORE	*L'Osservatore Romano, weekly edition in English.*
PG	*J.P. Migne, Patrologia, series graeca, 161 voll., Paris 1875ss.*
PL	*J.P. Migne, Patrologia, series latina, 217 voll., Paris 1875ss.*
RM	*Redemptoris Mater.*
ST	*St. Thomas Aquinas, Summa Theologiae.*
Theotokos	*Michael O'Carroll, C.S.Sp., Theotokos: A Theological Encyclopedia of the Blessed Virgin Mary (Wilmington: Michael Glazier, 1982).*

Works of Fulton Sheen

INTRODUCTION

I t was a hidden stroke of providence when I was first introduced to the works of Archbishop Fulton Sheen in 1998 and encouraged to listen to tape recordings of a retreat he gave for seminarians in 1972. I had no idea that God would use this servant of His to leave such an enduring impact on my intellectual and spiritual life. Like many others who have listened to his captivating and moving preaching, I felt as if I had found, in the fullest sense of the term, a spiritual father. His ability to make the deepest and seemingly complex truths of our Catholic faith easily intelligible and come alive became an inspiration for me to see and treat theology as a living science and thus one to which all can personally relate.

When Fulton Sheen's cause for canonization was formally accepted by the Holy See in 2002, coinciding with my discernment of a topic for my doctorate dissertation, I immediately knew that this was a unique opportunity to bring his significant theological contributions to the forefront of contemporary theological reflection. In particular I desired to expose the heart of his Mariological teaching, the role of the Blessed Virgin Mary in the history of salvation according to her role as Mediatrix (a title the Church has given her which sums up all aspects of Mary's unique mediatory role throughout salvation history).

Mary as Mediatrix has been in the forefront of the Church's reflection for at least a century, as we will see explained later in this work. Why? First, it naturally corresponds with the greatest Marian age in the Church's history of the last two hundred years. God is sending Mary to His people with urgent messages for the whole world in an unprecedented manner. In the midst of these revelations are accents of truths that focus our attention on *who* Mary is and *what* her role is in Redemption. She is visiting the world in the midst of a rapidly escalating cosmic confrontation between the Kingdom of Christ and the kingdom of anti-Christ. Sacred Scripture reveals at the heart of this cosmic war for souls is "the woman" (Gen. 3:15; Rev. 12). Mary is historically and theologically *in the middle* of God's salvific plan. It is not an overstatement, therefore, to describe Mary's place in salvation history truly as a "mystery"—a mystery of which the Church is receiving new insights by the grace of the Holy Spirit in our times.

This leads to a second point. The Holy Spirit always guides the *mens Ecclesiae* (the "mind of the Church") and the *sensus fidelii* (the "sense of the faithful"). And the Holy Spirit is putting the spotlight on the importance of understanding the person and role of His inseparable spouse in the world. We see this in the Church's declaration of two of the four Marian dogmas within a century and the current push for the fifth and final dogma of Mary that would define her role and title of "Mediatrix of All Graces." Unlike the first four dogmas, which concentrated on who Mary is as she relates to God, this fifth and final dogma would answer the important question, "How does Mary relate to all mankind, especially Christians?" Great Marian theologians of the twentieth century such as Cardinal Desiree Mercier, Reginald Garrigou-Lagrange, O.P., and St. Maximilian Maria Kolbe all agreed that the time was ripe for Mary as "Mediatrix of All Graces" to be solemnly defined as a dogma of the Catholic faith. Venerable Fulton J. Sheen also joined his voice to theirs when he said:

> One wonders if [the dogma of the Assumption] could not be the last of the great truths of Mary to be defined by the Church. Anything else might seem to be an anticlimax after she is declared to be in Heaven, body and soul. But actually there is one other truth left to be defined, and that is that she is the Mediatrix, under her Son, of all graces.[1]

---

[1] Fulton J. Sheen, *The World's First Love* (New York: McGraw-Hill Book Company, 1952; reprint, San Francisco: Ignatius Press, 1996), 141 (hereafter cited as *WFL*).

Lastly, the Church's doctrine of Mary as Mediatrix of all graces has significant implications for the spiritual life of the Christian. It is this doctrine alone that provides the theological foundation for the rapidly growing devotion of total consecration to Mary (which is also described as total consecration *to Jesus through Mary* [*ad Iesum per Mariam*]). This is a spiritual act that has been directly requested by the Blessed Virgin in her most notable visitations of the twentieth century, especially at Fatima where she called for the consecration of Russia to her Immaculate Heart. And the figure that put this devotion at the forefront of the Church's attention as it entered the third millennium was Pope St. John Paul II, who took for his papal motto "*Totus Tuus*" from the act of total consecration to Mary of St. Louis de Montfort (1673-1716): "*Totus tuus ego sum, et omnia mea tua sunt*" ("I am all thine, and all that I have belongs to thee"). This entire spirituality hinges on the truth that Mary, indeed, *is* the Mediatrix of all graces, all of which have their source in Jesus Christ.

I am, however, also keenly aware that Mary's mediation is the most contentiously debated subject in contemporary Mariology because of its undeniable implications for Christology, pneumatology, ecclesiology, spiritual theology and ecumenism. It is precisely because Mary's mediation plays a central role in each of these areas that I wanted to embark on this in-depth study of Fulton Sheen's Mariology; for I knew that Mary's mediation was at the heart of Sheen's Mariology, even though he often did not use the term "mediation" to express this doctrine. Sheen's tendency was to express the truth about Jesus Christ and His Mother in a manner to which we could *relate* since he understood Catholic theology as a living and personal truth.

In addition, it is undeniable that Sheen's teaching, either through his lectures or copious writings, was known for bringing an extraordinary clarity to seemingly complex theological topics. Therefore, in light of the opening of his cause for canonization and the contentious atmosphere surrounding the subject of Mary's mediation, it is opportune for a study such as this to offer the theological contributions of this Venerable Servant of God, deeply devoted to the Blessed Virgin, as they relate to Mary's mediation. It is the hope of this writer that Sheen's gift of successfully communicating the truths of the Catholic faith to peoples of all faiths will be equally applicable to his teaching on Mary's mediation.

While a study such as this, indeed, was an exciting endeavor, it posed a significant challenge. Fulton Sheen wrote few works that legitimately can be called theological treatises. That is because Sheen's audiences primarily were outside the academic classroom and found in the pews of churches, in retreats and on the receiving end of radios and televisions. While Sheen truly possessed a brilliant theological intellect, his real genius was his ability to make theological truths accessible to peoples of all faiths without them knowing that he was using the teaching of St. Thomas Aquinas or other theological fonts. Therefore, the great challenge of this study was constructing a systematic theology of Mary's mediation from the numerous sources of Sheen's teaching which were most often presented according to his customary preaching style.

This work accomplished this challenge by dividing the study into four chapters followed by a Conclusion and Appendix which follow an interior logic. The original arrangement of this work—in the form of a doctoral thesis—contained five chapters. What is now the Appendix in this work was originally Chapter II. The Appendix provides a helpful scrutiny of the historical and theological context pertaining to the contemporary debate surrounding Mary's mediation in which Sheen's teaching on the subject will have a positive, and perhaps resolving, contribution. However, since this work is intended not only for advanced students and teachers of theology, but also for those who simply have an interest in learning more about this important doctrine of Our Blessed Mother, the *status quaestionis* (the state of the question) of Mary's mediation within the present theological debate was moved to the Appendix. Thus, this new arrangement facilitates the flow of content, connecting more directly the person of Venerable Fulton Sheen to his teaching on Mary's mediation.

Chapter I serves as a necessary introduction to Archbishop Sheen to familiarize the reader with the extraordinary intellect and piety that left a lasting mark on the minds and hearts of millions of people around the world. In other words, it answers the question, "Why should we listen to Fulton Sheen?" The first chapter summarizes Sheen's intellectual capacity in philosophy and theology as well as his pastoral achievements to make the case that any study of his insightful teachings is a worthy endeavor. There are many teachings of Sheen which are undiscovered treasures that will greatly enrich the intellectual and spiritual life of the Church. This study will hopefully expose one of the greatest gems of this treasury.

Chapters II and III make up the main corpus of Sheen's theology of Mary's mediation, both of which compose an organic unity. Chapter IV presents Sheen's practical application of his theology of Mary's mediation in the modern world. It answers the question: "How do we understand Mary's activity in our extraordinary age?" Lastly, the Conclusion will summarize the many theological contributions Sheen's teaching brings to the contemporary debate on Mary's mediation.

It is a great privilege to be among the first who will introduce the profound theological contributions of this inspiring Servant of God. This book represents the first in-depth and systematic study into the heart of Sheen's Mariology, Mary's role in salvation history as Mediatrix. As such, it provides two significant contributions. The first is exposing the genius of Sheen's theological insights as they relate to Mary's mediation with the hope that they will provide a theological formula that will not only unite both sides of the theological debate on the issue, but also further advance the unity of all Christians and all peoples. Secondly, by exposing the significant theological contributions of Sheen's Mariology, it is the hope of this writer that the Church will see fit to further advance the cause of canonization of this extraordinary and now Venerable Servant of God and of Mary.

CHAPTER I

VENERABLE FULTON J. SHEEN

INTRODUCTION

The Catholic Church of the twentieth century witnessed the passing of many memorable figures, some of whom are already proclaimed saints. Others are on their way to canonization. In 1999, a poll was conducted by the Internet *Catholic Daily* to determine the top 100 Catholics of the twentieth century. There were 23,455 respondents.[1] The top three were no surprise to most: Pope St. John Paul II ranked first, Blessed Mother Teresa second, and St. Padre Pio third. The person who ranked fourth would be a surprise to those who did not know him, namely, Archbishop Fulton J. Sheen. Father Andrew Apostoli, C.F.R., the first priest to be ordained by Fulton Sheen after the Second Vatican Council, narrated a series on Fulton Sheen in 2003, whom he called "a prophet for our times." When referring to this survey he stated his positive amazement that Sheen was chosen even above the great popes of the twentieth century—even over many great saints of the twentieth century." Father Apostoli was correct when he commented that Sheen's rank in this survey "reflects the deep esteem and love the Catholic people had for Fulton Sheen."[2]

---

[1] Cf. Thomas Reeves, *America's Bishop: The Life and Times of Fulton J. Sheen* (San Francisco: Encounter Books, 2001), 1.

[2] Andrew Apostoli, C.F.R., *Archbishop Fulton J. Sheen: A Prophet for Our Times* (West Covina, CA: St. Joseph Communications, 2004), compact disc.

Those who wrote on the life of Fulton Sheen were not reserved in their acclaim of his impact on the world. At the time of Sheen's debut into the television medium in 1953, one author considered Sheen "the most influential voice in Christendom next to that of Pope Pius XII—and easily the most hypnotic since that of Peter the Hermit...."[3] The same author shortly after called Sheen the "twentieth century Chrysostom."[4] D.P. Noonan, Sheen's special assistant during most of his time as National Director of the Society for the Propagation of the Faith, referred to him in 1972 as "the best-known churchman in the world."[5] Sheen was known around the world as a brilliant thinker and communicator, and his lasting impact on the American church of the twentieth century is indisputable. A close friend of Fulton Sheen referred to him then as "the greatest orator of our time."[6]

On September 14, 2002, the Congregation for the Causes of Saints gave permission to Peoria Bishop Daniel R. Jenky, C.S.C., to open the cause of canonization for Archbishop Fulton J. Sheen (1895–1979), who was born, raised and later ordained a priest to serve in that diocese. Archbishop Sheen, therefore, is now referred to as a "Venerable." Should Fulton Sheen be canonized, he would become the first American-born male saint. It is, therefore, important that the Church give special attention to this Venerable Servant of God to understand how indelible a contribution his life and teaching was to the Church of the twentieth century and still is.

Now that Archbishop Sheen's cause is officially underway, it is time for the Church to discover Sheen "the theologian," as the investigation of his published and unpublished works (sermons, retreat lectures, et. al.) has now only just begun. As the great theologian, Melchior Cano, explained in his renowned work *De Locis Theologicis*, the writings of saints have always served as a *locus theo-*

---

[3] James C.G. Conniff, *The Bishop Sheen Story* (New York: Fawcett Publications, 1953), 1.
[4] Ibid., 2.
[5] D.P. Noonan, *The Passion of Fulton Sheen* (New York: Dodd, Mead & Company, 1972), 2.
[6] Ibid., 56.

logicus for the Church[7]. It is, therefore, opportune to give special consideration to those of Archbishop Fulton Sheen, considered "the most popular and influential American Catholic of the twentieth century" by at least one of his biographers,[8] and whose cause may bring him, too, to the altars.

It is important to know Fulton Sheen the man as much as it is to know his teachings. Saints are not canonized only for their theological contributions, but also (and primarily) because of their heroic virtue. The purpose of this chapter, therefore, is to provide insight into the life of this extraordinary man who fully lived out his vocation as a priest and victim of Christ. One will better understand Sheen's teachings when he understands the historical and personal context from which they came. It is important to know, for example, that Sheen's teachings arose not only out of assiduous study, but also out of deep contemplative prayer. Sheen's faith was deeply personal, not just intellectual. His extraordinary intellectual gifts, his passion for souls and love of truth made Fulton Sheen a perfect instrument to provide a fully Christian response to the many challenges of the twentieth century—challenges which have by no means left the Church, thus making the teachings of Fulton Sheen relevant in our own troubled times.

ONE OF THE GREATEST EVANGELIZERS OF THE TWENTIETH CENTURY

Fulton Sheen was one of the greatest evangelizers of his time. He was "the voice of the Catholic Church in the United States for over 30 years," hosting radio and television programs at the service of the Gospel which had an audience of over thirty million.[9] Sheen left such a mark on the Church in the United States that he has been invoked as "the greatest preacher and teacher…the most

---

[7] Cf. Melchior Cano, O.P., *Opera Theologica—Nova editio emendatissima* (Paris: Amabilem Auroy, 1704), 3, 287-311.

[8] Cf. Kathleen L. Riley, *Fulton Sheen: An American Catholic Response to the Twentieth Century* (New York: Alba House, 2004), xv.

[9] Apostoli, *Archbishop Fulton J. Sheen: A Prophet for Our Times*, compact disc.

popular, recognized and influential priest…the Catholic Church
in the United States has ever known."[10] Archbishop John Foley,
former head of the Pontifical Commission for Social Communications, praised Sheen for his ability to represent the Catholic faith
"with the intellectual clarity and eloquence of speech which the
true faith demanded," adding "no one figure in the history of the
United States…touched as many lives as did Archbishop Sheen."[11]

What characterizes Fulton Sheen above everything else are the
two pillars upon which his heroic dedication to evangelization was
built: his unfailing love for Jesus in the Blessed Sacrament and his
deep, filial devotion to His Blessed Mother. From this love of Jesus
and His Mother flowed his burning zeal to use every gift and talent
to bring Jesus and His Mother to everyone in the world; and to
bring the world to them. The instrument through which Sheen
was able to do this most effectively was what he called his "priest-
victimhood."[12] Sheen put his brilliant intellect, his tireless work
ethic and his love for souls at the service of the Gospel. Through his
priest-victimhood, he found he was able to especially identify with
the poor and suffering of the world. He preached Christ crucified and identified himself with the victim side of Jesus which had
the power to draw the entire world to Himself. Through Sheen's
extraordinary intellect, preaching and teaching, supported by his
deep devotion to the Blessed Sacrament and the Mother of Christ,
Sheen left a lasting mark on the world and became "a prophet for
our times."[13]

Fulton Sheen took very seriously Jesus' command to His apostles: "Go, therefore, and make disciples of all nations, baptizing

[10] Monsignor Timothy Dolan, "Archbishop Fulton J. Sheen, 1895-1995,"
(1995), 9-17, quoted in Kathleen L. Riley, *Fulton Sheen: An American Catholic
Response to the Twentieth Century*, xi.

[11] Archbishop John P. Foley, "Archbishop Fulton J. Sheen, 1895-1995,"
(1995), 12-13, quoted in Kathleen L. Riley, *Fulton Sheen: An American Catholic Response to the Twentieth Century*, xi.

[12] Fulton J. Sheen, *Treasure in Clay* (New York: Doubleday & Company,
1980), 22, 38 (hereafter cited as *TIC*).

[13] This became the title of a video series on the Eternal Word Television Net-
work hosted by Father Andrew Apostoli, C.F.R., in 2003.

them in the name of the Father and of the Son and of the Holy Spirit, teaching them to observe all that I have commanded you."[14] He literally carried out this commission.[15] The source of strength behind Sheen's heroic dedication to carrying out Christ's command was Jesus' final words before He ascended: "Behold, I am with you all days, even unto the consummation of the world."[16]

BACKGROUND

A trait common to almost every saint is the spiritual foundation they received from their families. Fulton Sheen was no exception. Born on May 8, 1895, in El Paso, Illinois, Fulton was baptized Peter, but during his early years of childhood, he took the name of Fulton after his mother's maiden name. Despite their very limited educations, Fulton's parents were determined to give each of their children the best education they could provide. This caused the Sheen family to move from El Paso to Peoria, Illinois, where there were strong Catholic schools. It was there that young Fulton became an altar boy at age eight and attended St. Mary's parochial school and then Spalding Institute, a Catholic secondary school named after the bishop of that time, John L. Spalding.

Throughout his childhood, Fulton had instilled in him an extraordinary work ethic that remained throughout the rest of his life. In his autobiography Sheen wrote: "Without expressing it in so many words, I was brought up on the ethic of work....Not only because it was parental training but perhaps because it was already ingrained in me, the habit of work was one I never got over, and I thank God I never did."[17] The truth of this statement is evident in Sheen's daily work schedule after he was ordained, which consisted of 19-hour days, seven days a week.[18]

---

[14] Mt. 28:19-20

[15] Cf. *TIC*, 107.

[16] Mt. 28:20

[17] *TIC*, 19-20.

[18] Apostoli, *Archbishop Fulton J. Sheen: A Prophet for Our Times*, compact disc.

One interesting occurrence during Fulton's days in elementary school occurred while he was serving Mass as an altar boy for whom he referred to as "the great Bishop John J. Spalding."[19] During the Mass, Fulton dropped the wine cruet on the marble floor. Sheen later recounted in his autobiography: "There is no atomic explosion that can equal in intensity of decibels the noise and explosive force of a wine cruet falling on a marble floor of a cathedral in the presence of a bishop."[20] After Mass had finished, Bishop Spalding,

When young Fulton graduated from Spalding Institute in 1913, Peoria, Illinois.

overlooking Fulton's embarrassing moment during Mass, asked Fulton where he was going to study after high school. Fulton did not know. Bishop Spalding then made a profound prophecy to Fulton: "Go home and tell your mother that I said when you get big you are to go to Louvain, and someday you will be just as I am."[21] At that time, Fulton had never heard of the University of Louvain and its reputation as one of the greatest universities in the world. Moreover, Sheen had forgotten this prophecy until two years after his ordination, when he had set foot in Louvain for his post-graduate studies in philosophy.[22]

Sheen excelled in his high school studies. He was the valedictorian of his graduating class,[23] and subsequently enrolled at St. Viator's College and Seminary in Bourbonnais, Illinois, which was run by the Viatorian Fathers. It was there that Sheen became very familiar with the works of Shakespeare and where he also learned a lesson that forever changed his approach to public speaking. He learned this from one of the Viatorian priests, Father William J.

---

[19] *TIC*, 10.
[20] *TIC*, 12.
[21] Ibid., 12.
[22] *TIC*, 12.
[23] Ibid., 14.

Bergan, whom Sheen called "one of my greatest inspirations."[24] Father Bergan was Fulton's debate team coach at St. Viator's. On one occasion Father Bergan severely criticized Fulton as being one of the worst speakers he had ever heard.[25] This deeply troubled Sheen and after deeply pondering why Father Bergan made this statement, Sheen realized that the key to being a successful speaker was just to "be natural."[26] This was to become one of Sheen's keys to a successful apostolate of preaching and teaching.

Father Bergan was also instrumental in Fulton's spiritual formation, in particular the practical side of the Catholic faith. In his

Graduation from St. Viator's College,
Bourbonnais, Illinois, c. 1917.

---

[24] Ibid., 14-15.
[25] Riley, *Fulton Sheen: An American Catholic Response to the Twentieth Century*, 3.
[26] Ibid., 3.

autobiography, Sheen recounted what he considered "a turning point" in his life as he finished his collegiate studies at St. Viator's.[27] This encounter with Father Bergan was one of those "few decisive moments" which Sheen believed determine one's course in life.[28] Father Bergan challenged him to make a great step in faith by tearing up a scholarship Sheen had won to attend graduate school in order that Fulton not delay pursuing his priestly vocation. Sheen obeyed Father Bergan's directive, trusting that God would provide the education he sought. This decision ultimately led to the fulfillment of Bishop Spalding's prophecy that Sheen would one day study at the University of Louvain.

Sheen pursued ordination to the priesthood as a seminarian of the Diocese of Peoria, Illinois. He attended St. Paul's Seminary in St. Paul, Minnesota, and was very pleased with his theological formation there. Fulton particularly excelled in Sacred Scripture,

---

[27] The following is Sheen's account of this pivotal point in his life: "The course of life is determined not by the trivial incidents of day to day, but by a few decisive moments…Certainly a turning point in my life happened when I finished college. A national examination was given to college students. The prize was a three-year university scholarship. I took the examination and won one of the scholarships. I was informed sometime during the summer and immediately went up to St. Viator's College to see Father William J. Bergan, by now my dear friend. He was on the tennis court when I arrived. With great glee and delight I announced: 'Father Bergan, I won the scholarship!' He put his hands on my shoulders, looked me straight in the eyes and said: 'Fulton, do you believe in God?' I replied: 'You know that I do.' He said: 'I mean *practically*, not from a theoretical point of view.' This time I was not so sure, and I said: 'Well, I *hope* I do.' 'Then tear up the scholarship.' 'Father Bergan, this scholarship entitles me to three years of university training with all expenses paid. It is worth about nine or ten thousand dollars.' He retorted: 'You know you have a vocation; you should be going to the seminary.' I countered with this proposal: 'I can go to the seminary after I get my Ph.D., because there will be little chance of getting a Ph.D. after I am ordained, and I would like very much to have a good education.' He repeated: 'Tear up the scholarship; go to the seminary. That is what the Lord wants you to do. And if you do it, trusting in Him, you will receive a far better university education after you are ordained than before.' I tore up the scholarship and went to the seminary. I have never regretted that visit and that decision" (*TIC*, 31-32).
[28] *TIC*, 31.

history, and moral theology.[29] Fulton later recounted a profound mystical experience while at the seminary:

> Every afternoon about five-thirty…the spiritual director would give us a conference. I was paying the usual amount of attention this particular day, when suddenly I stopped listening. My mind seemed to be suffused with light. I heard not a word he uttered, but during that experience—I don't know how long it lasted—there came to me an illumination of soul, a light that suffused my intellect, bringing with it an overwhelming conviction of the certitude of the Faith. The Creed and the affirmation "I believe" became not only an intellectual assent: I was momentarily possessed of the absolute and irrefutable character of Faith. As a result of that experience, I never in my life had any doubts about the Faith. My faith centered not just in the Creed, but in the Church, and it became personalized in the Pope as the Head of the Church and the Vicar of Christ.[30]

Fulton Sheen was ordained a priest on September 20, 1919, in St. Mary's Cathedral in Peoria, Illinois.

ACADEMIC ACHIEVEMENTS

The academic achievements of Fulton Sheen were impressive. After he completed his seminary studies in St. Paul, Sheen was sent to Catholic University of America in Washington, D.C., to pursue a doctorate in philosophy.[31] There he obtained Bachelor of Canon Law (J.C.B.) and Licentiate in Sacred Theology (S.T.L.) degrees. After two years of residency, the intellectually ambitious Sheen was not satisfied with his education. He confided his frustration to one of the professors at Catholic University: "I should like to know two things—first, what the modern world is thinking about; second,

---

[29] Reeves, *America's Bishop: The Life and Times of Fulton J. Sheen*, 35.
[30] *TIC*, 229.
[31] *TIC*, 22.

how to answer the errors of modern philosophy in the light of the philosophy of St. Thomas Aquinas." [32] Father Sheen was directed to the University of Louvain where "the professors were the most learned men in Europe at their time."[33]

The University of Louvain offered a unique academic program dedicated to understanding contemporary sciences and the philosophy of St. Thomas Aquinas, led by the renowned Désirée Cardinal Mercier. The purpose of the Institute was exactly what Fulton Sheen was seeking. Sheen excelled in his studies, becoming both a disciple and "devotee" of Cardinal Mercier and Dr. Leon Noel.[34] Fulton obtained a "license in the philosophy of St. Thomas" which served as a means for him to complete his Ph.D. in philosophy in 1923.

Subsequently, Sheen was offered and accepted a special and rare invitation from the faculty of Louvain to take the competitive examination for admission into the teaching staff of the university. In 1925, Sheen successfully passed the examination with its highest grade: "Very Highest Distinction."[35] This earned Fulton

---

[32] Ibid., 23.

[33] Noonan, *The Passion of Fulton Sheen*, 12.

[34] Miles P. Murphy, *The Life and Times of Archbishop Fulton J. Sheen* (New York: Alba House, 2000), 4.

[35] Cf. Murphy, *The Life and Times of Archbishop Fulton J. Sheen*, 4-5. In Fulton Sheen's autobiography, he explains his unique invitation to study for the *agrégé* degree and his experiences during his preparation: "There were several conditions to receiving the honor: one, the university must extend the invitation; second, a book must be written; and third, one had to pass a public examination before professors of other universities. I received an invitation to work for the agrégé. Since it was not necessary to stay at Louvain while one was working for the degree, I went to Rome for a year and entered the Angelicum, now referred to more properly as the University of St Thomas Aquinas, as well as the Jesuit Gregorian University, studying theology. Then I was invited to give a course in theology in the Westminster Seminary of London.

"The time came to take the agrégé examination before the invited professors of other universities. It began at nine o'clock in the morning and went on until five in the afternoon. A board was then selected from the visiting professors to decide on the grade with which one passed. They were always the same as they were for a doctorate: Satisfaction, Distinction, Great Distinction and Very Highest Distinction. That night the university would give a dinner to the

Sheen the post-doctoral degree: *Professeur Agrégé en Philosophie*, which included an invitation to join the teaching staff of the university. Sheen was the first American ever to earn this prestigious degree.[36] According to one biographer of Sheen: "Other than his love for the Blessed Mother, that degree may well have been the one thing Sheen is openly proudest of and inclined to make no bones about."[37]

It was not required that Sheen remain in Louvain while he prepared for the *Agrégé en Philosophie* degree. He, therefore, traveled to Rome for one year where he studied at the Angelicum and Gregorian universities, but did not seek or receive a degree from either institution. While studying at the Angelicum, Sheen "read through every single line that St. Thomas wrote at least once."[38] After Sheen's year in Rome, he was invited to teach a course in dogmatic theology at St. Edmund's College, the seminary of the Archdiocese of Westminster in England.

In 1926, Fulton Sheen received the Cardinal Mercier Prize for International Philosophy, issued by the University of Louvain every ten years for the best dissertation in Thomistic philosophy. The award was granted for his first published book: *God and Intelligence in Modern Philosophy*, which was based upon Sheen's dissertation for the *Professeur agrégé en philosophie* degree at Louvain. Sheen was also the first American to win this prestigious award.[39] Sheen finished his academic career a published scholar with impeccable academic credentials. He had also won "a fine reputation as a gifted orator on both sides of the Atlantic," as he preached at Westminster Cathedral and St. Patrick's Church in Soho Square, London.[40]

---

successful candidate and induct him into the faculty. If you passed with Satisfaction only water could be served at the dinner; if with Distinction, beer; if with Great Distinction, wine; and the Very Highest Distinction, champagne. The champagne tasted so good that night!" *TIC*, 27-28.

[36] Reeves, *America's Bishop: The Life and Times of Fulton J. Sheen*, 50.

[37] Conniff, *The Bishop Sheen Story*, 25.

[38] *TIC*, 27.

[39] Reeves, *America's Bishop: The Life and Times of Fulton J. Sheen*, 53.

[40] Riley, *Fulton Sheen: An American Catholic Response to the Twentieth Century*, 6.

Sheen was offered two prestigious teaching invitations—one at Oxford and the other at Columbia University in New York City.[41] When Fulton Sheen asked his bishop which offer he should take, he was given a very brief answer: "Come home."[42] Sheen was obedient without complaint and returned to Peoria. He later wrote: "The will of God was expressed through the Bishop as a successor of the Apostles and that was sufficient for me."[43] Fulton Sheen spent about one year of pastoral work at St. Patrick's Parish in Peoria before the bishop phoned him and communicated that he had already promised Sheen to the Catholic University of America three years prior and added: "I just wanted to see if you would be obedient. So run along now; you have my blessing."[44]

---

[41] *TIC*, 28.
[42] Ibid.
[43] *TIC*, 42.
[44] Ibid.

TEACHING CAREER

While Sheen had obtained his initial teaching experience in England during his preparatory studies for the *agrégé*, his teaching career really began when he was appointed to the Graduate School of Catholic University in 1926. Part of Sheen's appointment was that he was to lead a future school of apologetics that never materialized.[45] Within the first two years of Sheen teaching theology, tensions grew among his fellow theology professors.

The tensions began at the end of Fulton's first year at Catholic University. The rector, Bishop Shahan, whom Sheen described as a "brilliant, gifted, saintly rector,"[46] proposed to the theology faculty the possibility of beginning an undergraduate theology program for seminarians in order to attract more students. Prior to that meeting, all of the theology professors opposed such an idea. However, when they were each asked for their opinion on the matter in the presence of Bishop Shahan, they switched positions and expressed favor to the idea. Fulton Sheen was the only one who was not in favor of it. He recommended instituting higher standards for the graduate theology program which he believed would attract more students rather than lowering them to accommodate an undergraduate program. Bishop Shahan expressed dissatisfaction with the division expressed among the theology faculty (especially the opposition of Sheen), but later pulled Fulton Sheen aside and told him that the university had not "received into its ranks in recent years anyone who is destined to shed more light and luster upon it than yourself. God bless you."[47] Sheen, however, did not win favor with his colleagues.

The tension among the theology faculty and the rector, Bishop James T. Ryan, Bishop Shahan's successor, reached a climax during 1930 and 1931 over the constitutionality of the new seminary at Catholic University. This new statute would transfer the authority over the seminary from the School of Sacred Sciences to the

---

[45] Cf. *TIC*, 49-51.
[46] *TIC*, 42.
[47] *TIC*, 44.

university officials.[48] This would give Bishop Ryan much more power over the faculty. One new requirement Bishop Ryan wished to implement was that all professors in the School of Theology must have a Doctor of Divinity (D.D.) in order to keep up academic standards. This caused a problem when one of the professors, John A. Ryan, chose Dr. Francis J. Haas, who he believed was the best person to succeed him as professor of moral theology. Haas's doctorate was in philosophy, not theology, thus rendering him unqualified since he did not have the newly required D.D. degree. Dr. John Ryan refused to send his successor to Rome for further schooling to get a D.D. and decided to petition against the rector.

All professors in the School of Theology, with the exception of Fulton Sheen, signed a statement attacking the rector.[49] Sheen refused to sign the letter because he did not believe Bishop Ryan was given an opportunity to defend his position. Sheen recounted the consequences of his decision: "The next day there appeared on the bulletin board of the School of Theology a notice to the effect that all of the classes of Dr. Fulton J. Sheen had been suspended in the School of Theology."[50] He added: "James H. Ryan, the rector, knew the reason—namely, because I defended him. He then transferred me to the School of Philosophy, where I taught for more than twenty years [until 1950]."[51] Sheen's biographer Thomas Reeves stated that Sheen's transfer to the philosophy department was also to shield Sheen from "the field of fire" because the feud between the rector and the School of Theology took many more months to resolve. The investigative committee sided with the rector.[52]

When all of the dust settled, Sheen and the Catholic University administration "enjoyed an amicable relationship" and "Sheen was permitted to continue his frantic life as a writer, public speaker, retreat director, preacher, and spiritual director for untold numbers of converts, and the campus [of Catholic University] basked in his

---

[48] Cf. Reeves, *America's Bishop: The Life and Times of Fulton J. Sheen*, 72-73.
[49] Ibid., 72.
[50] *TIC*, 45-46.
[51] Ibid., 46.
[52] Reeves, *America's Bishop: The Life and Times of Fulton J. Sheen*, 73.

fame."[53] It is also worth noting that during Sheen's teaching career, he was appointed Papal Chamberlain in 1934 and subsequently elevated to Domestic Prelate in 1935.[54]

Fulton Sheen loved to teach and quickly became "one of the best-known professors at Catholic University, and his fame grew."[55] Fulton always felt a serious moral obligation to his students which contributed to the impressive amount of preparation that went into every course he taught. Sheen was known for putting in six hours of preparation for every hour of class.[56] Sheen observed two principles which he learned from one of his mentors, Cardinal Mercier, in Louvain: "Always keep current: know what the modern world is thinking about; read its poetry, its history, its literature; observe its architecture and its art; hear its music and its theater; and then plunge deeply into St. Thomas and the wisdom of the ancients and you will be able to refute its errors. The second suggestion: tear up your notes at the end of each year. There is nothing that so much destroys the intellectual growth of a teacher as the keeping of notes and the repetition of the same course the following year."[57]

It is very interesting to note the similarities in traits shared between Cardinal Mercier and Fulton Sheen. For example, the following was written of Cardinal Mercier by one of his biographers, John A. Gade:

> ...To Mercier things temporal were of trivial importance; things intellectual and spiritual were pearls of price. Small wonder, then, at thirty he knew his Latin as well as he knew his French, that he quoted Aristotle, Socrates, and Plato easily in Greek, knew Huxley, Spencer, and Darwin in English, Kant, Schopenhauer, and Fichte in German, and Balmes in Spanish. It would have been hard to trip him on a quotation from St. Thomas or St. Augustine. Somewhat of this learning Leo had heard, somewhat, too, of the

---

[53] Ibid., 73.
[54] *TIC*, 358.
[55] Noonan, *The Passion of Fulton Sheen*, 18.
[56] Apostoli, *Archbishop Fulton J. Sheen: A Prophet for Our Times*, compact disc.
[57] *TIC*, 51.

young Abbé's genius for teaching, [and] his compelling influence upon youth...[58]

If we compare what was just said of Cardinal Mercier with the traits found in Fulton Sheen, we will find many common elements. For example, Sheen openly confessed in his autobiography that he was completely detached from the extraordinary amount of money he received from his writing and media productions.[59] The millions of dollars he received over the years were donated to the Society for the Propagation of the Faith and to other needy souls he met along his path. Regarding Sheen's intellectual prowess, Reeves wrote:

> Sheen's expertise encompassed a wide variety of topics, from Aristotle, Augustine, and Thomas Aquinas to Karl Marx, Sigmund Freud, and John Dewey. In his *Philosophy of Science*, he revealed a sophisticated knowledge of the literature of physics and mathematics....His linguistic achievements were admirable: he read Greek, German, Italian, Latin, French, and spoke at least three fluently. (It was said that he "thought in Latin.")[60]

Gade goes on to describe other characteristics of Mercier which were also found in his disciple Sheen: "He was always a fisherman of men, always absorbed in the endeavor to inspire and lead them to the Truth....[Mercier] was an indefatigable worker, reading and writing at a prodigious rate....Besides original writing, he did a large amount of reading. He read both widely and thoroughly....How few men would have been as careful and thorough...in expressing an opinion."[61] Perhaps the best way to summarize their mutual love for Christ and zeal to bring others to Him is by the inscription which was found in Cardinal Mercier's mantelpiece: *Labora sicut bonus miles Christi* ("Work as a good soldier of Christ").[62] Anyone

---

[58] John A. Gade, *The Life of Cardinal Mercier* (New York: Charles Sribner's Sons, 1935), 32-33.

[59] Cf. *TIC*, 66, 92.

[60] Reeves, *America's Bishop: The Life and Times of Fulton J. Sheen*, 2-3.

[61] Ibid., 45, 68-69.

[62] Gade, *The Life of Cardinal Mercier*, 49.

who knew Fulton Sheen, even his adversaries, could not say anything less of him.

Sheen was the perpetual student. He never stopped reading books. His intellect sought truth in every field of study. In his autobiography, he lamented the fact that many priests neglect their need for a continuing education which will make their sermons more fruitful.[63] Sheen loved books and he read everything he could: "My reading embraces literature, science, philosophy of politics—in a word everything that would be useful for a priest in instructing or discoursing with others, or in supplying material for communication."[64]

The number of courses taught by Sheen at Catholic University was relatively low, so he was able to dedicate much of his spare time to preaching. As one biographer writes:

> By 1941, Monsignor Sheen was investing a good deal of his time and energy outside the university as well. Almost from the beginning of his tenure at Catholic University, Sheen spent a considerable amount of time away, lecturing and giving retreats, and preaching regular sermons at both the Paulist Church and St. Patrick's Cathedral in New York City. Also, he was a regular speaker on the "Catholic Hour" radio broadcasts, becoming one of American Catholicism's most famous and sought-after speakers....During the later thirties and early forties...it was estimated that Sheen filled over "150 speaking dates a year."[65]

---

[63] *TIC*, 76.

[64] *TIC*, 78.

[65] Riley, *Sheen: An American Catholic Response to the Twentieth Century*, 18-19; Cf. Conniff, *The Bishop Sheen Story*, 29. Conniff reported: "He used to deliver around 36 major addresses a year, and a convert friend estimates he sandwiched in 'at least several hundred more' of shorter duration."

SHEEN AND COMMUNISM

The times in which Fulton Sheen lived were the most violent in human history as his life witnessed the effects of World War I (1914-1918), the Bolshevik Revolution of 1917, the Spanish Civil War (1936), World War II (1939-1945), the Korean War (1950-1953), and the Vietnam War (1965-1973). It was providential that in a century marked by continuous bloodshed and war God sent the Church someone equipped to provide a hopeful response whose name in Gaelic means "war" (Fulton) and "peace" (Sheen).[66]

During his lifetime, Sheen believed the spread of communism posed more of a threat to Christendom, in general, and to the Church, in particular, than wars because communism aims at the eradication of all religion. While wars caused the death of the body, communism caused the death of the soul. For most of Fulton Sheen's life he sought to expose the truth about communism. Through his assiduous study and ardent preaching against communism he became one of its most dangerous enemies on the intellectual front.

Sheen became well known for his anti-Communist position from his university lectures and speaking presentations.[67] His knowledge of communism was extensive. As Reeves put it, Sheen was "a keen student of Communist literature and history," and "was not deceived by the Popular Front of 1935."[68] He understood communism more than many who professed it. In his autobiography, Sheen wrote, "As a preparation for communism, I have read through the writings of Marx, Lenin and Stalin."[69] The depth of his knowledge was well demonstrated in the five anti-Communist pamphlets he wrote in 1936-1937 as well as the many times he spoke on communism on his radio program the "Catholic Hour," which was very popular.[70]

---

[66] Cf. Noonan, *The Passion of Fulton Sheen*, 23.
[67] *TIC*, 86.
[68] Cf. Reeves, *America's Bishop: The Life and Times of Fulton J. Sheen*, 126.
[69] *TIC*, 81.
[70] Cf. Reeves, *America's Bishop: The Life and Times of Fulton J. Sheen*, 127.

Sheen at blackboard during his prime-time religious television program "Life Is Worth Living."

Sheen preached against communism before most realized communism was truly a threat to the Unites States. At the end of World War II, Sheen warned that Russia was not America's ally and that the Communists had every intention to take over Eastern Europe and impose their Marxist philosophy on the western world, especially the United States.[71] As concerned as Sheen was about the United States, he was more concerned about the threat that the Marxist philosophical disease posed to the Church.[72]

During World War II, Sheen's anti-Communist positions were well-known throughout the United States. They made him very unpopular, even with President Franklin Roosevelt who was sympathetic toward Russia as he saw the United States and Russia working together to eradicate Nazism.[73] Sheen was considered a threat by the Communist party and carefully monitored by them, especially by Communist agents in the United States. For example, Sheen learned from a defector of the Communist party that at one point, Sheen was called "Public Enemy No. 1."[74] Sheen traveled with a bodyguard when he lectured against communism.[75] Because a considerable number of alleged defectors were in contact with Sheen, he developed a good relationship with the United States Federal Bureau of Investigation (FBI). On one occasion, Sheen helped the FBI catch a "very well-known spy" of the Communists who attempted to persuade Sheen to allow him to follow Sheen on his anti-Communist speaking tour.[76]

---

[71] Cf. *TIC*, 87-88.
[72] Cf. Ibid., 89-90.
[73] Cf. Ibid., 82-84.
[74] Cf. Ibid., 86-87.
[75] Cf. Ibid., 87.
[76] Cf. Ibid., 84-85.

PREACHING AND MAKING CONVERTS

Stronger than his love for teaching in the classroom was Fulton Sheen's passion for souls. This was at the heart of his priesthood. As one of Sheen's earliest biographers wrote in 1953 at the height of Sheen's popularity: "With Sheen, souls are practically an obsession" as Sheen truly believed that all are "children of God."[77] No matter whether Sheen was teaching or preaching, his maxim for evangelization was to work out "a Christian response to the challenge of the times."[78] Through much gentle perseverance, study and prayer, one of Sheen's most celebrated converts was the former editor of the Communist *Daily Worker* newspaper in New York City, Louis Budenz.[79]

---

[77] James C. G. Conniff, *The Bishop Sheen Story*, 2.

[78] Riley, *Fulton Sheen: An American Catholic Response to the Twentieth Century*, ix.

[79] Cf. *TIC*, 265-266.

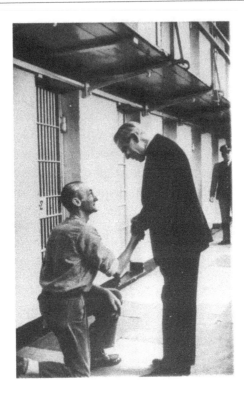

Sheen never wasted an opportunity to win over souls for Christ. During Sheen's twenty-five years of teaching at Catholic University, he would spend most of his weekends instructing converts to the Catholic faith: "All during my teaching career, I would travel to New York, Boston and other cities almost every weekend to instruct converts and preach. Evangelization took on other forms. I also built several churches in Alabama."[80] Many of Sheen's contemporaries could not understand where he received the energy to keep up with his many *other* apostolates in addition to his television program and countless speaking engagements. Sheen was a workaholic, as James Conniff wrote in 1953 concerning Sheen's work schedule:

> Besides taking care of its ["Life Is Worth Living" television program] unwritten script all by himself, he sees visiting laity and clergyman from all over the world every

---

[80] *TIC*, 105.

day between 10 and 1. He edits and writes copy for two mission magazines that bugged the eyes of full-time professional editors who know a hot item when they see it. He also prepares two weekly columns, one for Catholic newspapers, one for the secular press, when he has a spare moment from hammering away at his best-selling books. In between he passes his leisure time reading weighty philosophical and theological journals, as often as not in Latin, French, German, Italian, Spanish or Hebrew. The amazing part of it all is that he manages at the same time to keep holy and happy and altogether sane.[81]

Sheen was never shy to confess that he received this extraordinary energy from his commitment to his daily Holy Hour before Jesus in the Blessed Sacrament.

---

[81] Conniff, *The Bishop Sheen Story*, 14.

Sheen as a guest preacher in the 1930s for the Catholic Evidence Guild in Alabama.

Sheen firmly believed that Catholics have a responsibility to vitalize their faith within the secular environment where they lived. Kathleen Riley highlighted this quality of Sheen when speaking on Sheen's philosophy of education which Sheen also applied to his approach to evangelize his audiences. In her biography on Sheen, Riley described what Sheen referred to as "The Principle of Vitalization for the world of Peter, and the Principle of Integration for the world of Pan" which Sheen explained in his work "Educating for a Catholic Renaissance":

The principle of vitalization meant the presentation of Christian truth as an "organic whole" and a practical adaptation of that truth to make it the "very soul and unifying spirit" of the student's own experiences. Faith was to be a living reality, the vital center of life, and Christian doctrine a "living body of truth" (cf. Sheen, *Educating for a Catholic Renaissance*, p. 8)....Sheen suggested that religion should "enter into, permeate, and spiritualize life's activities" (cf. Sheen, *Educating for a Catholic Renaissance*, p. 10).[82]

Those who have listened to and watched his media broadcasts can attest to this approach of Sheen, who used every contemporary means of science and analogy to help communicate the underlying truths of the Catholic faith in a language they could understand—namely, from their own experiences. Once his audience could identify with the truth of Sheen's content, they were captivated and vitalized, and many were led to embrace the Catholic faith as the logical conclusion to all they had learned from Sheen.

Many sought Fulton Sheen simply because of his magnetic personality. D.P. Noonan wrote: "[Sheen] became the popular choice, the outstanding orator and apologist for the Catholic Church in America. Thousands who heard him on radio sought him out for personal guidance and counsel."[83] Fulton also met the great Catholic apologist G.K. Chesterton. Sheen impressed Chesterton enough that Chesterton agreed to write the introduction to Sheen's first book, *God and Intelligence*, which won the prestigious Cardinal Mercier Award in 1926.[84] The number of converts won over through Bishop Sheen's preaching and personal conversations is countless. Converts came from all walks of life, from different religious faiths, or from no faith at all. As Fulton Sheen put it: "I must remind you that there were hundreds of others besides these whom I recall: housekeepers, flight attendants, ministers, beggars at the door, businessmen, housewives, alcoholics and college students."[85]

---

[82] Riley, *Fulton Sheen: An American Catholic Response to the Twentieth Century*, 21-22.
[83] Noonan, *The Passion of Fulton Sheen*, 60.
[84] Reeves, *America's Bishop: The Life and Times of Fulton J. Sheen*, 52.
[85] *TIC*, 254.

SHEEN'S WRITINGS

Archbishop Sheen established himself as a reputable philosopher and theologian and was one of the American Church's most prolific writers. He authored 66 books and published 62 booklets, pamphlets, and printed radio talks—practically all of which he dedicated to the Blessed Mother.[86] Through his books, teaching, lectures and preaching Fulton Sheen demonstrated not only an expertise in philosophy and theology, but also a considerable knowledge and understanding in subjects such as psychology, mathematics, and physics. The appeal of Sheen's works was compared to that of C.S. Lewis.[87] Sheen even won praise from the Vatican newspaper *L'Osservatore Romano* for a series he wrote on the "New Paganism...gaining the attention of the highest Church officials."[88] Sheen also wrote an article that was published in the English edition of the *L'Osservatore Romano* in 1968. His article was written shortly after Pope Paul VI issued *Humanae Vitae*. In his article he voiced his strong support of the Pope's teaching as he stated, "We reaffirm our allegiance to the Voice of Peter in Paul VI, for we know that we share in Christ's prayer for His Church only to the extent that we are united with Peter."[89]

Beginning with his doctoral dissertation in philosophy at Louvain, Sheen demonstrated his writing ability and his potential to be a great scholar. Conniff wrote of Sheen: "In all fairness, Sheen's reputation for scholarly checking of facts deserves a bow too. It is part of the reason why editors look him up. His doctoral thesis at Louvain, and each of his books since then, have given page after page of exhaustive bibliography to show the many sources he has consulted before committing himself to print. As one close friend puts it, 'The Bishop doesn't just consult those sources, either, my friend. He *reads* them, cover to cover.'"[90]

---

[86] Cf. Riley, *Archbishop Fulton J. Sheen: An American Catholic Response to the Twentieth Century*, 319.

[87] Reeves, *America's Bishop: The Life and Times of Fulton J. Sheen*, 2-3.

[88] Ibid., 79.

[89] Ibid., 323.

[90] Conniff, *The Bishop Sheen Story*, 8.

In his autobiography Sheen revealed those figures who influenced his writing and preaching:

> Since my life has covered such a long span, it has undergone
> several influences in style. The greatest influence in writing
> was G.K. Chesterton, who never used a useless word, who
> saw the value of a paradox and avoided what was trite. At
> a later date came the writings of C.S. Lewis, who, with
> Chesterton and Belloc, became one of the leading apolo-
> gists of Christianity in the contemporary world. Lewis'
> style was concrete, pedestrian, full of examples, analogies,
> parables and always interesting. Malcolm Muggeridge, too,
> has become another inspiration to me. He is always spar-
> kling, brilliant, explosive, humorous. And I must not forget

poetry, particularly *The Oxford Book of Mystical Verse*—
especially the poems of Studdert Kennedy and, above all,
Francis Thompson. Through the years I have kept a file of
favorite poems, many of which I have learned by heart.[91]

PREACHING "THE ELECTRONIC GOSPEL"[92]

God blessed Sheen's desire to evangelize the world by equip-
ping him with an extraordinary intellect which would be able to
communicate the most profound truths of the Catholic faith and
philosophy to every kind of audience. Moreover, God gave Fulton

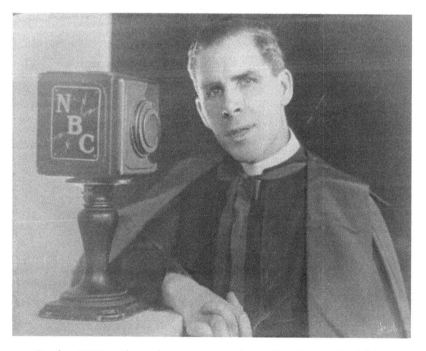

In the 1930s, Sheen hosted a popular radio show called "the
Catholic Hour" on NBC sponsored by The National Council of
Catholic Men.

---

[91] *TIC*, 79.
[92] Ibid., 63.

Sheen the means to be able to reach more people in half an hour than St. Paul could reach throughout all his years and missionary voyages.[93] Sheen liked to refer to radio and television as analogous to the two testaments of Sacred Scripture. "Radio," he stated, "is like the Old Testament, for it is the hearing of the Word without the seeing. "Television," he continued, "is like the New Testament, for the Word is seen as it becomes flesh and dwells among us."[94]

Sheen's career with the media began in 1928 while he was still teaching at Catholic University. His popularity was instantaneous, as his oratory skills won over the crowd who packed the church where Sheen delivered a series of sermons over the radio for the Paulist Fathers of New York.[95] Two years later a new program called the "Catholic Hour" appeared on national radio. Fulton Sheen was the obvious choice by the United States bishops to host the show which won instant success while running up against other popular radio programs. The content of each radio broadcast was based on a theme chosen by Fulton Sheen, namely, "a popular presentation of Christian doctrine on the existence of God, the divinity of Christ, the Church and the spiritual life."[96]

---

[93] Noonan, *The Passion of Fulton Sheen*, 60.
[94] *TIC*, 63.
[95] Ibid., 63.
[96] Ibid., 64.

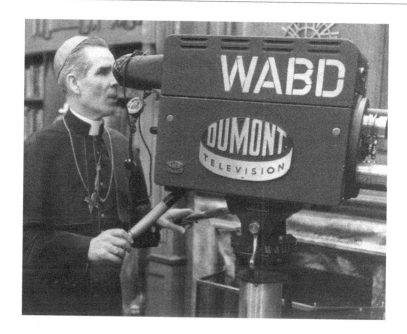

In 1950 Fulton Sheen was invited to become National Director of the Society for the Propagation of the Faith, supervising 129 diocesan directors throughout the United States. That same year, Sheen was consecrated auxiliary bishop of New York under Francis Cardinal Spellman. Sheen took great delight in his appointment as national director and his consecration to the episcopacy (a dream of Fulton since his ordination to the priesthood[97]). Bishop Sheen's responsibilities as national director afforded him many opportunities to meet with missionaries and the poor throughout the world. These encounters left a deep impression on Sheen that moved him to donate all of the proceeds which he would later make from his telecasts to the Society for the Propagation of the Faith. It is estimated that in Sheen's lifetime, his popularity and works (publications, telecasts, etc.) brought him an income that totaled about $100,000,000.[98] During Sheen's years on television, the fee he received was $26,000 a night—"every cent of which found its way

---

[97] Ibid., 91.

[98] Apostoli, *Archbishop Fulton J. Sheen: A Prophet for Our Times*, compact disc.

to some poor area of this earth for the building of hospitals and schools and the further communication of the Word."[99]

The appointment of Sheen as national director and his elevation to the episcopacy came at a most opportune time for Fulton. In 1951, Bishop Sheen made the transition from radio to television on which Sheen would host a show called "Life Is Worth Living." Similar to his radio program, "Life Is Worth Living" was an instant success, reaching an estimated 25 million viewers within its first two years of broadcasting. Sheen wrote in his autobiography that he would spend "about thirty hours preparing every telecast."[100] His audience was composed of people of all different faiths and some with no faith at all. Sheen's mystique even caught the attention of the White House.[101] One of Sheen's biographers reported: "In 1955 his television program was carried by 170 stations in the United States, and 17 in Canada. The viewers were in this order—Jewish, Protestant, and Catholic."[102]

This last fact reveals another important quality of Fulton Sheen's gift of evangelization—ecumenism. Many would agree with D.P. Noonan when he stated, "Sheen was way ahead of Vatican Council II as regards the ecumenical movement."[103] This ecumenical desire of Sheen closely resembled that of his mentor, Cardinal Mercier, who was known to have an ecumenical heartbeat until his final

[99] *TIC*, 66.
[100] *TIC*, 70.
[101] Ibid., 67.
[102] Noonan, *The Passion of Fulton Sheen*, 60. This statement from Noonan, as he presents it, cannot be factually accurate since Christians comprised the great majority of Americans in 1955. What I believe Noonan was trying to say is that proportionately, the percentage of Jewish viewers who watched "Life Is Worth Living" out of the total number of Jewish people was higher than the percentage of viewers among Protestants and Catholics. For example, current demographic statistics show that Christians compose 84.12% of the American population while 1.92% is Jewish. Those statistics could not have changed much since 1955 (accessed 27 May 2006); available from the Association of Religion Data Archives, http://www.thearda.com/internationalData/countries/Country_234_1.asp; Internet.
[103] Ibid., 56.

breath.[104] Sheen's efforts to evangelize peoples of different Christian faiths and different religions preceded the Second Vatican Council by over twenty years.[105] The fact that Sheen's viewers were primarily non-Catholic and his show remained among the most popular during its tenure reveal that Sheen had the incredible gift of articulating to the world a message which was truly Catholic and Thomistic in a language which was universally intelligible. Regarding his popular television show "Life Is Worth Living," Miles Murphy writes: "Basically, the television medium was a way for Sheen to get people to change not by telling them what they wanted to hear, but what they needed to hear."[106] Sheen's career with the media gave him the opportunity to evangelize the world according to the way he was trained, which was to refute the errors of the world using the philosophy of St. Thomas Aquinas in order to return the modern world to "the path of intellectual sobriety."[107]

SHEEN AND VATICAN II

Sheen considered his presence and participation at the Second Vatican Council as "one of the great blessings the Lord bestowed" on his life.[108] Sheen was named to one of the pre-conciliar commissions, namely, the Catholic Action Commission. He was later assigned by Pope St. John XXIII to the Conciliar Commission on the Missions.[109]

Sheen's contributions at the Council consisted of "applying his expertise on the Missions [sic] during discourses and in the interventions he submitted on several subjects. Those subjects included ecumenism, religious freedom, education, priestly formation, and the Decree on the Church's Missionary Activity."[110]

---

[104] Cf. Gade, *The Life of Cardinal Mercier*, 286-289.
[105] Apostoli, *Archbishop Fulton J. Sheen: A Prophet for Our Times*, compact disc.
[106] Murphy, *The Life and Times of Archbishop Fulton J. Sheen*, 66.
[107] Ibid., 9.
[108] *TIC*, 281.
[109] Cf. Ibid., 283-284.
[110] Murphy, *The Life and Times of Archbishop Fulton J. Sheen*, 79.

(Courtesy, Society for the Propagation of the Faith)

In his autobiography, Sheen described his opposition to a proposed document to treat the subject of tourism. Sheen thought the topic senseless unless it was going to remind Catholics of their obligation to go to Mass on Sunday while they traveled.[111] He believed there were much more important matters that should be discussed. One such matter was the role of the feminine principle in religion. Sheen stated: "I had a strong conviction that the feminine principle in religion had been neglected." He added: "Many world religions were without a feminine principle and we were beginning to live in an age when women were coming into their own. I still feel that it would have been well to have included a chapter on women – it certainly was far more important than tourism!"[112]

Fulton was a firm believer in the necessity of the Council. As we have already highlighted earlier, Sheen had a passion to know what the modern world was thinking and then provide the Catholic response to it. Sheen noted that the challenge of the Second Vatican Council was properly understanding what it meant for the

---

[111] Cf. *TIC*, 283.
[112] Ibid., 284.

Church to be *in* the world but not *of* the world.[113] He summarized the accomplishments of the Council concerning the Church's relation to the world when he wrote: "What the Council did was establish equilibrium or balance between these extremes – between evangelization and human progress, between soul-winning and society-saving, between divine salvation and human liberation. It made both inseparable."[114]

Sheen was not surprised when tensions developed after the Council. He stated such tensions always existed throughout the Church's history after such grace-filled events as ecumenical councils. He stated:

> The tensions which developed after the Council are not surprising to those who know the whole history of the Church. It is a historical fact that whenever there is an outpouring of the Holy Spirit as in a General Council of the Church, there is always an extra show of force by the anti-Spirit or the demonic. Even at the beginning, immediately after Pentecost and the descent of the Spirit upon the Apostles, there began a persecution and the murder of Stephen. If a General Council did not provoke the spirit of turbulence, one might almost doubt the operation of the Third Person of the Trinity over the Assembly.[115]

Soon after the Council, Sheen would directly face these tensions when he was elected Bishop of Rochester. Sheen would embrace his new pastorate in Rochester eager to put the Council's teachings into practice. Reeves pointed out that Bishop Sheen was "the first American bishop to attempt to implement in a diocese the full teachings of the Second Vatican Council, prompting severe criticism from conservatives and radicals alike."[116]

---

[113] Cf. Ibid., 290.
[114] Ibid., 290.
[115] Ibid., 292-293.
[116] Reeves, *America's Bishop: The Life and Times of Fulton J. Sheen*, 6.

THE HOUR WHICH MADE HIS DAY

Those who knew Sheen well attested to the depth of his prayer life. Although Fulton Sheen was constantly in the spotlight because of his media fame and countless speaking engagements, he was "a very interior and spiritual man, preferring silence to exterior noises, as he stated: 'The closer one gets to the spirit, the greater the silence.'"[117]

---

[117] Conniff, *The Bishop Sheen Story*, 4.

Sheen never considered himself a very ascetical man, although one of the earliest writers on Sheen wrote that Fulton was said "to wear something like a hair shirt, called a *silicio* [*sic*] next to his skin."[118] He was not one prone to fasting much more than what was already prescribed by Canon Law, which is why he would never really preach on the subject.[119] But there was one thing which Fulton did preach consistently throughout his many years in the media and giving retreats—the daily Holy Hour. For Sheen, it was "the hour that made my day."[120] This was the primary form of Sheen's asceticism and at the heart of his priestly life. Upon his priestly ordination, Sheen made two resolutions: "I would offer the Holy Eucharist every Saturday in honor of the Blessed Mother to solicit her protection on my priesthood" and "to spend a continuous Holy Hour every day in the presence of Our Lord in the Blessed Sacrament."[121] Sheen never failed in keeping these resolutions.

The daily Holy Hour was always a practice he recommended whenever he gave a series of retreat lectures. He could preach it forcefully and convincingly because he practiced it religiously. Sheen was convinced of the power and efficacy which spending a Holy Hour before the Blessed Sacrament had in the lives of those who made the hour, especially priests. Sheen summarized the significance of the daily Holy Hour: "The purpose of the Holy Hour is to encourage deep personal encounter with Christ." He preached the Holy Hour not as a devotion, but as "a sharing in the work of redemption."[122] Sheen explained that the word "hour" was used in the Gospel of St. John seven times, each in reference to "the demonic, and to the moments when Christ is no longer in the Father's Hands, but in the hands of men."[123] One of the reasons, therefore, Sheen encouraged his audience to make the daily Holy

---

[118] Ibid., 21. I believe the word Conniff meant to use was "cilicium" which is the Latin word for a type of hair shirt.
[119] Cf. *TIC*, 194.
[120] Ibid., 187.
[121] Ibid., 187.
[122] Ibid., 188.
[123] Cf. Ibid., 188.

Hour was to combat and make reparation for the evil in the world as the only time Jesus made this request was the night He entered into His agony. Another fruit of making the Holy Hour, according to Sheen, was that we grow more into the likeness of Jesus Christ, just as the face of Moses was transformed after spending time with God on the mountain.[124]

Sheen preached the daily Holy Hour even to Protestants, who do not believe in the real presence of Christ in the Eucharist. Following his usual ingenious pedagogy of prodding others toward the fullness of truth, he encouraged Protestant ministers to make the Holy Hour before God's presence in the Sacred Scriptures—a presence which Sheen related was given greater attention at the Second Vatican Council.[125] Sheen recounted, "Many came to me later to inquire about the Eucharist, some even asked to join with me in a Holy Hour before the Eucharist."[126]

Sheen attributed to his fidelity to the daily Holy Hour the preservation of his priesthood, for he believed: "Being tethered to a tabernacle, one's rope for finding other pastures is not so long."[127] More important to Sheen was his conviction that spending silent time before Jesus in the Blessed Sacrament always leads to a deeper intimacy with Christ. Sheen stressed that the Holy Hour was his *"magister"*; "...for although before we love anyone we must have a knowledge of that person, nevertheless, *after* we know, it is love that increases knowledge. Theological insights are gained not only from two covers of a treatise, but from two knees on a prie-dieu before a tabernacle."[128]

Sheen drew all his inspiration from Jesus in the Blessed Sacrament and he made it a priority to do as much work as he could in the presence of the Eucharist. In his autobiography Sheen wrote: "All my sermons are prepared in the presence of the Blessed Sacrament. As recreation is most pleasant and profitable in the sun,

---

[124] Cf. Ibid., 188-189.
[125] Cf. *TIC*, 196.
[126] Ibid., 196.
[127] Ibid., 192.
[128] Ibid., 192.

so homiletic creativity is best nourished before the Eucharist."[129] Sheen believed that "the most brilliant ideas" come from these intimate encounters with Christ truly present in the Blessed Sacrament adding, "The Holy Spirit which presided at the Incarnation is the best atmosphere for illumination."[130] In fact, Sheen wrote his entire autobiography in the presence of the Blessed Sacrament.[131]

"THE WOMAN"[132] SHEEN LOVED

Miles Murphy wrote: "Next to his desire of exposing the world to the dangers of Communism and [his passion for] the salvation of souls, was his conviction of the importance of Mary, the Mother of God, in Salvation History."[133] It was no secret to the world that Fulton Sheen always possessed a deep devotion to the Blessed Mother. From his earliest days Fulton always saw Mary as the most direct route to Jesus. Reflecting on his devotion to her in his autobiography, Sheen said, "I trust in her intercession to provide as direct a route as possible to Christ, my Savior, for 'she knows the way.'"[134] He also wrote:

> True, in the course of history, there have been exaggerations in devotion to Mary, but it was not the Church that made her important; it was Christ Himself. The Church has never adored Mary, because only God may be adored. But she, of all creatures, was closest to God. Without her as the key, it is difficult to discover the treasures in the vault of Faith.[135]

---

[129] Ibid., 75.

[130] Ibid., 75.

[131] Ibid., 198.

[132] Ibid., 315.

[133] Murphy, *The Life and Times of Archbishop Fulton J. Sheen*, 111.

[134] *TIC*, 324. Sheen's reference in this quotation is taken from the poem of Mary Thayer Dixon, "Lovely Lady Dressed in Blue," which Sheen made famous by frequently ending his lectures or programs on Mary with a dramatic recitation of this poem.

[135] Ibid., 315.

Sheen deeply believed in this and when it came to converting souls, he would simply tell his listeners that if you want the
conversion of a particular person, "pray to Mary."[136] Those who
knew Sheen and studied his life noted how the Blessed Mother
always came up in Sheen's conversations, especially with potential
converts "no matter what the subject."[137] Biographer James Conniff
recounts Sheen's perpetual request to families: "May I ask you husbands and wives and children in honor of this model love of the
Holy Family, to say the Rosary together every night."[138] Conniff
added that Sheen always asked the same of every newlywed couple
who stood before him at the altar.

As already stated, Fulton Sheen had two great loves: Jesus in the
Blessed Sacrament and the Blessed Virgin Mary, whom he often
referred to as "The Woman I love." His devotion to Mary was cul-
tivated from the strong Christian atmosphere that surrounded his
childhood. Fulton was raised in a very humble and devout Catholic family. As Fulton Sheen described it in his autobiography: "The
molding of the clay was done by great sacrifices on the part of my
father and my mother, who would deny themselves every personal
comfort and luxury in order that their sons be well clothed and
well cared for. Our family life was simple and the atmosphere of
our home Christian."[139] The Sheen household was devoted to the
Blessed Virgin; "the Rosary was said every evening."[140]

During Sheen's sixteen years as National Director of the Society
for the Propagation of the Faith, he encouraged his staff to pray
the Rosary daily. His secretary recounts the impact of this devotion among the staff of the Society. "The whole staff would gather,
at mid-afternoon, to pray the Rosary as well as to spend fifteen
minutes reflecting upon the Scriptures. It was really a family affair.
All visitors were invited to join us. Bishop Sheen would lead us in
prayer. For all of us it was the highlight of the day."[141] Sheen even

---

[136] Apostoli, *Archbishop Fulton J. Sheen: A Prophet for Our Time*, compact disc.
[137] Conniff, *The Bishop Sheen Story*, 18.
[138] Ibid., 31.
[139] *TIC*, 16.
[140] Ibid., 16.
[141] Miles P. Murphy, *The Life and Times of Archbishop Fulton J. Sheen*, 113.

designed a World Mission Rosary "with different color beads for each of the five continents Catholics pray may be converted to the true Faith."[142]

Fulton shared a special relationship with the Blessed Virgin Mary from his earliest days. Shortly after his birth, at his baptism, his mother laid him upon the altar of the Blessed Mother in St. Mary's Church, El Paso, Illinois, and consecrated him to her. As Fulton later recounted: "As an infant may be unconscious of a birthmark, so I was unconscious of the dedication—but the mark was always there. Like a piece of iron to the magnet, I was drawn to her before I knew her, but never drawn to her without Christ."[143]

When Fulton received his first Holy Communion at age 12, he made his infant consecration personal when he made "the conscious dedication" of himself to Mary, who would later play a special intercessory role in Fulton's pursuit of a priestly vocation.[144] Sheen wrote: "Though I cannot recall the exact words of my prayer, it was certainly similar to the motto which I chose for my coat of arms as bishop: *Da per matrem me venire* (Grant that I may come to Thee through Mary)."[145] Fulton added that he began the daily recitation of the Litany to the Blessed Virgin Mary found in his first Communion book and remained faithful to that practice until his death. Another devotion which Fulton preserved from his childhood was a practice he learned from his high school teachers, which was to pray three Hail Marys to St. Joseph for the grace of a happy death.[146]

---

[142] Conniff, *The Bishop Sheen Story*, 30.
[143] *TIC*, 316.
[144] Ibid., 316.
[145] Ibid., 316.
[146] Ibid., 324.

Archbisoph Sheen administering Holy Communion during one of his many visits to Lourdes, France.

Beginning with the earliest days of his priesthood, Sheen
expressed his deep devotion to Our Lady by visiting her shrine in
Lourdes about thirty times.[1] It was said, "Archbishop Sheen would
never visit Europe without making a pilgrimage to Lourdes."[2] Sheen
recorded in his autobiography two mystical experiences he had
during his pilgrimages to Lourdes. Both of these experiences reas-
sured him of the Blessed Mother's special care over him.[3] It is worth
sharing what may be considered the more remarkable story of the
two. At the end of Sheen's university studies, he made a pilgrimage
to Lourdes. This pilgrimage was shortly after Sheen received the
brief letter from his bishop telling him to "Come home." He had
no idea what his bishop had planned for him and he was worried
that he would not be able to return to Lourdes again. The rest of
the account is best described with Sheen's own words:

> I asked the Blessed Mother to give me some sign that
> despite the odds of returning to Lourdes, she would do
> what seemed impossible. The sign I asked was this: that
> after I offered the Holy Sacrifice of the Mass and before I
> would reach the outer gate of the shrine, a little girl aged
> about twelve, dressed in white, would give me a white
> rose. About twenty feet from the gate I could see no one. I
> remember saying: "You had better hurry, there is not much
> time left." As I arrived at the gate a little girl aged twelve,
> dressed in white, gave me a white rose.[4]

[1] Ibid., 317.
[2] Ibid., 320.
[3] Cf. Ibid., 318.
[4] Ibid., 318. In 1953, James Conniff provided a slightly different version of the
story which is more colorful, but inconsistent with Sheen's account. According to Conniff, Sheen prayed to Mary asking if she was displeased with him
because a prayer of his had thus far gone unanswered. He asked Mary to give
him a sign showing she was not displeased. The sign Sheen asked for was that
"a little girl ten years old, dressed in white, present him with a single red rose
before he should reach the gate in the church courtyard." Sheen had given up
hope that his prayer would be answered and the moment his hand pushed
the latch on the gate he heard a voice: "Father. Here." Conniff described what
followed: "Sheen felt a dizziness then, and turned to find a tiny child in a
white dress, smiling and offering him one red rose. She said he should take it

Fulton Sheen prayed that through the intercession of Mary he would one day be consecrated a bishop. His prayers were answered on June 11, 1951, when he was consecrated bishop in the Church of Sts. John and Paul in Rome. The first trip Fulton made after his consecration was to Lourdes. It was there that Sheen had previously purchased what became his first episcopal ring. At Lourdes he had an image of the Blessed Virgin engraved on it.[5] Sheen also made about ten pilgrimages to Mary's shrine in Fatima, a place which also held a special place in Sheen's heart and in his teaching about Mary.

In 1966, Sheen was appointed by Pope Paul VI to be the bishop of the Diocese of Rochester, New York. At his installation Sheen made a request of the congregation that revealed the heart of his Marian spirituality and theology. Sheen asked, "Pray for me daily to Mary, my patroness, that as she formed Jesus physically in her body, so may she form Jesus mystically in my soul."[6] As this book will demonstrate later, the heart of Sheen's theology of Marian mediation rests on Mary's spiritual maternity, which cooperates at every moment of every Christian's life with the Holy Spirit to form Christ mystically within each of the baptized, thus prolonging the incarnation until God is all in all. This teaching is central to Sheen's theology of Marian mediation and we will examine this teaching more closely in Chapter IV of this book.

Fulton meditated deeply throughout his priesthood on the mystery of Mary. He saw her as fulfilling the feminine principle of religion which would be an instrument in bringing other religions to Christianity. This is a topic which will be explained when the subject of Marian mediation is treated. Sheen saw Mary as "the ideal Woman in every truly Christian life." He felt that her presence in his life had always been very real as evidenced by his mys-

---

because he looked so sad. He took it. And then, temptation being what it is, he asked her, his great voice choked to a whisper, how old she was, for she was very small. Up came the bright little face in the morning sun. 'I'm ten years old today,' she said, and ran away before he could stop her." Cf. Conniff, *The Bishop Sheen Story*, 31-32.

[5] Miles P. Murphy, *The Life and Times of Archbishop Fulton J. Sheen*, 114.

[6] Ibid., 114.

tical experiences in Lourdes and by the countless times she had obtained special favors for Sheen for the conversion of souls.[7] Fulton believed that his devotion to Mary also taught him about the sacredness of suffering and what it meant to be not only a priest, but also a victim.

Fulton Sheen always saw an intrinsic relationship between Mary and the Church, the theology of which is at the heart of this book. He always saw how a decline in devotion to Mary led to a decline to devotion to the Church. This connection will be elaborated in Chapter IV.

Fulton Sheen encouraged all married couples and families to pray the Rosary every night in honor of the Holy Family.

---

[7] Cf. *TIC*, 324-325.

Fulton always found consolation in Mary, whom he always venerated as the Mother of "priest-victims." Sheen confessed in his autobiography that he suffered much throughout his priesthood. These sufferings were both spiritual and physical. The physical sufferings were due to serious illnesses Sheen battled during his life, especially in his later years, often occurring on Marian feast days, which he later saw as a "special predilection of Mary."[8] Sheen explained: "If I had expressed a love for her as the Mother of the Priesthood, why should she not, in maternal love, make me more like her Son by forcing me to become a victim? If she did not despise this conformity with Him on Calvary, why should she, whom I recognize as Heavenly Mother, be less solicitous about seeing the image of her Son stamped more indelibly on my soul? If my own earthly mother laid me on her altar at birth, why should not my Heavenly Mother lay me at His Cross as I come to the end of life?"[9]

Sheen's sufferings were also of a spiritual nature, which were much more intense than the physical. Many times this was caused by Sheen's knowledge of those priests who abandoned their priestly vocation.[10] However, biographers reveal that this suffering was largely due to Francis Cardinal Spellman who served as Archbishop of New York from 1939 to 1967. The suffering Sheen endured at the hands of Cardinal Spellman had such an impact on Sheen's spiritual life that it is important that we understand exactly what happened between the two.

Cardinal Spellman also served as chairman of the Propagation of the Faith in the United States and, as his biographer John Cooney described, "He treated the organization as part of his personal fiefdom."[11] The feud between these two figures lasted a

---

[8] *TIC*, 323.

[9] Ibid., 323.

[10] Cf. Ibid., 220-221. Sheen wrote: "Shortly after the Council and in the late sixties, it was possible for a period of about five years to predict those who were about to leave the priesthood. This condition existed only for a short time, but it was so very noticeable that I could not help but moan at its presence, and rejoice when it passed away."

[11] John Cooney, *The American Pope: The Life and Times of Francis Cardinal*

period of about ten years (1957-1967).[12] Sheen chose not to revisit this subject in his autobiography. There were two main incidents that fueled Cardinal Spellman's fury against Sheen which would last until Spellman's death in 1967. Both incidents occurred while Sheen was National Director of the Society for the Propagation of the Faith.

The first incident occurred in 1955 when Cardinal Spellman asked Sheen to use funds from the Society to pay for additional food that was being sent to people of all faiths in war-torn countries. These relief efforts were a joint venture of the United States government and the National Catholic Welfare Conference and the goods were distributed by Catholic missionaries. Sheen rejected Spellman's request on the grounds that he had not received orders by the Holy See for such a request. Spellman, who was considered by many the most powerful and well-connected Catholic in the country, was not used to being denied anything.[13] As Noonan put it, "Spellman was probably the only cardinal in the world with a direct line to the Vatican."[14] While Sheen strongly disapproved of any of the Society's money going to anyone but the poor, Cooney accurately observed that the real issue behind Spellman and Sheen's quarrels was not money, but authority. He wrote:

> Sheen did what no one else dared: he challenged a cardinal who was supposed to have absolute power....What Sheen resented was Spellman's habit of helping himself to Propagation money: On his frequent trips, Spellman gave donations to schools, hospitals, priest friends, bishops, cardinals, and other people and causes. On his trips to Rome he arrived laden with presents for all.[15]

Spellman then tried to go around Sheen's authority and appeal to Rome, which ultimately sided with Sheen and rejected Spellman's

---

Spellman (New York: Times Books, 1984), 253.
[12] Cf. Reeves, *America's Bishop: The Life and Times of Fulton J. Sheen*, 259.
[13] Cf. Noonan, *The Passion of Fulton Sheen*, 79-81.
[14] Ibid., 81.
[15] Cooney, *The American Pope: The Life and Times of Francis Cardinal Spellman*, 253.

request. Spellman was furious that anyone would reject him, let alone a bishop whom he helped elect. Spellman's fury grew to the point that he appealed to his friend Pope Pius XII to have Sheen removed as National Director and have himself elected as his successor. After months of deliberation, Pius XII refused to concede to Spellman's request.[16]

The second incident occurred in early 1957 and it revolved around Cardinal Spellman's "Milk Fund."[17] Spellman received a large amount of surplus food in the form of powdered milk. Spellman never paid for the supplies, which were worth millions of dollars. On one occasion, Spellman donated a large amount of powdered milk to the Society of the Propagation for the Faith while claiming to have paid for the supplies himself. He, therefore, asked Sheen to pay him what amounted to millions of dollars to cover the cost of the supplies. Sheen refused knowing very well that the milk was provided free of charge to Spellman. Cardinal Spellman became enraged and began attacking Sheen behind the scenes. For example, Sheen's television series "Life Is Worth Living" was suddenly cancelled. Although Sheen told his audiences that he was simply retiring from television, those on the inside knew that Spellman forced Sheen's retirement.[18]

The feud over the milk fund eventually reached Rome and Spellman and Sheen appeared before Pius XII. After an investigation of the facts, Sheen had documented evidence that Spellman received the milk for free. In front of Pope Pius XII, the most powerful bishop in the American church was caught lying and at that moment "he realized he had lost face with Pope Pius XII."[19] Sheen was vindicated by Rome, but the wrath that followed from Spellman over the next ten years would serve as a Calvary for Sheen as Spellman would make it his mission to ruin Sheen's reputation.[20] Thomas Reeves noted that Sheen's suffering at the hand of Spellman inspired Sheen to write his *Life of Christ* which is Sheen's nar-

---

[16] *TIC*, 254.
[17] Cf. Noonan, *The Passion of Fulton Sheen*, 81.
[18] Cf. Reeves, *America's Bishop: The Life and Times of Fulton J. Sheen*, 255.
[19] Noonan, *The Passion of Fulton Sheen*, 82.
[20] Cf. Ibid., 82.

ration of the life of Jesus Christ as testified by Sacred Scripture.[21]
Reeves stated that this is evident from words Sheen shared with his
priest secretary about his inspiration for writing the book. Moreover, this is evident in the preface of the 1977 reissue of *Life of
Christ* in which Sheen specifically refers to the "great trial" which
he endured from 1957-1967 (the year Cardinal Spellman died).[22]
Sheen did not need to mention Cardinal Spellman by name.

Many, including Sheen, believed that Cardinal Spellman was
responsible for Sheen being transferred from the Archdiocese of
New York to the Diocese of Rochester.[23] While Sheen only served
as the bishop of Rochester for thirty-four months, he suffered
much from his own people in Rochester during what some considered a failed episcopacy in that diocese.[24] At age 75, Bishop Sheen
resigned from the diocese, not to retire but only to "retread" in
order that he might dedicate his last years to doing what he loved
doing most—giving retreats to priests.[25]

THE POPES AND SHEEN: LOYAL SON OF THE CHURCH

Another of Sheen's hallmarks was his love for and fidelity to
the Pope. Even as a youth, he could not conceive of another ever
disagreeing with a position of a pope.[26] Sheen always believed that
when the Holy Father spoke, he "expressed the mind of Christ."[27]
Throughout his priesthood and episcopacy, Fulton Sheen shared a
close friendship with many of the popes. Sheen had a private audience with Pope Pius XII every year of his pontificate but two.[28]

---

[21] Cf. Reeves, *America's Bishop: The Life and Times of Fulton J. Sheen*, 257.

[22] Cf. Reeves, *America's Bishop: The Life and Times of Fulton J. Sheen*, 258-259.

[23] Cf. Ibid., 287-288.

[24] Cf. Ibid., 327.

[25] *TIC*, 183.

[26] Reeves, *America's Bishop: The Life and Times of Fulton J. Sheen*, 14-15.

[27] Ibid., 323.

[28] Cf. *TIC*, 230-232. "One of the special privileges of my life was to have private audiences with many Pontiffs. The first audience with a Vicar of Christ
was when I was a graduate student at the University of Louvain. The Pontiff

Fulton enjoyed private audiences with Pope St. John XXIII every year of his pontificate and "almost every year" of Pope Paul VI's pontificate.[29] Just as it was Sheen's intellectual philosophy to "stay current" with what the modern world was thinking, he was even more interested to stay current with the teaching of the popes.

then on the throne was Pius XI....

"...I knew [Pius XI's] successor, Pius XII, before he was chosen as the Vicar of Christ. I had dined with Cardinal Pacelli, spent more than an hour in his office when he was Secretary of State, discussing Nazism and condemning it violently. I met him again when, as Cardinal Pacelli, he visited the United States, and on one occasion had dinner with him in the city of Rome with a mutual friend, Duchess Brady. A private audience was accorded me every year when he became Pontiff, except twice when he refused to see any of the national directors of the Society for the Propagation of the Faith throughout the world when they met at their annual meeting in Rome. When that difficulty was resolved, we returned to our meetings."

[29] Cf. *TIC*, 233, 236.

Fulton Sheen was very explicit throughout his teaching and preaching, as well as in his autobiography, about his profound love and loyalty to the Vicar of Christ. Sheen always submitted his brilliant intellect to complete obedience to the teaching authority of the popes. Sheen's theology, therefore, was heavily influenced by writings of the papal magisterium and tradition of the Church.

Sheen shared close friendships with Popes Pius XII, John XXIII, and Paul VI. Although Sheen only lived to see the first year of the pontificate of John Paul II, it was enough for Sheen to prophesy that John Paul II would go down in history as one of the greatest popes of all time.[30]

Fulton Sheen during an audience with Pope Paul VI.

---

[30] *TIC*, 245.

Each year of Sheen's national radio broadcasts, he would visit with Pope Pius XII and discuss with him the subjects for the coming year.[31] During one visit, Pius XII explicitly called Fulton Sheen "a prophet of the times" and told Sheen that he would have "a high place in heaven" for all that he had done for the church.[32] Pope St. John XXIII was aware of Sheen's suffering at the hands of Cardinal Spellman and commenting on that he shared with Sheen his belief that Fulton's suffering would bring him "to a high place in heaven."[33] Pope Paul VI also had high esteem for Sheen, as was evident from their private correspondence, some of which Sheen reproduced in his autobiography.[34]

The apex of Sheen's sixty years of priestly service came just two months before his death. On 2 October 1979, Archbishop Sheen had a very personal encounter with Pope St. John Paul II at St. Patrick's Cathedral in New York. During an emotional embrace between the two, John Paul II conveyed to Sheen the words which Sheen had longed to hear. Sheen recounted what was said in his autobiography: "He told me that I had written and spoken well of the Lord Jesus, and that I was a loyal son of the Church."[35] Shortly after John Paul II's return to Rome, Sheen received a letter from him thanking Sheen for his six decades of priestly service. John Paul stated in that letter: "And so with Saint Paul, 'I thank my God whenever I think of you; and every time I pray for…you, I pray with joy, remembering how you have helped to spread the Good News.'"[36]

CONCLUSION

After Pope St. John Paul II and Mother Teresa, there is hardly another figure of the 20th century who has had as great an impact

---

[32] Ibid., 232.
[33] Ibid., 234.
[34] Ibid., 239-241.
[35] Ibid., 357.
[36] Ibid., 357.

on the evangelization of the world as Fulton Sheen. The similarities between Sheen and John Paul II, who grew up thousands of miles apart, are striking. Both were known as superior philosophers before they were known as superior theologians (it is the position of this writer that Sheen will also one day be universally recognized by the church as a superior theologian). John Paul II and Fulton each spent considerable time before the Blessed Sacrament for inspiration (both always had a pad of paper to take notes of any insights they received while in the presence of Our Lord).[37] According to Father Andrew Apostoli, Sheen was aware that Pope St. John Paul II often watched Bishop Sheen's videos (most likely the "Life Is Worth Living" series) in order to "keep up with his English."[38]

Like John Paul II, Sheen was a prophetic voice of the Church. Sheen demonstrated through his ceaseless teaching the organic unity of truth throughout the storms of the twentieth century. As Kathleen Riley wrote: "Sheen built a bridge which helped American Catholics make the transition from the 'pre' to the 'post' Vatican II Church. This analysis meshes well with Sheen's perception of himself as one who always tried to maintain a sense of balance, theologically orthodox yet progressive and open to new ideas as he dedicated his life as an American Catholic priest and spokesman to 'reading the signs of the times,' and responding with boldness and creativity to the challenges he encountered."[39]

Sheen was prophetic regarding the crucial importance of the culture of life,[40] and he was prophetic regarding Mary's mediatory role in the church of our times. Moreover, much of what John Paul II would teach on Mary through his audiences and encyclicals was preached already by this Venerable Servant of God who was always ahead of his times.

---

[37] *TIC*, 75.

[38] Apostoli, *Archbishop Fulton J. Sheen: A Prophet for Our Time*, compact disc.

[39] Riley, *Fulton Sheen: An American Catholic Response to the Twentieth Century*, xiv.

[40] Reeves, *America's Bishop: The Life and Times of Fulton J. Sheen*, 335-337.

CHAPTER II

THE RELEVANCE OF VENERABLE FULTON J. SHEEN AND HIS THEOLOGICAL APPROACH TO MARY'S MEDIATION

INTRODUCTION

To date there has been neither an in-depth study of Fulton Sheen's Mariology, in general, nor of his teaching on Mary's mediation as it relates to her inseparable role in Redemption, in particular. Fulton Sheen's teaching on Mary's mediation has been chosen as the subject of this study because it is at the heart of his Mariological thought which is essential to understanding his teaching on the mystery of Christ. In addition, there is no more important Marian topic in contemporary Mariology than properly understanding Mary's mediation because it further reveals Mary's inseparable relation to Christ in the mystery of Redemption and her relationship with Christians. The theological and spiritual consequences in the life of every Christian which emerge from the Church's understanding of this mystery are incalculable.

For Fulton Sheen, Mary's maternal mediation was central to his understanding of the mystery of Christ and, hence, the mystery of his priesthood. If the Church wishes to understand the priestly life of Archbishop Sheen, then an in-depth study of his Marian teaching is essential. In addition, this study will illustrate the unique depth and insight into Mary's mediation which Sheen possessed that was at the same time rooted in over eighteen centuries of theological tradition and yet ahead of the Church in its Mariological reflection of the twentieth century, in particular the theological direction established by the Second Vatican Council.

RELEVANCE OF FULTON SHEEN IN THE CONTEMPORARY THEOLOGICAL DEBATE

The Appendix of this work presents the primary theological questions surrounding the contemporary debate on Mary's mediation and the suitability of defining Mary's mediation as a dogma of the Catholic faith. In summary, the contemporary debate stems from the theological climate that followed the Second Vatican Council pertaining to Mary's role in salvation history. The conciliar document which established the Mariological direction after Vatican II was *Lumen Gentium*, in particular its eighth chapter, which called for continued theological studies into Mary's role in salvation history, including her role as "Mediatrix." The momentum of the pre-conciliar dogmatic movement was impeded by the tempestuous events following Vatican II[1] until Pope St. John Paul II put Mary's mediation back into the forefront of the Church's theological reflection both by taking as his papal motto *"Totus tuus"* (taken from St. Louis de Montfort's act of consecration to Mary), his papal program of Marian consecration,[2] his consecration of the world to the Immaculate Heart of Mary in 1984 and his 1987 Encyclical Letter *Redemptoris Mater*.

---

[1] The theological, social and moral climate in the decades following the Second Vatican Council led to mass misinterpretations and even blatant counter-agendas to what Vatican II actually taught. As Archbishop Sheen frequently commented on those times, "the demonic" was especially loosed in the Church and the world after the Council and brought about division in the priesthood, religious life, marriages, families and in the minds of many theologians who sought to cut off the Council's teaching from the organic Tradition to which it was inseparably attached.

[2] An excellent study which thoroughly presents Pope St. John Paul II's papal program of Marian consecration is that of Arthur B. Calkins, *Totus Tuus: John Paul II's Program of Marian Consecration and Entrustment* (Libertyville, Illinois: Academy of the Immaculate, 1992).

The Marian pontificate of Pope St. John Paul II gave rise to a movement *Vox Populi Mariae Mediatrici*, which reignited the pre-conciliar dogmatic movement calling for a dogma of Mary's mediation. This movement sparked a theological response by the unofficial Czestochowa Commission of 1996, the Marianum, Stefano De Fiores, and Salvatore Perrella—all of which opposed a new dogma concerning Mary's mediation. This opposition was accompanied by a renewed call of the Second Vatican Council to continue studies into Mary's mediation from Trinitarian, Christological, ecclesiological, pneumatological, and anthropological perspectives.

This exposition of the teaching of Fulton Sheen on Mary's mediation will provide a positive and insightful response to the theological questions underlying the contemporary debate. What many do not yet realize is that the aforementioned theological studies into Mary's mediation called for by Vatican II, the Czestochowa Commission, the Marianum, Stefano De Fiores and Salvatore Perrella were already given significant attention in the Marian teaching of Fulton Sheen decades before Vatican II. Moreover, Sheen presents his Marian teaching within a profoundly biblical framework, an approach later adopted and emphasized by Vatican II, and one with which he would remain consistent until his death. This same rich approach would be adopted by Pope St. John Paul II two decades after Vatican II, who significantly developed Vatican II's emphasis on Mary's spiritual maternity as it relates to her mediation.[3]

---

[3] Many rightly acclaim John Paul II as the champion of Marian mediation of the post-Conciliar era, especially in his explication of the doctrine on Mary's maternal mediation, articulated above all in *Redemptoris Mater*. He also deliberately brought back into usage pre-Conciliar theological titles such as Coredemptrix and Mediatrix to describe Mary's inseparable role in the mystery of Redemption and to emphasize their theological compatibility with post-Conciliar Mariology. While his use of these terms is significant, John Paul, however, was more concerned with explaining the meaning of Mary's role in Redemption, especially her mediation, in terms of her spiritual maternity; thus giving Mary's mediation a more personal quality that is both at the heart of her mediation and expressed in what will be more appealing to Christians.

What many do not yet know is that John Paul II's teaching on Mary's *maternal* mediation was already significantly developed half a century earlier by Fulton Sheen. In fact, the similarity in approach (especially biblical) which they share is extraordinary as we will see. Moreover, Sheen's Marian teaching spans a period of over four decades (1934–1979), thus demonstrating his thought before and after the Second Vatican Council. It is worth noting at this early stage of our study that Sheen's thought on Mary's maternal mediation remained remarkably consistent from his earliest recorded thoughts in 1934 in his work *The Eternal Galilean* to his final lectures given up to the year of his death in 1979.

As this study highlighted in Chapter I, Sheen's writings and preaching were found convincing to millions of Catholics and non-Catholics around the world. It is time to present his rich Mariological contribution as it relates to Mary's mediation in the hope that it, too, will provide the clarity sought by contemporary Mariologists.

SHEEN'S THEOLOGICAL APPROACH TO MARY'S MEDIATION

The Mystery of Mary in Christ is a Living Theology

Fulton Sheen's approach to the mystery of Mary's maternal mediation derived from "piously meditating on her and contemplating her in the light of the Word made man," and through this reverent approach, he entered "more intimately into the great mystery of the Incarnation."[4] Moreover, Sheen treated the mystery of Mary's mediation as a *vital* doctrine. Sheen writes:

> Unfortunately, many of our dogmas become static. Words are so fixed in their meaning that when we hear "crucified," our minds go back to a hill outside Jerusalem which, like the Battle of Waterloo, is gone forever. A doctrine that is

---

[4] *LG*, 65.

only a doctrine has a poor chance indeed to create a glowing enthusiasm or a faith that can move mountains.[5]

He understood Mary's mediation, therefore, as an "inner truth;"[6] a truth that speaks of Mary as a living subject influencing the life of Christians today, not as an historical object. In other words, Mary's mediation has a relational reality with every person, especially Christians. We will see how Sheen develops this in the fourth chapter of our study when we see how Sheen understood Mary's mediation from heaven.

Mary in the Mystery of the Fullness of Christ

How to treat Mary within the mystery of Christ depends on one's understanding of what the mystery of Christ entails. As we will see in the following chapters, for Sheen, the mystery of Christ is fully understood only by a proper understanding of the mystery of the Incarnation, its redemptive mission, and how it continues in the Church today. In other words, Sheen understood that the mystery of Christ comprised of both the historical Christ beginning with the Incarnation at Nazareth and lasting until His Ascension at Mount Olivet, and what he called the "Mystical Christ," which is the Incarnation of Christ mystically prolonged in His Church. Together they comprise the whole Christ or the fullness of Christ. Sheen understood that Mary played an essential and central role in the mystery of the Incarnation and its continuation in the Mystical Body of Christ, the Church, as the Mother of Christ. For Sheen, if we understand the full theological significance of Mary as Mother of the fullness of Christ, then we will begin to grasp the profound significance of this living doctrine. Therefore, Sheen knew that in order to understand Mary in the mystery of Christ, one must, first, have an accurate understanding of what the mystery of Christ fully

---

[5] Fulton J. Sheen, *Those Mysterious Priests* (New York: Doubleday & Company, 1974; reprint, Staten Island: Society of St. Paul, 2005), 99 (hereafter cited as *TMP*).

[6] Fulton J. Sheen, "Spirituality" (from a series of retreat lectures given at Holy Trinity Seminary, Irving, Texas, 1972, recorded by and in the possession of Mr. Daniel B. Steffen of Plano, Texas), compact disc.

encompassed. This was later outlined in the Marian doctrine of Vatican II, reaffirmed by Paul VI, and developed significantly by John Paul II, who wrote:

> The Second Vatican Council prepares us[7] for [Mary's unique presence in history] by presenting in its teaching the Mother of God in the mystery of Christ and of the Church. If it is true, as the Council itself proclaims, that "only in the mystery of the Incarnate Word does the mystery of man take on light," then this principle must be applied in a very particular way to that exceptional "daughter of the human race," that extraordinary "woman" who became the Mother of Christ. Only in the mystery of Christ is her mystery fully made clear. Thus has the Church sought to interpret it from the very beginning: the mystery of the Incarnation has enabled her to penetrate and to make ever clearer the mystery of the Mother of the Incarnate Word.[8]

Sheen's first major theological work in 1935, *The Mystical Body of Christ*, addressed this very question of what is meant by the mystery of Christ and how we are best to understand the Church in relation to this mystery. As we will see in Chapter IV of this study, Sheen's ecclesiology is an extension of his Christology. He further developed Mary's mediatory role within the mystery of Christ in his major treatise on Mary, *The World's First Love*, written in 1952. The Marian doctrine in these two works provides an insightful treatise on Mary's mediation that can serve as a rich commentary on the Marian doctrine of Vatican II found in *Lumen Gentium* Chapter VIII.

---

[7] "Wherefore this Holy Synod, in expounding the doctrine on the Church, in which the divine Redeemer works salvation, intends to describe with diligence both the role of the Blessed Virgin in the mystery of the Incarnate Word and the Mystical Body, and the duties of redeemed mankind toward the Mother of God, who is mother of Christ and mother of men, particularly of the faithful. It does not, however, have it in mind to give a complete doctrine on Mary, nor does it wish to decide those questions which the work of theologians has not yet fully clarified" (*LG*, 54).

[8] *RM*, 4.

Ascending and Descending Mediation of Christ

At the heart of the mystery of Christ is His role as the Mediator between God and man (cf. 1 Tim. 2:5). Sheen spoke of two dimensions to Christ's one mediation: "ascending" and "descending" mediation. For Sheen, at the heart of Christ's mediation is His role as Priest and Victim. Sheen repeatedly emphasized in his teaching and preaching on the nature of Christ that the reason He is Mediator between God and man is because He is both Priest and Victim due to being the God-Man.[9] Although we will treat this subject fully in the following chapter, it suffices to say that Sheen saw it impossible to understand the one mediation of Christ without a proper understanding of His mediation as the "Priest-Victim."

In particular, Sheen explained Christ's "ascending" mediation in terms of His Priest-Victimhood where Christ's mediation as High Priest is "consummated on Calvary," and through which He offers His Life for our Redemption which "is brought before the Heavenly Father."[10] The "descending mediation of Christ" is that "by which His merits are conferred on us."[11]

Sheen treats Mary's mediation within the same theological context as Christ's ascending and descending mediation, since hers is a participation in the one mediation of Christ. Therefore, if Christ's mediation is one exercised through His Priest-Victimhood, Mary's mediation would be a unique participation in the Priesthood and Victimhood of Christ. We will see how Sheen explains this in the next chapter, especially in terms of understanding what is meant by the *kenosis* of Christ—a *kenosis* of God in which Mary's

---

[9] Fulton Sheen preached extensively on the importance of understanding the nature of Christ as Priest and Victim, especially after the Second Vatican Council when he saw a crisis in understanding of the nature of the priesthood. His mature thought on this subject is found throughout one of his final theological works, *Those Mysterious Priests*, in particular, pages 13-57.

[10] Fulton J. Sheen, "Theandric Actions in Christ" (undated typescript within folder labeled "Mystical Body"), Archbishop Fulton J. Sheen Archives, Catholic Diocese of Rochester, Rochester, New York (all subsequent references to the archives of Fulton Sheen are hereafter cited as "Sheen Archives").

[11] Ibid.

role and participation would be both "essential" and "indissoluble," as Paul VI would later affirm.[12]

Deepening Our Understanding of Mary as the New Eve

For Sheen, the theological framework which best expresses Mary's participation in the one mediation of Christ is Mary as the New Eve, who was created to be the Mother of the Redeemer and of the new humanity regenerated in Christ. In order to be worthy of these sublime privileges, Mary would have to participate in Christ's mediation as Priest-Victim in a way unique to her vocation. Sheen's theological development of Mary as the New Eve from a primarily biblical perspective illustrates how Mary's participation in both the ascending and descending mediation of Christ is best understood by a renewed and deeper understanding of this most ancient Mariology which stemmed from St. Paul's theology of Christ as the New Adam, which St. Paul developed in the fifth chapter of his Letter to the Romans.[13]

---

[12] "It was with a view to Christ that God the Father from all eternity chose her to be the all-holy Mother and adorned her with gifts of the Spirit granted to no one else. Certainly genuine Christian piety has never failed to highlight the indissoluble link and essential relationship of the Virgin to the divine Savior" (*MC,* 25).

[13] "Therefore, since we are justified by faith, we have peace with God through our Lord Jesus Christ. Through him we have obtained access to this grace in which we stand, and we rejoice in our hope of sharing the glory of God. More than that, we rejoice in our sufferings, knowing that suffering produces endurance, and endurance produces character, and character produces hope, and hope does not disappoint us, because God's love has been poured into our hearts through the Holy Spirit which has been given to us. While we were still weak, at the right time Christ died for the ungodly. Why, one will hardly die for a righteous man—though perhaps for a good man one will dare even to die. But God shows his love for us in that while we were yet sinners Christ died for us. Since, therefore, we are now justified by his blood, much more shall we be saved by him from the wrath of God. For if while we were enemies we were reconciled to God by the death of his Son, much more, now that we are reconciled, shall we be saved by his life. Not only so, but we also rejoice in God through our Lord Jesus Christ, through whom we have now received our reconciliation. Therefore as sin came into the world through one man and death through sin, and so death spread to all men because all men

St. Paul was clearly emphasizing that Jesus Christ is the Source of the grace of our Justification and Redemption just as the first Adam is the source of the transmission of Original Sin, although he was not the first to sin. St. Thomas explains this when he teaches that had Adam not sinned, then Eve's transgression would not have been transmitted to all humanity since it is the man's seed which carries the generative power.[14]

The early Church Fathers, however, understood that as the first Adam did not act alone in the Fall, neither did the Second Adam. Thus, beginning with St. Justin Martyr († c. 165) and St. Irenaeus († c. 200) the early Fathers began to understand Mary as the Second Eve who cooperated with Christ, the New Adam,

---

sinned—sin indeed was in the world before the law was given, but sin is not counted where there is no law. Yet death reigned from Adam to Moses, even over those whose sins were not like the transgression of Adam, who was a type of the one who was to come. But the free gift is not like the trespass. For if many died through one man's trespass, much more have the grace of God and the free gift in the grace of that one man Jesus Christ abounded for many. And the free gift is not like the effect of that one man's sin. For the judgment following one trespass brought condemnation, but the free gift following many trespasses brings justification. If, because of one man's trespass, death reigned through that one man, much more will those who receive the abundance of grace and the free gift of righteousness reign in life through the one man Jesus Christ. Then as one man's trespass led to condemnation for all men, so one man's act of righteousness leads to acquittal and life for all men. For as by one man's disobedience many were made sinners, so by one man's obedience many will be made righteous. Law came in, to increase the trespass; but where sin increased, grace abounded all the more, so that, as sin reigned in death, grace also might reign through righteousness to eternal life through Jesus Christ our Lord" (Rm. 5:1-21).

[14] "…Original sin is transmitted by the first parent in so far as he is the mover in the begetting of his children: wherefore it has been said [*ST*, I-II, q. 81, a. 4] that if anyone were begotten materially only, of human flesh, they would not contract original sin. Now it is evident that in the opinion of philosophers, the active principle of generation is from the father, while the mother provides the matter. Therefore original sin is contracted, not from the mother, but from the father: so that, accordingly, if Eve, and not Adam, had sinned, their children would not contract original sin: whereas, if Adam, and not Eve, had sinned, they would contract it" (*ST*, I-II, q. 81, a.5).

for the Redemption of humanity, which included its regeneration through the Suffering, Death, and Resurrection of Christ.[15]

---

[15] Mary as the New Eve is a doctrine that was first alluded to in the second century by St. Justin Martyr in his famous "Dialogue with Trypho" in which he speaks of the fittingness of God's plan of Redemption that it would involve a Second Eve (Mary) through whom the world would receive its Redeemer:

> ...He became man [by the Virgin], in order that the disobedience which proceeded from the serpent might receive its destruction in the same manner in which it derived its origin. For Eve, who was a virgin and undefiled, having conceived the word of the serpent, brought forth disobedience and death. But the Virgin Mary received faith and joy, when the angel Gabriel announced the good tidings to her that the Spirit of the Lord would come upon her, and the power of the Highest would overshadow her: wherefore also the Holy Thing begotten of her is the Son of God; and she replied, "Be it unto me according to your word."

> ...χαὶ διὰ τᾶς Παρθένου ἄνθρωπος γεγοωέναι, ἵνα χαὶ δι' ἧς ὁδοῦ ἡ ἀπὸ τοῦ ὄφεως παραχοὴ τὴν ἀπχὴν ἔλαβε, χαὶ διὰ ταύτης τᾶς ὁδοῦ χαὶ κατάλυσιν λάβη. Παρθένος γὰρ οὖσα. Εὔα χαὶ ἄφθορος, τὸν λόγον τὸν ἀπὸ τοῦ ὄφεως συλλαζοῦσα, παραχοὴν χαὶ θάνατον ἔτεχε. Πίστιν δὲ χαὶ χαρὰν λαζοῦσα Μαρία ἡ Παρθένος, εὐαγγελιζομένου αὐτῖ Γαβπιὴλ ἀγγέλου, ὅτι Πνεῦμα Κυρίου ἐπ' α'θτὴν ἐπελεύσεται, χαὶ δύναμις Ὑψίστου ἐπισχιάσει αὐτὴν διὸ χαὶ τὸ γεννώμενον ἐξ αὐτᾶς ἁγιόν ἐστιν Υἱὸς Θεοῦ, ἀπεχρίνατο "Γένοιτό μοι χατὰ τὸ ῥᾶμά σου" (St. Justin Martyr, *Dialogus cum Tryphone Judaeo*, PG 6, 709D-712A; English trans. from http://www.newadvent.org/fathers/01283.htm; Internet).

From the earliest centuries, therefore, Mary was seen as playing an inseparable role in God's plan of Redemption. This truth is especially evident by St. Irenaeus, who continued St. Justin's teaching on Mary as the Second Eve and is noted for his famous statement: "Mary, espoused but yet a virgin, became by her obedience a cause of salvation for herself and the whole human race" [*Maria habens praedestinatum virum, et tamen virgo, obediens, et sibi, et universo generi humano causa facta est salutis*] (St. Irenaeus, *Contra Haereses III*, PG 7, 959; cf. Michael O'Carroll, C.S.Sp., "Mediation, Mary Mediatress," *Theotokos*, 239). The title "New Eve," therefore, associates Mary to Christ, the "New Adam," and His universal work of Redemption. On the one hand, St. Irenaeus saw Christ's obedience as the efficient cause of mediating our salvation and making atonement for our disobedience. On the other hand, Mary's obedience to the redemptive plan of God, especially through her *fiat* at the Annunciation, made her inseparably associated with Christ's work of Redemption. This intimate connection between Mary and her Son in God's plan of Redemption was expressed by St. Jerome's formula: "Death *through*

Eve, life *through* Mary" [*Mors per Evam: vita per Mariam*] (St. Jerome, *Epistola 22, PL* 22, 408).

Among the Medieval Scholastics, no theologian better articulated this doctrine and its significance than St. Bernard. At the beginning of his sermon on the twelve stars of Mary's mystical crown, St. Bernard provides an excellent summary of Mary as the "New Eve" and the significance of this reality in order to explain Mary's inseparable role with Jesus Christ, the "New Adam," in God's plan of Redemption. St. Bernard explains that Mary continues her cooperation with her Son today by offering a fallen humanity "the remedy of salvation" which is the Redemptive graces from her Son:

> It is true, most dearly beloved, that the first man and the first woman did us grievous harm, but—thanks be to God!—by another Man and another Woman all that was lost has been restored to us, not without the addition of abundant grace. For "not as the offence, so also the gift" (Rm. 5:15): the magnitude of the grace won for us by Christ exceeds beyond all proportion the ruin wrought by Adam. Instead of breaking that which was injured (Matt. 22:20), the Almighty Creator in His infinite wisdom and goodness restored it to its original perfection, yea, made it better than it had been before, forming a new Adam from the ancient and giving us in Mary a second Eve. Christ alone would no doubt have been sufficient, for even now "all our sufficiency is from Him" (2 Cor. 3:5); but it was not good for us that the Man should be alone (Gen. 2:18). It seemed more congruous that as both sexes contributed to the ruin of our race, so should both have a part in the work of reparation. A truly faithful and powerful, "Mediator of God and men is the Man Christ Jesus" (1 Tim. 2:5); but the Majesty of His Godhead inspires mortals with fear....

> From this, therefore, it ought to appear evident that the Woman pronounced "blessed among women" (Lk. 1:28) is not without her proper function: for her also is found something to do in the work of reconciliation. So great a Mediator is Christ that we have need of another to mediate between Him and us, and for this we can find none so well qualified as Mary. A most cruel Mediatrix [*Crudelis nimium mediatrix Eva*] was our mother Eve, through whom the "old serpent" (Rev. 12:9) communicated the mortal poison of sin even to the man; but Mary is faithful, Mary offers the remedy of salvation both to men and women. The former became the means of our seduction, the latter co-operated in our reconciliation; the former was made the instrument of temptation, the latter the channel of redemption [*...sed fidelis Maria, quae salutis antidotum et viris, et mulieribus propinavit. Illa enim ministra seductionis; haec, propitiationis: illa suggessit praevaricationem, haec ingessit redemptionem*] (St. Bernard of Clairveaux, *In Dominica infra Octavam Assumptionis B. V. Mariae Sermo, PL* 183, 429-430; cf. *St. Bernard's Sermons for the Seasons & Principal*

Mary as the New Eve stresses her unique role and active participation under Christ and with Christ, the New Adam, in bringing about the Redemption of mankind. Vatican II stressed Mary as the New Eve for the same reason.[16] As this study will illustrate, Sheen develops Mary as the New Eve as she fulfills the place in Redemption which fittingly corresponds to the role Eve played in the Fall. As Eve was created for Adam to be a "helper fit for him" (Gn. 2:18) and become "mother of all living (Gn. 3:20)," so did God create Mary to be fittingly "the handmaid of the Lord (Lk. 1:38)," Spouse of the Holy Spirit, Mother of the Redeemer and Mother of the new humanity. As the first Adam and first Eve formed a unity in the flesh, so did there exist in a more elevated way a "unity of the two"[17] between the New Adam and the New Eve in God's

---

Festivals of the Year, vol. 3, trans. anon. [Westminster, MD: Carroll Press, 1950], 258-259).

[16] "'...Behold the handmaid of the Lord, be it done unto me according to thy word.' Thus Mary, a daughter of Adam, consenting to the divine Word, became the mother of Jesus, the one and only Mediator. Embracing God's salvific will with a full heart and impeded by no sin, she devoted herself totally as a handmaid of the Lord to the person and work of her Son, under Him and with Him, by the grace of almighty God, serving the mystery of redemption. Rightly therefore the holy Fathers see her as used by God not merely in a passive way, but as freely cooperating in the work of human salvation through faith and obedience. For, as St. Irenaeus says, she 'being obedient, became the cause of salvation for herself and for the whole human race.' Hence not a few of the early Fathers gladly assert in their preaching, 'The knot of Eve's disobedience was untied by Mary's obedience; what the virgin Eve bound through her unbelief, the Virgin Mary loosened by her faith.' Comparing Mary with Eve, they call her 'the Mother of the living,' and still more often they say: 'death through Eve, life through Mary'" (*LG*, 56). John Paul II further developed the importance and fittingness of Christ, the New Adam, working with a New Eve to accentuate the nuptial context within which the new humanity would come into being through a "unity of the two" (cf. *MD*, 6-8, 10, 23, 25). John Paul is not speaking of a hypostatic union between Mary and Christ, but a spousal union between Mary and the Spirit of Christ, which renders her virginity fruitful as our "mother in the order of grace" (cf. *LG*, 61-63).

[17] The phrase "unity of the two" is borrowed from John Paul II's Apostolic Letter *Mulieris Dignitatem* in which he significantly developed the spousal theme which runs throughout Sacred Scripture and applies it to God's plan of Redemption which would fittingly involve a nuptial union between God and

plan of Redemption. We will see shortly how Sheen unpacks these profound mysteries as he explains Mary as the New Eve in her role as the *ideal* woman who acts with and for God as His Spouse and Virgin-Mother in His plan of Redemption.

Sheen explains this unique role of Mary as central to the entire history of salvation, where Mary, as the Second Vatican Council says, "is already prophetically foreshadowed in that promise of victory over the serpent, which was given to our first parents after their fall into sin (cf. Gn. 3:15)."[18] In light of the Genesis account of the fall of Adam and Eve, Sheen demonstrates that the mystery of Mary's role as the New Eve, or maternal Mediatrix, is only understood by closely examining her inseparable role in the mystery of the Incarnation, which Sheen taught encompassed the messianic mission of Christ beginning at the Annunciation, culminating at Calvary, and continuing in her maternal role from heaven by her universal intercession and dispensing of all graces to mankind.

This recapitulation theology is particularly ecclesiological since it deals with the role of the Church as the instrument through which the members of the Mystical Body receive the Divine Life of Christ through grace. For Sheen, however, this recapitulation is merely an extension, or continuation of Christ's Incarnation on earth.[19] Sheen's ecclesiology is therefore part of his Christology. In Sheen's teaching on both, Mary plays a central mediatory role as Mother of Christ and Mother of His Mystical Body, or as Sheen combines the two, Mary is the Mother of the *fullness* of Christ.[20] He explains the significance of Mary's Divine and spiritual motherhood in terms of Mary's unique role in salvation history as the New Eve.

While St. Irenaeus's theological parallel between Eve and Mary was integrated into the Mariological thought of the Fathers and Medieval Scholastics, there was little development of what those parallels contained. Important questions remained without any

humanity through the cooperation of a New Adam and a new "woman," or New Eve. Mary, who is the Mother and type of the Church, fulfills this role.
[18] *LG*, 55; *RM*, 7.
[19] Cf. Ibid., 69-72.
[20] Cf. Ibid., 314-316.

significant treatment. For example, of what exactly did Eve's "knot" consist? How exactly did Mary untie this knot? How do we understand better this mystery, especially Irenaeus's bold words that Mary "became for herself and for the whole human race a cause of salvation [*causa salutis*]? How are we better to understand the parallel drawn between Eve and Mary? These are very important questions that must be adequately addressed if we are to understand how Mary mediates salvation and of what this mediation truly consists.

Sheen's teaching of Mary in the mystery of Christ fills in the theological gaps. He found the answers to these questions by returning to a careful study and reflection on Mary's relationship to the mystery of the Incarnation as revealed in Sacred Scripture. He understood the mystery of the Incarnation as inseparably linked to the mysteries of Redemption (soteriology), the Church as the mystical prolongation of the Incarnation (ecclesiology), and the sanctifying mission of the Holy Spirit (pneumatology). Sheen knew that since Mary is inseparably related to the Incarnation as Mother of Christ and Mother of Christians, a study into her mediatory role in salvation history would necessitate reflection on her relation to each of these mysteries. This study will therefore illustrate Sheen's position that Mary's mediation was—and remains—primarily a *salvific* mediation since it is bound up in the mystery of Christ's Incarnation and His messianic mission.[21]

Therefore, the Mariology of Fulton Sheen presents in a new light a deeper understanding of the mystery of Mary's mediation in her role as the New Eve. It is a Mariology which, for Sheen, expresses her role as maternal Mediatrix and inseparable cooperator with Christ in Redemption (what is referred to by some as Mary's role as the "Coredemptrix"). Therefore, understanding *who* Mary is as the New Eve (or maternal Mediatrix) is as important as understanding *how she acts* as maternal Mediatrix. They are both at the heart of the mystery of Mary according to Sheen, who will demonstrate in our study how the four Marian dogmas are directly related to making her a fitting Mediatrix of all graces because they inseparably unite her to the mystery of the Incarnation.

---

[21] Cf. *WFL*, 73-74; *MBC*, 326.

Sheen's approach to Mary's role as maternal Mediatrix is also anthropological because understanding Mary as the New Eve is at the heart of understanding her vocation as the *new* "woman" in relation to the *new* "Man." The two are oriented toward each other to achieve a new communion of love in Christ. This plays out not only in the human order, but also according to God's salvific plan. That is why, as we shall see, Sheen emphasizes that the spiritual relationship between Christ and Mary in the work of Redemption is best understood within the context of the Bride and Bridegroom.

Mary's Relationship to the Incarnation is the Paradigm of Her Relationship to its Mystical Prolongation

A proper and complete understanding of the Incarnation was critical for Sheen, for as we will see in Chapter IV of this study, Sheen presents the theology of the Church as the "mystical prolongation of the Incarnation." For Sheen, this means that the Church is the life of Christ extended or continued in His Mystical Body, the Church, until His fullness is achieved in His Body. His teaching is a profound development of St. Irenaeus's recapitulation theology, especially as it applies to Mary.

Sheen's understanding of the Incarnation prolonged in and through the Church, therefore, provides necessary insight into what it means to say Mary is "Mother of Christ." As we will see Sheen explain in Chapter IV, Mary is the Mother of the fullness of Christ, or Mother of the *whole* Christ. What this means for Sheen is that what is revealed about Mary's motherhood to Christ during His historical life will apply equally to all those who will make up His Mystical Body. This is another way of explaining St. Irenaeus's theology of recapitulation, for whatever applies to Christ the Head in relation to Mary, applies equally to His Mystical Body because they constitute one Person, although our union with Christ is through grace, not hypostatically. John Paul II later taught that the life of the Church is a recapitulation of the life of Christ, as was affirmed by Vatican II:

> [Mary's] "pilgrimage of faith" in which "the Blessed Virgin advanced," faithfully preserving her union with Christ

[*LG*, 58]. In this way the "twofold bond" which unites the Mother of God with Christ and with the Church takes on historical significance. Nor is it just a question of the Virgin Mother's life-story, of her personal journey of faith and "the better part" which is hers in the mystery of salvation; it is also a question of the history of the whole People of God, of all those who take part in the same "pilgrimage of faith."

The Council expresses this when it states in another passage that Mary "has gone before," becoming "a model of the Church in the matter of faith, charity and perfect union with Christ" [*LG*, 63]. This "going before" as a figure or model is in reference to the intimate mystery of the Church, as she actuates and accomplishes her own saving mission by uniting in herself—as Mary did—the qualities of mother and virgin. She is a virgin who "keeps whole and pure the fidelity she has pledged to her Spouse" and "becomes herself a mother," for "she brings forth to a new and immortal life children who are conceived of the Holy Spirit and born of God" [*LG*, 64].[22]

We will see, therefore, that what the Second Vatican Council and John Paul II will later refer to as Mary's "motherhood in the order of grace," Sheen had explained in terms of Mary's motherhood of the whole Christ, or Mary's continued role as Mother in the mystical prolongation of the Incarnation in the Church. Like Vatican II and John Paul II, Sheen will explain how Mary's maternal influence not only pertains to the faithful, but to all humanity.

METHODOLOGY USED BY FULTON SHEEN AND FOR THIS STUDY

Sheen's approach to Mary's mediation is primarily biblical, rooted in Sacred Tradition, and it is essentially Christological. Sheen's biblical approach is noteworthy, not only because it provides a positive response to the wishes of the Czestochowa Commission

---

[22] *RM*, 5.

(mentioned earlier in this chapter), but also because it anticipated the renewed biblical approach to theology which Vatican II would emphasize decades later in Articles 24 and 25 of *Dei Verbum*.[23]

Starting with Sacred Scripture is precisely what marked Sheen's theological method. This was especially true in his approach to explaining the mystery of Mary in salvation history. Although he does not always explicitly reference his sources, a careful study such as ours into his Mariology will reveal that Sheen's approach was a return *ad fontes*, beginning with Sacred Scripture and supported with the teachings from the Fathers and Doctors of the Church. With special adherence to the teachings of the papal Magisterium of his time, Sheen would then find reasonable ways to articulate the mystery of Mary drawing upon his knowledge of philosophy, the natural sciences, his masterful use of analogy and biblical typology. In this light, Sheen's contribution to the theology of Mary's mediation is of great value.

In presenting his doctrine on Mary's mediation Sheen brings us through the key events of salvation history as they relate to Mary's role in the mystery of the Incarnation. Through these events Sheen demonstrates how they provide critical insight into Mary's role as maternal Mediatrix in God's plan of Redemption. He also emphasizes that since the Church is the mystical prolongation of the Incarnation, what is revealed about Mary's relationship to the Incarnation will also be prolonged in her ongoing relationship to humanity as Mother of the Mystical Body of Christ. The biblical events thus reveal God's blueprint for how Mary will exercise her mediation once she is assumed gloriously into heaven.

---

[23] "Sacred theology relies on the written Word of God, taken together with sacred Tradition, as on a permanent foundation. By this Word it is most firmly strengthened and constantly rejuvenated, as it searches out, under the light of faith, the full truth stored up in the mystery of Christ. The Sacred Scriptures contain the Word of God, and, because they are inspired, they are truly the Word of God. Therefore, the 'study of the sacred page' should be the very soul of sacred theology. The ministry of the Word, too—pastoral preaching, catechetics and all forms of Christian instruction, among which the liturgical homily should hold pride of place—is healthily nourished and thrives in holiness through the Word of Scripture."

The division of this study, therefore, reflects Sheen's two-fold approach to understanding Mary's mediation. The first half is dedicated to understanding the blueprint of Mary's mediation as revealed in her relationship with Christ throughout His redemptive mission. The second half of the study is an explication of Sheen's teaching on how we can best understand Mary's descending mediation in terms of her role as Mother of the Mystical Body of Christ. For Sheen, everything revealed about Mary's role with her Son in acquiring the graces of Redemption is paradigmatic for how Mary will act in the distribution of those redemptive graces. In both aspects of her mediation, Sheen illustrates how Mary acts as both Spouse and Mother. A special chapter will be added to these two in which we will examine Sheen's thought on Mary's mediation in the modern world.

In this study, therefore, we will draw out what is both explicit and implicit in Sheen's teaching on Mary's mediation in the mystery of the Incarnation. In the concluding chapter of this study, we will return to the primary theological questions of the debate presented in the second chapter. We will summarize how this study of Sheen's teaching on Mary's ascending and descending mediation from a biblical and Christological perspective provides a rich and positive contribution to the ongoing debate.

FULTON SHEEN'S STYLE

It is important that something be said of Sheen's style of teaching. As we described in the previous chapter, Sheen was an incredibly gifted and effective communicator of the truths of the Catholic faith. He knew how to reach his audiences. In order to accomplish that goal, for example, Sheen would utilize rhetorical devices such as hyperbole to reinforce a theological point. Thus, there are times in his lectures and in his writings where Sheen may seem to lack theological precision in order that he may convey the overall theological point to his audience. This distinction will be duly noted where appropriate throughout our study.

Sources for Our Study on Fulton Sheen's Teaching on Marian Mediation

It is fortunate for the Church that Sheen provided for us his thoughts through various media on this important doctrine of Mary's mediation. The fullness of Sheen's Marian thought is only found by a careful study of his abundant writing, teaching and preaching, which literally span his entire sixty years of priesthood. It is important to note that the great majority of Sheen's published works were written prior to the Second Vatican Council as Sheen was already 67 years old at the time the Council convened in 1962. Among these are his most significant and comprehensive works on the Church and the Blessed Virgin Mary which necessarily serve as the primary theological sources of Sheen's thought on Mary's maternal mediation. However, while the majority of Sheen's insights are found in his works before the Second Vatican Council, Sheen's later publications on the priesthood and his many recorded lectures demonstrate the consistency and accuracy of his thought which was later confirmed by the Marian teaching of Vatican II.

In light of the debate we have examined in this chapter—in particular, the relevance of pre-conciliar teaching and terminology on Mary's mediation—it is important that brief attention be given to the significance of Sheen's pre-conciliar works on Mary. The Second Vatican Council did not intend to discard the organic, theological tradition of the Church which led up to it (and essentially served as the foundations for its teachings). One of these *loci theologici* which was given special attention by the Council was the papal Magisterium.

During an address given to the bishops of Chile in 1988, Joseph Cardinal Ratzinger addressed a misconception among some bishops and theologians according to which the Second Vatican Council marked a new era of theology disconnected from pre-conciliar teachings. Cardinal Ratzinger asserted that this indeed was not the case. Rather, the teachings of the Council make sense only in light of the tradition from which they came:

The Second Vatican Council has not been treated as a part
of the entire living Tradition of the Church, but as an end
of Tradition, a new start from zero. The truth is that this
particular Council defined no dogma at all, and deliberately chose to remain on a modest level, as a merely pastoral
council; and yet many treat it as though it had made itself
into a sort of superdogma which takes away the importance
of all the rest....

...The one way in which Vatican II can be made plausible
is to present it as it is; one part of the unbroken, the unique
Tradition of the Church and of her faith.[24]

Four years later, Cardinal Ratzinger shared additional thoughts
on this matter:

The Church does not have the right to exchange the faith
for something else and at the same time to expect the faithful to stay with her. Councils can therefore neither discover ecclesiologies or other doctrines nor can they repudi-
ate them. In the words of Vatican II, the Church is "not
higher than the Word of God but serves it and therefore
teaches only what is handed on to it." Our understanding of the depth and breadth of the tradition develops
because the Holy Spirit broadens and deepens the memory
of the Church in order to guide her "into all the truth"
(Jn 16:13). According to the Council, growth in the perception (*Wahrnehmung, perceptio*) of what is inherent to
the tradition occurs in three ways: through the meditation
and study of the faithful, through an interior understanding which stems from the spiritual life, and through the
proclamation of those "who have received the sure charism
of truth by succeeding to the office of the bishop." The following words basically paraphrase the spiritual position of
a council as well as its possibilities and tasks: the council

[24] Joseph Cardinal Ratzinger, Address to the Bishops of Chile Regarding the
Lefebvre Schism (13 July 1988, accessed 10 July 2007); available from http://
www.unavoce.org/cardinal_ratzinger_chile.htm; Internet.

is committed from within to the Word of God and to the tradition. It can only teach what is handed on. As a rule, it must find new language to hand on the tradition in each new context so that—to put it a different way—the tradition remains genuinely the same.[25]

These citations from *Lumen Gentium* and then from Cardinal Ratzinger emphasize the vital importance of pre-conciliar teachings and how understanding these pre-conciliar teachings is essential to any authentic interpretation of the Second Vatican Council. This is why both the pre-conciliar and post-conciliar Marian thought of Fulton Sheen needs to be studied. They form a whole which faithfully unites and clearly articulates his theological reflection on Mary's mediation which, remarkably, remained largely unchanged.

The first major theological treatise of Sheen was on the Church, *The Mystical Body of Christ*. Written in 1935, almost a decade before Pope Pius XII's *Mystici Corporis*, Sheen's treatise on the Church contained a special chapter which examined exclusively Mary's maternal and ecclesial mediation within the Mystical Body of Christ, the Church. Sheen emphasized an ecclesiology where Mary plays an essential role acting as both mother of the Redeemer and spiritual mother of the redeemed in the order of grace. In fact, Sheen's understanding of Mary's spiritual maternity can only be understood in conjunction with his ecclesiology that centers on understanding the Church as the Mystical Body of Christ and Mary as the mother of the Mystical Body of Christ.

Almost twenty years later, in 1952, Sheen wrote *The World's First Love*. In this remarkable and comprehensive treatise on the Blessed Virgin Mary, the Marian ecclesiology Sheen presented in *The Mystical Body of Christ* was articulated anew, but within the broader context of Mary's role in salvation history. This work was written only two years after the solemn definition of Mary's Assumption, which had special significance for Sheen. This work not only represents Sheen's comprehensive thought on Mary's mediation, but provides an interesting application of his theology as it applies to

---

[25] Joseph Cardinal Ratzinger, "Communio: A Program," *Communio: International Catholic Review* 19 (Fall 1992): 436-49.

Mary's mediation in the modern world, a subject we will treat in greater depth later in the final chapter of our study.

By the beginning of the Second Vatican Council, Sheen had already written most of his theological works. The last two decades of his life were devoted primarily to preaching and giving lectures around the United States and various parts of the world. Most of his preaching was part of a series which commonly contained at least one presentation dedicated to the Blessed Virgin. We are fortunate that much of Sheen's post-conciliar preaching, often in the form of retreat lectures, was recorded on audio cassette and is generally accessible to the public. These recordings illustrate Sheen's consistency of thought throughout his priesthood as well as the influence that the Second Vatican Council had on his Mariology, in particular Mary's relationship with the Church as "Mother of the Church," a title proposed by Pope Paul VI during the Council and accepted by the conciliar bishops.

The last primary source is Sheen's significant work on the priesthood entitled *Those Mysterious Priests*, which Sheen published in 1974, only five years before his death. In *Those Mysterious Priests*, which is largely a mature summary of his Christology, Sheen dedicated a special section to the Blessed Virgin Mary. In this section, representing forty years of pious reflection and study on the mystery of Mary, Sheen summarizes the main points of his teaching on Mary's maternal mediation in the mystery of Christ. The work also demonstrates Sheen's consistency of thought on Mary's mediation over four decades and how Sheen's pre-conciliar thought anticipated the theological direction of Vatican II.

This study will also examine important sources of Sheen's Marian thought which, although secondary to the above treatises, include publications and audio recordings of Sheen throughout his life in which he wrote and spoke of the Blessed Virgin Mary. Lastly, this study includes related elements from Sheen's unpublished thought on Mary, which he used in preparation for many of his lectures.

CONCLUSION

While both sides of the debate have not yet found mutually acceptable terms for accurately articulating the theological significance of Mary's mediation, both sides of the argument point to the fact that Mary's mediation has a central place in the mystery of Redemption. Therefore, a proper understanding of Mary's mediation is critical for the Church because of its "undeniable consequences" on our understanding for the mystery of Christ. The debate also revolves around the important question of the theological direction of Vatican II as it relates to Mary's mediation. What both sides concede is that Vatican II placed a renewed emphasis on the maternal dimension of Mary's mediation from a Scriptural standpoint and on Mary's inseparable role in God's plan of Redemption. In an attempt to reconcile the pre-conciliar and post-conciliar teaching on Mary's mediation, the contemporary debate has called for deeper reflection and study of Mary's mediatory role in salvation history according to its Trinitarian, Christological, pneumatological, soteriological, ecclesiological and anthropological perspectives.

This study of Fulton Sheen's theology of Mary's mediation provides a rich and positive response to the theological challenge posed by the debate. In the following chapters we will see how Sheen uses Sacred Scripture as his theological foundation upon which one can accurately develop a correct understanding of the unique mediation of Jesus Christ, the New Adam—a mediation which possesses ascending and descending characteristics corresponding to the objective and subjective dimensions of Redemption. Mary's mediation derives from and is a participation in Christ's mediation, thus also possessing ascending and descending dimensions. Sheen believed that one can best understand how Mary exercises her ascending and descending mediation by a renewed understanding of the ancient typology of Mary as the New Eve and the relation of the New Eve as spouse and mother to the mystery of the Incarnation. While preserving pre-conciliar Marian terminology, Sheen is less concerned with promoting terminology than with explaining the nature of Mary's mediation, which he will explain in terms of Mary's personal relationships to the mystery of the Incarnation as spouse and mother in her role as the New Eve.

CHAPTER III
MARY'S MEDIATION IN THE MYSTERY OF THE INCARNATION

Adam, Eve, and the Fall

In order to properly contextualize Fulton Sheen's approach to Mary as the New Eve, it is important that we give due attention to understanding the created state and fall of Eve. The parallel would not work if the two were not essentially identical in their original state. If Mary had an advantage over Eve, then the parallel fails. How was the original state of Eve and Mary's sinless state the same? How were they different? How did Eve fall into sin and Mary did not? How *could* Eve fall into sin, and could Mary sin considering she, like Eve, was created without Original Sin? Did they both share the same grace? These are important questions to answer as we begin our study of Mary entering into salvation history as early as the allusion to her in the Protoevangelium in Genesis 3:15. We begin our study, therefore, analyzing the significance of Eve's fall from grace through one disobedient act and the universal consequences which resulted after Eve seduced Adam to sin. When we later examine Sheen's explanation of the events of the Annunciation, we will contrast Eve's fall to Mary's *fiat*, examining its full significance, its relation to Christ the New Adam and its universal consequences in relation to her Divine Maternity.

First, St. Thomas Aquinas teaches that both Adam and Eve were created in the state of "original righteousness,"[1] which meant their reason was subjected to God and the lower powers to reason.[2] St. Thomas explains that this state of original righteousness (or "original justice"[3]) was made possible because Adam and Eve were created in "sanctifying grace," which St. Thomas defines as the grace "whereby man himself is united to God."[4] Article 56 of *Lumen Gentium* refers to this created state of Adam and Eve as "original holiness," where Adam and Eve were filled with the divine life.

If Eve was created in sanctifying grace, how could she be tempted to sin? St. Thomas explains that Adam and Eve were created with an intellect and free will.[5] As St. Thomas explains, because both were endowed with reason, this allowed man to make free judgments derived "from some act of comparison in the reason."[6] St. Thomas, therefore, says, "Forasmuch as man is rational is it necessary that man have a free will," which is what separates us from the "brute animals."[7] This is very important because without free will, "counsels, exhortations, commands, prohibitions, rewards and punishments would be in vain."[8] This teaching is especially important when we treat the question of *merit* in regards to Mary's *fiat* at the Annunciation.

In addition to free will, St. Thomas explains that another condition of human nature is that "one creature can be helped or impeded by another." For this reason, St. Thomas explains, "It was fitting that God should both allow man in the state of innocence to be tempted by evil angels, and should cause him to be helped by good angels." He adds, "And by a special favor of grace, it was granted him that no creature outside himself could harm him against his own will, whereby he was able even to resist the

---

[1] *ST*, I, q. 100, a. 1.
[2] Cf. *ST*, I, q. 95, a. 1.
[3] Cf. *CCC*, 376.
[4] *ST*, I-II, q. 111, a. 1; cf. *CCC*, 375.
[5] *ST*, I, q. 83, a. 1.
[6] Ibid.
[7] Ibid; cf. *ST*, I-II, q. 114.
[8] Ibid.

temptation of the demon."[9] St. Thomas even goes as far as to say, "In the state of innocence, man was able, *without any difficulty*, to resist temptation. Consequently, the tempter's assault was not a punishment to man."[10]

If it would have been easy to resist the temptation of Satan, how did Adam and Eve fall into sin and, from the account in Scripture, rather easily? St. Thomas answers by quoting the Book of Sirach: "Pride is the beginning of sin."[11] But how was pride possible when, as St. Thomas says, "man was so appointed in the state of innocence, that there was no rebellion of the flesh against the spirit"?[12] St. Thomas responds by saying that any "inordinateness" begins in the soul and, while there was no rebellion of the flesh against the spirit, "it was possible for his appetite (a faculty of the soul) to be directed to an inordinate end."[13] In the case of the temptation of Adam of Eve, the temptation targeted Adam and Eve's "coveting inordinately some spiritual good…above his measure: and this pertains to pride."[14] He explains this further:

> Man's disobedience to the Divine command was not willed by man for his own sake, for this could not happen unless one presupposes inordinateness in his will. It remains therefore that he willed it for the sake of something else. Now the first thing he coveted inordinately was his own excellence; and consequently his disobedience was the result of his pride.[15]

St. Thomas explains that Eve coveted the serpent's promise upon eating the fruit of the tree of the knowledge of good and evil: "Your eyes shall be opened and you shall be as Gods (Gn. 3:5)."[16] The serpent was cunning and knew how to tempt Adam and Eve:

---

[9] *ST*, II-II, q. 165, a. 1.

[10] *ST*, II-II, q. 165, a. 1, ad 3.

[11] Sir. 10:15; *ST*, II-II, q. 163, a. 1.

[12] *ST*, II-II, q. 163, a. 1.

[13] Ibid.

[14] Ibid.

[15] *ST*, II-II, q. 163, a. 1, ad 1.

[16] *ST*, II-II, q. 163, a. 1, ad. 2.

"The desire for knowledge resulted in our first parents from their inordinate desire for excellence. Hence the serpent began by saying: 'You shall be as Gods,' and added: 'Knowing good and evil.'"[17]

St. Thomas explains, however, that this inordinate desire for excellence (pride) did not precede the promptings of the serpent, "but that as soon as the serpent had spoken his words of persuasion, her mind was puffed up, the result being that she believed the demon to have spoken truly."[18] Later, Thomas explains that Eve coveted this knowledge because she wanted according to her own terms to acquire the Divine likeness according to knowledge, for which she had the potential, but "had not yet received this likeness in actuality."[19] Therefore,

> The first man sinned chiefly by coveting God's likeness as regards "knowledge of good and evil," *according to the serpent's instigation*, namely that by his own natural power he might decide what was good, and what was evil for him to do; or again that he should of himself foreknow what good and what evil would befall him. Secondarily, he sinned by coveting God's likeness as regards his own power of operation, namely that by his own natural power he might act so as to obtain happiness....Both coveted somewhat to be equal to God, in so far as each wished to rely on himself in contempt of the order of the Divine rule.[20]

St. Thomas summarizes the reason for the fall of Adam and Eve by saying; "To covet [God's] likeness inordinately, that is, above one's measure, this is a sin....Thus did the devil, who was unwilling to be subject to Him, and man who refused to be, as a servant, bound by His command."[21] Fulton Sheen interpreted the "Divine rule" to which St. Thomas refers as the Divine law of love to which our created free will was originally oriented. Thus freedom is associated with loving according to God's rule, thereby

[17] *ST*, II-II, q. 163, a. 1, ad. 3.
[18] *ST*, II-II, q. 163, a. 1, ad. 4.
[19] *ST*, II-II, q. 163, a. 2.
[20] Ibid.
[21] *ST*, II-II, q. 163, a. 2, ad. 2.

making the coveting and disobedience of Adam and Eve the fruit of their misuse of their free will influenced by an inordinate love of self over God. The ability to love, therefore, is God's greatest gift to man and woman because it allows them to choose Him first and receive the gifts which God promises to those who obey His law of love. Sheen explains the significance of the intrinsic relation between freedom and love and its central place in understanding God's plan for humanity:

> An interesting insight into love is this—that, to just the extent that we reject love, we lose our gifts. No refugee from Russia sends a gift back to a dictator; God's gifts, too, are dependent on our love. Adam and Eve could have passed on to posterity extraordinary gifts of body and soul had they but loved. They were not *forced* to love; they were not asked to say, "I love", because words can be empty; they were merely asked to make an act of choice between what is God's and what is not God's, between the choices symbolized in the alternatives of the garden and the tree. If they had had no freedom, they would have turned to God as the sunflower does to the sun; but, being free, they could reject the whole for the part, the garden for the tree, the future joy for the immediate pleasure. The result was that mankind lost those gifts that God would have passed on to it, had it only been true in love.[22]

One can already begin to see how humility and faith in God's plan will play a central role in Mary when she is tested as the second Eve.

Although Adam was guilty of the same sin as Eve, he did not share the same severity as Eve. This is primarily due to the fact, as St. Thomas points out, that she "was employed as an instrument of temptation in bringing about the downfall of the man, both because the woman was weaker than the man, and consequently more liable to be deceived, and because, on account of her union with man, the devil was able to deceive the man especially through

---

[22] *WFL*, 26.

her."[23] This is why St. Bernard, as we have already seen, referred to Eve as "a most cruel Mediatrix [*Crudelis nimium mediatrix Eva*]…through whom the 'old serpent' (Rev. 12:9) communicated the mortal poison of sin even to the man." Eve, therefore, had a double sin in comparison to the sin of Adam. This is why Eve's punishment was more severe, as is evident in Genesis 3:16. But the universal consequences of Eve's sin—what Irenaeus referred to as "the knot of Eve's disobedience"[24]—is revealed immediately after God, in His mercy, promises Redemption through a New Adam. God reveals that the Redeemer of humanity would fittingly come through the cooperation of a New Eve ("the *woman*"), who would mediate the antidote (Jesus Christ) for the poison of sin and its consequences. In addition, this second Eve would have the mission of redeeming the shattered image of womanhood—especially in her role as servant of God and faithful spouse of man. Sheen provided interesting insights into how Mary was God's special creation chosen to undo the knot of Eve's disobedience, which we will now illuminate.

A New Eve Acting as Mediatrix to the Mediator was Necessary to Satisfy Justice

Fulton Sheen stressed that there were two sides to God's plan of Redemption. The first side pertains to God's mercy. It was impossible for man alone to atone for the universal consequences of Adam and Eve's Original Sin. Mankind does not possess the power to forgive sins. Therefore, God Himself, out of His infinite mercy, intervened to offer Redemption to a fallen humanity. The other side to God's plan of Redemption pertained to satisfying the conditions of His Justice. It would not have been just if God had imposed Redemption upon humanity whose Original Sin arose out

---

[23] *ST*, II-II, q. 165, a. 2.
[24] St. Irenaeus, *Contra Haereses III, PL* 7, 958-959.

of its free choice to disobey Him. Mankind's freedom would there-fore have to play an inseparable part in God's plan of Redemption.

How, therefore, would God mediate Redemption in a way that perfectly fulfilled the exigencies of His Justice? If the Original Sin was introduced through the misuse of freedom of a woman who then seduced her husband to sin, then Divine Justice demands that Redemption be mediated in a manner that also involves the free cooperation of a new *woman* with God whose obedience of faith and love will mediate the means of Redemption, a New Adam. Sheen explains this dilemma with the following analogy:

> What concerns us now is the restoration of these gifts through another act of freedom. God could have restored man to himself by simply forgiving man's sin, but then there would have been mercy without justice. The problem confronting man was something like that which confronts an orchestra leader. The score is written and given to an excellent director. The musicians, well skilled in their art, are free to follow the director or to rebel against him. Suppose that one of the musicians decides to hit a wrong note. The director might do either of two things: either he might ignore the mistake, or he might strike his baton and order the measure to be replayed. It would make little dif-ference, for that note has already gone winging into space, and since time cannot be reversed, the discord goes on and on through the universe, even to the end of time. Is there any possible way by which this voluntary disharmony can be stopped? Certainly not by anyone in time. It could be corrected on condition that someone would reach out from eternity, would seize that note in time and arrest it in its mad flight. But would it still not be a discord? No, it could be made the first note in a new symphony and thus be made harmonious!

When our first parents were created, God gave them a con-science, a moral law, and an original justice. They were not compelled to follow Him as the director of the symphony of creation. Yet they chose to rebel, and that sour note of

original revolution was passed on to humanity, through
human generation. How could that original disorder be
stopped? It could be arrested in the same way as the sour
note, by having eternity come into time and lay hold of a
man by force, compelling him to enter into a new order
where the original gifts would be restored and harmony
would be the law. But this would not be God's way, for
it would mean the destruction of human freedom. God
could lay hold of a note, but He could not lay hold of
a man by force without abusing the greatest gift that He
gave to man—namely, freedom, which alone makes love
possible.[25]

We therefore see from Sheen's analogy that although God had
no absolute need for an intermediary to redeem humanity, justice
demanded that the restoration of humanity be accomplished
through the free cooperation of one its members. In this sense,
Mary as Mediatrix and the New Eve was necessary as she was predestined to fulfill this central and indispensable role on behalf of
fallen humanity. She would be the one with whom, through whom
and from whom God would become the one Mediator between
God and man by means of the Incarnation. Sheen further explains
the significance of Mary's role as Mediatrix as it relates to the instrument of Redemption, the Incarnation, by a renewed examination
of the significance of the Protoevangelium.

The Woman, the Seed and the Shedding of Blood

After the Fall of Adam and Eve through their pride and disobedience, God revealed His promise of Redemption that would come
through "the seed" of "the woman." In other words, God would
create a new humanity that would come about through a second

---

[25] *WFL*, 26-27.

Adam and a second Eve, whose holiness and progeny will be in total opposition with sin and the devil.

> I will put enmity between you and the woman,
> and between your seed and her seed:
> he shall bruise your head,
> and you shall bruise his heel.[26]

We see, therefore, that immediately after the Fall, God promised Redemption to Adam and Eve and their progeny. But this Redemption would come at a great price. The price of Redemption is explicitly revealed in the ninth chapter of the Letter to the Hebrews, verse 23: "Without the shedding of blood there is no forgiveness of sins." Commenting on this passage Sheen said:

> Why the shedding of blood? What is the relationship between sin and the shedding of blood? Sin is in the blood…and therefore if it is in the blood, if it is ever to be done away with, it has to be poured out….
>
> …And another reason: sin is serious. It requires expiation and sacrifice.[27]

Sheen goes on to point out that Hebrews 9 is implicitly revealed immediately after God promises Redemption and covers up Adam and Eve's shame with the skins of animals. We read in Genesis 3: 21,

> And the Lord God made for Adam and his wife
> garments of skins, and clothed them.

Sheen explained that this one line in Scripture has great importance in understanding God's plan of Redemption:

> In order to have the skins of animals, there had to be the shedding of blood. Note here, three characteristics of this covering of shame. First of all, it came from God Himself.

---

[26] Gn. 3:15.

[27] Fulton J. Sheen, "The Remission of Sin" (from a series of retreat lectures given at Holy Trinity Seminary, Irving, Texas, 1972, recorded by and in the possession of Mr. Daniel B. Steffen of Plano, Texas), compact disc (hereafter cited as "Remission of Sin").

Secondly, there was a vicarious victim, an animal. And
thirdly, there was the shedding of blood. And this is what
runs all through Sacred Scripture.[28]

The sacrifice of blood also introduced another new reality into
the life of fallen humanity—intermediaries. Sheen pointed out that
after the Fall, humanity would no longer enjoy a direct relationship
with God. Before the Fall, God acted directly on the First Parents.
There was no intermediary—"no curtain, no wall, no priesthood,
no sacraments."[29] After the Fall, God introduced "intermediaries"
who would mediate between God and humans in a limited fashion.
Such were Noah and Moses, who Sheen said were "symbols—sacraments for mediators to come" until the coming of the one Mediator who alone could satisfy the infinite debt of sin.[30]

Sheen described how in the Old Testament the "offering of
Blood was the privilege of the priesthood as the priest was the
mediator between God and man (e.g. Ex. 29:1-46; Lev. 8:1-36)."[31]
This type of priesthood was not complete, in that what the priest
offered only served as a substitute. Man alone could not satisfy an
infinite debt.

The Book of Genesis, therefore, reveals that there would need
to be a mediator who can satisfy the infinite debt of sin, and at the
same time, this mediation would involve the shedding of blood for
the remission of sin. Clearly, no human being could act as such a
mediator, as St. Thomas affirms:

> Properly speaking, the office of a mediator is to join together
> and unite those between whom he mediates: for extremes
> are united in the mean (*medio*). Now to unite men to God
> perfectively belongs to Christ, through Whom men are rec-
> onciled to God, according to 2 Cor. 5:19: *God was in Christ
> reconciling the world to Himself.* And, consequently, Christ
> alone is the perfect Mediator of God and men, inasmuch

---

[28] Sheen, "The Remission of Sin."
[29] Cf. Fulton J. Sheen, "Church" (undated manuscript), Sheen Archives.
[30] Cf. Ibid.
[31] Fulton J. Sheen, "Priests and the Blood of Christ" (undated manuscript of
outline and notes for sermon in green notebook), Sheen Archives.

as, by His death, He reconciled the human race to God. Hence the Apostle, after saying, *Mediator of God and man Christ Jesus*, added: *Who Himself gave a redemption for all.*[32]

The Redeemer would, therefore have to be a priest who can mediate fully between both God and man in order to satisfy Divine justice. In other words, *the* mediator between God and man would have to be both priest *and* victim. Sheen explains:

> The value of any life is determined by the value of the blood that is shed. The blood of a rat is not as precious as the blood of a man. And if, therefore, you have the blood of the God-Man, you have a complete remission of sin.[33]

Sheen saw that the satisfaction for sin and the regeneration of mankind would require suffering and sacrifice, which was symbolized by the flaming sword with the cherubim:

> He drove out the man; and at the east of the garden of Eden
> He placed the cherubim, and a flaming sword
> Which turned every way,
> To guard the way to the tree of life.[34]

Both Adam and Eve suffered the punishment of expulsion from the Garden of Eden and the sacrificial price of return to Paradise was symbolized by the "flaming sword" of which Sheen found great significance:

> The sword has an interesting history in Scripture. When our first parents sinned and lost Paradise, God "stationed the cherubim and a sword whirling and flashing to guard the way to the tree of life" (Gen 3:24). Literally, it was "the flame of a sword turning itself." Its purpose was to protect Paradise, to keep the way open to the Tree of Life, for God is the God of Mercy. "Paradise Lost" is not "Paradise Destroyed," for there shall be a "Paradise Regained." That sword was a symbol of sacrifice; it was flaming because

---

[32] *ST*, III, q. 26, a.1.
[33] Sheen, "The Remission of Sin."
[34] Gn. 3:24.

sacrificial love would be the condition of getting back into Paradise—"Without the shedding of blood there is no forgiveness" (Heb 9:22). Every Jewish high priest who was allowed to enter the Holy of Holies once a year was commanded to bear the sword and the fire, namely, by sacrifice of the lamb.[35]

As we will see later in this chapter, the "sword" has central importance in understanding Mary's role as Mediatrix. For Sheen, it will be the particular symbol of Mary's inseparable union and unique participation in Christ's mediation as Priest and Victim.

In order that God might be able to suffer, He needed to assume a human nature. This is where Sheen's attention turned to Mary. Sheen saw that Genesis 3:15 announced that the Second Adam would not be acting alone in redeeming humanity. God's plan of Redemption would also involve, fittingly, a second Eve who would become the "mother of all living"[36] in the new order of Redemption. Sheen writes, therefore:

> Some dim suggestion and hint of the part Mary plays in the regeneration of the human race is to be found in the part Eve played in its fall. Sacred Scripture tells us that Christ is the second Adam, who by His obedience on the tree of the cross undid the wrong of the first and disobedient Adam under the tree of the knowledge of good and evil [cf. Rm. 5:12-21]. If Christ is the spiritual counterpart of Adam and the new head of the human race, then Mary, the Mother of those who live in Christ, is the counterpart of Eve, the mother of those who die in Adam. A fitting parallel indeed, for if a woman played such an important role in the fall of the human race, then it is fitting that she be assigned no less eminence in its redemption.[37]

---

[35] Fulton J. Sheen, "Mary and the Tabernacle" [corrected copy] (typescript of address given at the Eucharistic Congress, Philadelphia, Pennsylvania, 6 August 1976), Sheen Archives.

[36] Gn. 3:20.

[37] Fulton J. Sheen, *The Mystical Body of Christ* (New York: Sheed and Ward, 1935), 313 (hereafter referred to as *MBC*). John Paul II developed this further

Mary's role as the New Eve, therefore, serves as Sheen's point of departure in his reflection and teaching on Mary's role as Mediatrix. What kind of Mediatrix would Mary be in relation to the New Adam? First, it must be said that Mary can rightly be called Mediatrix because, as St. Thomas reminds us, although Christ is the one Mediator between God and man, there can be secondary and subordinate mediators: "Nothing hinders certain others from being called mediators, in some respect, between God and man, forasmuch as they cooperate in uniting men to God, dispositively or ministerially."[38] Therefore, as Eve became a "most cruel Mediatrix" to Adam, communicating the poison of sin to him and through him, all humanity, Mary, who Sheen said would "be assigned no less eminence its redemption," would be a most faithful Mediatrix whose fidelity and cooperation with God would be the means through which the Redeemer would obtain and transmit the merits of Redemption to the new humanity. Therefore, the New Eve would be a mediatrix to the New Adam as spouse and mother similar to Eve who was a mediatrix as spouse of Adam and mother of humanity. Also, as Eve would have her decisive *moment* in the Garden, Mary, the New Eve, would have hers at the Annunciation. Unlike Eve, however, Mary will have to sustain her decision from Nazareth to Calvary as that was the price the New Eve would need to pay to restore what the first Eve lost.[39] The New

---

in *Mulieris Dignitatem* when he repeatedly emphasized that as Adam and Eve were created to be a "unity of the two," so are the New Adam and the New Eve (Mary-Church) to reflect that intended communion (Cf. *Mulieris Dignitatem* (*MD*), 6-8, 10-11, 14, 23, 26, 29). They cooperate together as one for the same purpose according the role assigned to them.

[38] *ST*, III, q. 26, a. 1.

[39] René Laurentin accurately summarizes how the New Eve theology of St. Irenaeus expresses that Mary's part in the mystery of Redemption necessarily involved Mary's participation beyond her consent at the Annunciation; for the New Eve had a unique role in the "radical restoration each one of the elements marred by the fall":

Irenaeus gives bold relief to a theme only outlined by Justin. With Irenaeus the Eve-Mary parallel is not simply a literary effect nor a gratuitous improvisation, but an integral part of his theology of salvation. One idea is the key to this theology: God's saving plan is not a mending or a "patch-up

Eve would, therefore, have to be specially prepared by God for this
eminent role as maternal Mediatrix of the Redeemer in God's plan
of Redemption.

Mary Created as the Fitting Maternal Mediatrix: The Immaculate Conception

In this section we will analyze what Sheen saw as two critical qualities that were necessary for Mary to be a fitting maternal Mediatrix—Mary's Immaculate Conception and her lifelong
virginity. Sheen understood these qualities as illustrating both the
Divine initiative and Mary's cooperation with God to become His

---

job" done on his first product; it is a resumption of the work from the
beginning, a regeneration from head downwards, a *recapitulation* in Christ.
In this radical restoration each one of the elements marred by the fall is
renewed in its very root. In terms of the symbol developed by Irenaeus, the
knot badly tied at the beginning is unknotted, untied in reverse *(recircula-
tion):* Christ takes up anew the role of Adam, the cross that of the tree of
life. In this ensemble, Mary who corresponds to Eve, holds a place of first
importance. According to Irenaeus her role is necessary to the logic of the
divine plan. After having announced the broad outlines of the divine program, he links up Mary's role with it by the adverb *consequenter...*
Consequently,...there is Mary, the obedient virgin....Eve, still a virgin, was
disobedient and became for herself and for the whole human race a cause
of death. Mary, a virgin and obedient, became for herself and for the whole
human race a cause of salvation....From Mary to Eve there is a taking up
again of the same path *(recirculationem)....*For what is tied together could
not otherwise be untied than by untangling the knot from which the tie-
up had arisen....That is why in beginning his genealogy with the Savior
Luke went backwards to Adam, showing thereby that [the true movement
of generation] does not run from these ancestors toward the Savior but
from him toward them, according to regeneration in the gospel of life.
And thus it is that Eve's disobedience was untied by Mary's obedience: for
what the virgin Eve tied up by her disbelief, the virgin Mary, untied by her
faith *(Adversus Haereses III,* 22; PL 7, 958-959) (René Laurentin, *A Short
Treatise on the Blessed Virgin Mary,* trans. Charles Neumann, S.M. [Wash-
ington, New Jersey: Ami Press, 1991], 54-55).

Mother and the New Eve through whom He would create a new humanity.

MARY THE NEW EDEN

How was God to prepare for the entrance into the world of the Redeemer Who would be both God and man? He would need a sinless and perfect human nature to accomplish this. Sheen explains God's solution in terms of God creating a new Eden through which he would undo all that was ruined in the first garden. Therefore, Mary's role as the New Eve first entailed her to become the immaculate, maternal Mediatrix through whom God would assume a human nature.

Sheen described how in this new Eden He would cultivate a new garden in which and through which He would establish "a beachhead in humanity."[40] Unlike the first Adam, the New Adam was to enter the world through the womb of a woman. Therefore, God would make sure that she was the most beautiful and most perfect Mother of all. Sheen goes on to explain that the first Immaculate Conception, therefore, existed in the mind of God when He dreamed of His ideal creature whom He would call His Mother. Sheen writes:

Through the centuries, Christian liturgy has applied to her the words of the Book of Proverbs.[41] Because she is

---

[40] Fulton J. Sheen, *The Priest Is Not His Own* (New York: McGraw-Hill Book Company, 1963; reprint, San Francisco: Ignatius Press, 2005), 272 (hereafter cited as *PNHO*).

[41] Proverbs 8:22-35. The Lord possessed me in the beginning of His ways, before He made anything, from the beginning. I was set up from eternity, and of old, before the earth was made. The depths were not as yet, and I was already conceived; neither had the fountains of waters as yet sprung out; the mountains with their huge bulk had not as yet been established: before the hills I was brought forth. He had not yet made the earth, or the rivers, or the poles of the world. When He prepared the heavens, I was present; when with a certain law and compass He enclosed the depths; when He established the sky above and poised the fountains of waters; when He compassed the sea with its bounds and set a law to the waters that they should not pass their limits; when

what God wanted us all to be, she speaks of herself [*sic*] as
the Eternal Blueprint in the Mind of God, the one whom
God loved before she was a creature. She is even pictured as
being with Him not only at creation, but before creation.
She existed in the Divine Mind as an Eternal Thought
before there were any mothers—SHE IS THE WORLD'S
FIRST LOVE.[42]

In another place Sheen adds:

God not only thought of her in eternity; He also had her in
mind at the beginning of time. In the beginning of history,
when the human race fell through the solicitation of a
woman, God spoke to the Devil and said, "I will establish
a feud between you and the woman, between thy offspring
and hers; she is to crush thy head, while thou dost lie in
wait at her heels" (Gen 3:15). God was saying that, if it was
by a woman that man fell, it would be through a woman
that God would be revenged.[43]

Sheen described how God prepared Mary to be His new Paradise through her unique privilege of the Immaculate Conception:

God never does anything without exceeding preparation.
The two great masterpieces of God are the Creation of
man and the Re-creation or Redemption of man. Creation
was made for unfallen men; His Mystical Body, for fallen
men....In that Paradise of Creation there was celebrated
the first nuptials of man and woman. But man willed not

He balanced the foundations of the earth; I was with Him, forming all things,
and was delighted every day, playing before Him at all times, playing in the
world: and my delights were to be with the children of men. Now, therefore,
ye children, hear me: Blessed are they that keep my ways. Hear instruction,
and be wise, and refuse it not. Blessed is the man that heareth me and that
watcheth daily at my gates and waiteth at the posts of my doors. He that shall
find me shall find life and shall have salvation from the Lord [Translation from
WFL, 13-14]; cf. *RM*, 8.

[42] *TMP*, 305-306.
[43] *WFL*, 14.

to have blessings except according to his lower nature.[44] Not only did he lose his happiness, he even wounded his own mind and will. Then God planned the remaking or redeeming of man. But before doing so, He would make another Garden. This new one would not be of earth, but of flesh; it would be a Garden over whose portals the name of sin would never be written—a Garden in which there would grow no weeds of rebellion to choke the growth of the flowers of grace—a Garden from which there would flow four rivers of redemption to the four corners of the earth—a Garden so pure that the Heavenly Father would not blush at sending His Own Son into it—and this "flesh-girt Paradise to be gardened by the Adam new" was Our Blessed Mother. As Eden was the Paradise of Creation, Mary is the Paradise of the Incarnation, and in her as a Garden was celebrated the first nuptials of God and man....This special purity of hers we call the Immaculate Conception.[45]

Sheen holds that Mary's Immaculate Conception, therefore, is directly related to her pre-ordained role of becoming the maternal Mediatrix of the Redeemer.

Mary the New Eve—The Fittingness of God Renewing Woman

Sheen's words above raise an interesting point as to another important reason why God chose to redeem humanity with the cooperation of an ideal woman—Mary's special role in the restoration of the fallen image of woman. Commenting on the anthropological importance of a new Eve in God's Redemptive plan, Sheen says:

There *had* to be some such creature as Mary—otherwise God would have found no one in whom He could fittingly

---

[44] Cf. *ST*, II-II, q. 163, a. 2.
[45] *TMP*, 307.

have taken His human origin…There would have been, in some minds, a doubt about the Power of God if He had not shown a special favor to the woman who was to be His Mother. Certainly what God gave to Eve, He would not refuse to His Own Mother [*sic*].

Suppose that God in making over man did not also make over woman into a New Eve!

…Had there been no Immaculate Conception, then Christ would have been said to be less beautiful, for He would have taken His Body from one who was not humanly perfect.…

…Oh, yes! He is our Model, but He is also the Person of God! There ought to be on the human level, someone who would give humans hope, someone who could lead us to Christ, someone who would mediate between us and Christ as He mediates between us and the Father.[46]

Hence, as it is true that "only in the mystery of the incarnate Word does the mystery of man take on light,"[47] Sheen affirms to us that Mary was included in this mystery in order to reveal the fullness of the mystery of womanhood to women. Mary's role in the Redemption as the New Eve will have a special character in restoring womanhood, thus making her the model and ideal of all women. These insights are later found and further developed by the teaching of Pope St. John Paul II.[48]

---

[46] *TMP*, 309-310.

[47] *Gaudium et Spes*, 22.

[48] "The 'woman' of the Proto-evangelium fits into the perspective of the Redemption. The comparison Eve-Mary can be understood also in the sense that Mary assumes in herself and embraces the mystery of the 'woman' whose beginning is Eve, 'the mother of all the living' (Gen 3:20). First of all she assumes and embraces it within the mystery of Christ, 'the new and the last Adam' (cf. 1 Cor 15:45), who assumed in his own person the nature of the first Adam.…

"…In the tradition of faith and of Christian reflection throughout the ages, the coupling Adam-Christ is often linked with that of Eve-Mary. If Mary is described also as the 'new Eve,' what are the meanings of this analogy? Certainly there are many. Particularly noteworthy is the meaning which sees Mary as the full revelation of all that is included in the biblical word 'woman': a

The Immaculate Conception and Mary's Passive *Kenosis-Pleroma*

Fulton Sheen emphasizes a central theological theme in the mystery of Christ and His Mystical Body, the Church—the mystery of *kenosis* and *pleroma*. This teaching is important because it is at the heart of the mystery of Mary's Immaculate Conception, her *fiat* at the Annunciation, and her union with her Son in His work of Redemption. Sheen developed his teaching on *kenosis* and *pleroma* from the doctrine of St. Paul:

> Pleroma is a word of common usage. Used absolutely in Colossians 1:19, it emphasizes contrast to emptiness or kenosis or completeness in relationship to incompleteness or deficiency (Colossians 1:24; 2 Corinthians 11:9; Romans 11:12). Pleroma is embodied in the Incarnation (Colossians 1:19). It dwells permanently in His glorified Body (Colossians 2:9; Ephesians 4:13). It is also the perfection to which Christians aspire and with which they ought to be filled (Ephesians 4:13; Colossians 2:9; John 1:16; 1:14).
>
> It is the completeness or the fullness of life which makes Christ the representative without any other mediary of the universe. It is the fullness of moral and intellectual protection which is communicable through Him to man.
>
> The term is also used of the Church in Ephesians 1:23 to emphasize the thoroughness with which the Church is the

revelation commensurate with the mystery of the Redemption. Mary means, in a sense, a going beyond the limit spoken of in the Book of Genesis (3:16) and a return to that 'beginning' in which one finds the 'woman' as she was intended to be in creation, and therefore in the eternal mind of God: in the bosom of the Most Holy Trinity. Mary is 'the new beginning' of the dignity and vocation of women, of each and every woman....In Mary, Eve discovers the nature of the true dignity of woman, of feminine humanity. This discovery must continually reach the heart of every woman and shape her vocation and her life" (*MD*, 11); cf. John Paul II, Apostolic Exhortation *Familiaris Consortio* (22 November 1981) 22.

receptacle of His power and represents Him on earth. It also represents the compliment [sic] of Christ which fills up His activities. His withdrawal into heaven would have left undone [sic] had it not been for the Church (Ephesians 3:10; 3:21).[49]

These words of Sheen lead to another important insight he had into the Incarnation. In order for the Word to be conceived in Mary, there had to be a mutual *kenosis* of God *and* of Mary. St. Paul speaks of this *kenosis* of Christ in Philippians 2:5-11, where God emptied Himself by assuming the vulnerabilities and limitations of a human nature, but moreover, so that He could assume the role as a slave and undergo suffering.[50] But Sheen teaches that Mary, too, had her *kenosis* as well. It was a *kenosis* that was both passive and active.

Passively, God provided for Mary's complete emptiness of self, or *kenosis*, by means of her Immaculate Conception. As Mary matured and exercised her free will to a greater degree, she would grow in her cooperation with God to remain in this sinless and grace-filled state. This was necessary in order that Mary would become a fitting Mediatrix to become the Mother of God, where what she possessed by grace would now become incarnate in her and from her. Sheen explains that Mary's Divine Maternity involved the mutual cooperation of Mary's *kenosis* and that of God: "Since there was no self there [in Mary], He filled it with His very Self....

---

[49] Fulton J. Sheen, "Pleroma" (notes from folder labeled "Mystical Body"), Sheen Archives.

[50] "Have this mind among yourselves, which is yours in Christ Jesus, who, though he was in the form of God, did not count equality with God a thing to be grasped, but emptied himself, taking the form of a servant, being born in the likeness of men. And being found in human form he humbled himself and became obedient unto death, even death on a cross. Therefore God has highly exalted him and bestowed on him the name which is above every name, that at the name of Jesus every knee should bow, in heaven and on earth and under the earth, and every tongue confess that Jesus Christ is Lord, to the glory of God the Father" (Phil. 2:5-11).

Mary's self-emptying, alone, would not have been enough, had not He Who is her God, her Lord and Savior, 'humbled Himself.'"[51]

According to Sheen, this *kenosis* of Mary, therefore, by virtue of her Immaculate Conception, made her the perfect Mediatrix through which God would re-create humanity from her *nothingness*: "Lowliness and exaltation are one in her: lowliness because, judging herself to be unworthy of being the Mother of Our Lord, she took the vow of virginity;[52] exalted because God, looking upon what Mary believed was her nothingness, once more created the world out of 'nothing.'"[53] This complete filling up of Mary with God in virtue of her complete emptiness of self, which St. Luke captures by use of the verb κεχαριτωμένη in the Angelic Salutation, thus represents Mary's passive *kenosis*. Therefore, in Mary the mystery of *kenosis-pleroma* has already taken place in Mary by the Divine initiative, but, as we will see shortly, this privilege was given only in light of the unique role Mary would be asked to play in Redemption in which she would then be asked to merit the unique place in salvation history which God had preordained for her.

The mystery of Mary's *kenosis-pleroma* (emptiness and fullness of grace) by means of her Immaculate Conception is also related to her mediation because it pertains to Mary's perfect participation in the priestly mediation of Christ from the moment of her Immaculate Conception, when she was made full of *redemptive* grace. Sheen reminds us that Mary, too, despite her unique privilege of the Immaculate Conception, was in need of redemption:

> If we exempted her from the need of redemption, we would also have to exempt her from membership in humanity. The Immaculate Conception, therefore, in no way implies that she needed no redemption. She did! Mary is the first effect of redemption, in the sense that it was applied to her

---

[51] *WFL*, 43.

[52] The tradition and significance of Mary's vow of virginity is addressed later in pages 114-116.

[53] *WFL*, 45.

at the moment of her conception and to us in another and diminished fashion only after our birth.[54]

In addition, St. Thomas teaches that at Baptism we receive a character, which is "nothing else than [a certain participation] of Christ's Priesthood, flowing from Christ Himself."[55] The Second Vatican Council developed this teaching when it expounded on the significance of the priesthood of the baptized, which is a participation in the one Priesthood of Jesus Christ.[56] Applying this reality to Mary, her Immaculate Conception and fullness of grace allowed her to participate perfectly in the Priesthood of Christ—a participation which was initially passive until the Annunciation, the pivotal point of salvation history.

Key New Testament Passages Revealing Mary as Maternal Mediatrix and the New Eve in the Mystery of the Incarnation

Thus far, we have focused on Sheen's teaching and understanding of how Mary was preordained from the beginning of time and specially prepared by God for her central role as Mediatrix in His plan of Redemption. We now move to the primary New Testament Scripture passages from which Sheen composed his theology of Marian mediation, where Mary's passive role in redemption would now assume its central and active participation beginning with her consent at the Annunciation. These passages are important because Sheen believed that what is revealed about the relationship of Jesus

---

[54] *WFL*, 18.

[55] *ST*, III, q. 63, a. 3.

[56] "The baptized, by regeneration and the anointing of the Holy Spirit, are consecrated as a spiritual house and a holy priesthood.…Though they differ from one another in essence and not only in degree, the common priesthood of the faithful and the ministerial or hierarchical priesthood are nonetheless interrelated: each of them in its own special way is a participation in the one priesthood of Christ" (*LG*, 10); See also *LG*, 9-11, 62.

and Mary during their earthly lives serves as paradigms for how they continue that relationship from heaven. In other words, what is revealed about Mary's mediation in relation to Christ the Head will continue in her maternal relationship with His Mystical Body.

The following New Testament passages serve as the primary biblical foundations for Sheen's theology of Mary as maternal Mediatrix:

1. The Annunciation and Incarnation (Lk. 1:26-38)
2. The Visitation (Lk. 1:39-56)
3. The Nativity of Our Lord—Mary's "first-born" (Lk. 2:7)
4. The Presentation and Simeon's Prophecy of the Sword and Mary (Lk. 2:22-35)
5. The Finding of Jesus in the Temple at Age 12 (Lk. 2:41-51)
6. The Marriage Feast at Cana (Jn. 2:1-11)
7. Mary at the Foot of the Cross (Jn. 19:25-30)
8. Mary Present with the Apostles at Pentecost (Acts 1:14)

It is interesting to note that these biblical passages became the foundations for the Mariology of Vatican II[57] and John Paul II.[58]

Significance of the Genealogies of Matthew and Luke Regarding Mary's Universal Mediation

Sheen points out that the genealogies of Matthew and Luke—especially Luke—provide insight into Mary's universal maternal mediation. He states:

She [Mary] brings to the [sic] fulfillment the faithful remnant of Israel through its history. The geneology [sic] in Luke goes back to Adam, and not to Abraham, and inasmuch as she is the one who has begotten the Savior she is to

---

[57] Cf. *LG*, 57-61.
[58] The first half of *Redemptoris Mater* is dedicated to explaining Mary's role in salvation history according to the biblical narrative (cf. *RM*, 1-24).

some extent also tied up with humanity. It will be recalled that St. Thomas said that when she gave her consent to the angel to become the Mother of God that she spoke in the name of all humanity [*ST*, III, q. 30, a. 1], the whole human race. It may, therefore, be said that she spoke in the name of the quahal [*sic*] in Matthew, and in the name of humanity in the geneology [*sic*] of Luke. Matthew was writing for the Jews, therefore, he goes back to Abraham. Luke was writing for the Greeks and the Romans, therefore, he goes back to the beginning of humanity. But inasmuch as Christ is mentioned as the goal of both geneologies [*sic*], His mother who was the means of His coming into the world is tied up with them. The Gospel of Matthew begins with the word that it is the book of the generation of Jesus Christ, the Son of David, the Son of Abraham. Matthew mentions the real progenitors according to the flesh; Luke the adopted and reputed relatives of Joseph, for Christ was the reputed and adopted Son of Joseph as we are the adopted and reputed sons of God. Matthew, therefore, is tied up with the past, and Luke suggests the future reign of grace by which is produced the adopted sons of God.[59]

Mary's Divine Motherhood, therefore, marks the beginning of an inseparable union of Mary with her Son in God's plan of Redemption. This central teaching of Sheen was later confirmed and stressed by *Lumen Gentium*[60] and John Paul II.[61]

---

[59] Fulton J. Sheen, "The Marriage Feast of Cana and Christ the Bridegroom" (notes from folder labeled "Mystical Body"), Sheen Archives, 4.

[60] "The union of the Mother with the Son in the work of salvation is made manifest from the time of Christ's virginal conception up to His death" (*LG*, 57).

[61] "From the first moment of her divine motherhood, of her union with the Son whom 'the Father sent into the world, that the world might be saved through him' [cf. Jn. 3:17]. Mary takes her places within Christ's messianic service" (*MD*, 5); "This role [Mary's mediation] is at the same time special and extraordinary. It flows from her divine motherhood and can be understood and lived in faith only on the basis of the full truth of this motherhood. Since by virtue of divine election Mary is the earthly Mother of the Father's consubstantial Son and his 'generous companion' in the work of redemption 'she is

The Incarnation: "Mary Is Mediatrix between Christ and Us"[62] as *Theotokos* and the New Eve

All that we have just presented from Sheen's teaching prepares us to understand the significance of the dialogue between Mary and the angel, followed by Mary's response, at the Annunciation. This event carried central theological significance in Sheen's teaching on Mary's mediation. The context surrounding Mary's *fiat* and all the implications contained within it depend on an accurate understanding of the nature of Christ's messianic mission and His redemptive mediation as Priest-Victim. We will now illustrate the main theological themes which Sheen saw present in Mary's role in the mystery of the Incarnation.

MARY'S PREPARATION TO ACCEPT THE ANNUNCIATION

We return to Sheen's emphasis on the importance of human freedom and its cooperation with God in satisfying the demands of justice that would be integral to His plan of Redemption. For Sheen, human freedom is a central theme in the mystery of Redemption, as he explained in regard to the Annunciation:

> Now we come to the greatest act of freedom the world has ever known—the reversal of that free act which the Head [*sic*] of humanity performed in Paradise when he chose non-God against God. It was the moment in which that unfortunate choice was reversed, when God in His Mercy [*sic*] willed to remake man and to give him a fresh start in a *new* birth of freedom under God. God *could* have made a perfect man to start humanity out of dust as He had done

---

a mother to us in the order of grace.' This role constitutes a real dimension of her presence in the saving mystery of Christ and the Church" (*RM*, 38).
[62] *WFL*, 72.

in the beginning. He could have made the new man start
the new humanity from nothing as He had done in making
the world. And He could have done it without consulting
humanity, but this would have been the invasion of human
privilege. God would not take a man out of the world of
freedom without the free act of a free being. God's way
with man is not dictatorship, but cooperation. If He would
redeem humanity, it would be *with* human consent and
not *against it*. God could destroy evil, but only at the cost
of human freedom, and that would be too high a price to
pay for the destruction of dictatorship on earth—to have a
dictator in Heaven.

Before remaking humanity, God willed to consult with
humanity, so that there would be no destruction of human
dignity; the particular person whom He consulted was a
woman. In the beginning it was man who was asked to
ratify the gift; this time it is a woman. The mystery of the
Incarnation is very simply that of God's asking a woman
freely to give Him a human nature. In so many words,
through the angel, He was saying: "Will you make Me a
man?" As from the first Adam came the first Eve, so now,
in the rebirth of man's dignity, the new Adam will come
from the new Eve. And in Mary's free consent we have the
only human nature that was ever born in perfect liberty.[63]

How, then, was Mary free to make a decision of such magni-
tude? Sheen noted that in order for Mary's consent to be truly free,
she needed to know in a most profound manner the significance
of her *fiat*. This would have been possible only by a deep understanding of Divine revelation through the Hebrew Scriptures. The
theological tradition of the Church attributes Mary's unparalleled
insight into the Divine mysteries as a consequence of her fullness
of grace and Immaculate Conception,[64] and the knowledge and
wisdom which flowed from Mary's consecrated life of virginity at

---

[63] *WFL*, 27-28.
[64] Reginald Garrigou-Lagrange, O.P., summarizes this theological tradition:

The consequences of the Immaculate Conception have been developed by the great spiritual writers. Mary has been preserved from the two baneful fruits of original sin, concupiscence and darkness of understanding....

...Mary was never subject to error or illusion. Her judgment was always enlightened and correct. If she did not understand a thing fully she suspended her judgment upon it, and thus avoided the precipitation which might have been the cause of error...She is, as the Litanies say, the Seat of Wisdom, the Queen of Doctors, the Virgin most prudent, the Mother of good counsel...She had, too, an eminent and wonderfully simple knowledge of what the Scriptures said of the Messiah, the Incarnation, and the Redemption. Thus she was fully exempt from concupiscence and error (57-58)....

...We may say...that it is at least very probable, according to the teaching of the majority of theologians, that Mary had the use of her free will through her infused knowledge from the first manner of her conception, at least in a passing manner. Such is the teaching of St. Vincent Ferrer, St. Bernardine of Sienna, St. Francis de Sales, St. Alphonsus, Suarez, Vega, Contenson, Justin de Miéchow, and most modern theologians....

...The following are the reasons that can be adduced in favour of the privilege:

1st—It is not becoming to hold that Mary, Queen of patriarchs, prophets, apostles, and all the saints, lacked a privilege [cf. *ST*, III, q. 27, a. 6] granted to St. John the Baptist [at the Visitation]...St. Irenaeus, St. Ambrose, St. Leo the Great, and St. Gregory the Great have noted that the joy of St. John the Baptist before his birth was not merely of the sense order, but was elicited by the coming of the Saviour, Whose precursor he was. Thus Cajetan notes that this joy, being a spiritual order, presupposes the use of reason and will, and at the same time there could be no question of acquired but only of infused knowledge (*Comment. in IIIa*, P., q. 27, a.6)...If, therefore, St. John the Baptist had the use of reason and will before birth, because of his vocation as precursor of Christ, the same privilege can hardly be denied to Christ's mother....

...2nd—Since Mary received the grace and the infused virtues and the gifts in the first instant in a degree higher than that of the final grace of the saints, she must have been sanctified in the way proper to adults, that is, by disposing her through actual grace for habitual grace, and by using this latter as a principle of merit from the moment she received it; in other words, she offered herself to God as her Son did on His entry to the world....

...3rd—Mary's fulness of grace, virtues, and gifts which surpassed already the final fulness of all the saints, could not have remained inactive at the beginning of her life. Such inactivity would appear opposed to the sweet and generous dispositions of Divine Providence in favour of the Mother

the Temple from an early age.[65] While Sheen accepted the former,

---

of the Saviour. But unless she had the use of her free will through infused knowledge, the virtues and gifts which she possessed in so high a degree would have remained inactive for a considerable part of her life (that is, the beginning).

Almost all present-day theologians admit that it is at least very probable that, in her mother's womb, Mary had the use of her free will through infused knowledge—transitorily, at any rate. They admit too that she had the use of this infused knowledge on certain occasions, such as the Incarnation, the Passion, the Resurrection, the Ascension; also that she had the use of it for the purpose of acquiring a more perfect knowledge of the divine perfections and of the mystery of the Blessed Trinity...Even those theologians who are most conservative in their views do not hesitate to admit this much of Mary....(Reginald Garrigou-Lagrange, O.P., *The Mother of the Saviour and Our Interior Life*, trans. Bernard J. Kelly, C.S.Sp. [Rockford, IL: Tan Books and Publishers, Inc., 1993], 57-58; 81-83).

[65] There exists a strong theological tradition which supports that Mary not only took a vow of virginity, but also led a consecrated life at the Temple from the age of three. In addition to the early Christian writing *Protoevangelium of James*, which seems to have been written to defend this claim, St. Alphonsus de Liguori summarizes this theological tradition:

There never was, and never will be, an offering on the part of a pure creature greater or more perfect than that which Mary made to God when, at the age of three years, she presented herself in the temple to offer Him, not aromatic spices, nor calves, nor gold, but her entire self, consecrating herself as a perpetual victim in His honour. She well understood the voice of God, calling her to devote herself entirely to His love when He said, "Arise, make haste, my love, my dove, my beautiful one, and come!" [Cant. 2:10]. Therefore her Lord willed that from that time she should forget her country, and all, to think only of loving and pleasing Him: "Hearken, O daughter, and see, and incline thine ear; and forget thy people, and thy father's house" [Ps. 44:11]. She with promptitude and at once obeyed the divine call....Mary's offering was prompt and without delay; secondly, it was entire and without reserve.

Mary's offering was prompt. From the first moment that this heavenly child was sanctified in her mother's womb, which was in the instant of her Immaculate Conception, she received the perfect use of reason, that she might begin to merit. This is in accordance with the general opinion of theologians, and with that of Father Suarez in particular, who says, that as the most perfect way in which God sanctifies a soul is by its own merit, as St. Thomas also teaches, it is thus we must believe that the Blessed Virgin was sanctified: "To be sanctified by one's own act is the more perfect way.

Therefore it is to be believed that the Blessed Virgin was thus sanctified"
[*De Incarn.* p. 22 q. xxvii. art. 6, disp. 4 §8]. And if this privilege was
granted to the angels, and to Adam, as the angelic Doctor says [*ST*, I,
q. 43, a. 5], much more ought we to believe that it was granted to the
Divine Mother, on whom, certainly, we must suppose that God, having
condescended to make her His Mother, also conferred greater gifts than
on all other creatures....

...Thus, from the beginning of her life, Mary knew God, and knew Him
so that 'no tongue' (as the angel declared to Saint Briget) 'will ever express
how clearly this Blessed Virgin understood His greatness in that very
moment of her existence. And thus enlightened, she instantly offered her
entire self to her Lord, dedicating herself, without reserve, to His love and
glory. 'Immediately,' the angel went on to say, 'our Queen determined to
sacrifice her will to God, and to give Him all her love for the whole of her
life. No one can understand how entire was the subjection in which she
then placed her will, and how fully she was determined to do all according
to His pleasure.'

But the Immaculate Child, afterwards understanding that her holy parents, Joachim and Anne, had promised God, even by vow, as many authors
relate, that if He granted them issue, they would consecrate it to His service in the temple; as it was, moreover, an ancient custom amongst the
Jews to take their daughters to the temple, and there to leave them for their
education (for which purpose there were cells contiguous), as it is recorded
by Baronius, Nicephorus, Cedrenus, and Suarez, with Joseph, the Jewish
historian, and also on the authority of Saint John Damascen [*sic*], Saint
George of Nicomedia, Saint Anselm, and Saint Ambrose, and, as we may
easily gather from the Second Book of Machabees [*sic*], where, speaking
of Heliodorus, who besieged the temple, that he might gain possession of
the treasure there deposited, says, "Because the place was like to come into
contempt...and the virgins also that were shut up came forth, some to
Onias" [2 Mac. 3:18-19]. Mary hearing this, I say, having scarcely attained
the age of three years, as Saint Germanus and Saint Epiphanius attest—the
latter of whom says, 'In her third year she was brought to the temple'—an
age at which children are the most desirous and stand in the greatest need
of their parents' care, she desired to offer and solemnly to consecrate herself to God, by presenting herself in the temple. Hence, of her own accord,
she requested her parents, with earnestness, to take her there, that they
might thus accomplish their promise. And her holy mother, says Saint
Gregory of Nyssa, 'did not long delay leading her to the temple, and offering her to God....'

...St. Anselm also speaks of the life of the Blessed Virgin in the temple,
and says that 'Mary was docile, spoke little, was always composed, did

he specifically addressed the significance of the latter as it applied to Mary's knowledge and freedom at the time of Annunciation.

In accord with the tradition of the Fathers and Doctors of the Church—in particular, St. Augustine—Sheen taught that Mary took a vow of virginity at a young age and dedicated herself to a life consecrated to God alone.[66] Such a decision, according to Sheen,

---

not laugh, and that her mind was never disturbed. She also persevered in prayer, in the study of the sacred Scriptures, in fastings, and all virtuous works.' St. Jerome enters more into detail....She was always the first in watchings, the most exact in the observance of the Divine law, the most profoundly humble, and the most perfect in every virtue.

[Mary reportedly told St. Elizabeth of Hungary]: "Dost thou think that I possessed grace and virtue without effort? Know that I obtained no grace from God without great effort, constant prayer, ardent desire, and many tears and mortifications."

But above all we should consider the revelation made to Saint Bridget of the virtues and practices of the Blessed Virgin in her childhood: 'From her childhood Mary was full of the Holy Ghost and as she advanced in age she advanced also in grace....Afterwards, on discovering in the sacred Scriptures that God was to be born of a Virgin, that He might redeem the world, her soul was to such a degree inflamed with Divine love, that she could desire and think nothing but God....She desired, with the greatest ardour, to live until the time of the coming of the Messiah, that she might be the servant of that happy Virgin, who merited to be His Mother' (St. Alphonsus de Liguori, *The Glories of Mary* [Rockford, IL: Tan Books and Publishers, Inc., 1977], 305-308, 312-313).

[66] Cf. *WFL*, 45; Sheen's teaching that Mary took a vow of virginity at a young age reflects the theological tradition of the Church on this subject. The primary Scriptural passage used for this argument is Mary's response to the Archangel Gabriel, "How can this be since I know not man" (Lk. 1:34). St. Augustine explained that Mary's response to the Archangel Gabriel referred to a previous vow she had made to the Lord to remain a virgin—a vow she had no intention of breaking. St. Augustine wrote:

Indeed, her [Mary's] virginity was itself more beautiful and more pleasing, because Christ, in His conception, did not Himself take away that which He was preserving from violation from man; but, before He was conceived He chose one already consecrated to God of whom He would be born. The words which Mary addressed to the angel who announced her Child to her indicate this. 'How shall this happen,' she asked, 'since I do not know man?' [Lk. 1:34] And this she would certainly not have said unless she had previously vowed herself to God as a virgin. But, because the customs of

would have been the natural inclination for Mary, considering Mary's highest vocation to be the Mother of God and her singular privilege of being the Immaculate Conception. He pointed out that in the Old Testament "proximity to God implied virginity" and that "virginity made possible one's role in religious functions" (Lv. 21:7, 13; Ez. 44:22).[67] Therefore, such unparalleled proximity to God would imply that Mary was consecrated to God and that she willed to live for Him alone; thus her vow of virginity.

Sheen also saw this highest level of purity as a reflection of the highest form of love, what Sheen called "*sacral*" or "*sacrificial*" love. Of this love Sheen writes: "The lover sacrifices himself for the beloved, counts himself most free when he is a 'slave' to the object of his love, and desires even to immolate self so that the other might

---

the Jews as yet forbade this, she was espoused to a just man; not to one who would ravage by violence, but to one who would protect against violent men that which she had already vowed.

Although, even if she had only said: 'How shall this happen?' and had not added 'since I do not know man,' she would never have asked at all how a woman was to bear the son promised to her if she had married with the intention of cohabiting.

Again, she could have been commanded to remain a virgin in whom the Son of God would, by a fitting miracle, take upon Himself the nature of a slave, but, in order to be a model for holy virgins, lest it be thought that only she ought to be a virgin who had merited to conceive a child even without carnal intercourse, she consecrated her virginity to God while she was still ignorant of what she would conceive, so that the imitation of the heavenly life in her earthly and mortal body might come about by vow, not by precept, but a love of her own choice, not by the compulsion of obedience.

Thus, Christ, in being born of a virgin who, before she knew who was to be born of her, had resolved to remain a virgin, chose rather to approve holy virginity than to impose it. So, even in that woman in whom He took upon Himself the nature of a slave, He desired virginity to be free" (St. Augustine, *De Sancta Virginitate* 4, *PL* 40, 398; Cf. *The Fathers of the Church: St. Augustine – Treatises on Marriage and Other Subjects*, ed. Roy J. Deferrari, trans. Charles T. Wilcox et. al. [New York: Fathers of the Church, Inc., 1955], 146-147).

[67] Fulton J. Sheen, "Immaculate Conception" (from spiral notebook marked "Vol. 1: Notes for Sermons in Novena at Dublin, Ireland, July 16-25 [no year]), Sheen Archives (hereafter cited as "Immaculate Conception").

be glorified....Consecrated virginity is the highest form of *sacral* or *sacrificial* love; it seeks nothing for itself but only the will of the beloved."[68] Sheen affirmed that this *sacral* love led to her taking a vow of virginity. He writes:

> A woman can be a virgin in one of three ways: first, because she never had a chance to marry....[Secondly,] because she decided not to marry. This can be for social or economic reasons and, therefore, may have no religious value, but it can also be meritorious, if it is done for a religious motive—for example, the better to serve a sick member of a family or to dedicate oneself to neighbor for the love of God. Thirdly, a woman can be a virgin because she made a vow or a promise to God to keep herself pure for His sake although she has a hundred chances to marry.
>
> Mary was a virgin in the third way. She fell in love at a very early age, and it was with God—one of those beautiful loves where the first love is the last love, and the last love is Eternal Love. She must have been very wise, as well as good, as a young girl of fifteen or sixteen, to have made such a choice.[69]

Moreover, Sheen saw Mary's free decision to take the vow of virginity as a reflection of a profound understanding of her lineage and its possible link with the messianic plan of God; for Sheen says she took the vow with the hope of hastening the coming of the Messiah:

> ...The Blessed Mother had a better chance than most women to become the Mother of God, for the Bible said that Our Lord would be born of the House of David, the great King who lived a thousand years before. And Mary belonged to that royal family. Without doubt Mary knew the prophecy of Isaias, which some had forgotten, namely, that the Messias would be born of a Virgin [Is. 7:14]. But it is more likely, from what she said later, that she considered

---

[68] *WFL*, 166-167.
[69] Ibid., 78.

herself too lowly for such dignity and took the vow in the hope that, through her sacrifice and prayers, the coming of the Messias might be hastened.

How do we know that Mary took a vow? We know it from her answer to the angel Gabriel....Mary says: "How shall this be, seeing I know not man?" Mary did not say: "I will never marry; therefore I cannot become the Mother of Jesus." That would have been disobedient to the angel who asked her to become the Mother of Jesus. Neither did she say: "I do not want a husband, but let the will of God be fulfilled," for that would have been untrue to herself and her vow. Mary merely wanted to be enlightened concerning her duty. The problem was not her virginity. She was familiar enough with the prophecy of Isaias to know that God would be born of a virgin. Mary's only concern was— since up to this point in history motherhood and virginity had been irreconcilable—how will God arrange it?...The angel answers that, in her case, birth will come without human love, but not without Divine Love, for the...Holy Spirit, Who is the Love of God will descend into her, and He that will be born of her will be "the Son of God."

Mary saw at once that this allowed her to keep her vow.[70]

Sheen also found an important relationship between Mary's virginity and the effects that it would have had on her clarity of understanding of Divine mysteries. He writes:

There is an intrinsic relation between virginity and intelligence....In a more positive way, we may say that the purer the love, the less disturbance of the mind. But since there can be no greater love than that of the soul in union with the Infinite, it follows that the mind free from anxieties and fear should have the greatest clearness of intellectual insights. The concentration on *spiritual* fecundity should by its very nature produce a high degree of intellectual fecundity. Here one speaks not of knowledge *about things*,

---

[70] *WFL*, 78-81.

for that depends on effort, but of judgment, counsel, decision, which are the marks of a keen intelligence. One finds a suggestion of this in Mary, whose virginity is associated with wisdom in the highest degree, not only because she owned it in her new right but also because she begot Intelligence Itself in her flesh.[71]

Therefore, considering Sheen's affirmation that Mary possessed profound knowledge and understanding of Divine revelation through both infused and acquired knowledge—due to the graces from her Immaculate Conception and consecrated life— Mary not only would have known the prophecy of Isaiah of the Virgin birth of the Messiah, but also Isaiah's prophecy of the Suffering Servant (Is. 53) and the popular story of the bronze serpent (Nm. 21:9). Therefore, Mary knew that while her consent would lead to "the greatest ecstasy of love,"[72] from which the Word would be conceived in her womb, her joy would be turned to sorrow. If her association with the Redeemer was to reflect Eve's inseparable association with Adam in the Fall, then Mary was destined for intense suffering; for Sheen described the antiphon of the Redeemer: "Everyone else came into the world to live; He came into the world to die."[73]

---

[71] *WFL*, 168-169.

[72] Fulton J. Sheen, "Immaculate Conception" (from spiral notebook marked "Vol. 1: Notes for Sermons in Novena at Dublin, Ireland, July 16-25 [no year]), Sheen Archives (hereafter cited as "Immaculate Conception").

[73] *LC*, 79. St. Alphonsus de Liguori summarizes the theological tradition which speaks of Mary's entire life as an ongoing martyrdom. While there is no evidence to suggest that Mary had infused knowledge informing her she was to be the Mother of the Christ, her life-long contemplation and anticipation of the coming of the Priest-Victim Messiah caused her great suffering—a suffering which was intensified after her *fiat* to become Mother of the Redeemer and the New Eve. He writes:

> ...Mary was not only a real martyr, but...her martyrdom surpassed all others, and her whole life may be said to have been a prolonged death.

> 'The passion of Jesus,' as Saint Bernard says, 'commenced with His birth.' So also did Mary, in all things like unto her Son, endure her martyrdom throughout her life. Amongst other significations of the name of Mary, as Blessed Albert the Great asserts, is that of 'a bitter sea.' Hence to her is applicable the text of Jeremias: "great as the sea is thy destruction" [Lam.

INCARNATION IN THE CONTEXT OF NUPTIALS

Sheen says that the context of the Incarnation was that of nuptials. He commented:

> The Blessed Mother knew there could be no conception without fire and passion. How could there be a son, since she had 'no knowledge of man'? Heaven had the answer. Certainly, there would be fire and passion and love, but that fire and that love would be the Holy Spirit.[74]

Sheen is suggesting that implicit in God's request for Mary's consent to become the Mother of God was that in doing so, she would also become the Spouse of the Holy Spirit, Who alone had the power to render her fruitful in her virginity. Herein was the solution to the problem of God entering humanity without being in contact with its fallen nature. The Holy Spirit would espouse the Immaculate Virgin and form within her womb, as the New Eden, the Redeemer of mankind. Sheen explains how this fruitful espousal between Mary and the Holy Spirit was something that she seemingly did not anticipate because of her humility:

> [Mary was asked] if she was willing to give God a human nature. Her answer was that she 'knew not man' and,

---

2:13]. For as the sea is all bitter and salt, so also was the life of Mary always full of bitterness at the sight of the passion of the Redeemer, which was ever present to her mind. 'There can be no doubt, that enlightened by the Holy Ghost in a far higher degree than all the prophets, she, far better than they, understood the predictions recorded by them in the sacred Scriptures concerning the Messias.' This is precisely what the angel revealed to Saint Bridget; and he also added, 'that the Blessed Virgin, even before she became His Mother, knowing how much the Incarnate Word was to suffer for the salvation of men, and compassionating this innocent Saviour, who was to be so cruelly put to death for crimes not His own, even then began her great martyrdom.'

Her grief was immeasurably increased when she became the Mother of this Saviour; so that at the sad sight of the many torments which were to be endured by her poor Son, she indeed suffered a long martyrdom, a martyrdom which lasted her whole life (*The Glories of Mary*, 405-406).

[74] *PNHO*, 272.

therefore, could not be the mother of the "Expected of the Nations."

There never came a birth without love. In this the maiden was right. The begetting of new life requires the fires of love. But besides the human passion which begets life, there is the "passionless passion and wild tranquility" of the Holy Spirit; and it was this that overshadowed the woman and begot her Emmanuel or "God is with us."

By pronouncing *Fiat* Mary achieved the full role of womanhood, namely, to be the bearer of God's gifts to man.[75]

This nuptial consent of Mary introduced into history the only motherhood in which both the Mother and child willed each other:

> Children come into the world not always as a result of a distinct act of love of man and woman. Though the love between the two be willed, the fruit of their love, which is the child, is not willed in the same way as their love one for another. There is an undetermined element in human love. The parents do not know whether the child will be a boy or a girl, or the exact time of its birth, for conception is lost in some unknown night of love. Children are later accepted and loved by their parents, but they were never directly willed into being with them. But, in the Annunciation, the Child was not accepted in any unforeseen way; *the Child was willed.* There was a collaboration between a woman and the Spirit of Divine Love. The consent was voluntary under the *Fiat*; the physical cooperation was freely offered by the same word.[76]

---

[75] Fulton J. Sheen, *Life of Christ* (New York: McGraw-Hill Book Company, 1958), 16 (hereafter cited as *LC*).
[76] *LC*, 16.

"CONCEPTION BY PERCEPTION"

Sheen provided a unique perspective in which to consider the Incarnation. He applied to Mary the following words of St. Paul: "Faith is awakened by the message and the message that awakens it comes through the Word of God" (Romans 10:17). At the time of the Annunciation, Sheen suggested that because Mary already enjoyed such a union with God through her Immaculate Conception and fullness of grace, in a certain sense, the Son of God was only one "Word" away from becoming incarnate in her; so that when the Word did come to Mary, she immediately conceived of the Word in her body. This is what Sheen called "conception by perception." He explains:

> Everyone who is a Christian has Christ in him. Christ is born, conceived, in him by Baptism. There is first of all the renewal [of Christ] in the intellect, so that Paul says, "We put on the *mind* of Christ" [1 Cor. 2:16]; and that He is in the will as grace and power. And He is in our body because our body becomes the temple of God....It is easy to understand this in a convert because one can always distinguish the before and after state....A convert...can say, "This precise date I heard the Word of God, and the Word was born in me, so that I have His truth and His grace, and he is living inside of my body;" so, that there is *conception by perception*—conception by the hearing of the Word of God. But not everyone possesses Christ in exactly the same way. Some, for example, have a greater possession of intellect by Christ than others, not only by knowledge, but by obedience to truth. And then there is more power in the will of some than in others. In fact, Christ is the motive, motor force, of certain individuals. And then there is the purity of the body, too, and in some much greater than in others. So, if therefore, there are degrees of the possession of Christ in virtue of the hearing of the Word of God, is it unthinkable that there might be one creature in all the world whose mind would be so absorbed in Christ, whose will was so totally committed to Him, and whose body was

so very pure, that when the Word came to her, it would be not only in the intellect entirely, not only in the will, but in the *body*? And the Word was made flesh and dwelt in her. This is conception by perception.[77]

This teaching of Sheen is also suggested by the words of *Lumen Gentium* which expressed the immediacy of the Word becoming incarnate in Mary upon her hearing the Angelic Salutation: "The Virgin Mary,...*at the message of the angel* received the Word of God in her heart and in her body and gave Life to the world."[78]

FIAT MIHI SECUNDUM VERBUM TUUM

We will now examine how Sheen's teaching on Mary and the Incarnation reveals three ways in which Mary's *fiat* relates to her pre-ordained role as maternal Mediatrix: Mary's *fiat* was her free appropriation of her Redemption; it was her free consent to become *Theotokos* and Mediatrix of the Mediator; and it was her free consent to assume the full extent of her role as the New Eve in which she would endure all in the Divine plan that is necessary to undo the "knot of Eve's disobedience" (*LG*, 56) and become the mother of a redeemed humanity. This last consequence of Mary's *fiat* refers to Mary's ascending mediation in the form of her *active kenosis* in and with Christ, the New Adam. Another way of expressing Mary's active *kenosis* is her active participation in the priest-victimhood of Christ. Let us examine these points more closely.

As the New Eve, Mary Had to Ratify Her Redemption in Total Freedom

Sheen understood that what was asked of Mary by the angel was more than becoming a passive instrument through which

---

[77] Sheen, *Renewal and Reconciliation*.

[78] *LG*, 53 (emphasis mine). This teaching of Sheen is also hinted at by John Paul II who stated, "As the Fathers of the Church teach—she conceived this Son in her mind before she conceived him in her womb: precisely in faith!" (*RM*, 13).

God would enter humanity. Mary understood that her *fiat* was her consent to, or ratification of, the extraordinary privileges of grace which she received in her Immaculate Conception and what she would receive in grace and honor by becoming Mother of God and Mother of the Church. Mary's appropriation of her Redemption, however, would come at an extraordinary price proportionate to her privileges. In order for Mary truly to merit her privileges, she would have to be totally free in her consent. Sheen writes:

> If she were so prepared,[79] would she be free to accept or to reject, and would her answer be the full fruit of her free will? The answer is that her redemption was already completed but that she had not yet accepted or ratified it....She was planned for a role in the drama of redemption by God...but it was not fulfilled until that moment....Before Mary could claim as her own the great gifts of God, she had to ratify those gifts by an act of will in the Annunciation.[80]

If Mary was truly to be the New Eve, then she, too, needed to be tempted (as is fitting since she, like Eve, had a free will[81]), so that she could demonstrate her fidelity and submission to God. If anything, Mary's trial was more difficult than that of Eve because she could perceive that her *fiat* to become the mother of the Suffering Servant (Is. 53) and Priest-Victim would bring about intense suffering. Mary's vocation, indeed, was greater than Eve's because her vocation required a more intense denial of self (*kenosis*) in the form of extraordinary spiritual suffering on a universal scale to correspond to her fullness of grace and her universal motherhood,

---

[79] Cf. *ST*, III, q. 27, a. 4: "God so prepares and endows those, whom He chooses for some particular office, that they are rendered capable of fulfilling it, according to 2 Cor. Iii. 6: *(Who) hath made us fit ministers of the New Testament*. Now the Blessed Virgin was chosen by God to be His Mother. Therefore there can be no doubt that God, by His grace, made her worthy of that office, according to the words spoken to her by the angel (Luke i. 30, 31): *Thou hast found grace with God: behold thou shalt conceive*, etc."

[80] *WFL*, 30-31.

[81] The reason for this is that the kind of elevation by grace Mary enjoyed does not seem to be "no different" from that of Eve.

through which she would identify with all the struggles of fallen humanity. This was not asked of Eve. Sheen wrote:

> She paid dearly for the privilege of the Immaculate Conception as one wonders how many would have accepted it at the cost of a sword thrust through the heart, the Son holding the hilt. Mary's life was one of conflict, somewhat like our own; between the Spirit and the flesh. It is precisely because of this dynamic warfare that she becomes our inspiration, not because of a static devotion to her....She cannot encourage purity unless she struggled to do so— not in a petty battle provoked by the thousand uprisings of concupiscence which meet one in the street and the printed page, but a battle of more cosmic proportions. No woman ever fought so much to master the flesh. She, therefore, can speak to us for celibacy in a priest, chastity in nuns, purity in the laity do not come easily....No one is crowned unless he has struggled (2 Timothy 2:5).[82]

Therefore, Mary's sinlessness and purity were not to exempt her from the temptations and struggles of the flesh. On the contrary, Sheen is saying that this privilege allowed her to identify more perfectly with the Redemptive role of her Son of whom the Letter to the Hebrews says: "For we have not a high priest who is unable to sympathize with our weaknesses, but one who in every respect has been tempted as we are, yet without sin."[83] He is applying this to Mary's associative role with Christ in Redemption because if she is to become Mother of the new humanity in the order of grace, she must be able to identify with all of their needs and serve as their model. In other words, it was not enough for Mary to be passively created as maternal Mediatrix; she needed to be a "worthy and acceptable Mediatrix to the Mediator [Mediatrix ad Mediatorem]," as Pope Leo XIII referred to Mary; "for no single individual can even be imagined who has ever contributed or ever will contribute so much toward reconciling man with God."[84] This is why Vatican II

---

[82] Ibid., 313-314.
[83] Heb. 4:15.
[84] Pope Leo XIII, Encyclical Letter *Fidentem Piumque* of 20 September 1896,

speaks of Mary's *fiat* as an all-encompassing consent to her indissoluble participation in the entire Redemptive mission of Christ from Nazareth to Calvary.[85]

Mary's Fiat Mediates the Mediator, Making Her Mediatrix of the Source of All Graces

St. Paul wrote: "For there is one God, and there is one mediator between God and men, the man Jesus Christ, who gave himself a redemption for all."[86] These words of St. Paul serve as the Scriptural foundation for the Church's affirmation that Jesus Christ is the one Mediator. Commenting on this teaching of St. Paul, St. Thomas adds that Jesus Christ acts as Mediator *as man*, as his humanity is hypostatically united to His Divinity.[87] Moreover, St. Thomas explains that the human nature of Christ serves the purpose of Him to be Mediator as Priest and Victim, the necessary condition for Redemption.[88]

ASS 29 (1896-1897), 206 [*OL* #194].

[85] Cf. *LG*, 62.

[86] 1 Tm. 2:5. The Revised Standard Version, Catholic Edition of the Bible translates the Vulgate's *redemptio* as "ransom." In order to remain faithful to the literal translation which provides greater insight into our subject, "*redemptio*" is translated as "redemption."

[87] Cf. *ST*, III, q. 26, a. 2.

[88] Cf. *ST*, III, q. 22, a. 1, 2. (a. 1) "The office proper to a priest is to be mediator between God and the people: to wit, inasmuch as He bestows Divine things on the people, wherefore, *sacerdos* (priest) means a giver of sacred things (*sacra dans*)....*Every high-priest taken from among men is ordained for men in the things that appertain to God, that he may offer up gifts and sacrifices for sins.* Now this is most fitting to Christ. For through Him are gifts bestowed on men, according to 2 Pet. i. 4: *By Whom* (i.e. Christ) *He hath given us most great and precious promises, that by these you may be made partakers of the Divine Nature.* Moreover, He reconciled the human race to God, according to Col. 1:19, 20: *In Him* (i.e. Christ) *it hath well pleased (the Father) that all fulness should dwell, and through Him to reconcile all things unto Himself.* Therefore it is most fitting that Christ should be a priest. (a. 2) Now man is required to offer sacrifice for three reasons. First, for the remission of sin, by which he is turned away from God. Hence, the Apostle says (Heb. v. 1) that it appertains to the priest *to offer gifts and sacrifices for sins.* Secondly, that man may be preserved in a state of grace, by ever adhering to God, wherein his peace and

Calling to mind the Letter to the Hebrews, Sheen confirms the significance of this truth in that only as man could God act as Priest and victim: "As priest had He not been man He could not have shed His blood, if He had not been God, it would have been of no value to us (Hebrews 2:17; Acts 20:28)."[89] Hence, Sheen affirmed that Mary's *fiat* inaugurated Christ's priestly mission, for "the priesthood of Christ began, namely, when His human nature was anointed with the oil of Divinity in the Incarnation."[90] Sheen also affirmed that "[Christ's] victimhood was never divorced from His Priesthood."[91] This is evidenced by those who sought to kill Him shortly after His birth (Mt. 2:13, 16-18) and later by the prophecy of Simeon (Lk. 2:34-35).

The Annunciation, therefore, is the pivotal moment in salvation history where God asks Mary, who represented all humanity, to give Him that human nature—the human nature that would allow Him to act as Mediator—Priest and Victim—between God and man. This is why Mary, alone, from among all those who acted as mediators between God and man throughout salvation history,

---

salvation consist. Wherefore under the Old Law the sacrifice of peace-offerings was offered up for the salvation of the offerers, as is prescribed in the third chapter of Leviticus. Thirdly, in order that the spirit of man be perfectly united to God: which will be most perfectly realized in glory. Hence, under the Old Law, the holocaust was offered, so called because the victim was wholly burnt, as we read in the first chapter of Leviticus.

"Now, these effects were conferred on us by the humanity of Christ. For, in the first place, our sins were blotted out, according to Rom. iv. 25: *Who was delivered up for our sins.* Secondly, through Him we received the grace of salvation, according to Heb. v. 9: *He became to all that obey Him the cause of eternal salvation.* Thirdly, through Him we have acquired the perfection of glory, according to Heb. x. 19: *We have* (Vulg.,--*Having*) *a confidence in the entering into Holies* (i.e. the heavenly glory) *through His Blood.* Therefore Christ Himself, as man, was not only priest, but also a perfect victim, being at the same time victim for sin, victim for a peace-offering, and a holocaust."

[89] Fulton J. Sheen, "Priest Prophet and King" (undated notes from folder labeled "Mystical Body"), Sheen Archives.

[90] Sheen, "The Priesthood of Christ in Heaven" (undated typescript from folder labeled "Mystical Body"), Sheen Archives.

[91] *TMP*, 27.

in a secondary and subordinate sense, merits the singular title "Mediatrix."[92]

Sheen reinforced the truth that while Mary mediates the Incarnation of the Mediator, she is not equal to Christ. Mary's union with God was not a hypostatic union like Christ. Rather, it was one by grace and her espousal to the Holy Spirit in a very unique and perfect way via her Immaculate Conception. Mary, therefore, did not have a divine personality, which belongs exclusively to the Persons of the Trinity. Sheen reinforced this important point:

> Christ is the mediator between God and man....What makes it possible for Christ to be the Head of the human race is the fact that He had no human personality. Human personality is the limitation of nature, for example, the nature that belonged to George Washington, was eminent by the personality of George Washington....But Christ

---

[92] Pope Leo XIII, basing himself on St. Thomas Aquinas, writes:

> And who could think or say that the confidence so strongly felt in the patronage and protection of the Blessed Virgin is excessive? Undoubtedly the name and attributes of the absolute Mediator belong to no other than to Christ, for being one person, and yet both man and God, He restored the human race to the favour of the Heavenly Father: *One Mediator of God and men, the man Christ Jesus, who gave Himself a redemption for all* (1 Tim. ii. 5, 6). And yet, as the Angelic Doctor teaches, *there is no reason why certain others should not be called in a certain way mediators between God and man, that is to say, in so far as they co-operate by predisposing and ministering in the union of man with God* (*Summa*, p. III, q. xxvi., articles 1, 2). Such are the angels and saints, the prophets and priests of both Testaments; but especially has the Blessed Virgin a claim to the glory of this title. For no single individual can even be imagined who has ever contributed or ever will contribute so much towards reconciling man with God. She offered to mankind, hastening to eternal ruin, a Saviour, at that moment when she received the announcement of the mystery of peace brought to this earth by the Angel, with that admirable act of consent *in the name of the whole human race* (*Summa*, p. III, q. xxx., art. 1). She it is *from whom is born Jesus*; she is therefore truly His mother, and for this reason a worthy and acceptable "Mediatrix to the Mediator" [Encyclical Letter *Fidentem Piumque* of 20 September 1896, *ASS* 29 (1896-1897), 206; English trans. available from http://www.vatican.va/holy_father/leo_xiii/encyclicals/documents/hf_l-xiii_enc_20091896_fidentem-piumque-animum_en.html].

wanting a human personality was able to subsume all human natures under Himself. It is this ability to incorporate all humanity to Himself which makes possible the Mystical Body, or the Church."[93]

Mary's role as Mediatrix, therefore, is secondary and subordinate to the one Mediation of Christ due partly to the fact that she was a human person, unlike the Divine Personality of her Son, the Word made flesh.[94] However, God made Mary's cooperation in mediating the physical means through which He would redeem humanity an essential element in His plan of Redemption. He made Mary's role so essential that without her *fiat* there is no assurance that God would have offered an alternative plan of salvation. Sheen writes:

> If He had never taken on our human flesh, we would never have heard His Sermon on the Mount or have seen Him forgive those who dug His hands and feet with nails on the Cross. But the Woman gave Our Lord His human nature. He asked her to give Him a human life—to give Him hands with which to bless children, feet with which to go in search of stray sheep, eyes with which to weep over dead friends, and a body with which to suffer—that He might give us a rebirth in freedom and love....
>
> ...It was through her that He became the bridge between the Divine and the human. If we take her away, then either

---

[93] Fulton J. Sheen, "Christ the Head of the Church," (undated typescript from folder labeled "Mystical Body"), Sheen Archives (hereafter cited as "Christ the Head of the Church").

[94] Mary's secondary and subordinate mediation is also understood from her role as the New Eve. The very fact that Mary is the New Eve indicates that Mary, like Eve, was not the Head of their spousal relationship. In addition, Mary is not *the* Mediator by the fact that she is woman because the Mediator mediates the remission of sins *and* the generation of new life according to the Spirit. As St. Thomas reminds us, "The active power of generation invariably accompanies the passive power...; the active power of generation belongs to the male sex, and the passive power to the female" (*ST*, I, q. 92, a. 1). Therefore, we see the spousal complementarity at the Incarnation between the New Adam and the New Eve according to the Spirit.

God does not become man, or He that is born of her is a
man and not God. Without her we would no longer have
Our Lord! If we have a box in which we keep our money,
we know that one thing we must always give attention to is
the key; we never think that the key is the money, but we
know that without the key we cannot get our money. Our
Blessed Mother is like the key. Without her we can never
get to Our Lord, because He came through her. She is not
to be compared to Our Lord, for she is a creature and He
is a Creator. But if we lose her, we cannot get to Him. That
is why we pay so much attention to her; without her we
could never understand how that bridge was built between
Heaven and earth.[95]

Sheen therefore concludes, "Christ is Mediator between God
and humanity; Mary is Mediatrix between Christ and us."[96]

MARY BECOMES *THEOTOKOS* AND MOTHER OF THE *TOTUS CHRISTUS*

Sheen understood Mary's *fiat* as Mary's consent not only to
become Mother of the Redeemer, but also Mother of the Redeemed.
In other words, Mary accepted in one *fiat* her role as *Theotokos* and
the New Eve. The full realization of this mystery was gradually
revealed throughout Christ's historical life and fully manifested
only at Calvary (as we will see later in this chapter). Sheen writes:

Since the Head and the Body are inseparable, it is therefore
true to say that as Mary bore Christ in her womb she was
virtually carrying the whole Mystical Body. The mother
earth that bears the vine also bears the branches.[97]

Hence, Sheen connects the Divine Maternity and the origin
of her spiritual maternity. We find this teaching in Leo XIII

---

[95] *WFL*, 73-74.
[96] Ibid., 72.
[97] Sheen, notes from "Immaculate Conception" (emphasis mine).

(*Fidentem Piumque*),[98] Pius X (*Ad diem illum*),[99] Pius XII (*Per Christi Matrem*)[100] and also in *Lumen Gentium*, which affirmed

---

[98] "For no single individual can even be imagined who has ever contributed or ever will contribute so much toward reconciling man with God. To mankind heading for eternal ruin, she offered a Savior when she received the announcement of the mystery brought to this earth by the Angel, and in giving her consent gave it 'in the name of the whole human race' (*ST*, III, q. 30, a. 1). She is from whom Jesus is born; she is therefore truly His Mother and for this reason a worthy and acceptable 'Mediatrix to the Mediator' ('*ad Mediatorem Mediatrix*')" [*ASS* 29 (1896-1897), 206 (*OL* #194)].

[99] "For is not Mary the Mother of Christ? Then she is our Mother also. And we must in truth hold that Christ, the Word made Flesh, is also the Savior of mankind. He had a physical body like that of any other man: and again as Savior of the human family, he had a spiritual and mystical body, the society, namely, of those who believe in Christ. 'We are many, but one sole body in Christ' (Rom. 12, 5). Now the Blessed Virgin did not conceive the Eternal Son of God merely in order that He might be made man taking His human nature from her, but also in order that by means of the nature assumed from her He might be the Redeemer of men. For which reason the Angel said to the Shepherds: 'Today there is born to you a Savior who is Christ the Lord' (Lk. 2, 11). Wherefore in the same holy bosom of his most chaste Mother Christ took to Himself flesh, and united to Himself the spiritual body formed by those who were to believe in Him. Hence Mary, carrying the Savior within her, may be said to have also carried all those whose life was contained in the life of the Savior. Therefore all we who are united to Christ, and as the Apostle says are members of His body, of His flesh, and of His bones (Eph. 5, 30), have issued from the womb of Mary like a body united to its head. Hence, though in a spiritual and mystical fashion, we are all children of Mary, and she is Mother of us all. Mother, spiritually indeed, but truly Mother of the members of Christ, who are we (St. Augustine, *De S. Virginitate*, 6).

"If then the most Blessed Virgin is the Mother at once of God and men, who can doubt that she will work with all diligence to procure that Christ, Head of the Body of the Church (Col. 1, 18), may transfuse His gifts into us, His members, and above all that of knowing Him and living through Him (1 Jn 4, 9)?" [*ASS* 36 (1903-1904), 452-453].

[100] "The grace of Christ comes to us through the Mother of Christ. She in fact 'Sumens illud ave Gabrielis ore,' who greeted her as full of grace, became at the same time Mother of Christ and Mother of divine grace. The maternal office of 'Mediatrix' really began at the very moment of her consent to the Incarnation; it was manifested for the first time by the first sign of Christ's grace, at Cana in Galilee; from that moment it rapidly spread down through the ages with the growth of the Church" [*AAS* 40 (1948), 536-537; *OL* #428].

that Mary was at one and the same time "Mother of the Son of God" and "the mother of the members of Christ"[101] because "by reason of the gift and role of divine maternity, by which she is united with her Son, the Redeemer, and with his singular graces and functions, the Blessed Virgin is also intimately united with the Church....This maternity of Mary in the order of grace began with the consent which she gave in faith at the Annunciation and which she sustained without wavering beneath the cross, and lasts until the eternal fulfillment of all the elect."[102] This is an important teaching of Sheen that we will examine in greater depth in the following chapter when we look at Mary's mediation as Mother of the Mystical Body of Christ. It is important to note, however, that the beginning of Mary's mediation as Mother of the Church really began, although implicitly, when she became Mother of God.

MARY'S *FIAT* INAUGURATES HER *ASCENDING* MEDIATION THROUGH HER ACTIVE *KENOSIS* BY PARTICIPATING IN THE PRIEST-VICTIMHOOD OF CHRIST

Mary's need to ratify her Immaculate Conception and fullness of grace (*pleroma*) resulted in her *active kenosis*, which began with her *fiat*. In other words, the passive character of her participation in the priest-victimhood of Christ which began at her Immaculate Conception will now take on a conscious and active dimension in Mary's role in Redemption. Vatican II expressed Mary's active

---

[101] *LG,* 53. This phrase was included in response to Pope Paul VI's request to the Council Fathers that Mary's role as "Mother of the Church"—a title close to the heart of Paul VI—explicitly be worked into the final text of *Lumen Gentium.*

[102] *LG,* 63, 62. John Paul II affirmed this same teaching when he said: "The Second Vatican Council, by presenting Mary in the mystery of Christ, also finds the path to a deeper understanding of the mystery of the Church. Mary, as the Mother of Christ, is in a particular way united to the Church, 'which the Lord established as his own body [*LG,* 52]'" (*RM,* 5).

cooperation with God in Redemption in terms of Mary's faith and obedience to God's plan for her as the New Eve:

> Rightly therefore the holy Fathers see her as used by God not merely in a passive way, but as freely cooperating in the work of human salvation through faith and obedience. For, as St. Irenaeus says, she "being obedient, became the cause of salvation for herself and for the whole human race."[103]

As we have already seen from Sheen (and St. Thomas), Christ's one mediation as Priest and Victim began at the moment of His Incarnation. In Chapter II, we saw how Sheen referred to Christ's mediation in terms of His priest-victimhood, which culminated at Calvary, as Christ's "ascending mediation." Another way Sheen explains this ascending mediation of Christ as Priest and Victim is in terms of His active *kenosis*. Sheen explained that "the *kenosis* was the emptying of Christ as a Victim," and that it was "a long historical 'emptying.'"[104] In other words, it was an emptying that began with Mary's *fiat* at Nazareth and culminated on the Cross at Calvary. Sheen explains the mystery of *kenosis* in Christ the Priest-Victim and how it especially applies to priests, but which also applies equally to the priesthood of the laity:

> The "making Himself nothing" or as in some versions, "He emptied Himself," has been known in the theology as *kenosis*. Our concern here is only the understanding of the text in the relation to priest-victimhood....
>
> ...*Kenosis* imposes participation on all of Christ's ambassadors. As a priest, one "fills" himself up with holiness; as a victim, one "empties" himself in service to mankind and the world. Emptiness is of two kinds: *Sterile emptiness* like the Grand Canyon or a deep ditch; *Fertile emptiness* like a flute through which the breath may pipe a tune; or like an empty nest which can be filled with new life and song. The latter implies excentration of the self, or the de-egotization of personality that Christ may exalt us in our humiliation.

---

[103] *LG,* 56.
[104] *TMP,* 131.

Kenosis in a priest-servant will express itself in two resolutions: (1) humility, and (2) compassion.

Humility: "As He grows greater, I must grow less" (John 3:30). The increase of Christ in the soul of a priest is in direct relation to the decrease of the self-will....

...*Emptiness* as regards self, is balanced by compassion for others. The less stress on the ego, the more care there is for neighbor.... *The emptiness of self is in order that Christ may get in; compassion and service is in order that Christ may get out to others.*[105]

No one more perfectly fulfilled this mystery than Mary. Applying this teaching to her, who participated perfectly and uniquely in the priest-victimhood of Christ, Mary participated in the Priesthood of Christ by her perfect humility, her fullness of grace and her consent worthily to become the Mother of God and give Him the human nature through which He would redeem all humanity. She also participated in the Priesthood of Christ in her ongoing *fiat* to offer her Son for the salvation of the world. We will see this more explicitly in Sheen's reflection on the Presentation of Jesus in the Temple.

Mary's *kenosis*, as it relates to her compassion for others, is seen in her *fiat* which was her free consent on behalf of the entire human race to become the mother of the Messiah. Mary's *kenosis*, or ascending mediation, is evidenced also by her consent to undergo a unique co-passion, or co-victimhood, with Christ, the New Adam, in her role as the New Eve. Since Christ's *kenosis*, or victimhood, began with His Priesthood, namely at the Incarnation, then Mary's *active* participation in the ascending mediation of Christ via His *kenosis*/victimhood began at the moment of her *fiat* and, too, culminated at the Cross.[106]

---

[105] *TMP*, 36, 38-40.
[106] Cf. Alphonsus de Liguori, *The Glories of Mary*, 404-405.

MARY'S *FIAT* TO GOD HAS AN ANTHROPOLOGICAL SIGNIFICANCE

Sheen also found an anthropological significance to Mary's *fiat* as the representative of all women as the New Eve. Whereas Eve's disobedience led to death, Mary's *fiat* gave us Life, which is the fullness of the gift of motherhood. He stated, "By pronouncing *Fiat* Mary achieved the full role of womanhood, namely, to be the bearer of God's gifts to man."[107] He elaborates on the significance of this elsewhere:

> Mary is here recapturing woman's vocation from the beginning, namely, to be to humanity the bearer of the Divine. Every mother is this when she gives birth to a child, for the soul of every child is infused by God. She thus becomes a co-worker with Divinity; she bears what God alone can give....
>
> ...The hidden wish of every woman in history, the secret desire of every feminine heart, is fulfilled in that instant when Mary says: "*Fiat*"—"Be it done unto me according thy word."
>
> Here is cooperation at its best. Here is the essence of womanhood—*acceptance, resignation, submission*: "Be it done unto me."...[Throughout history there are heroic examples of women] making the Total Gift, accepting a Divine assignment, being submissive for Heaven's holy purposes. Mary calls herself *ancilla Domini*, the handmaid of the Lord. *Not* to be this for any woman lowers her dignity. Woman's unhappiest moments are when she is unable to give; her most hellish moments are when she refuses to give....
>
> ...Closely allied with this submission is sacrifice. For submission is not passivity but action—the action of self-forgetfulness. Woman is capable of greater sacrifices than man partly because her love is less intermittent, and also

---

[107] *LC*, 16.

because she is unhappy without total and complete dedication. Woman is made for the sacred. She is Heaven's instrument on earth. Mary is the prototype, the pattern-woman who fulfills in herself the deepest aspirations of the heart of every daughter of Eve. [108]

This anthropological dimension of Mary as perfectly fulfilling the vocation of womanhood was later developed further by Pope St. John Paul II in his insightful Apostolic Letter *Mulieris Dignitatem*.[109] We will see this truth confirmed and revealed in greater depth when Mary has what Sheen calls another great *fiat*, or, more accurately, a renewal of her original *fiat* at the Annunciation, while at the foot of the Cross. We will examine this later in the chapter.

SUMMARY OF THE THEOLOGICAL SIGNIFICANCE OF MARY'S MEDIATION IN RELATION TO THE INCARNATION, ACCORDING TO THE TEACHING OF FULTON SHEEN

1. Mary's role as Mediatrix and the New Eve satisfied the demands of God's justice as it related to His plan of Redemption fittingly requiring the free cooperation of one who could choose and mediate the means of Redemption—the Incarnation—on behalf of fallen humanity. Fulfilling this role at the Annunciation, Mary became the fitting Mediatrix to the Mediator.

2. Christ is the one Mediator between God and Man because of His hypostatic union, making Him the only one who can satisfy the infinite debt of sin by mediating as Priest and Victim. Christ's mediation, therefore, is intrinsically related to His priest-victimhood.

3. Mary's mediation, therefore, must be understood according to her relationship to the priest-victimhood

---

[108] *WFL*, 82-85.
[109] Cf. *MD*, 11.

of Christ, which Sheen refers to as Christ's *ascending* mediation.

4. Mary relates to the priest-victimhood, or ascending mediation, of Christ in two ways: *Theotokos* and her singular role as the New Eve. In both roles, Mary mediates as spouse and mother.

5. Mary was specially prepared to become maternal Mediatrix as *Theotokos* and the New Eve by her singular privilege of the Immaculate Conception and her fullness of redemptive grace, which was her passive participation in the priest-victimhood of Christ which had yet to become Incarnate.

6. Christ's priest-victimhood began at the moment of Mary's *fiat* to become at the same time *Theotokos* and the New Eve. Therefore, Mary's active mediation began at the moment she gave her *fiat*, which consented to have God assume from her His human nature in which He would begin His messianic mission as Priest-Victim and the New Adam. Of particular significance is Mary's mediation which gave God the blood through which He would redeem man from sin.

7. Mary's *fiat* mediated her role as *Theotokos* and her predestined role of the New Eve which would involve her inseparable association and participation in the redemptive victimhood of Christ (Christ's ascending mediation) which endured from Nazareth to Calvary. Sheen characterized Christ's victimhood as a lifelong *kenosis* in which Mary would be perfectly united as the New Eve with the New Adam.

8. Mary's *fiat* to a lifelong victimhood with Christ also served as her free and active appropriation of her Redemption, which she had already received by her Immaculate Conception. Secondly, Mary's *fiat* was her humble submission to suffer with Christ to prepare

her and make her a worthy Mediatrix to Christ and
Mother of the Church.

9. The events which are associated with the priest-victim-
    hood, or *kenosis*, of Christ from the Annunciation to
    Calvary represent the ascending mediation of Christ,
    the New Adam, and Mary, the New Eve.

10. Mary's Divine Maternity is the cause for her spiritual
    maternity: "Since Mary is the Mother of God, then she
    can be Mother of everyone whom Christ redeemed."[110]

11. The Incarnation of Jesus Christ resulted from the
    mutual consent and nuptial union of Mary and
    the Holy Spirit. This truth will be revisited again at
    Calvary when the prolongation of the Incarnation in
    the Church begins.

The Visitation (Lk. 1:39-56): Mary Mediates Christ and the Holy Spirit to John the Baptist

The next *locus* for Sheen's teaching on Mary's mediation is the
Visitation. Mary is not mentioned often in Scripture, but Sheen
notes that when she is, she is never mentioned apart from Christ.[111]
Sheen concludes, therefore, that each reference to Mary in Scripture
carries with it great significance as to her association with Christ's
Redemptive mission. Also, the revealed relationship between Jesus
and Mary is paradigmatic of their relationship to Christ's Mystical
Body, the Church.

Immediately after the Incarnation, Scripture reveals that Mary
"arose and went with haste" to visit her cousin, Elizabeth, until the
birth of John the Baptist (cf. Lk. 1:39). Mary's visit to Elizabeth

---

[110] *WFL*, 63.
[111] Cf. *MBC*, 313-314.

represented for Sheen the meeting of the Old Testament and the New Testament as he writes:

> On hearing the woman's greeting, the child whom Elizabeth bore within her "leaped in her womb." The Old Testament is here meeting the New Testament....All the longings and expectations of thousands of years as to Him Who would be the Savior are now fulfilled in this one ecstatic moment when John the Baptist greets Christ, the Son of the Living God.[112]

Sheen saw the Visitation as a revelation of Mary's mediation of the Holy Spirit. Sheen especially noted that while Christ alone sanctifies, it was "*Mary's visit* [which] sanctified John the Baptist,"[113] as he "leaped with joy at the mother who brought the Christ into her home."[114] Sheen saw this as a foreshadowing of Mary's mediation of the Holy Spirit at Pentecost:

> "The child leaped in her womb, and Elizabeth herself was filled with the Holy Ghost." A Pentecost came before Pentecost. The physical boy of Christ within Mary now fills John the Baptist with the Spirit of Christ; thirty-three years later the Mystical Body of Christ, His Church, will be filled with the Holy Spirit, as Mary, too, will be, in the midst of the Apostles abiding in prayer....Mary received the Spirit of God through an angel; Elizabeth was the first to receive it through Mary.[115]

---

[112] *WFL*, 36.

[113] *PNHO*, 273. The sanctification of St. John was when he was "filled with the Holy Spirit" (Lk. 1:15); *ST*, III, q. 27, a. 1. This teaching is also affirmed in the great Marian treatise *True Devotion* by St. Louis de Montfort: "If we examine closely the remainder of the life of Jesus Christ, we see that he chose to begin his miracles through Mary. It was by her word that he sanctified Saint John the Baptist in the womb of his mother, Saint Elizabeth; no sooner had Mary spoken than John was sanctified" (St. Louis de Montfort, *True Devotion to Mary*, in *God Alone: The Collected Writings of St. Louis Marie de Montfort* [Bay Shore, NY: Montfort Publications, 1995], 295).

[114] *LC*, 18.

[115] *WFL*, 36-37.

Mary as the Mediatrix of the Holy Spirit at the Visitation was also taught by St. Louis Marie de Montfort who wrote:

> If we examine closely the remainder of the life of Jesus Christ, we see that he chose to begin his miracles through Mary. It was by her word that he sanctified St. John the Baptist in the womb of his mother, St. Elizabeth; no sooner had Mary spoken than John was sanctified.[116]

Here at Ain Karem does Sheen see Mary's active mediation revealed with greater clarity. He saw Mary's visit to Elizabeth as the paradigm of her mediation with us. Sheen highlights that, as at Ain Karem, it is "the role of Mary" to bring Our Lord and the Holy Spirit to us as she did to Elizabeth and John (Scripture references this when Elizabeth called Mary "Mother of my Lord" and when it stated that Elizabeth was "filled with the Holy Spirit").[117] It is interesting to note that while God could have waited to sanctify John the Baptist until Jesus was old enough to do it on His own, He chose to do it through the mediation of His mother while still in her womb.

Sheen also understood Mary's mediation at the Visitation served as a foreshadowing of the role of the Mystical Body, the Church, which not only bears Christ in her (e.g. substantially in the Eucharist and accidentally by grace), but also brings Christ to others. Moreover, Sheen emphasized that the Visitation also serves to highlight Mary's mediation as secondary to the one mediation of Christ from Whom all graces flow:

> This is a beautiful example of how our communion with Christ unites us inseparably not only to Him but to our neighbor. Union with Christ is inseparable from union with His Church and union with humanity....Here [Mary mediating Christ to John the Baptist], too, is a hint that there are graces that flow to us through Mary, for the virgin at that particular time was mediating in a secondary way

---

[116] St. Louis de Montfort, *True Devotion to Mary*, in *God Alone: The Collected Writings of St. Louis Marie de Montfort*, 295.
[117] Cf. Sheen, "Immaculate Conception," Sheen Archives.

the blessing of the Divinity of Christ within her to John the Baptist.[118]

Sheen further explains how Elizabeth's actions toward Jesus and Mary highlight the inseparable, but subordinate relationship that exists between Jesus and His Mother:

> In the Visitation there was not only an <u>adoration</u> of the Holy of Holies or the Real Presence in Mary, but there was also the <u>veneration</u> of the Tabernacle: "the Mother of my Lord." The Eucharistic Lord is to be <u>adored</u>; the mother of the Lord is only to be <u>honored</u>...[However,] you cannot go to a marble statue of a mother with a babe, hack away the babe without destroying the mother.[119]

Sheen understood St. Luke's reference to Mary remaining with her cousin "about three months" to signify that Mary remained with Elizabeth until the birth of John the Baptist. Based upon this, Sheen observed, "Mary is present at three births: at the birth of John the Baptist, at the birth of her own Divine Son, and at the 'birth' of John the Evangelist, at the foot of the Cross, as the Master saluted him: 'Behold thy mother!'"[120] While the full significance of this insight is not revealed until Calvary, Sheen is highlighting a definite connection between one's "birth" in Christ and the role Mary plays in bringing that about.

Lastly, Sheen noted that while some may perceive that the spotlight is predominantly on Mary in this scene, her reaction to Elizabeth's praise points to the contrary. Mary immediately deflects it to her Son, emphasizing that she is what she is only in light of her special relationship with her Son. Sheen writes:

> When Elizabeth extols Mary, Mary glorifies her God. Mary receives praise as a mirror receives light: she stores it not, nor even acknowledges it, but makes it pass from her to God to Whom is due all praise, all honor and thanksgiving.... The love of God is reflected in the soul of the just, as

---

[118] Sheen, "Mary and the Tabernacle," Sheen Archives.
[119] Ibid.
[120] *WFL*, 36.

the light of the sun is magnified by a mirror. So Mary's Son is the Sun, for she is the moon.[121]

The Virgin Birth of Christ (Lk. 2:1-20): Mary's "first-born"

There is one passage of the Nativity narrative of St. Luke that carried great significance in Sheen's understanding of Mary's maternal mediation: "And she gave birth to her *first-born* son..." (Luke 2:7). Sheen found the timing of St. Luke's usage of this phrase significant:

> As is evidence that Christ is the Head of the human race, St. Paul says that He was the first-born among many brethren (Romans 8:29). The name of the unique Son of God belongs to Him as the Word, and remains after His union with the flesh. The name, however of first-born among humanity comes to Him after His Incarnation, when He became inserted in the humanity so that what He did affected all humanity.[122]

Here, at the birth of the Head of the Mystical Body, the Church, Sheen sees an implicit reference that Mary's Virgin Birth of Christ will continue in the Virgin Birth of Christ's Mystical Body, a mystery that is fully revealed only at Calvary:

> Mary had no other children in the flesh. But "firstborn" could mean Our Lady's relation to other children she would have according to the Spirit. In this sense, her Divine Son called John her "son" at the foot of the Cross. Spiritually, John was her "second son."[123]

These words of Sheen illustrate a direct relationship among the Annunciation at Nazareth, Nativity at Bethlehem and Calvary. In

---

[121] *WFL*, 41.

[122] Fulton J. Sheen, "Christ the First Born Among the Brethren" (undated manuscript from folder labeled "Mystical Body"), Sheen Archives.

[123] *LC*, 29.

each of these moments, the virginal motherhood of Mary is empha-
sized. At Nazareth, Mary becomes the Virgin Mother of Christ; at
Bethlehem she bears Christ; and at Calvary, as we will soon see,
Mary becomes the Virgin Mother of Christians as the "New Eve."
Sheen further explains the significance of "first-born":

> It suggests that she was to have a spiritual progeny which
> would make up the Mystical Body of her Divine Son, just
> as Eve is called the "mother of all living" (Gen. 3:20) or the
> mother of men in the natural order. Sara gave only one son
> to the father of believers, Abraham, and yet she is called the
> mother of all Israel (Isaiah 51:21). There is a clear sugges-
> tion in the words "first-born" that she who begot corporally
> the Head of the Church, was also to beget spiritually the
> members of the Church.[124]

The Prophecy of Simeon
and the Sword (Lk. 2:22-35)

Sheen understood that the earliest events of Jesus' life provide
significant insight into and serve to remind us of the sacrificial
mission He was undertaking for the Redemption of the world.
The first of these was represented by the myrrh given at His birth.
Sheen comments: "They brought three gifts: gold to honor His
Kingship, frankincense to honor His Divinity, and myrrh to honor
His Humanity which was destined for death. Myrrh was used at
His burial. The crib and the Cross are related again, for there is
myrrh at both."[125] The second event, only eight days after His
birth, was Christ's circumcision. Sheen did not view Christ's cir-
cumcision as merely the fulfillment of Jewish law. Since He was the
Son of God, there was greater significance behind this event. Referring to circumcision as a "knife's stroke upon natural life,"[126] Sheen

---

[124] MBC, 318.
[125] LC, 40.
[126] Sheen, "Immaculate Conception," Sheen Archives.

highlighted that the shedding of blood at Christ's circumcision served as a foreshadowing of His shedding of blood on Calvary:

> In the Circumcision of the Divine Child there was a dim suggestion and hint of Calvary, in the precocious surrendering of blood....But whenever there was an indication of Calvary, there was also some sign of glory; and it was at this moment when He was anticipating Calvary by shedding His blood that the name of Jesus was bestowed on Him.

> A Child only eight days old was already beginning the blood shedding that would fulfill His perfect manhood. The cradle was tinged with crimson, a token of Calvary. The Precious Blood was beginning its long pilgrimage. Within an octave of His birth, Christ obeyed a law of which He Himself was the Author, a law which was to find its last application with Him. There had been sin in human blood, and now blood was already being poured out to do away with sin....

> ...Coming straight from the Father's arms to the arms of His earthly mother, He is carried in her arms to His first Calvary. Many years later, he will be taken from her arms again, after the bruising of the flesh on the Cross, when the Father's work is done.[127]

Further insight into the Redemptive mystery of Christ and the role Mary would play in it is revealed only thirty-two days after Christ's circumcision when Mary presents Jesus in the temple in Jerusalem. The presentation of Jesus and the words addressed to Mary by Simeon carried great theological significance for Sheen as it is here at the temple where "Mary's role in the Redemption becomes even clearer."[128]

First, Sheen describes the significance of Mary's consecration of Jesus at the temple:

> In the Book of Numbers, the tribe of Levi was set apart for the priestly function, and this priestly dedication was

---

[127] *LC*, 33.
[128] *MBC*, 319.

understood as a substitute for the sacrifice of the firstborn, a rite which was never practiced. But when the Divine Child was taken to the temple by Mary, the law of the consecration of the firstborn was observed in its fullness; for this Child's dedication to the Father was absolute, and would lead Him to the Cross.[129]

These words of Sheen underscore, once again, that while Mary herself was not a priest, her role in the Redemption was certainly priestly in character. Sheen highlights this when he comments on Mary's consecration of Jesus: "The Mother who brought the Lamb of God into the world had no lamb to offer—except the Lamb of God. God was presented in the temple at the age of 40 days."[130] This is an important point that sheds additional insight into the mystery of Mary's maternal mediation as a profound sharing in the priest-victimhood of Christ. Not only was her life an offering through her *kenosis* (which represents Mary's participation in the victimhood of Christ) in order that she might untie Eve's knot of disobedience, but she did freely *offer* her Son for the salvation of the world. The Presentation of Jesus in the Temple thus reveals another dimension of Mary's participation in the Priesthood of Christ as Christ offered Himself to the Father through the offering of Mary, who freely offered Jesus and surrendered her maternal rights to the will of the Father. Pope Paul VI in his Apostolic Exhortation *Marialis Cultus* confirmed this priestly dimension of Mary's actions at the Presentation of Jesus when he wrote:

> Mary is, finally, *the Virgin presenting offerings*. In the episode of the Presentation of Jesus in the Temple (cf. Lk. 2:22-35), the Church, guided by the Spirit, has detected, over and above the fulfillment of the laws regarding the offering of the firstborn (cf. Ex. 13:11-16) and the purification of the mother (cf. Lv. 12:6-8), a mystery of salvation related to the history of salvation. That is, she has noted the continuity of the fundamental offering that the Incarnate Word made to

---

[129] *LC*, 34.
[130] Ibid., 34.

the Father when He entered the world (cf. Heb. 15:5-7)....
The Church herself, in particular from the Middle Ages
onwards, has detected in the heart of the Virgin taking
her Son to Jerusalem to present Him to the Lord (cf. Lk.
2:22) a desire to make an offering, a desire that exceeds the
ordinary meaning of the rite. A witness to this intuition is
found in the loving prayer of Saint Bernard "Offer your
Son, holy Virgin, and present to the Lord the blessed fruit
of your womb. Offer for the reconciliation of us all the
holy Victim which is pleasing to God" (*In Purificatione B.
Mariae., Sermo III*, 2: *PL* 183, 370).[131]

The one who would illuminate the mystery of Mary's intimate association with the Redemption of her Son was the Prophet
Simeon, who had waited his whole life to see the Redeemer of
mankind. Sheen observed that the passing of the baby Jesus from
the arms of Mary to those of Simeon accompanied by Simeon's
Nunc dimittis represented the passage from the Old Testament to
the New Testament where "all the promises of the Old Testament
were accomplished and all the prophecies of God's chosen people
fulfilled."[132] But Sheen also noted: "Simeon's words of joy turned
into sorrow, as he spoke of the part Mother and Son were to play
in the Redemption of the world."[133]

At the heart of this encounter are the prophetic words of
Simeon directed only at Mary: "*And a sword will pierce through
your own soul also.*"[134] Sheen comments on the significance of these
words:

Simeon, full of the prophetic spirit, was looking forward to
the day when this Babe, the new Adam, would atone for
sin on the Cross, as the Man of Sorrows, and where she as
the new Eve would co-operate in that Redemption as the

---

[131] Pope Paul VI, *MC*, 20.
[132] Fulton J. Sheen, *The Eternal Galilean* (New York: D. Appleton-Century
Company, 1934; reprint, Garden City, NY: Garden City Books, 1950), 224
(hereafter cited as *EG*).
[133] Ibid., 225.
[134] Lk. 2:35.

Woman of sorrows. Simeon was practically telling her that
Eden would become Calvary, the tree would be the Cross,
and she would be the Mother of the Redeemer. But if she is
the Mother of the Redeemer, then was she not called to be
the Mother of the Redeemed.[135]

Sheen points out that the Greek word used by Simeon for
sword is ρομφαία, which refers not to a dagger but to a large,
curved two-edged sword. This signified that in her role as Mother
of the Redeemer and Mother of the Redeemed, Mary "would be
destined to great suffering."[136] According to Sheen, the "sword"
became the sign of Mary's "co-victimhood" (Mary's ascending
mediation in and with Christ) in her inseparable role as the New
Eve in Redemption.[137]

There is also a deeper significance to Simeon's use of the word
"sword." Reading this event in the greater context of Sacred Scripture, Sheen immediately recalled the flaming sword held by the
cherubim outside Paradise. As we saw earlier in this chapter, the
sword signified that while the entrance back into Paradise would
not be sealed off, the condition for admittance would involve sacrifice and the destruction of "every vestige of the old humanity."[138]
He added:

> It was an echo back to the Garden of Eden, where a tree
> brought the ruin of the first Adam, and at whose gates
> stood an angel with a flaming sword to guard the gates until
> the appointed hour of salvation. Simeon was now saying
> that the hour had come. The tree of Paradise that brought
> ruin would be transplanted to Calvary and be His cross;
> the sword of the angel would be lifted from his hands and
> driven into Mary's heart, as a first witness that only those

---

[135] *MBC*, 319.
[136] Sheen, "Our Blessed Mother" (from a series of retreat lectures given at Holy
Trinity Seminary, Irving, Texas, 1972, recorded by and in the possession of
Mr. Daniel B. Steffen of Plano, Texas), compact disc.
[137] Cf. Sheen, "Mary and the Tabernacle," Sheen Archives.
[138] Sheen, "Immaculate Conception," Sheen Archives.

who are pierced through and through with the sword of sacrificial love shall enter the everlasting Eden of heaven.[139]

Sheen develops the significance of the sword into a central theological doctrine which highlights two important elements of Mary's association in Redemption. First, Sheen takes the position, combining the teachings of St. Paul and St. Thomas Aquinas on the significance of the sword, that "the sword that pierced [Mary's] soul was Christ Himself" and that "this sword has a double edge: one edge ran into His Own Sacred Heart, the other into her Immaculate Heart." He explains this further:

> How is Christ a sword? First of all, the Epistle to the Hebrews tells us the word of God is a two-edged sword. "God's word to us is something alive, full of energy; it can penetrate deeper than any two-edged sword, reaching the very division between soul and spirit, between joints and marrow, quick to distinguish every thought and design in our hearts. From him, no creature can be hidden; everything lies bare, everything is brought face to face with him, this God to whom we must give our account" (Heb. 4:12, 13). The "word here is undoubtedly Scripture and the living voice of the Church. But the root, the source, is the Divine Word, Who is Christ Himself. St. Thomas in his *Commentary* on this passage makes that identification. Furthermore, St. Thomas quotes St. Ambrose as giving the same interpretation: "For the Word of God is living and effectual and more piercing than any two-edged sword."[140]

Sheen saw this identification confirmed by the words of Christ Himself Who would later say, "I came to bring the sword" (cf. Mt. 10:34).[141] The identification of Christ with the two-edged sword has central significance to Sheen's soteriological thought. First, it emphasizes that in the work of Redemption, Christ is the primary cause. This also implicitly reinforces Christ's Headship as the New

---

[139] *EG*, 226.
[140] *WFL*, 239.
[141] *LC*, 38.

Adam. In order not to confuse his audience, Sheen clarifies his teaching on Christ as the cause of His own death referring to the teaching of St. Thomas:

> One edge of this sword—to speak metaphorically—Christ ran into His Own Sacred Heart, in the sense that He willed all the sufferings from Bethlehem to Calvary. He was the cause of His own death, St. Thomas tells us, and in two ways: *directly*, by being in such antagonism to the world that the world could not endure His Presence. Simeon foretold this by saying He was "a sign to be contradicted."...*Indirectly*, Christ was the cause of His own death, as St. Thomas tells us, "by not preventing it when He could do so...."[142]

Secondly, Sheen's identification highlights the inseparability between the New Adam and the New Eve in the work of Redemption. It is one sword with two edges, and as Sheen will later point out when commenting on the Passion, Christ always made sure that His edge of the sword was sharper. Sheen stated, "With His Passion there must be her compassion....A mother who did not share in His sufferings would be unworthy of her great role.[143] He explains the significance of this:

> [Christ] also willed that His Mother should be as closely associated with Him as any human person could be associated with a Divine Person. Pius X declared that the bond between them was so intimate that the words of the Prophet could be applied to both: *Defecit in dolore vita mea, et anni mei in gemitibus* (Ps. 30:11). If it be granted with Leo XIII that "God willed that the grace and truth which Christ won for us should be bestowed on us in no other way than through Mary," then she, too, had to will cooperation in redemption, as Christ willed it as the Redeemer Himself. Christ willed that she should suffer with Him, some theologians say *per modum unius*. If He willed His death, He willed her Dolors....But it was no imposed will; she

---

[142] Ibid., 239-240; cf. *ST*, III, q. 47, a. 1.
[143] Ibid., 38.

accepted it all in her original *Fiat* in the Annunciation. The Sword He plunged into His Heart, He, with cooperation, plunged into her own. He could hardly have done this if she were not His Mother and if they were not in a spiritual sense "two in one flesh", "two in one mind." The sorrows of His Passion were His, but His Mother considered them her own, too, for this is the meaning of compassion.[144]

Sheen explained further why it was necessary for Mary to share so deeply in the priest-victimhood of her Son:

> She also had to suffer for our sakes as well as for His. As Our Lord learned obedience by which He suffered, so Mary had to learn motherhood, not by appointment but by experience with the burdens of the human heart. The rich cannot console the poor unless they become less rich for the sake of the poor; Mary cannot wipe away human tears unless she herself has been their fountain. The title "Mother of the Afflicted" had to be earned in the school of affliction. She does not expiate for sins; she does not redeem; she is not a savior—but by His will and by her own, she is so much bound up with Him that His Passion would have been entirely different had there not been her compassion.

> He also plunged the sword into her own soul in the sense that He called her to be a cooperator with Him, as the new Eve, in the regeneration of humanity....St. Paul tells us that we cannot be partakers of His glory unless we partake also of His crucifixion. If, then, the sons of Mary are not exempt from the law of sacrifice, certainly Mary herself, who is the Mother of God, shall be less exempt.[145]

Hence, already at the Presentation of Jesus, Sheen reaffirms the theological foundations upon which Mary's mediation is understood. She mediates, first, in her unique participation in the priest-victimhood of Christ in a way necessary for her worthily to merit the privilege of her fullness of grace, her vocation to be Mother

---

[144] Ibid., 240-241.
[145] *WFL*, 242.

of God, and her vocation to be Mother of the new humanity. She would, therefore, have to suffer in an unfathomable capacity. Referring to Pope Pius XII, Sheen writes, "Pius XII says that [Mary], as the true Queen of Martyrs, more than any of the faithful, filled up for His Body the Church the sufferings that were wanting to the Passion of Christ!" (cf. Col. 1:24).[146] Another keen insight Sheen offers as to the significance of Mary's sufferings pertains to the nature of the Church as the prolongation of Christ's Incarnation, in particular, His Passion. He writes, "This was the first reason, why God permitted her Dolors, that she might be the first after the Redeemer Himself to continue His Passion and death in His Mystical Body."[147] These words of Sheen provide greater insight into what he stated on page 125, "[Mary's] redemption was already completed [through her privilege of the Immaculate Conception] but that she had not yet accepted or ratified it."[148] Each of the sufferings Mary would endure through her union with the victimhood of Christ was her appropriation of the fullness of redemptive grace she already received from her privilege of the Immaculate Conception. In addition, Mary's sufferings served as her unique part in the recapitulation of the Church in Christ that corresponded to her vocation as Mother and model of the Church.

Elaborating on this insight further, Sheen explains how the sword becomes representative of such an intimate association of Mary with the Redemptive suffering of her Son that the word he chose to best represent this unique role and relationship of Mary with Jesus was "Co-Redemptrix":

> As Mary left the Temple that day she understood as she never understood before why the Magi brought with their joyous gifts of gold and incense, the bitter, sad, and sorrowful gift of myrrh. She saw now that the law that bound Him would also bind her, and that while He would have the tree, she would have the sword; that as He was the new Adam, she would be the new Eve; and as Eve was instrumental in

---

[146] Ibid., 241.
[147] Ibid., 241.
[148] WFL, 30-31.

the fall, so she would be instrumental in the salvation as the
Co-Redemptrix of the Redeemer Christ.[149]

The Finding of Jesus
in the Temple (Lk. 2:41-51)

Mary experienced the sword of deep sorrow when for three
days she lost her Son, Who was only twelve years old at the time.
Continuing the metaphor of the sword, Sheen noted the significance of this loss of Jesus: "In those three days, Mary came to know
one of the effects of sin, namely, the loss of God. Though she was
without sin, nevertheless she knew the feats and the loneliness, the
darkness and the isolation which every sinner experiences when
he loses God."[150] Commenting further in another place, Sheen
stated that "in this dolor both His natures were fastening her to
make her a co-Redemptrix under His causality: His human nature
in the physical loss, His Divine nature in the Dark Night of her
soul."[151]

Sheen also found deep significance in the first recorded words
of Jesus addressed to Mary in response to her question:

> Son, why have you treated us so?
> Behold, your father and I have been looking for you anx-
> iously.

Jesus' response to Mary was:

> How is it that you sought me?
> Did you not know that I must be in my Father's house?[152]

Sheen understood that these words of Jesus served as a sword
to Mary and Joseph. As they express their anxiety He seemingly
rebukes them and reminds them of His real Father and that now

---

[149] *EG*, 227-228.
[150] *LC*, 45.
[151] *WFL*, 251.
[152] Lk. 2:48-49.

as a "Son of the Commandments"[153] He is to be about His Father's
business. These words especially affected His relationship with
Joseph. As Sheen says, "Jesus takes the name 'father' away from
Joseph."[154] These words also hint at a future separation in His
earthly relationship with His Mother, an insight shared by John
Paul II three decades later.[155] Sheen writes:

> The Divine Child answered by making a distinction
> between the one whom He honored as a father on earth
> and the Eternal Father. This answer affirmed a parting of
> the ways; it did not diminish the filial duty that He owed
> to Mary and Joseph, for He became immediately subject to
> them again, but it decisively put them in a second place.[156]

Sheen noted that the Gospels reinforce this point by never
mentioning Joseph again from this moment on.[157] Eighteen years

---

[153] Sheen, "Our Blessed Mother" (from a series of retreat lectures given at Holy
Trinity Seminary, Irving, Texas, 1972, recorded by and in the possession of
Mr. Daniel B. Steffen of Plano, Texas), compact disc. Sheen explained how
Jesus could become "Son of the Commandments" (giving Him the authority to teach) at age 12 (the normal age was 13) because of an exception that
was made in Jewish law for children of widows. He explained that since Jesus
was born of a Virgin, then that would mean that He had no earthly Father.
Lacking an earthly father would thereby qualify Him to become Son of the
Commandments at age 12.
[154] Sheen, "Immaculate Conception," Sheen Archives.
[155] "Now, when Jesus left Nazareth and began his public life throughout Pales-
tine, he was completely and exclusively 'concerned with his Father's business'
(cf. Lk. 2:49). He announced the Kingdom: the 'Kingdom of God' and 'his
Father's business,' which add a new dimension and meaning to everything
human, and therefore to every human bond, insofar as these things relate to
the goals and tasks assigned to every human being. Within this new dimension, also a bond such as that of 'brotherhood' means something different
from 'brotherhood according to the flesh' deriving from a common origin
from the same set of parents. 'Motherhood,' too, in the dimension of the
Kingdom of God and in the radius of the fatherhood of God himself, takes on
another meaning. In the words reported by Luke, Jesus teaches precisely this
new meaning of motherhood" (*RM,* 20).
[156] *LC,* 46.
[157] Ibid., 47.

later at the Wedding Feast at Cana, Jesus will revisit this point, but then it will concern His relationship with His mother.

Cana: Mary Mediates Jesus' "Hour" and Begins a New Relationship with Him and with Humanity (Jn. 2:1-11)

In the second chapter of St. John's Gospel we read:

On the third day there was a marriage at Cana in Galilee,
And the mother of Jesus was there;
Jesus also was invited to the marriage, with the disciples.
When the wine failed, the mother of Jesus said to him,
They have no wine.
And Jesus said to her, "O woman, what have you to do with me?
My hour has not yet come."
His mother said to the servants, "Do whatever he tells you."

The events that take place at the Wedding Feast of Cana are of monumental importance in Sheen's theology of Mary as Mediatrix. He saw Cana as serving as the mid-point between two phases in the lives and relationship between Jesus and Mary. He writes:

There are two great periods in the relations of Jesus and Mary, the first extending from the Crib to Cana, and the second, from Cana to the Cross. In the first, she is the Mother of Jesus; in the second, she begins to be the Mother of all whom Jesus would redeem—in other words, to become the Mother of men.[158]

As we will see from his teaching on Cana, Sheen would have agreed with the words of John Paul II that "the episode at Cana in Galilee offers us a sort of first announcement of Mary's mediation, wholly oriented towards Christ and tending to the revelation of

---

[158] *WFL*, 125.

his salvific power."[159] Since the Wedding of Cana represents for Sheen a new manifestation of Mary's role as maternal Mediatrix, it deserves special attention.

"THE MOTHER OF JESUS WAS THERE"

St. John's separate reference to Mary as "the mother of Jesus" at the beginning of the account carried special significance for Sheen. Sheen pointed out that "this is the only occasion in the life of Our Lord where Mary is mentioned before her Son."[160] Sheen saw that this introduction to the Wedding at Cana served as a literary device to alert the reader that Mary is about to exercise her mediation in a special way as she did when she was "the instrument for the sanctification of John the Baptist in his mother's womb."[161] In addition, St. John's reference to Mary as "the mother of Jesus," a title Sheen points out was used four times of Mary, was indicative that whatever was to take place during the marriage feast would reveal greater insight into Mary's relationship with Jesus and her role in His plan of Redemption. He writes:

> It is very much to the point to indicate that John in (2:1) does not give Mary her personal name, but describes her as "the Mother of Jesus." This is exactly the same description that is given to her in (Acts 1:14). This indicates that she is in a representative character....It is through her the long promised seed had come....The only time the Blessed Mother is identified as the Mother of Jesus is when she is inaugurating either the public life of the physical Christ or the life of the Mystical Christ....Therefore, whenever she is described as the Mother of Jesus there seems to be some connection: one, with the whole Abrahamic background or else, the whole foreground of the Church on Pentecost,

---

[159] RM, 22.

[160] LC, 74. John Paul also noted the significance of Mary's presence mentioned before that of Jesus: "From the text it appears that Jesus and his disciples were invited because of his mother" (RM, 21).

[161] Ibid., 74.

and at this first miracle the Mother and the disciples were gathered together.[162]

He saw Mary as representing the Old Testament as the Daughter of Zion, who was about to meet the New Testament in the Person of her Divine Son and His disciples.[163] Once again, Mary's presence and subsequent role will serve as a bridge by which Old and New Testaments meet. The fact that this event takes place within the context of a marriage was also significant to Sheen:

> In the Old Testament, the relation between God and Israel was compared to the relation between a bridegroom and his bride. Our Lord suggested that the same relation would henceforth exist between Himself and the new spiritual Israel, which He was going to found. He would be the Bridegroom, His Church would be the bride. And since He came to establish this kind of union between Himself and redeemed humanity, it was fitting that He should commence His public ministry by assisting at a marriage. St. Paul was not introducing a new idea when he wrote to the Ephesians [5:25] later on that the union of man and woman was the symbol of the union of Christ and His Church.[164]

MARY MEDIATES THE "HOUR" OF CHRIST'S PASSION AND DEATH

Mary's seemingly insignificant request or "prayer," as Sheen refers to it, of "They have no wine," carried great significance as the immediate and profound response from Jesus indicates. Before we explore Sheen's explanation of Jesus' response, let us look at the

---

[162] Fulton J. Sheen, "The Marriage Feast of Cana and Christ the Bridegroom" (notes from folder labeled "Mystical Body"), Sheen Archives.

[163] Sheen, "Our Blessed Mother" (from a series of retreat lectures given at Holy Trinity Seminary, Irving, Texas, 1972, recorded by and in the possession of Mr. Daniel B. Steffen of Plano, Texas), compact disc.

[164] LC, 73.

significance of Mary's request as it relates to her mediation. First, Sheen points out that Mary notices one's needs before He does:

> One of the most amazing features of this marriage is that it was not the wine servant, whose business it was to service [*sic*] the wine, who noticed the shortage, but rather Our Blessed Mother. (She notes our needs before we ourselves feel them.) She made a very simple prayer to her Divine Son about the empty wine pots when she said: "They have no wine." Hidden in the words was not only a consciousness of the power of her Divine Son but also an expression of her desire to remedy an awkward situation.[165]

While this request shows her solicitude for our natural and seemingly insignificant needs—which shows the depth of her love for us—the deeper significance of Mary's request lies in the fact, as Sheen just pointed out—that she knew her Son's Divine power to perform miracles and that she believed *now was the time* to manifest this to the world. The implications of this request for a miracle were enormous as is evidenced by Jesus' response to His mother, commonly translated in English as "O woman, what have you to do with me? My hour has not yet come" (Jn. 2:4). This translation of the first part of Jesus' response (O woman, what have you to do with me?) falls short of capturing the theological significance of the original text. The Greek text of Jesus' response reads, "Τί ἐμοὶ καὶ σοί, γύναι," which is accurately translated in the Vulgate as "*Quid mihi et tibi, mulier?*" Sheen therefore based his commentary on the corresponding English translation: "Woman, what to me is to thee. My hour is not yet come."

---

[165] *WFL*, 113. In another place Sheen further described the significance of Mary's request: "It was not a personal request; she was already mediatrix for all who were seeking the fullness of joy. She has never been a spectator, but a full participant willingly involving herself in the needs of others. The mother used the special power which she had as a mother over her Son, a power generated by mutual love" (*LC*, 75).

"WOMAN" AND "THE HOUR": THE ANNOUNCE-
MENT TO MARY OF HER ROLE AS THE NEW EVE

Jesus' response to Mary referring to her as "Woman" is extremely significant for Sheen, for he saw it as the first explicit connection Jesus makes of Mary with Eve.[166] Therefore, the events of Cana provide important insight into how Mary will fulfill her vocation as the New Eve. "Woman" indicated that a new relationship was now beginning between Mary and her Son. As Sheen put it, "He [Jesus] makes it plain to her that He can no longer act under her author-ity. She is now about to lose Him as a Son."[167] The title "Woman" hearkened back to Genesis when the first *woman* was given the title mother. Jesus was telling Mary that she was now going to bear that great title by becoming the new universal mother of humanity as Mother of the Redeemed.[168] Therefore, Jesus' response was not a rebuke, but rather a proclamation or salutation of Mary's new role, as Sheen explains: "These words did not mean a denial of His Blessed Mother whom He loved next to His own heavenly Father; rather did they mean that there are other ties than those of the flesh, and that in the spiritual order, she who is my Mother may be like Eve, 'mother of all the living.'"[169]

---

[166] Cf. *MBC*, 320; *LC*, 396.

[167] *TMP*, 315.

[168] Earlier in this chapter (see pp. 98-100), we saw that Mary possessed pro-found insight into the salvific mysteries of Divine revelation from an unusually young age. The graces from her Immaculate Conception, her vow of virginity, and education in the Hebrew Scriptures from her earliest years contributed to Mary's extraordinary knowledge and understanding of Divine revelation. In this light, we also recall Sheen's teaching that Mary's consent at the Annun-ciation to become the mother of the Redeemer also included her consent to become the mother of the redeemed (in other words, mother of the *totus Christus*). It is reasonable to conclude, therefore, that Mary would certainly have understood that Jesus' response to her at Cana was an announcement that what she consented to at the Annunciation (to be Mother of God and the New Eve) would begin its realization at the moment Christ manifests His Divinity and messianic mission. The full realization of Mary's universal moth-erhood would only be accomplished at Calvary when Jesus repeated this title.

[169] *MBC*, 320.

Sheen noted the significance that at the same time Jesus called His mother "Woman," it was in the context of His "hour." Sheen explained that the word "hour" was used always in reference to His Passion. He states: "Whenever the word 'Hour' [*sic*] is used in the New Testament, it is used in relation to His Passion, death, and glory. References to this 'Hour' [*sic*] are made seven times in John alone (Jn. 2:4; Jn. 7:30; Jn. 8:20; Jn. 12:23; Jn. 12:27; Jn. 16:32; Jn. 17:1)."[170]

This meant that Mary's request for a miracle was really a request for Jesus to begin His Redemptive mission to the Cross. And Jesus' words to Mary, "What to me is to thee; My hour is not yet come," served both as a statement and as a question. To emphasize all the implications of Jesus' words, Sheen translates them into common language:

> My dear mother, do you realize that you are asking Me to proclaim My Divinity—to appear before the world as the Son of God, and to prove My Divinity by My works and My miracles? The moment that I do this, I begin the royal road to the Cross. When I am no longer known among men as the son of a carpenter, but as the Son of God, that will be My first step toward Calvary. My Hour [*sic*] is not yet come; but would you have Me anticipate it? Is it your will that I go to the Cross? If I do, your relationship with me changes. You are now My mother. You are known everywhere in our little village as the mother of Jesus. But if I appear now as the Savior of men, and begin the work of Redemption, your role will change too. Once I undertake the salvation of mankind, you will not only be My mother, but you will also be the mother of everyone whom I redeem. I am the Head of humanity; as soon as I save the body of humanity, you who are the mother of the Head will become also the mother of My Mystical Body or the Church. You will then be the universal mother, the new Eve, as I am the new Adam.

---

[170] *LC*, 76.

To indicate the role that you will play in Redemption, I now bestow upon you that title of universal motherhood; I call you—*Woman*. It was to you that I referred when I said to Satan that I would put enmity between him and the woman, between his brood of evil and your seed, which I am. That great title of woman I dignify you with now. And I shall dignify you with it again when My Hour [*sic*] comes and when I am unfurled upon the Cross like a wounded eagle. We are in this work of Redemption together. What is yours is mine. From this Hour [*sic*] on, we are not just Mary and Jesus, we are the new Adam and the new Eve, beginning a new humanity, changing the water of sin into the wine of life. Knowing all this, My dear mother, is it your will that I anticipate the Cross and that I go to Calvary?[171]

Sheen, therefore, understood that Jesus was asking Mary not only if she knew what her request would mean for her Son, but also what the cost of that miracle would mean for her as well. Jesus' Redemptive road would lead to His Crucifixion. Mary's sharing in that would lead to her mystical transfixion by the sword.

Mary's response confirmed her deep understanding of the implications of her request as it would elevate her *fiat* from the Annunciation to a greater level of participation in the Redemptive work of her Son. Sheen notes how this response of Mary served as her last recorded words in Sacred Scripture and that they would be among her most significant: "Do whatever He tells you." Sheen described these words as "a magnificent valedictory!"[172] That response of Mary indicated full confidence and surrender to Him. It became yet another great *fiat* as it inaugurated Mary into her new role as the New Eve, the spiritual mother of the redeemed, which would be fulfilled at Calvary. Sheen adds:

At Cana, the prophecy that Simeon had made to her in the temple was confirmed: henceforth, whatever involved her Son would involve her, too; whatever happened to Him

---

[171] *LC*, 396.
[172] *WFL*, 115.

would happen to her. If He was destined to go to the Cross, so was she; and if He was now beginning His Public Life, then she would begin a new life too, no longer as just the mother of Jesus, but as the mother of all whom Jesus the Savior would redeem. He called Himself "Son of Man," a title embracing all humanity; she would be henceforth the "Mother of Men."[173] Just as she was at His side as He began His Hour, so would she be at His side at its climactic finish.[174]

A PIVOTAL POINT IN THE RELATIONS BETWEEN JESUS AND MARY

Hence, Sheen notes that Cana marks a pivotal point in the relationship between Jesus and Mary. Sheen writes: "From Cana on, there is a growing detachment, which Mary helps to bring on herself. She induced her Son to work His first miracle, as He changed her name from Mother to Woman, the significance of which will not become clear until the Cross."[175] In another place he adds: "Here, Mary passes from Theotokos to 'Bride of Christ,'"[176] and "as Joseph disappears at the Temple, so Mary, as the Mother of Jesus, disappears to become the Mother of all whom He will redeem."[177] Mary is now entirely associated with the Church as Sheen interpreted the first verse after Cana: "He went down to Caphernaum with his mother, his brethren and his disciples" (John 2:12).

---

[173] "Henceforth" in this statement of Sheen refers to the beginning of the actualization of Mary's role as Mother of the Redeemed. It would not be fully manifested until Calvary when Mary would have fully merited the title "Mother of Men" through her compassion with her Son. This will be explained on pages 152-172.

[174] *LC,* 77-78.

[175] *WFL,* 125.

[176] Sheen, "Immaculate Conception," Sheen Archives.

[177] *PNHO,* 274-275.

Lastly, Sheen notes that Cana emphasizes that the kind of relationship which Jesus came to establish was in the order of the Spirit, not of the flesh. He reinforced this point when, some time after Cana, the disciples of Jesus informed Him that "his mother and his brethren" were waiting to speak to Him, and Jesus immediately responded, "Who is my mother, and who are my brethren?"[178] In his customary language of preaching, Sheen explains that with this response, "He took all relationships out of the order of blood. For Christ, they no longer exist."[179] Only those who do the will of His Father are His brother, sister and mother. This teaching was also affirmed by John Paul II.[180]

CONCLUSIONS ABOUT MARY'S MEDIATION AT CANA

Mary's mediation at Cana reveals, first of all, a profound love in her maternal heart for humanity. As her role as the New Eve becomes more manifest, we begin to see more explicitly the power of her maternal intercession for both our material and, most importantly, redemptive needs is revealed in Mary's mediation on

---

[178] Mt. 12:46, 48.

[179] Sheen, "The Blessed Mother," *Renewal and Reconciliation*, 1974.

[180] "The Gospel of Luke records the moment when 'a woman in the crowd raised her voice' and said to Jesus: 'Blessed is the womb that bore you, and the breasts that you sucked!' (Lk. 11:27) These words were an expression of praise of Mary as Jesus' mother according to the flesh....But to the blessing uttered by that woman upon her who was his mother according to the flesh, Jesus replies in a significant way: 'Blessed rather are those who hear the word of God and keep it' (Lk. 11:28). He wishes to divert attention from motherhood understood only as a fleshly bond, in order to direct it towards those mysterious bonds of the spirit which develop from hearing and keeping God's word.

"This same shift into the sphere of spiritual values is seen even more clearly in another response of Jesus reported by all the Synoptics. When Jesus is told that 'his mother and brothers are standing outside and wish to see him,' he replies: 'My mother and my brothers are those who hear the word of God and do it' (cf. Lk. 8:20-21). This he said 'looking around on those who sat about him,' as we read in Mark (3:34) or, according to Mathew (12:49), 'stretching out his hand towards his disciples' (*RM*, 20).

behalf of all those present at the wedding. This is evidenced not only by Mary's noticing of and interceding for our small, material needs ("they have no wine"), but moreover, by Mary's apparent impatience to bring to us the graces of Redemption. This is why she anticipated her Son's Hour.[181]

Secondly, Sheen points out that Mary is our Mediatrix to Christ by means of substitution:

> The Marriage Feast of Cana reveals how Mary makes up for our battered and weak wills; she does this by substituting herself for us....Mary comes into this crisis of life to substitute for us in the same way that a mother substitutes for a sick child....The Mother thus puts herself in the place of the child, who does not have the knowledge to know what is best or cannot will to do anything to help himself. She "doubles," as it were for the freedom of the child. Thus does the mother dispose the child to receive what is best.... As the baby needs the doctor, so the Blessed Mother knows we need her Divine Son. As Our Lord mediates between us and the Heavenly Father, so the Blessed Mother mediates between us and Our Divine Lord.[182]

These words of Sheen remind us of the words spoken by the Second Vatican Council which said: "The maternal duty of Mary

---

[181] John Paul II's commentary on this passage confirms the teaching of Sheen: "At Cana in Galilee there is shown only one concrete aspect of human need, apparently a small one of little importance ('They have no wine'). But it has a symbolic value: this coming to the aid of human needs means, at the same time, bringing those needs within the radius of Christ's messianic mission and salvific power. Thus there is a mediation: Mary places herself between her Son and mankind in the reality of their wants, needs and sufferings. She puts herself 'in the middle,' that is to say she acts as a mediatrix not as an outsider, but in her position as mother. She knows that as such she can point out to her Son the needs of mankind, and in fact, she 'has the right' to do so. Her mediation is thus in the nature of intercession: Mary 'intercedes' for mankind. And that is not all. As a mother she also wishes the messianic power of her Son to be manifested, that salvific power of his which is meant to help man in his misfortunes, to free him from the evil which in various forms and degrees weighs heavily upon his life" (*RM*, 20).

[182] *WFL*, 117-118.

toward men in no wise obscures or diminishes this unique mediation of Christ, but rather shows his power....In no way does it
impede, but rather does it foster the immediate union of the
faithful with Christ."[183] Sheen anticipated this teaching when he
affirmed: "Mary is not our salvation—let us not be absurd on that.
The mother is not the doctor, and neither is Mary the Savior. But
Mary brings us the Savior!"[184]

Thus, at Cana, Mary mediates the manifestation of the Divinity of her Son when her prayer moves her Son to turn water into
wine, thus sending her Son toward the Cross. Sheen offers an
interesting insight into the deeper significance of this miracle. He
writes that since this miracle was directly related to the "Hour," the
"change of water into wine was oriented to the change of wine into
His Blood." Sheen, therefore, observed a relation between Mary
and the Eucharist because her intervention resulted in the transubstantiation of water into wine, which was a foreshadowing of
Christ's greater miracle, the transubstantiation of wine into Blood
at the Last Supper.[185]

Sheen's insights into Mary's role as the New Eve, as revealed
at Cana, provide a stronger biblical basis for Mary's title "Mother
of the Church." It was at Cana where this role is announced for
the first time when Jesus called His Mother, "Woman," the new
mother of those who will live in Christ. It will be announced to the
rest of the world at Calvary.

Lastly, Mary always points and takes us to her Son. Sheen writes:
"No one will ever call on her without being heard or without being
finally led to her Divine Son, Jesus Christ, for Whose sake she
alone exists—for Whose sake she was made pure—and for Whose
sake she was given to us."[186] Faith in Mary's intercessory power and
role was found in the earliest expressions of devotion among the
first Christians. This is evidenced by the ancient prayer to Mary,
the *Sub tuum praesidium*, which experts date back to the third or

---

[183] *LG*, 60.
[184] *WFL*, 118.
[185] Fulton J. Sheen, "Mary and Institution of Eucharist" (outline and notes for
sermon in green notebook), Sheen Archives.
[186] *WFL*, 117.

fourth century and which remains as part of the *lex orandi* of the Church:

> We fly to your patronage,
> O holy Theotokos;
> Despise not our petitions
> In our necessities,
> But from all dangers
> Deliver us always,
> O glorious and blessed Virgin.[187]

The Second Vatican Council made direct reference to it in its teaching on Mary in *Lumen Gentium*.[188]

Calvary: Mary, the New Eve— Spouse of Christ and Mother of the Mystical Body of Christ

NUPTIAL CONTEXT OF CALVARY: THE NEW ADAM AND THE NEW EVE

What takes place at Calvary reveals the heart of Fulton Sheen's understanding of Mary's maternal mediation. All that we have studied thus far of the key moments in salvation history and Mary's central role in it serve as snapshots of the full revelation of their significance as they converge at the foot of the Cross. The predominant theme for Sheen in viewing the events of Calvary is that of

---

[187] "*Sub tuum praesidium confugimus, Sancta Dei Genitrix; nostras deprecationes ne despicias in necessitatibus nostris, sed a periculis cunctis libera nos semper, Virgo gloriosa et benedicta (ex Brevario Romano)*"; *The Raccolta*, eds. Joseph P. Christopher, Charles E. Spence, and John F. Rown (New York: Benziger Brothers, Inc., 1952), 234-235.

[188] "Clearly from earliest times the Blessed Virgin is honored under the title of Mother of God, under whose protection the faithful took refuge in all their dangers and necessities" (*LG*, 66; cf. *Flannery*, 421).

nuptials, which he reminds us is the main theme throughout God's relationship with mankind:

> There's something different here. This moment on the Cross we no longer have Jesus and Mary. We have the New Adam and the New Eve. What is the idea that runs all through Scripture? It is nuptials. The covenant is based on nuptials....There was the nuptials of man and woman in the Garden of Eden. There was the nuptials of Divinity and humanity in the Blessed Mother; the nuptials of Israel and God in the Old Testament. In the Prophet Isaiah: "I, your Creator, am your husband" (Is. 54:1). God is the husband of Israel. And in the beautiful Book of Hosea, God tells Hosea to marry a prostitute—an absolutely worthless woman. She leaves him, betrays him, commits adultery, has children by other men, and when the heart of Hosea is broken, God said to Hosea, "Take her back....She is the symbol of Israel. Israel has been my unworthy spouse, but I love Israel and I will never let her go." And Hosea taking back the prostitute is the symbol of God's love for His quahal [*sic*], his ecclesia of the Old Testament.[189]

We are therefore witnessing a marriage covenant taking place at the Cross between the New Adam and the New Eve, the Bridegroom and His Bride. Sheen notes that Christ referred to Himself as the Bridegroom (cf. Mt. 9:15; Mt. 25:1-10; Mk. 2:19-20; Lk. 5:34-35). Now the Bridegroom carrying "the transplanted tree of Eden" meets His Bride, who waits for Him "wearing the angel's transplanted sword" from Eden.[190] Who is the Bride? Mary's spousal and maternal relationship is so enmeshed within the complete mystery of the Incarnation that when its mystical prolongation begins with the birth of the Church at Calvary, the Church herself assumes the same identity—the New Eve. To emphasize this mystery, Sheen often quoted the following passage of St. Augustine († 430) which Sheen saw as applicable both to the Church (which

---

[189] Sheen, "The Blessed Mother," *Renewal and Reconciliation*, 1974.
[190] *EG*, 240-241.

was the original context of St. Augustine) and to Mary because they both act as a New Eve to Christ the New Adam, at Calvary:

> The Cross is the scene of nuptials and generation....[The Bridegroom] now meets His Bride, the Woman at the Cross. As from the side of Adam is drawn Eve, so now from the New Adam on the Cross is begotten the New Eve, which is the Church or His Body. As St. Augustine describes this mystical marriage: "Like a Bridegroom Christ went out from His Heavenly chambers. He went with a presage of His Nuptials into the field of the world. He came to the marriage bed of the Cross; there, mounting it, He consummated His marriage. And when He perceived the sighs of His creature, He lovingly gave Himself up and joined Himself to the woman forever" (*Sermo CXX, In Natali Domini IV, PL* 39, 1987).

> Mary is first "Woman," or the New Eve, in relation to Christ, the New Adam. Then she is called "Mother" but the Motherhood is of John. She who was the Mother of Jesus the Son of God now became the Mother of the son of Zebedee. But John is unnamed in the word from the Cross, and stands for all the children of Mary yet to be born [in the order of grace].[191]

What Sheen's teaching emphasizes is that the Church's relationship as the New Eve with Christ is the mystical extension and reflection of Mary's relationship as the New Eve with Christ. At Calvary, Mary achieved the fullness of the reality which the Church herself will one day achieve at the end of time. John Paul II explained the significance of this mystery when he commented on the teaching of the Second Vatican Council describing Mary as type and model of the Church.[192]

---

[191] *TMP*, 318-319.

[192] "The Dogmatic Constitution *Lumen gentium* of the Second Vatican Council, after presenting Mary as 'pre-eminent and as a wholly unique member of the Church', declares her to be the Church's 'type and outstanding model in faith and charity' (*Lumen gentium*, n. 53).

The Covenantal Sacrifice of Marriage Manifested at Calvary: a Union of Suffering, Love and Glory

Building upon the words of St. Augustine just quoted, Sheen explains the importance of the nuptial union between the New Adam and the New Eve taking place within the context of the

---

"The Council Fathers attribute to Mary the function of 'type,' that is, figure, 'of the Church,' borrowing the term from St Ambrose who expresses himself thus in his commentary on the Annunciation: 'Yes, she [Mary] is betrothed, but she is a virgin because she is a type of the Church which is immaculate but a bride: a virgin, she conceived us by the Spirit; a virgin, she gave birth to us without pain' (*In Ev. sec. Luc.*, II, 7, *CCL*, 14, 33, 102-106). Thus Mary is a type of the Church because of her immaculate holiness, her virginity, her betrothal and her motherhood.

"1. ...By defining Mary as a type of the Church, the Council invites us to see in her the visible figure of the Church's spiritual reality, and in her spotless motherhood, the announcement of the Church's virginal motherhood.

"2. ...unlike the Old Testament images or types, which are only prefigurations of future realities, in Mary the spiritual reality signified is already eminently present.

"3. ...In affirming that Mary is a type of the Church, the Council does not intend to equate her with the figures or types of the Old Testament, but instead to affirm that in her the spiritual reality proclaimed and represented is completely fulfilled.

"In fact, the Blessed Virgin is a type of the Church, not as an imperfect prefiguration, but as the spiritual fullness which will be found in various ways in the Church's life. The particular relationship that exists here between the image and the reality represented is based on the divine plan, which establishes a close bond between Mary and the Church. The plan of salvation which orders the prefigurations of the Old Testament to fulfilment in the New Covenant likewise determines that Mary would live in a perfect way what was later to be fulfilled in the Church.

"The perfection God conferred upon Mary, therefore, acquires its most authentic meaning if it is interpreted as a prelude to divine life in the Church.

"4. ...The functions of 'type and model of the Church' refer in particular to Mary's virginal motherhood and shed light on her particular place in the work of salvation. This basic structure of Mary's being is reflected in the motherhood and virginity of the Church" (Pope St. John Paul II, "Mary is Outstanding Figure of Church," *ORE*, 13 August 1997, 11).

Sacrifice on Calvary. He writes: "Christ was considered the Bridegroom and the Church the bride....This is important because when a new covenant is made it too is consummated in a sacrifice."[193] With this in mind, Sheen goes on to explain that even the covenant (or sacrament) of marriage involves a sacrifice "because the lover dies to himself and submits to the beloved. The beloved dies to herself and submits to the lover. And out of that mutual death, there comes the ecstasy of love. That is the sacrifice."[194] The sacrifice of Christ was complete in that it was both corporal and spiritual involving a total *kenosis* and immolation of body and soul for His Bride, the Church (cf. Eph. 5), whose fullness was already achieved in Mary the mother and model of the Church.

Not only did Mary cooperate in Redemption by giving God the human nature He would use as the instrument of our Redemption, but she would cooperate in a unique manner by means of the special sharing she had in the victimhood of Christ. In his customary oratorical style, Sheen brings out this often overlooked aspect of Mary's union with Christ's suffering:

> The Sword He drove into her soul made her identify herself with His redemptive sufferings, forced her to tread the streets over her own Son's blood. His wounds bled; hers did not. Mothers, seeing their sons suffer, wish it could be their own blood instead of their sons' that is shed. In her case, it was her blood that He shed. Every crimson drop of that blood, every cell of that flesh, she had given to Him. Jesus had no human father. It was always her blood that He was shedding; it was only her blood that she was treading.[195]

This mystery of Mary's material relationship in Christ's Redemption is a subject worthy of further reflection. St. Paul wrote: "I fill up in my flesh what is lacking to the sufferings of Christ" (Col. 1:24). Sheen emphasizes that this is St. Paul's way of describing the universal call of Christians to share in the victimhood of Christ

---

[193] Sheen, "The Church as a Bride of the Bridegroom Christ," (undated notes from folder labeled "Mystical Body"), Sheen Archives.

[194] Sheen, "The Blessed Mother," *Renewal and Reconciliation*.

[195] *WFL*, 254.

and that Mary, as the Mother of Christians, was not exempt from this. He writes:

> The Lord has called us not only to be members of his priesthood but also members of His Victimhood. His death is finished, for He can never die again; but our death and the death of the Church is not yet finished. Christ is on the cross until the end of the world (cf. Col 1:24)....If every priest and every Christian is called to be a co-victim with Christ, is it not particularly true of His Mother?[196]

As we have already established, it is this priest-victimhood of Christ which characterized His mediation between God and humanity. Therefore, Mary is *the* Mediatrix because she alone was asked by God to be uniquely associated with His Redemption as *Theotokos* and the New Eve. This union in suffering would fittingly merit her a unique sharing in the glory of her Son and worthily make her Mother of the Church. In a way unique to one who was the Mother of God and Mother of the Church, Mary completed in her flesh what is lacking in the sufferings of Christ in His Mystical Body. This teaching of St. Paul also has importance in Sheen's Marian ecclesiology which we will examine in Chapter IV.

In another place,[197] Sheen highlights the related teaching of St. Paul that basically puts forth the spiritual law of reciprocity between suffering and glory. He explains that the measure in which we suffer is the measure in which we are united to Christ the Head. Applying this to Mary, her union of suffering would have reached an incomprehensible level to match the fullness of grace which she possessed as well as the universal role she would assume as Mother of Men.

---

[196] Sheen, "Mary and the Tabernacle," Sheen Archives.

[197] Sheen, "The Church Both Temporal and Eternal" (undated typescript from folder labeled "Mystical Body"), Sheen Archives. "St. Paul in the Epistle to the Colossians speaks of the sufferings of Christ which unite the Church to the Head (Colossians 1:24; 2:19; Ephesians 4:11-16). Hence, the Church is both *suffering* and *glorified*. Christ, Who is the Head of the Church, is the first-born among the dead and since His Resurrection is above them all in heaven (Ephesians 1:20-21)."

MARY AND THE SWORD

We recall that only forty days after the birth of Christ, Mary was told her heart would be pierced by a long, two-edged sword, which Sheen believed was Christ Himself. Sheen insists on the sword as the symbol of Mary's co-victimhood also to highlight that her victimhood in Redemption would not be the same as Christ's. It would symbolize Mary's *kenosis* which would be unlike any other follower of Christ,[198] but her kenosis could not equal that of the *kenosis* of the God-Man. Sheen was insistent on this distinction. Sheen explains that this illustrates that the suffering He would endure would always be greater than that of His mother, but that she would fully share in it according to her own capacity.

In each dolor it is the Son Who is the executioner, but He always makes His edge the sharper. His edge was not only to bear the sins of man on the Cross but also to permit her, who was innocent of it all, to share it as her own.[199]

STABAT MATER DOLOROSA

Sheen saw the intensity of Mary's victimhood in St. John's description of her as "standing" at the foot of the Cross. Sheen

---

[198] John Paul II described Mary's union of suffering with her Son at Calvary as the culmination of her *kenosis*: "*Through this faith Mary is perfectly united with Christ in his self-emptying.* For 'Christ Jesus, who, though he was in the form of God, did not count equality with God a thing to be grasped, but emptied himself, taking the form of a servant, being born in the likeness of men': precisely on Golgotha 'humbled himself and became obedient unto death, even death on a cross' (cf. Phil. 2:5-8). At the foot of the Cross Mary shares through faith in the shocking mystery of this self-emptying. This is perhaps the deepest '*kenosis*' *of faith* in human history. Through faith the Mother shares in the death of her Son, in his redeeming death; but in contrast with the faith of the disciples who fled, hers was far more enlightened. On Golgotha, Jesus through the Cross definitively confirmed that he was the 'sign of contradiction' foretold by Simeon. At the same time, there were also fulfilled on Golgotha the words which Simeon had addressed to Mary: 'and a sword will pierce through your own soul also'" (*RM,* 18; cf. *MD,* 19) (emphases mine).

[199] *WFL,* 253.

understood that this action of Mary reinforced the reality that
Jesus willed His mother to be "a cooperator in His Redemption."[200]
Sheen also emphasized that this was not a passive posture of Mary.
On the contrary, it indicated Mary's "active participation and
sharing [in] His Passion."[201] Sheen explained that as the New Eve,
Mary had not only to suffer the consequences of Eve's sin, but she
also had to engage in spiritual battle to undo the "knot of Eve's
disobedience"[202] by her steadfast obedience:

> Woman appears in Scripture in two ways: as one who pulls
> man down to collapse, and as one who lifts him up to a sac-
> rifice. Eve was seduced and she seduced. But in the Genesis
> story there is the Creator's pity for this frail woman who
> could not resist what was pleasurable and pleasing to the
> eye. In Mary, there is a "yes" too—not to man, but to the
> angel. That is why she is pictured as "standing" at the foot
> of the Cross to carry on the combat at a tree where Eve
> yielded.[203]

"Woman, behold your son...Behold your Mother"—Mary, the New Eve, Becomes Mother of the Church

We recall Sheen's description of Calvary, where at the Cross
there are the nuptials of the New Adam and the New Eve. There is
also St. John, who is unnamed and only referred to as the "disciple
whom Jesus loved." Sheen understood John's anonymity as representative of "all the children of Mary yet to be born."[204]

These words of Our Lord to Mary and John, therefore, have
central importance to understanding the full significance of
Redemption. When Christ addresses Mary as "Woman," He is

---

[200] *TMP*, 28.
[201] Sheen, "Mary and the Tabernacle," Sheen Archives.
[202] Cf. *LG*, 56; *RM*, 19.
[203] *TMP*, 315.
[204] *TMP*, 319.

indicating that He is addressing His spouse. As soon as Christ adds, "Behold your son," and then to John, "Behold your mother," Mary, according to Sheen, becomes Mother of the Church and "receives the maternal function among the 'children' begotten through the mystical union with the New Adam."[205] Sheen also understood these words as unveiling the mystery of St. Luke's reference to the Virgin Birth of Christ as Mary's "first-born":

> Here is the answer, after all these years, to the mysterious words in the Gospel of the Incarnation which stated that Our Blessed Mother laid her "firstborn" in the manger....Our Divine Lord and Savior Jesus Christ was the unique Son of Our Blessed Mother by the flesh. But Our Lady was to have other children, not according to the flesh, but according to the spirit![206]

Sheen saw these words of Christ as a "second Annunciation."[207] As Mary was asked by the angel whether she would give God a human nature to become Priest and Victim, so now John is asked by Christ, "Will you give me another human nature through which I will continue to teach, govern, and sanctify?" Sheen, therefore, describes this Virgin Birth of the Church as Christ's mystical prolongation of His Incarnation.[208] The grace which St. John received at the Cross looked forward to what the *ecclesia*, gathered with Mary in the Upper Room, would receive at Pentecost. In other words, at the Annunciation, Mary conceived the *totus Christus*—Christ the Head and His Mystical Body—and the Mystical Body of Christ which Sheen described earlier as virtually present in Mary's womb when she gave her *fiat*, is now born at Calvary when Mary has fulfilled her compassion with Christ; thus meriting to exercise worthily and fully her role as Mother of the Church. Later, Pentecost becomes the corporate manifestation of this spiritual reality. Thus, the mystery of the Incarnation at the Annunciation is organically

[205] *TMP*, 320.
[206] *LC*, 396-397.
[207] Cf. *EG*, 246-247.
[208] Cf. *MBC*, 8, 69-71.

linked to the mystery of its mystical prolongation at Calvary and Pentecost. We will examine this more closely in the next chapter.

Here at the Cross we also have the paradigm of Sheen's *conception by perception* in the life of every Christian, represented by St. John, who, as Sheen explains, represents not just all humanity, but especially those who wish to be "the beloved disciple."[209] As Jesus was truly and fully the Son of Mary, those who would participate in His Divine Sonship through grace, too, will share the same Mother because all who enter into the Sonship of Christ "are one in Christ" (cf. Gal. 3:24).

It is worth noting that the words heard by John that became associated with the Word being born in him were "Behold your Mother." Sheen's teaching highlights, therefore, that Mary plays a central role in the regeneration of every Christian, in particular the grace of Baptism when they are reborn in Christ. As Sheen said: "If Christ was her first-born, would not the Redeemed be her other-born, brothers of Christ and sons of the heavenly Father?"[210] Sheen's teaching emphasizes that Mary's active, spiritual maternity is at the heart of the mystery of sanctifying grace. John, too, was so disposed to Christ, that when he heard the Word of Christ to take Mary as his Mother, he gave his *fiat* to accept Mary as his mother, who immediately assumed her role as spiritual mother in the order of grace. Thus, John's *fiat* to accept Mary as his mother was his *fiat* to Christ to continue His Incarnation and become mystically present in the life of St. John.

Jesus' announcement to Mary, as Sheen asserted, "[n]ow installs her as the new Eve."[211] As the mother of all those who will be redeemed, or Mother of Mystical Body of Christ, Mary would mother the Body of Christ in the order of grace as she mothered Christ, the Head, in the order of His human nature. Hence, these words of Christ highlight two important roles Mary exercises in relation to Christ: Spouse of Christ and Mother of the Mystical

---

[209] Cf. *TMP*, 320-321.
[210] *MBC*, 319. "If Christ was her first-born, would not the Redeemed be her other-born, brothers of Christ and sons of the heavenly Father?"
[211] *WFL*, 238.

Body. As Spouse of Christ, Mary is the New Eve and Bride of
Christ, the New Adam whose mystical and spousal union continues to bring forth members into the Church.[212] The same can be
said of the Church, which is also referred to as the Spouse of Christ
and the Mother of Christians. Therefore, there is an inseparable
relationship between Mary and the Church according to which
each is a figure of the other. We will develop this further in the next
section.

Sheen explains the significance of what is actually taking place
during the mutual entrustment of John (the beloved disciple) and
Mary (Spouse of Christ and Mother of the Church) to each other:

> Mary the spouse acquired by the price of His Blood, has
> been vivified by His Spirit; in her bosom, the *Maria-Ecclesia*
> or Mother Church [*sic*] is born by baptism, nourished by
> the milk of the Word (1 Peter 2:2), fortified by the Bread of
> Life. John was the "youngest"—the first son of the Church.
> John designated as the "disciple whom Jesus loved" is the
> personification of the true disciple who has received the
> Spirit of Christ. John represented total fidelity of all Christ's
> disciples [*sic*]. That is why only after the Resurrection did
> Jesus call His disciples "brothers" as He said to Magdalene:
> "Go to My brothers and tell them I am now ascending to
> My Father and your Father, My God and your God" (John

---

[212] John Paul II made a similar reflection on the significance of these words
from Christ to Mary and John: "The words uttered by Jesus from the Cross
signify that the motherhood of her who bore Christ finds a 'new' continuation
in the Church and through the Church, symbolized and represented by John.
In this way, she who as the one 'full of grace' was brought into the mystery of
Christ in order to be his Mother and thus the Holy Mother of God, through
the Church remains in that mystery as 'the woman' spoken of by the Book
of Genesis (3:15) at the beginning and by the Apocalypse (12:1) at the end
of the history of salvation. In accordance with the eternal plan of Providence,
Mary's divine motherhood is to be poured out upon the Church, as indicated
by statements of Tradition, according to which Mary's 'motherhood' of the
Church is the reflection and the extension of her motherhood of the Son of
God [t. Leo the Great, Tractatus 26, *de natale Domini*, 2; *CCL* 138, 126]"
(*RM*, 24).

20:18). Mary the symbol of the Church–Mother receives the disciple and the disciple receives her as his own.

Mary, then, is first the spouse of Christ, the New Eve who has another Virgin Birth which is the Church growing in John.[213]

Sheen's teaching is similar to that of St. Augustine who saw Mary's spiritual maternity in the order of grace as the model upon which the Church exercises her spiritual maternity. This is based on the mystical union between Christ and the faithful, where Mary is the mother of the Head and the Mystical Body:

That one woman, therefore, is both Mother and Virgin, not only in spirit, but also in body. She is mother, indeed, in the spirit, not of our Head, who is our Saviour Himself, of whom she was rather born spiritually, since all who believe in Him (among whom she, too, is included) are rightly called children of the bridegroom, but she is evidently the mother of us who are His members, because she has co-operated by charity that the faithful, who are members of that Head, might be born in the Church. Indeed, she is Mother of the Head Himself in the body.

It behooved our Head to be born of a virgin according to the flesh, for the sake of a wonderful miracle by which He might signify that His members would be born according to the spirit, of a virgin, the Church.

Mary alone, therefore, is mother and virgin both in spirit and in body, both Mother of Christ and Virgin of Christ. The Church, on the other hand, in the saints who are to possess the kingdom of God, is indeed wholly the mother of Christ, wholly the virgin of Christ in the spirit.[214]

---

[213] *TMP*, 320-321.
[214] St. Augustine, *De Sancta Virginitate* 6, *PL* 40, 399; Cf. *The Fathers of the Church: St. Augustine – Treatises on Marriage and Other Subjects*, ed. Roy J. Deferrari, trans. Charles T. Wilcox et. al. (New York: Fathers of the Church, Inc., 1955), 149.

Hence, every Christian (and the Church collectively) is directly tied to Mary's spiritual motherhood, which indissolubly binds us to her loving, maternal care. This is another reason why Mary is literally, as Sheen already put it, "Mediatrix between Christ and us;" for the mystical life of Christ comes to us *through* Mary. We will address this in greater detail in the next chapter.

Unlike the joy experienced at the Virgin Birth of Mary's "First-born" Son at Bethlehem, Mary had to bear the curse of Eve meaning that her "other-born" would be born in great pain. Sheen writes, therefore, that "although [Mary] brought forth the Innocent without pain, she could not bring forth sinners without sorrow."[215] In another place he adds: "At that moment Mary suffered the pangs of childbirth for the millions of souls who would ever be called to the adoptive sonship of the Father, the motherhood of Christ and the joy of calling her Mother....No one knows how much she suffered to become our spiritual mother or the Mother of the Mystical Body of the Divine Son." Sheen also writes, "One wonders if she did not undergo a labor-pain surpassing all the agonies of birth from the beginning of time."[216] Sheen therefore concludes:

> In [John] all humanity was commended to Mary, who became the Mother of men,[217] not by metaphor, or figure of speech, but by pangs of birth....The import of these words were spiritual and became fulfilled on the day of Pentecost when Christ's Mystical Body became visible and operative. Mary as the mother of the redeemed and regenerated humanity was in the midst of the Apostles.[218]

Sheen develops Mary's universal motherhood further: "St. Thomas Aquinas tells us that Mary at the Annunciation spoke in

---

[215] *EG*, 247.

[216] *TMP*, 319.

[217] Vatican II confirms that Mary can be called "Mother of Men" (Mother of all humanity) where Mary's spiritual motherhood is not limited only to the redeemed, but extends to all humanity: "[Mary] is mother of Christ and mother of men, particularly the faithful" (*LG*, 54). We will explain how Mary's motherhood in the order of grace applies to the non-baptized and others outside full communion with the Church in Chapter V.

[218] *LC*, 398.

the name of all humanity [*ST*, III, q. 30, a. 1]. At Cana she is given to humanity; at the foot of the Cross, she is confirmed as the Mother of mankind."[219] All of what Mary endured, therefore, was a prolongation of Mary's *fiat* to become *Theotokos* and the New Eve. As Sheen explained earlier, Mary possessed a profound understanding of the consequences which her consent to the angel would entail. From Nazareth to Bethlehem, from Bethlehem to Cana, from Cana to Calvary, Sheen described how the suffering endured throughout her life was to serve as a widening of her love in order that she would eventually be prepared to embrace all humanity's suffering through a corresponding love.[220] By the time Mary was standing at the foot of Cross, Mary's love and will were so conformed to those of Christ that her *fiat* to Christ the Bridegroom on the Cross did not require words:

> It was a new love, or perhaps the same love expanded over the wider area of humanity....The *Fiat* she pronounced when she became the Mother of God now becomes another *Fiat*, like unto Creation in the immensity of what she brought forth. It was also a *Fiat* that so enlarged her affections as to increase her pains. The bitterness of Eve's curse—that she would bring forth her children in sorrow—is now fulfilled, and not by the opening of a womb, but by the piercing of a heart, as Simeon had foretold....As the Annunciation tied her up with Divinity before the coming of her Divine Son, so this word from the Cross tied her up with all humanity until His Second Coming.[221]

---

[219] *PNHO*, 275.

[220] Cf. *EG*, 238-239; 247-248; *LC*, 397-398.

[221] *WFL*, 126-127; cf. *RM*, 22, 39. "Along the path of this collaboration with the work of her Son, the Redeemer, Mary's motherhood itself underwent a singular transformation, becoming ever more imbued with 'burning charity' towards all those to whom Christ's mission was directed. Through this 'burning charity,' which sought to achieve, in union with Christ, the restoration of 'supernatural life to souls [*LG*, 61]....' This maternity of Mary in the order of grace...will last without interruption until the eternal fulfillment of the elect [*LG*, 62]" (*RM*, 38, 22).

THE PIERCING OF THE TWO HEARTS— FULFILLMENT OF THE *KENOSIS* OF CHRIST AND THE BIRTH OF THE CHURCH

After Christ makes Mary Mother of His Mystical Body, represented by John, the totality of God's plan of Redemption is accomplished. Christ then offers His Spirit back to the Father, and dies on the Cross. What happens next is of great significance to Fulton Sheen. The spear of Longinus acts as the final thrust of the sword into the Sacred Heart of Jesus, out of which flows blood and water. Sheen reminds us that it is "Christ, Who is the Sword of His own death, [Who] continues the thrusts after His own death, by making Longinus the instrument for opening the treasures of His Sacred Heart, which becomes the Ark into which souls to be saved from the flood and deluge of sin might enter."[222] He immediately reminds us, though, of Simeon's prophecy that the (same) sword will also pierce the Immaculate Heart of Mary. He adds:

> But, as the one edge opened the treasures of His heart, the other edge went through Mary's soul. Simeon had foretold that a sword her own heart would pierce; this time it came through the riven side of Her Son. Literally in His case, metaphorically in hers. It was a piercing of two hearts with one sword.[223]

Sheen described that while her Son's suffering had ended, Mary's suffering was not yet finished. The piercing of the heart of Christ not only had mystical effects on Mary's soul, but it also caused intense physical and moral suffering because of their union of hearts:

> No mother ever stands at a gallows without feeling the rope about her own neck, too. Since no one else in all the world gave Him body and blood and heart but her, it was her own body and blood and heart that was feeling the thrust of the steel. The sword that pierced the Heart of Christ physically,

---

[222] *WFL*, 261.
[223] *WFL*, 261-262.

pierced the heart of Mary mystically. No separate stab was necessary to impale two hearts on a single blade or to yoke two hearts with a single plunge. As the moon reflects the light of the sun, so the creature, Mary, reflected in her Compassion the Passion of her Son. *Mater Dolorosa*, the Mother of Sorrows, capable of embracing every agony and loneliness in a universe of broken hearts.[224]

"At once, there came out blood and water" (Jn. 19:34). Sheen described the blood and water in terms of the consummation between spouses. He explained: "At the very opening of the side of Christ and the shedding of the blood and water was as a kind of spiritual semen fecundating the Church; for our Blessed Mother stood there as the Mother of the Church. And here, John, unnamed, is the first-born, the beginning of the great and tremendous progeny. Our Blessed Lord called Himself the Word and the Word is the seed...."[225]

Sheen immediately saw the sacramental symbolism in the blood and water, writing, "Blood [was] the price of Redemption and the symbol of the Eucharist; water, the symbol of regeneration

---

[224] Sheen, "Mary and the Tabernacle," Sheen Archives.

[225] Sheen, "Our Blessed Mother" (from a series of retreat lectures given at Holy Trinity Seminary, Irving, Texas, 1972, recorded by and in the possession of Mr. Daniel B. Steffen of Plano, Texas), compact disc. Incidentally, Sheen explains that this event reveals one of the reasons women cannot be priests. Sheen writes: "Here is one of the reasons why women cannot become priests. Man and woman play a role in Divine Covenants, which are based on the analogy of marriage. We meet nuptials everywhere in Scripture; the nuptials of man and woman in Eden; the nuptials of man and woman in Israel and God in the Old Testament; the nuptials of Divinity and humanity in Mary; the nuptials of Christ the Bridegroom and the Church the Bride and the nuptials of the Lamb and the Church in heaven. In marriage, it is man who gives the seed; it is the woman who receives it, nourishes it, brings it to life and educates it. 'The sower of the good seed is the Son of Man' (Matthew 13:37). 'The seed is the Word of God' (Luke 8:12). The man in his capacity as the seed-giver preaches the Word of God, administers it in sacraments; and for that reason he is the symbol of Christ, or the Word Who is the seed. The woman receiving and nourishing the seed is the symbol of the Church which receives: 'Husbands love your wives as Christ also loved the Church and gave Himself up for it' (Ephesians 5:25)" (*TMP*, 319-320).

and baptism."[226] Sheen believed St. John supports this interpretation of the blood and water when he later reflected on what he witnessed on Calvary: "This is he who came by water and blood, Jesus Christ, not with the water only but with the water and the blood" (1 Jn. 5:6). Commenting on this, Sheen wrote:

> There was something more than a natural phenomenon here inasmuch as John gave it a mysterious and sacramental significance. Water stood at the beginning of Our Lord's ministry when He was baptized, Blood stood at the close of it when He offered Himself as a spotless oblation.[227]

Sheen, therefore, in a manner similar to that of St. Augustine,[228] associated the symbolism of the blood and water with the birth of the Church:

> There was some mysterious Divine purpose in the opening of the Sacred Heart of God....When Adam slept, Eve was taken from his side and was called the mother of all living. Now as the second Adam inclined His head and slept on the Cross under the figure of Blood and water there came from His side His bride, the Church. The open heart

---

[226] *LC*, 419.

[227] *LC*, 419.

[228] "The Evangelist used a wide awake word so that he did not say, 'pierced his side' or 'wounded' or anything else, but 'opened,' so that there, in a manner of speaking, the door of life was thrown open from which the mystical rites of the Church flowed, without which one does not enter into the life which is the true life. That blood was shed for the remission of sins; that water provides the proper mix for the health-giving cup; it offers both bath and drink. There was a foretelling of this in that Noe was ordered to make a door in the side of the ark where the animals that were not going to perish in the flood might enter, and in these [animals] the Church was prefigured. For this reason the first woman was made from the side of a sleeping man, and she was called the life and the mother of the living....Here the second Adam, his head bowed, slept on the cross in order that from there might be found for him a wife— that one who flowed from the side of the One sleeping. O death from which the dead live again! What is cleaner that this blood? What is more healthful than this wound?" (St. Augustine, "Tractate 120," in *The Fathers of the Church*, trans. John W. Rettig, vol. 92, *Tractates on the Gospel of John* (Washington, D.C.: The Catholic University of America Press, 1995), 50-51.

fulfilled His words: *I am the door; a man will find salvation if he makes his way in through Me* (Jn. 10:9).[229]

Sheen posited that the birth of the Church from the side of Christ was even hinted at by Christ during the Last Supper when He instituted the Holy Eucharist. He suggests that the words Christ used for consecration of the Eucharist had special relevance to His blood and water flowing from His pierced Heart. Sheen writes. "There is here…the birth of the new quahal [*sic*] at the Cross. There is even a suggestion of it at the Last Supper, when Our Lord gave Himself: 'This is My Body, and this is My Blood.'"[230] We know from Sacred Scripture and Tradition that Mary was not among those ordained by Christ to what the Church now calls the "ministerial priesthood." However, Mary exercised a priesthood unique among all others by literally offering her Son to the Father from infancy to the Cross. As Sheen writes:

> Thirty years with the Redeemer had taught her that she must love men as He loved them—enough to suffer and die for them, and still live on.…Even in sorrow peace was hers, for she was joined to an Eternal Father in the offering of a common Son.[231]

Mary's victimhood was also unique among all others in that her motherhood morally and materially united her with the Redeemer. She freely provided the Redeemer with the human nature, in particular His Body and Blood, which He would use as the instrument for our Redemption; thus meriting a relationship with the Redeemer like no other. Providing a profound insight into Mary's inseparability with Christ in the mystery of Redemption that merits our personal reflection, Sheen writes:

> Mary was not a priest, but because she is the Mother of Christ the Priest-Victim, she is our Mother. When her Son was taken down from the Cross and laid in her arms as a

---

[229] *LC*, 420.

[230] Sheen, "The Marriage Feast of Cana and Christ the Bridegroom" (undated typescript from folder labeled "Mystical Body"), Sheen Archives, 12.

[231] *EG*, 247-248.

paten and drained chalice, she could say the words of consecration as no priest can say them: "This is my Body; This
is my Blood." No one in all the world gave Him a human
nature, he was passible and, therefore, Victim. But because
she generated the Son of God [in the flesh], He was Holy
and, therefore, Priest.[232]

Another interesting observation Sheen made was the manner
in which the pouring of the blood and water from the side of Christ
was described according to the Vulgate translation of St. Jerome.
Sheen noted that St. Jerome describes the pouring as an *ongoing
action*: "When the side is open there pours forth blood and water.
The Vulgate [expresses it] as a *continuo exivit*, that is to say, blood
and water continued to flow forth, these symbolizing Baptism and
the Eucharist."[233] The symbolism here is profound because Sheen
notes that it was not enough for Christ to give His Spirit. He was
not done giving Himself until He truly gave Himself to us Body,
Blood, Soul and Divinity. In other words, Christ's *kenosis* was complete when He had given over to His Church every part of Himself
in order to fill up His Mystical Body. Christ's complete emptying
of Himself also expressed the fullness of identification between His
earthly Life and His Mystical Life. We will examine this profound
teaching of Sheen in the next chapter.

The emptying, or *kenosis*, of Christ into His Church at Calvary
also illustrated that the communion He desired with the redeemed
would be a family bond through which they would share the same
Body, Blood and Spirit as Christ. As Christ is the New Adam and
Mary is the New Eve (a title which can equally be attributed to
the Church which acts as Spouse[234] and Mother), Christ wanted

---

[232] *TMP*, 324. These words of Sheen are addressed to priests to emphasize that
Mary shares a unique relationship with them because they are more perfectly
conformed to Christ, the Priest-Victim, by means of their sacramental character.
[233] Fulton J. Sheen, "The Church and the Side of Christ" (undated typescript
from folder labeled "Mystical Body"), Sheen Archives.
[234] Cf. Fulton J. Sheen, "The Church as Spouse" (undated typescript from
folder labeled "Mystical Body"), Sheen Archives. In this commentary by Sheen
on Ephesians 5, he develops St. Paul's teaching on the spousal relationship

a union that reflected the two-in-one-flesh of the first nuptials, Adam and Eve. Sheen writes, "Scripture describes the first Eve as bone of my bone, and flesh of my flesh. Everything comes from its principle of origin and [here at the Cross] the curve is completed and returns again."[235] In other words, Calvary becomes the beginning and end of our earthly "pilgrimage of faith" involving the *kenosis*, or victimhood, of Christians until they have fully lived the Paschal mystery and receive the fullness of Christ (*pleroma*) with the saints in heaven. This is affirmed in the teaching of *Sacrosanctum Concilium*,[236] and Paul VI,[237] and is a central theme in our next chapter when we examine Mary's mediation as it relates to the recapitulation of the Church in Christ.

Now that Mary had suffered as much as she could to fulfill her part in the Redemption, Christ installed His Mother as the Mother of His Mystical Body, the Church. Sheen explains that only at Calvary did Mary fully understand the meaning of her Son's words at Cana: "What is mine is thine and what is thine is mine," since they "are fulfilled at the foot of the Cross where...the unity that she finally achieved was the unity of suffering."[238]

Sheen concludes: "The Resurrection will be the sheathing of the sword for both, as the debt of sin is paid and man is redeemed. No one can tell the griefs that either bore, and no one can tell the holiness that she achieved through sharing, as much as she could as

---

between Christ and the Church.

[235] Fulton J. Sheen, "The Church and the Side of Christ," (undated typescript from folder labeled "Mystical Body"), Sheen Archives.

[236] "By celebrating their anniversaries the Church proclaims [the] achievement of the paschal mystery in the saints who have suffered and have been glorified with Christ. She proposes them to the faithful as examples who draw all men to the Father through Christ, and through their merits she begs for God's favors" (*Sacrosanctum Concilium* 104; cf. *Flannery*, 29).

[237] "Worship is rightly extended, though in a substantially different way, first and foremost and in a special manner, to the Mother of the Lord and then to the saints, in whom the Church proclaims the Paschal Mystery, for they have suffered with Christ and have been glorified with Him" (*MC*, 25).

[238] Fulton J. Sheen, "The Marriage Feast of Cana and Christ the Bridegroom" (undated typescript from folder labeled "Mystical Body"), Sheen Archives, 11-12.

a creature, in His act of redemption."[239] Now that the Redemptive
mission had been accomplished and the curtain of Our Lord's flesh
pierced, "the gates of Paradise were thrown wide again."[240]

Mary's Maternal Mediation at Pentecost

Christ died on the Cross, but He left His Mother behind. Sheen
noted that the reason for this was so that Mary would be sent ahead
to beget the Church. Just as she anticipated the Incarnation, so she
would anticipate its mystical prolongation in the Church.[241] Sheen
explains how the baptism and growth of the Church at Pentecost
is Scriptural evidence of the Mystical Body re-living the "pattern"
of the Incarnation, which began with Mary being overshadowed
with the Holy Spirit. In the first Annunciation, God assumed a
human nature through Mary in order to accomplish the Redemption of mankind. Now at Pentecost, a type of Annunciation of the
Church, Christ begins to pour into His Mystical Body the merits
of Redemption, namely, His sanctifying grace, through the spiritual maternity of Mary. Sheen writes:

> *Her Divine Son willed that since she was the nurse and Mother*
> *of the Physical Body with which He redeemed the world, so*
> *she should be left behind to be the nurse and Mother of His*
> *Mystical Body with which He would pour forth the fruits of*
> *the redemption upon the souls of men.* As she had been the
> Mother of the Head, so she should be the Mother of the
> Body.[242]

---

[239] *WFL*, 266; cf. Sheen, "Mary and the Tabernacle," Sheen Archives.

[240] Sheen, "Mary and the Tabernacle," Sheen Archives.

[241] Cf. Sheen, "Mary and Institution of Eucharist," Sheen Archives.

[242] *MBC*, 322 (emphasis in the original). John Paul II echoed Sheen's teaching
when he wrote: "In the redemptive economy of grace, brought about through
the action of the Holy Spirit, there is a unique correspondence between the
moment of the Incarnation of the Word and the moment of the birth of the
Church. The person who links these two moments is Mary: Mary at Nazareth
and Mary in the Upper Room at Jerusalem. In both cases her discreet yet
essential presence indicates the path of 'birth from the Holy Spirit.' Thus she

He explains further:

> The Mystical Christ of Pentecost, like the physical Christ of Bethlehem, was small, delicate, and frail like any new-born thing. Its members were small; its organs were in the process of formation, and though life was there it was yet to grow in "age and grace and wisdom before God and men" (Lk. 2:52)....Every infant needs a mother's care, even an infant Church. The mystery of Jesus did not begin without her, neither could it finish without her. Our Blessed Lord had kept His promise: He did not leave us orphans. He gave us His Father as our Father: His Spirit as our Spirit and His Mother as our Mother.[243]

Sheen, therefore, concludes: "There is every reason to believe that we who are members of the Mystical Body now receive the Divine Life of her Son through her, just as we [members of the Church] first received the Divine Life of her Son in Bethlehem [through Mary]."[244] Pentecost, therefore, confirms Christ's plan that just as His earthly Life was inseparably bound up with His Mother, so would His Mystical Life (the Church) be inseparably bound up with Mary as its Mother in the order of grace.

Sheen characteristically describes the beginning of one's regeneration in Christ as a kind of "Annunciation." He described St. John's at the Cross as a "second Annunciation." This is an interesting point because it calls to mind the event which brought about the Incarnation. Since Baptism is its mystical prolongation, what takes place must reflect what took place when the Word became Incarnate in Mary, namely the nuptial union of Mary and the Holy Spirit. Sheen implies this nuptial reality when He describes the *ecclesia* in the Upper Room at Pentecost (a notable point of interest in that the Upper Room is where Christ instituted the Eucharist,

---

who is present in the mystery of Christ as Mother becomes—by the will of the Son and the power of the Holy Spirit—present in the mystery of the Church. In the Church too she continues to be a maternal presence, as is shown by the words spoken from the Cross: 'Woman, behold your son!'; 'Behold, your mother'" (*RM*, 24).

[243] Ibid., 323.

[244] *MBC*, 326.

which was realized at Calvary; thus underlining the connection between Pentecost and Calvary):

> Ten days after the Ascension we find the apostles "persevering with one mind in prayer with Mary the Mother of Jesus;" awaiting the descent of the Holy Spirit. He had descended upon her at Nazareth to make her the Mother of Jesus [first-born]; now He descends upon the apostles to make them His new Body and her the Mother of that Body....In both instances it is the Holy Spirit which renders her fruitful.[245]

He develops this further in another place:

> This idea of the commitment of Mary to a role in the new quahal [sic] [Church] is reinforced at Pentecost, then there was a parallel of the Annunciation, now the Mystical Body is made visible. Once more the same phrase is used as is used at Cana: "The mother of Jesus was there." She was there abiding in prayer as it was her prayer that made her worthy *de congruo* to become the Mother of God. So, too, it is her prayer in the midst of the disciples that made her now the Mother of the New Quahal [sic]. The separation [between Jesus and Mary after Cana], therefore, was actually to raise her to a new level of love, because love never rises to a new level without the death to a lower one. Cana and subsequent events up to the Cross were the death of the old love, the death of the old quahal [sic] and the cross and Pentecost are the birth of the new quahal [sic] with Mary presiding.[246]

Sheen, therefore, is highlighting the spousal relationship between Mary and the Holy Spirit which brought forth the Incarnation at Nazareth and its mystical prolongation at Calvary in St. John. Sheen also underscores the reality that every baptism is an

---

[245] *MBC*, 323-323.
[246] Sheen, "The Marriage Feast of Cana and Christ the Bridegroom" (undated typescript from folder labeled "Mystical Body"), Sheen Archives.

extension of Calvary because every baptism received its efficacy from the Passion of Christ as St. Thomas affirms.[247]

Mary's presence and intercession at Pentecost also reveal her mediation in the form of the "Apostle *par excellence*," as Sheen explains:

> From the very beginning she was the apostle *par excellence* of her Divine Son. She it was who first made Jesus known to His precursor John the Baptist on the occasion of her visit to Elizabeth; she it was who first made Jesus known to the Jews in the person of the shepherds, and to the Gentiles in the person of the Wise Men. It was therefore in keeping with her vocation that she be with the apostles on Pentecost, to make the Mystical Christ known to the world, as she had made known the physical Christ to Judea and Galilee. She brought into the world apostolocity itself— He who came to cast fire on earth and willed that it be enkindled. Her role would now have been incomplete if she had not been in the very centre of the tongues of fire which the Spirit of her Son sent upon the apostles to make them burn with the message even to the consummation of the world.[248]

---

[247] "Even before Christ's Passion, Baptism, inasmuch as it foreshadowed it, derived its efficacy therefrom…" (*ST*, III, q. 66, a. 2).

[248] *MBC*, 324-325. We see the same teaching underlying St. Cyril's famous *Homily II*: "I salute you, O Mary, *Theotokos: through you* the prophets speak out and the shepherds sing God's praises…, the angels dance and the archangels sing tremendous hymns…, the Magi prostrate themselves in adoration…, the dignity of the twelve apostles has been exalted…, John exulted while still in his mother's womb, and the lamp adored the everlasting light…, grace ineffable came forth…, the true light came into the world, our Lord Jesus Christ…, light shone on those sitting in darkness and in the shadow of death….*Because of you* the Gospels proclaim, 'Blessed is he who comes in the name of the Lord' (Lk 19:38); *through you,* the churches of those who possess the orthodox faith have been founded in the cities, in the villages, in the isles…, the Conqueror of death and Destroyer of hell has come forth… *Through you,* the beauty of the Resurrection flowered, and its brilliance shone out…, the tremendous baptism of holiness in the Jordan has shone out…, John and the river Jordan are made holy, and the devil is cast out….*Through*

Sheen emphasized that at Pentecost, Mary truly became the "Mother of each soul [which is] not a figure of speech."[249] Sheen points out that the Book of Revelation confirms this in its twelfth chapter, referring to "the woman" [Mary] who is depicted as suffering the "pangs of birth."[250] This passage thus confirms Sheen's teaching that the birth of every Christian is tied to the Cross, where Mary suffered the birth-pangs of all those who would be re-born in Christ.

Conclusion

In this chapter we examined the heart of Sheen's theology of Mary's mediation according to its firm Scriptural and Christo-centric foundations as well as his accurate presentation of the doctrine within a renewed understanding of the ancient soteriology of Christ the New Adam and Mary the New Eve. By doing so, Sheen proved that Mary's mediation plays a central and inseparable role in God's plan of Redemption; for just as the fall of humanity occurred through the cooperation of the first Adam and Eve, so God found it fitting that Redemption be accomplished by the cooperation of a New Adam and a New Eve. Therefore, understanding God's plan for the first parents of humanity, their fall from grace and the consequences of their Original Sin provide the necessary context to understand the role of the New Adam and the New Eve in mediating God's plan for restoring a fallen humanity.

God's plan of Redemption, immediately promised after the fall from grace of humanity's first spouses and parents, fittingly involved a New Adam and a New Eve. Sheen therefore emphasized the nuptial context within which the drama of Redemption would take place and thus the nuptial context within which Christ the

---

you, every faithful soul finds salvation" [Cyril of Alexandria, *Homily I, PG 77*, 1033; English trans. in Luigi Gambero, *Mary and the Fathers of the Church: The Blessed Virgin Mary in Patristic Thought*, trans. Thomas Buffer (San Francisco: Ignatius Press, 1999), 244-245 (emphases mine)].

[249] Sheen, "Mary and Institution of Eucharist," Sheen Archives.

[250] Rev. 12:2f.

New Adam and Mary the New Eve would mediate. Hence, just as Eve's mediation was exercised in her inseparable roles as spouse of Adam and mother of all living, Mary exercised her mediation in a similar and more exalted manner in her role as the New Eve as Spouse of the New Adam and Mother of the total Christ, Head and Mystical Body.

Therefore, Sheen's teaching on Mary's mediation according to her role as the New Eve takes us back to Genesis so that we can properly understand the soteriological nature and purpose of her mediation as it is derived from and participates in the one saving mediation of Christ, the New Adam. We therefore learn the following from Sheen's teaching:

1. "There is one Mediator between God and men, the man Christ Jesus" (1 Tm. 2:5). This is the starting point of Sheen's understanding of Mary's mediation, especially within the context of a renewed understanding of the mystery of the Incarnation as it relates to the mediation of the New Adam. According to Sheen, Genesis reveals that as the first Adam was the head of fallen humanity and transmitted the Original Sin of the first parents, so also would a New Adam assume the role of establishing the capitulation of a redeemed, regenerated humanity and transmitting the fruits of Redemption. Since there could be no forgiveness of sin without the shedding of blood (cf. Heb. 9:23), the New Adam would need to be one who could represent all humanity and act as Priest and Victim, emptying (*kenosis*) and offering Himself in order to mediate a complete expiation for sin. This mediation was made possible because God became man in the Incarnation, and since there is only one God-Man, there is only one Mediator, Jesus Christ (cf. 1 Tm 2:5). For Sheen, therefore, the soteriological nature and purpose of the Incarnation is at the heart of the theology of mediation because it was only through God becoming man that Christ could become the fitting and worthy Mediator

of Redemption, both Priest and Victim. Therefore, all other mediations, theologically speaking, are so-called only to the extent that they relate to and participate in the one mediation of Jesus Christ. Sheen's approach to Mary's mediation, therefore, is in light of its relationship to the one mediation of the Christ exercised through the Incarnation.

2. The one mediation of Jesus Christ, the New Adam, has two dimensions—ascending and descending, corresponding to the objective and subjective dimensions of Redemption. Since the New Eve was predestined to play a central role in both dimensions of Redemption, she participated in both dimensions of Christ's mediation. Therefore, a proper understanding of the nature and purpose of Christ's ascending mediation is critical to understanding properly the nature and purpose of His descending mediation because, according to Sheen, the former is the blueprint according to which the latter is exercised (as we will see in the next chapter). The key passages of Sacred Scripture which provide us with this blueprint for understanding Mary's mediation as spouse are the Annunciation (Lk. 1:26-38), the Visitation (Lk. 1:39-56), the Nativity of the Lord (Lk. 2:7), the Presentation of the Lord and Simeon's Prophecy (Lk. 2:22-35), the Finding of Jesus in the Temple at age 12 (Lk. 2:41-51), the Marriage Feast at Cana (Jn. 2:1-11), Mary at the Foot of the Cross (Jn. 19:25-30) and Mary present with the Apostles at Pentecost (Acts 1:14).

3. Mary's ascending mediation consisted in her cooperation with God in her role as the New Eve who would untie the knot of Eve's disobedience by her lifelong obedience of faith. Mary's obedience was especially tested at the Annunciation when she was asked to serve as the New Eve, first, by giving God the human nature through which He would become the universal

Victim to make expiation for the sins of mankind and, secondly, be uniting herself to His redemptive mission in His mediatory role as Priest and Victim. Mary's *fiat* therefore united her forever, materially and morally, to the mystery of the Incarnation in a singular way because she freely gave God the instrument through which He would use to mediate humanity's Redemption, the flesh and blood of Christ. Henceforth, Mary would be inseparably united to the one mediation of Christ according to her unique relationships to God in the order of Redemption: Spouse of the Holy Spirit, Mother of God, Mother of the Redeemer, Mother of the Total Christ (Head and Mystical Body)

4. Sheen's teaching significantly developed how Mary's ascending mediation in her role as the New Eve did not end with her cooperation with the Holy Spirit to bring about the Incarnation; for just as the New Adam had the redemptive mission of capitulating a new humanity, so also did the New Eve have a special and inseparable role in that soteriological mission. Her mission was to redeem the image of womanhood—in both spousal and maternal dimensions—shattered by the disobedience of Eve. Through a lifelong obedience of faith and through union with the priest-victimhood of the New Adam, she would become the worthy mother of the new humanity regenerated in Christ; for like Christ the New Adam, Mary the New Eve learned obedience by what she suffered. Mary's *fiat*, therefore, was an informed and free consent to accept God's entire plan for the New Eve from the Annunciation to Calvary and to the end of time. Predestined to be the parents of redeemed humanity, the New Adam and the New Eve would cooperate according to their respective and joint roles—Mary's always secondary and subordinate to Christ's—to restore the images of the Adam and Eve,

untie the effects of their disobedience and mediate as a unity of the two a regenerated humanity.

5.   Sheen also explained how Mary's ascending mediation through her union with the priest-victimhood of Christ was her personal appropriation of the singular privileges granted her by God—the Immaculate Conception and fullness of grace. Sheen explained how Mary's free and faithful cooperation with God's plan indicated her worthiness to fulfill her predestined vocation to be a *worthy* New Eve and, hence, a *worthy* Spouse of the Spirit, *worthy* Mother of the Total Christ—Head and Mystical Body—and *worthy* model of the Church. Only when Mary had proven her worthiness of such a vocation by restoring the shattered image of Eve through her active union with the priest-victimhood of Christ from the Annunciation to Calvary was she installed as the worthy Mother of the redeemed at Calvary. Therefore, only at Calvary do we see the full manifestation and exercise of Mary's spousal and maternal mediation as the New Eve in both its ascending and descending dimensions as she fully and worthily exercises her role as the faithful Spouse of Christ the New Adam in the work of Redemption as Mother of all the redeemed as she continues her spousal and maternal mediation in the recapitulation of humanity in Christ until the end of time.

CHAPTER IV

MARY AS MATERNAL MEDIATRIX IN THE MYSTICAL PROLONGATION OF THE INCARNATION

INTRODUCTION

The previous chapter explained the heart of Sheen's theology of Mary's mediation as it relates to the mystery of the Incarnation. It centers on understanding Mary's unique relationship to Christ, the New Adam, in her role as the New Eve. The manifestation of Mary's role as the New Eve was revealed at Calvary where Mary worthily began to exercise the fullness of her role as Mother of Christ and Mother of the His Mystical Body, the Church. Sheen explained that at Calvary, we see the full manifestation and exercise of Mary's mediation of the *totus Christus*.

In this chapter, we will examine how Sheen understood that Mary's mediation as Mother of the Mystical Body of Christ is a continuation, or prolongation, of her mediation as the mother of Christ, the Head of the Mystical Body. In other words, what we have learned of Mary's mediation as it related to Christ, the Head, is foundational to understanding how Mary mediates in relation to His Mystical Body, the Church, which Sheen understood as the recapitulation of the earthly life of Christ. Therefore, in this chapter we will examine Sheen's ecclesiology as it relates to the mystery of the Incarnation of Christ and the central role Mary continues to play in that mystery as Mother of the Mystical Christ, the Church.

THE INCARNATION: THE "PATTERN" OF CHRIST'S MYSTICAL PROLONGATION

As we saw in the last chapter, the mystery of the Incarnation is a paradoxical mystery of *kenosis* and *pleroma* that is directly related to the mystery of the priest-victimhood of Christ. Sheen emphasized that we witness the full revelation of this mystery at the Cross, where Christ's *kenosis* was accomplished by fully emptying and offering Himself as *the* Priest and Victim for the remission of sins and to establish and fill up His Mystical Body with the full treasury of Redemptive graces. Sheen explained that the Church, represented by St. John, received the fullness of Christ only after it received Mary as its Mother.

In addition, the exchange between Jesus, Mary and John revealed that Christ identified the Church with His very Self. For this reason John was called Mary's "son" and Mary, now acting as the New Eve, was referred to as "mother" of "the beloved disciple," or the Church. The fruit of this mutual giving was the birth of the Church. Pentecost was the *ecclesial* expression of this reality as all the Apostles with Mary were present in the Upper Room. As Sheen illustrated, Mary is at the heart of the mystery of the birth of the Church in St. John and in its ecclesial expression at Pentecost because she is at the heart of the mystery of the Incarnation, of which the Church, as we will soon explain from Sheen's teachings, is its mystical prolongation.

As we now explore the mystery of Mary's maternal relationship with the Church, we note that Sheen teaches that the life which the Church now lives is what St. Irenaeus referred to as the recapitulation of Christ in each of its members, singularly, and in the Church corporately. It builds upon the teaching of St. Paul who wrote: "He has made known to us in all wisdom and insight the mystery of his will, according to his purpose which he set forth in Christ as a plan for the fullness of time, to unite all things in him, things in heaven and things on earth" (Eph. 1:9-10). The way in which Christ was united to humanity was, first, through His Incarnation. The way in which He *continues* to unite Himself and increase His presence within humanity is by incorporating others into His life, which is mystically prolonged in His Mystical Body, the Church. The mystery of the Church, therefore, is inextricably bound up in the mystery of the Incarnation. That is why this study has as its focus a proper understanding of Sheen's teaching—and its application—of Mary in the mystery of the Incarnation. Without this understanding, any teaching on Mary's mediation as it relates to the Church is fundamentally incomplete, for the life of the Church is the reliving of the life of Christ. Sheen summarizes:

> The Church was in existence before Peter or James or John or the other apostles became believers. It was in actual existence the very moment when the Word was made flesh and dwelt among us, for at that moment Christ assumed a human nature, the "pattern-man," like unto which He would mould us by the fingers of His love and the power of His grace....
>
> ...In the eyes of every member of the Church, the Eternal Galilean re-lives the events and crises of His Life [*sic*] in Judea and Galilee. The written Gospel is the record of His historical life. The Church is the living Gospel and record of His present Life [*sic*]. The life of the Church is the Life [*sic*] of the Mystical Christ—a life whose history is already written because it has been lived in pattern by the Christ who is its Head. The Church is the only thing in the world whose history was written before it was lived.[1]

In terms of the mystery of *kenosis* and *pleroma* which is central to the mystery of the Incarnation, Sheen illustrates how this mystery applied to the Church:

> Never in the Divine order is there a humiliation without an exaltation, and an emptying without a filling, a *kenosis* without a *pleroma*....Since there was the *kenosis* of Christ, which was the climax of a long historical "emptying," it follows that there will then be the *pleroma* of Christ when: "Christ is all and in all" (Colossians 3:11)....If there was an emptying of the Word in assuming a human nature, then

---

[1] *MBC*, 72-74.

there will also be the filling up of that enfleshment by the
incorporation of other human natures to Himself in the
Church....If the *kenosis* was the emptying of Christ as a
Victim, then the *pleroma* of Christ is the Church. "For it
is in Christ that the complete being of the Godhead dwells
embodied, and in Him you have been brought to completion" (Colossians 2:9).[2]

In other words, those who are incorporated into the life of
Christ enter into such a communion with Him that the words
which He used at Cana to Mary, the disciple *par excellence*, now
apply to them: "What to me is to thee."

In this chapter, therefore, we will examine Sheen's presentation of the pattern, or blueprint, of Mary's mediation as it relates
to the Mystical Body of Christ, the Church. Sheen's starting point
is making sure we have an accurate and complete understanding
of the Church. He was emphatic that unless we understand how
true and real is Christ's identification with His Church, we will not
understand how true, real, and active is Mary's spiritual motherhood of the Church and of each member of humanity. We will
now explore the core elements of Sheen's ecclesiological thought
which shed important light on the union between the Head and
the Body.

THE CHURCH IS THE "MYSTICAL BODY OF CHRIST" OR THE "MYSTICAL CHRIST"

Fulton Sheen's ecclesiological thought is the natural continuation of His understanding on the Incarnation. For this reason,
Sheen preferred to refer to the Church as the "Mystical Body of
Christ" because he believed those words best express the Church's
organic unity with the Divine Person of Christ which differs from
all other unions. In 1935 Sheen completed an insightful, theological work on the Church called *The Mystical Body of Christ*.[3]

---

[2] *TMP*, 131-132.
[3] In the early 1930s, Fulton Sheen took a keen interest in studying and reflect-

Sheen's ecclesiology is mostly influenced by the Gospel of
St. John and the teachings of St. Paul. St. John's description of
the Church as "life" and his emphasis on the begetting of the

---

ing on the nature of the Church. In 1935, the fruits of his labors were published
in his ecclesiological treatise, *The Mystical Body of Christ*. This work immediately followed his first work on the life of Christ, which was not intended to be
a Christological manual. *The Mystical Body of Christ*, however, could serve as
a theological treatise for our own times. The work, then, served to emphasize
that the life of Christ continues in His Mystical Body, the Church. Sheen's
work, while not alone on the subject, was oriented toward a rediscovery of
the Church as a living organism, rather than an institution. He explained how
the Church was already moving in that same direction as evidenced from a
schema drawn up on the Church as "the Mystical Body" during the Vatican
Council (*MBC*, 9). Sheen gave further evidence in referencing Pope Pius XI's
Encyclical Letter of 1928 *Miserentissimus Redemptor* of which he said:

> His Holiness does not give an *ex professo* treatment of the Mystical Body, but
> rather assumes it, in treating of devotion to the Sacred Heart. Having spoken
> of the union of the members one with another, and with their Head, Christ,
> he goes on to say: "The Passion of Christ is renewed, and in a certain manner
> continued and completed in His Mystical Body which is the Church. Thus
> Christ who suffers still in His Mystical Body asks us to be His companions of
> expiation. Our union with Him demands this" (*MBC*, 9-10).

At the beginning of his work, Sheen prophetically stated, "We are about
to witness the most intensive study of the Church since the Reformation…
and within the next twenty years we will witness a general revision of our *De
Ecclesia* manuals" (*MBC*, 3). Sheen's words were proven true. Within a decade
of Sheen's work, Pius XII wrote in 1943 his Encyclical Letter *Mystici Corporis
Christi*, a milestone treatise on the Church as the "Mystical Body of Christ,"
in which he extensively developed the subject. Twenty years later, the subject
would be brought up again at the Second Vatican Council which gave attention to the subject in its treatise on the Church, *Lumen Gentium*; in particular,
articles 7 and 8.

Sheen's contributions to ecclesiology are worthy of a separate study, which
hopefully this work will stimulate among its readers. It is worth noting two
theologians whom Sheen referenced as influencing his ecclesiological thought.
The first is the Marian ecclesiology of Emil Mersch, S.J., which can be found
in his work *The Theology of the Mystical Body* (New York: B. Herder Book Co.,
1951). The second is the ecclesiological teaching of his contemporary, Charles
Cardinal Journet (1891–1975), of which Sheen was familiar. For the purposes
of this study, we will highlight only those subjects from Sheen's ecclesiological
thought which provide the necessary context to help us better understand his
teaching on Mary's mediation.

Church and its members through nuptials are themes central to Sheen's understanding of the Church. St. John presents the Church as an organism which possesses unity and growth.[4] This, Sheen explained, is especially illustrated in Christ's analogy of the vine and the branches (cf. Jn. 15:1-5), which expressed the organic unity of His life and the life of His Church. Sheen explains how the emphasis on *life* "shows Christianity in its interior aspects, as closer to us than we are to ourselves...of a rejuvenation...and that we are incorporated into Christ, made children of His kingdom and beneficiaries of the 'mystery' hidden from the ages."[5] We have already seen these emphases in Sheen's teaching on the Incarnation and the role Mary played, not only in making the Incarnation possible by giving God His human nature, but also the role she plays in the prolongation of that life as at Calvary.

Sheen explained that the words "Mystical Body" best represent the true nature of the Church, for "Body," borrowed from St. Paul (cf. Rm. 12:4-5; 1 Cor. 12:12-27), emphasizes that while the Church is not only *"one, hierarchical,* and *possessed of solidarity,* like a living body;" she also possesses a "unity existing between the head and the members."[6] The term "mystical" expresses "the transcendent unity of Christ and His Church which is effected not by external bonds, but by an internal bond of charity diffused in our souls by the Third Person of the Blessed Trinity."[7]

Sheen explained that "mystical" also differentiates the life of the Church from Christ's historical and glorified life. He writes:

[Christ] must live on earth to-day [*sic*] in a way different from His Life [*sic*] of nineteen hundred years ago, and in a way other than that in which He inhabits heaven. This new way is called His Mystical Life. There are therefore three phases in the complete Life of Christ or in the Life of the

---

[4] Cf. Jn. 6; 15:1-5, 7-10.
[5] *MBC,* 7.
[6] *MBC,* 6, 51.
[7] Ibid., 52.

whole Christ: first, His Earthly Life; second, His Glorified Life; third; His Mystical Life.[8]

Later in this work, he develops this further:

The new presence of Christ on earth in His Church is the third phase of the complete Life of Christ, and in order to demarcate it from His physical Life and from His Glorified Life tradition has called it the Mystical Life. Just as in His earthly Life He took a human body as an instrument for the exercise of His office as Prophet, King, and Priest, so now on Pentecost He assumes a new body, His Church, through the instrumentality of which He still fulfils the same triple role of teaching, governing, and sanctifying. In His earthly Life, He had only one human nature united to Him; in His Mystical Life, He unites to Himself all those human natures throughout the world who receive His Spirit. In His earthly Life, He was redeeming; in His Mystical Life, He is bestowing the fruits of Redemption on the members of His Mystical Body. In His earthly Life, *He* possessed the fullness of the Godhead; in His Mystical Life, *we* receive of Its fullness.... The complete Life of Christ must include these three phases.[9]

Sheen also favored St. Paul's use of the word "body" to express the unity between the Head and member, not only from a corporate point of view, but moreover from a spousal point of view. St. Paul, in his Letter to the Ephesians, particularly employed the word "body" to describe the Church when he likened Christ's mystical relationship with His Body, the Church, to spouses who become one body in marriage.[10] Commenting on this passage,

---

[8] Ibid., 19. The inconsistent use of capital letters throughout this quotation is that of Sheen. Rather than overuse "[*sic*]" throughout quotations taken from Sheen, especially from his work *The Mystical Body of Christ*, this note acknowledges that Sheen's erratic use of capitalization in adjectives and nouns referring to Christ and Mary is found in many of his quotations throughout this chapter.

[9] Ibid., 24-25.

[10] Eph. 5:22-32.

Sheen concludes from St. Paul, "The Church and Christ, therefore, constitute one Person."[11] He explains this truth another way: "There are many men but they make but one humanity, there are many Christians but they make but one Christ. And the Christians united to their Head Who is in Heaven make only one Christ, '*unus Christus.*'"[12]

Developing St. Paul's analogy further, Sheen explains:

Under the idea of body, the Church is represented with Christ as forming *one Mystical Person.*[13] The word spouse identifies a moral person distinct from the Church, but [*sic*] still imperfect, but [*sic*] a person who finds its [*sic*] perfection in the union of love with Christ....

...The body and spouse idea seem to melt in the text of St. Paul (Eph. 5:28), where he says that husbands do not [*sic*] love their wives as their own flesh...The name of body shows us how much the Church belongs to Christ. The spouse indicates how much the Church was a stranger to Him, and how much it was sought.[14]

Sheen explains that the reality of the Church and Christ constituting one Mystical Person can be expressed by applying to the Church a Latin axiom he called "*actiones sunt suppositorum.*" St. Thomas indirectly uses this axiom when speaking of how Original Sin is passed on through Adam to humanity because the movement of generation originates from him:

---

[11] Fulton J. Sheen, "The Church and Christ or the Head and Body Are One Person" (undated typescript from folder labeled "Mystical Body"), Sheen Archives.

[12] Ibid.

[13] Pope Pius XII would later state this in *Mystici Corporis Christi,* 67.

[14] Fulton J. Sheen, "The Church as Spouse" (undated typescript from folder labeled "Mystical Body"), Sheen Archives. St. Paul's actual words were: "Husbands *should* love their wives as their own bodies. He who loves his wife loves himself" (emphasis mine). Sheen interpreted these words of St. Paul as an indication that the husbands of Ephesus were *not* living accordingly; hence, the need for St. Paul to issue such a directive in his letter to them.

All men born of Adam may be considered as one man, inasmuch as they have one common nature, which they receive from their first parents; even as in civil matters, all who are members of one community are reputed as one body, and the whole community as one man. Indeed Porphyry says (*Praedic., De Specie*) that "by sharing the same species, many men are one man." Accordingly the multitude of men born of Adam, are as so many members of one body. Now the action of one member of the body, of the hand for instance, is voluntary not by the will of that hand, but by the will of the soul, the first mover of the members. Wherefore a murder which the hand commits would not be imputed as a sin to the hand, considered by itself as apart from the body, but is imputed to it as something belonging to man and moved by man's first moving principle. In this way, then, the disorder which is in this man born of Adam, is voluntary, not by his will, but by the will of his first parent, who, by the movement of generation, moves all who originate from him, even as the soul's will moves all the members to their actions.[15]

The same principle applies to the New Adam and His connection with the new humanity, His Mystical Body, the Church; for one can say, "all men *reborn* of the New Adam may be considered as one Man." Adam is the head of corporate humanity and Christ is the Head of the corporate regenerated humanity, where all who are reborn in Christ may be considered as one new man in Christ. Using this axiom, the point Sheen wants to stress is that the actions of the Church, Christ's Mystical Body, are so tied up with the Person of Christ that what happens to Christ's Mystical Body applies equally to Christ and vice versa; for the Church and Christ are truly one. Sheen explains:

> In a certain sense, therefore, the actions of the Mystical Body are the actions of Christ. *Actiones sunt suppositorum* ["actions are attributed to the person"]. Actions are

---

[15] *ST*, I-II, q. 81, a. 1.

attributed not to a nature, but to a person....Now since
the Church and Christ are one, does not the same principle apply with reservations?...The human elements in the
Church are merely the instruments with which Christ continues to teach, to govern, and to sanctify, as His human
nature was the "conjoined instrument of His Divinity." The
actions of the members in this triple work are to be attributed to the Person of Christ.[16]

Sheen adds the following interesting point on this subject:

In the Incarnation the human nature of Christ was without
a human personality, but was subject to the Divine. In like
manner, the members of the Mystical Body are without
a human personality, not because they have none, but
because by an act of their will and with the help of grace,
they become identified with their Head—Christ. His will
is their will. His Person is their law: "I live, now not I, but
Christ liveth in me," says St. Paul (Gal. 2:20). I have no
human personality, and yet I have it not, because Christ is
my life: such is the attitude of a Christian.[17]

No person better exemplified this teaching for Sheen than
St. Paul, who experienced how literal this truth is as to the union
between Christ the Head and His Mystical Body. Commenting on
the conversion of St. Paul, Sheen writes:

The risen Christ, only four or five years after He had left
this earth, broke open the heavens in order to declare to
Saul and the world that the Church is His Body, that in
striking that body you strike its Head, that He and the
Church are one Person...so when the Body of the Church
is persecuted it is Christ who arises to speak....What does
all this mean, but that Calvary may be prolonged[18] even

[16] *MBC*, 67.
[17] Ibid.
[18] Pius XII also affirmed that Calvary mystically continues in the Church
which is the continuation and "complement" of the redeeming life of Christ
on earth: "The Church becomes, as it were, the filling out and the complement of the Redeemer, while Christ in a sense attains through the Church a

beyond Jerusalem's walls; and the Life of Christ in His Church extended beyond the sands of a Galilean seashore and the memorial of an upper-room? No wonder that the transformed Saul, St. Paul, understood so well the nature of the Church! He too knew Christ as well as the other apostles, for he too had touched His Body.[19]

This revelation to St. Paul is of central importance to Sheen's ecclesiological thought as well as to the Church's understanding of her own nature. It confirms that Ecclesiology is really an *extension* of Christology. Both are part of the same "Subject," Christ [understanding the Church as the Incarnation of Christ mystically prolonged will have great and positive consequences on how we understand Mary as related to the *complete* Christ]. Sheen concludes on this point:

> The Church, then, is in the truest sense of the term the prolongation of the Incarnation; it is the new Body which Christ assumes after His Ascension, with which to extend His Kingship throughout the kingdoms of the world; it is the new living instrument through which He teaches, governs, and sanctifies; it is His new corporate human nature under the headship of His Divine Person, of whose plenitude we have all received; it is His fullness [*pleroma*], without which His life would be but a memory and His Kingship only a name....
>
> ...Anyone who understands the Scriptures will see that the Church does not stand between Christ and me. The Church *is Christ....* The Church no more stands between the Divine Life of Christ and my soul, than His physical Body stands between me and His Divinity. It was through

---

fulness in all things.[159] Herein we find the reason why, according to the opinion of Augustine already referred to, the mystical Head, which is Christ, and the Church, which here below as another Christ shows forth His person, constitute one new man, in whom heaven and earth are joined together in perpetuating the saving work of the Cross: Christ We mean, the Head and the Body, the whole Christ" (*Mystici Corporis Christi*, 77).

[19] *MBC*, 69-70.

His human Body that He came to me in His individual Life; it is through His Mystical Body that He comes to me in His corporate Life. Christ *is the Church:* her real, inner self is His Body permeated through and through with His Redemptive Life....We are the cells in that very Body which is Christ![20]

This teaching of Sheen emphasizing the unity between and identification of Christ and His Mystical Body is central to understanding Sheen's teaching on Mary as the Mother of the Church. The interior logic arising from this teaching serves to support his subsequent teaching on Mary's *one* motherhood of the *one* Christ. If one does not see the Church as Christ's mystical prolongation, then it becomes more difficult for one to see Mary as Mother of the whole Christ.

MARY IS THE "MOTHER OF THE MYSTICAL BODY OF CHRIST"

At the end of the Second Vatican Council, Pope Paul VI proclaimed Mary "Mother of the Church"—a title with an interesting history revealing the theological controversy over Mary's mediation that took place before and after Vatican II. Although it was a title over which the Council fathers were divided for theological reasons as well as ecumenical sensitivities, the declaration was indeed a milestone moment in the history of the Church as it highlighted Mary's mediation in terms of her spiritual maternity and her role as the New Eve. The Marian ecclesiology of the Council, accompanied by Paul VI's proclamation,[21] put the mystery of Mary in

---

[20] *MBC*, 70-72.

[21] Cf. Luis Antonio G. Tagle, "The 'Black Week' of Vatican II (November 14-21 1964)," *History of Vatican II*, ed. Joseph A. Komonchak, vol. 4, *Church as Communion—Third Period and Intercession: September 1964–September 1965* (Maryknoll, NY: Orbis Books, 2000), 395, 446; cf. Evangelista Vilanova, "The Intersession (1963-1964)," *History of Vatican II*, ed. Joseph A. Komonchak, vol. 3, *The Mature Council—Second Period and Intercession: September 1963–September 1964* (Maryknoll, NY: Orbis Books, 2000), 367.

relation to the Church into the forefront of contemporary Mariological reflection.

It is important to note that Fulton Sheen anticipated this magisterial intervention in the Church by almost three decades. Sheen's insights into Mary's relationship to the Church are evidenced by his dedication of a special chapter on Mary within his treatise on the Mystical Body of Christ—a theological direction the Second Vatican Council would later adopt as its own. Sheen placed his chapter on Mary near the end of his ecclesiological work because he knew that once one had a proper understanding of the Church as the mystical prolongation of Christ's Incarnation, or the Church as the Mystical Body of Christ, then the application of that truth to Mary's spiritual maternity becomes logical. Once one understands the Church as the mystical prolongation of the life of Christ, then naturally, the inseparable relationship Mary had to Christ during His earthly life will continue with His Mystical life in the Church, which, as Sheen already explained "re-lives" the life of Christ. Therefore, the inseparability between Jesus and Mary during the historical life of Christ will continue in Mary's spiritual maternity over His Mystical Body, since these two constitute one Mystical Person, as we have already seen Sheen explain. Continuing on this topic he writes:

> Mary is the Mother of the Mystical Body of Christ: the Church. In order to understand how literal and real this truth is, dwell for a moment on the primary fact that Mary is the Mother of Christ. He who from all eternity was begotten of the Father, is generated in time of the Blessed Mother without man but by the overshadowing of the Holy Spirit. Her life from that point on is inseparably bound up with His; never does Scripture mention her apart from Him. She is with Her Divine Son in the flight to Egypt; she is with Him in the Temple praying the perfect prayer to the heavenly Father; she is with Him during His labours [*sic*] as a carpenter and years of obedience in the humble Nazarene home; she is with Him in His preaching and stands at

the foot of the Cross as He dies for the redemption of the world.[22]

MARY IS THE MOTHER OF THE *TOTAL CHRIST* (*CHRISTUS TOTUS*)

All of what we have examined of Sheen's ecclesiology converges on the fundamental truth that there is only one Christ with one life divided into what Sheen has already described as "three phases": earthly, glorious and mystical. Mary's maternal relationship to Christ, therefore, extends over all of these phases simply because she is the Mother of the total Christ. Sheen repeats the importance of this understanding:

> She was more than the mother of the historical Christ. If her Divine Son were only a man, then her maternity might be purely a corporal one. But recall that her Son is the Son of God as well as the son of man. Recall, furthermore, that during His earthly Life He promised to assume a new body after His Ascension into heaven, a body which would be made up of countless faithful who believed in Him; recall, too, that through this Body would flow His Life and Truth and Love as the sap of the vine flows through the branches. Once He ascended into heaven it was no longer possible for His physical Body to grow and develop, for it possessed the fruits of glory. But the other Body which He assumed on Pentecost, which is His Church, could grow. He said it would grow like the mustard seed, and St. Paul, building on that thought, speaks of it as the "increase of God" (1 Cor. 1:2-19)....
>
> ...This means that in addition to the physical Christ whose Life began at Bethlehem and ended with the Ascension, there is also the Mystical Christ which began with Pentecost and which will endure through all eternity. Now if

---

[22] *MBC*, 313-314.

the fullness of Christ embraces not only His historical Life in Galilee but also His Mystical Life in the Church, then should not Mary be not only the Mother of the physical Christ, but also the Mother of the fullness of Christ or the Mother of the Church? The Mother of Jesus should therefore be our Mother, otherwise the whole Christ would not be entirely the Son of Mary. She would be His Mother in the physical sense, but she would not be His Mother in the mystical sense. She would be the Mother of the Head, but she would not be the Mother of His Body....She who is the Mother of the Vine which is the historical Christ, must also be the Mother of the Branches which is the Church. As the Mystical Body is the complement and fullness of the natural Body of Christ, so too the Divine Motherhood of the Head should have its fullness in the Motherhood of the Mystical Body. Since she co-operated [*sic*] in the Incarnation by her consent, she should also co-operate [*sic*] in the prolongation of the Incarnation or the Church.[23]

ASSUMPTION AND CORONATION OF MARY AND HER UNIVERSAL MEDIATION OF GRACE—MARY'S DESCENDING MEDIATION

Mary's inseparable relationship with her Son in the mystery of Redemption was further evidenced in her singular privilege of the Assumption and consequent coronation as Queen of Heaven. Sheen connected Mary's Assumption to her singular privilege of the Divine Maternity and as the fitting reward of her inseparable and faithful association in Christ's Passion:

> Mary had her crucifixion as the sword of sorrow pierced her heart on Calvary. But now she was to have the counterpart of His Ascension, and that was her Assumption into heaven....She had begotten Eternal Life; how then could

---

[23] *MBC*, 314-316. When Sheen writes that Christ's physical life "ended," he is referring to the historical life of Christ before His Ascension into glory.

she be subject to corruption of the tomb? The Assumption of Mary into heaven was the natural consequence of her Divine maternity, the counterpart of her Son's Ascension.[24]

Just as Christ said that it was better for Him that He go (cf. Jn. 16:7) in order that He might assume His salvific role in heaven as Head of His Mystical Body from where He would distribute the fruits of His Redemption—what Sheen referred to as *descending mediation* (see Chapter II)—Sheen saw that it was fitting that Mary, after her Assumption, would assume a cooperative role with Christ in this ministry (or descending mediation) as she had cooperated in acquiring them (ascending mediation)—a teaching which had already found strong expression in the Apostolic Letter of Pope Benedict XV, *Inter Sodalicia*, of 22 May 1918.[25] In his *Mystical Body of Christ*, Sheen writes: "Inseparably united at the Cross when the reservoirs of redemption were filled, Jesus and Mary are now inseparably united in heaven as those merits are poured out upon all who believe in Him as Brother, in her as Mother, and in God as Father. Called to co-operate with Him in the acquisition of graces on Calvary, she is now called to co-operate with Him in the dispensation of those same graces to the Mystical Body."[26] Sheen grounds his teaching in that of St. Pius X, who shared a similar understand-

---

[24] *MBC*, 325.
[25] "The choosing and invoking of Our Lady of Sorrows as patroness of a happy death is in full conformity with Catholic Doctrine and with the pious sentiment of the Church. It is also based on a wise and well-founded hope. In fact, according to the common teaching of the Doctors it was God's design that the Blessed Virgin Mary, apparently absent from the public life of Jesus, should assist Him when He was dying nailed to the Cross. Mary suffered and, as it were, nearly died with her suffering Son; for the salvation of mankind she renounced her mother's rights and, as far as it depended on her, offered her Son to placate divine justice; so we may well say that she with Christ [*cum Christo*] redeemed mankind.

"Consequently, if the graces which we receive from the treasury of the Redemption are distributed, so to speak, by the hands of this sorrowful Virgin, no one can deny that the grace of a happy death must come from Mary because, in fact, it is by means of this preeminent grace that the work of Redemption reaches its fulfillment in every man" [*AAS* 10 (1918), 181-182; *OL* #267-68].
[26] Ibid., 326.

ing of Mary's unique and inseparable role in the Redemption. Paraphrasing the words of Pius X, Sheen writes:

> Because of the association of suffering and of love between Mary and Jesus, Mary has rightly merited to be the co-Redemptrix[27] of fallen humanity, the most powerful mediatrix in the whole world and, consequently, the dispenser of all the riches which Christ Jesus has won for us by His Blood and by His Death....She merits for us *de congruo*, in the language of the theologians, what Jesus Christ merits *de condigno*, and she is the supreme minister of the distribution of graces.[28]

He immediately follows these words of St. Pius X with a quotation he credits to Pope Leo XIII explaining that because Mary is inseparably associated with Christ's work of Redemption she, fittingly, is thereby associated with the distribution of the graces of Redemption:

> Christ is the Head of the Church; Mary the channel therein of Christ's graces. All benefits, all graces, all heavenly favours [*sic*] come from Christ as from a Head. All descend into the Body of the Church through Mary, as through the neck of the human body the head vivifies the members. Every grace given to the world comes by three steps in perfect order; from the Father to Christ; from Christ to the Virgin; from the Virgin to us.[29]

----

[27] While it is to be noted that Sheen's translation of Pius X's "*reparatrix*" was "co-Redemptrix," a title debated today as to its theological accuracy and suitability in describing Mary's inseparable cooperation with Christ in Redemption, this title was used in the teaching of the papal Magisterium at the time he wrote his work. Pius XI, for example, used "Coredemptrix" at least twice in his teaching; Cf. *OR*, 1 December 1933, 1; *OR*, 25 March 1934, 1.

[28] *ASS* 36 (1903), 453-454. *Ex hac autem Mariam inter et Christum communione dolorum ac voluntatis, promeruit illa ut reparatrix perditi orbis dignissime fieret, atque ideo universorum munerum dispensatrix quae nobis Iesus nece et sanguine comparavit...Ea de congruo promeret nobis quae Christus de condigno promeruit, estque princeps largiendarum gratiarum ministra*; cf. *MBC*, 326.

[29] *MBC*, 326-327. Sheen mistakenly attributed this quotation to Leo XIII's encyclical *Magnae Dei Matris*. The text is not found therein. Unfortunately,

Sheen was not equating Mary's mediation with the one mediation of Christ. However, he understood with the theological tradition of the Church that in the Divine order of causality, Mary was
given an extraordinary and central role. He grounds his doctrine
in a teaching which he attributed to St. Albert the Great. The text
attributed to St. Albert reads:

Mary is after God and with God and under God the *efficient*
cause of our regeneration because she begot our Redeemer,
and because by her virtue, she merited by a merit of con-
gruity this incomparable honour. She is the *material* cause,
because the Holy Ghost through the intermediary of her
consent took from her pure flesh and blood, the flesh and
blood from which was made the Body immolated for the
Redemption of the world. She is the *final* cause, for the
great work of Redemption which is ordained principally

---

he did not provide in his notes a specific reference for his quotation other
than "*Magnae Dei Matris.*" Sheen, however, was accurate in associating that
teaching with Leo XIII, who addressed the same content with only minor dif-
ferences in his Encyclical Letter *Jucunda Semper*, which states:

The recourse we have to Mary in prayer follows upon the office she con-
tinuously fills by the side of the throne of God as Mediatrix of divine
grace, being by worthiness and by merit more acceptable to Him, and for
that reason surpassing in power all the angels and saints in heaven. Now,
this merciful office of hers appears perhaps in no other form of prayer
as manifestly as it does in the Rosary....No one can meditate upon this
without feeling a new awakening in his heart of confidence that he will
certainly obtain through Mary the fullness of the mercies of God....Thus
is confirmed that *law of merciful mediation* of which we have spoken,
and which St. Bernardine of Siena thus expresses: "Every grace granted
to man has three successive steps: By God it is communicated to Christ,
from Christ it passes to the Virgin, and from the Virgin it descends to us"
(*Sermo 6, 1, in Fest. B.M.V. de Annun.* a. I, s. 2)....Now may God, who *in
His most merciful providence gave us this Mediatrix* [*Mediatricem*] (St. Bernard, *De XII prærogativis B.M.V.*, n. 2) "and decreed that all good should
come to us by the hands of Mary" (St. Bernard, *In Nativitate B. Mariae
Virginis Sermo*) receive propitiously our common prayers and fulfill our
common hopes [Leo XIII, Encyclical Letter *Jucunda Semper* (8 September
1894), *ASS* 27 (1894-1895), 178-80, 182-84; *OL* #149, 154-55, 161, 163
(emphases mine)].

for the glory of God, is ordained secondarily for the honour of this same Virgin. She is the *formal* cause, for by the Light of a Light so very deiform she is the universal exemplar which shows us the way out of darkness to the vision of the Eternal Light" (St. Albert the Great, *Quaest.*, q. 146, t. XX, p. 100).[30]

In the quotation Sheen references from Leo XIII, there is a clear reference to the two most popular teachings on Mary's mediation from the Medieval Scholastics, St. Bernard of Clairveaux and St. Bernardine of Sienna. With these two citations from Popes Pius X and Leo XIII, Sheen manages to express a summary of his doctrine of Mary's mediation in the theological language of the most accepted teachings on Mary's mediation by the Medieval Scholastics—teachings that were adopted into the consistent doctrine of the papal Magisterium at the time he wrote his theological treatise on Mary's relationship with the Church, *The Mystical Body of Christ* (1935). These references to St. Bernard, St. Bernardine, and the

---

[30] "*Et nota, quod Dominus beatissimae Virginis opus recreationis secundum quatuor genera causarum communicavit. Causa efficiens nostrae regenerationis post Deum, sub Deo, et cum Deo ipsa fuit: quia illa illum nobis genuit, qui nos omnes regeneravit, et ipsum gignere suis virtutibus de congruo promeruit. Item, causa materialis: quia Spiritus sanctus se purissimis carnibus ejus et sanguinibus, ipsius consensu mediante, carnem sumpsit: quamin corpus transformavit, per quod redemptio nostra facta fuit. Item, causa finalis fuit: quia per totum opus redemptionis post Deum in ipsius gloriam et honorem ordinatum fuit*" ([B. Alberti Magni], *Mariale, sive quaestiones super Evangelium*, q. 146, in *Opera Omnia*, vol. 37 (Paris, 1898); *MBC*, 324.] The scholarship of Father Albert Fries, C.Ss.R., who served as a member of the papal commission established in the 1940s to prepare critical editions of Albert's authentic writings, provided persuasive arguments against his authorship of the *Mariale* in his 1954 work *Die unter dem Namen des Albertus Magnus überlieferten mariologischen Schriften*, Beiträge zur Geschichte der Philosophie und Theologie des Mittelalters, Band XXXVII, Heft 4 (Münster: Aschendorff, 1954); cf. Martin J. Tracey, "St. Albert the Great and the Conception of Mary" (date unknown, accessed 16 July 2007); available from http://www.catholic.net/RCC/Periodicals/Dossier/0506-96/Article5.html; Internet. Despite the conclusions of recent scholarship, the esteemed and authoritative use of the theological content of *Mariale* throughout the centuries gives its teaching a certain authoritative value and should not be undervalued.

papal Magisterium on Mary's mediation highlight two key points of Sheen's doctrine regarding Mary's universal mediation of grace. First, it derives from her inseparable association and cooperation with Christ in Redemption during the earthly period of the Incarnation. Secondly, as a result of Mary's cooperation in Redemption she continues her association and cooperation with Christ in the distribution of the graces of Redemption in her unique role as Mediatrix between Christ the Head of the Church and His Mystical Body.

Hence, we see the solidarity of Sheen's teaching on Mary's universal mediation of graces with the Tradition of the Church. Sheen employed these teachings in order to further ground his position that "the role of Mary in the Church is therefore just as active as her role in the Incarnation," which he develops in a theological language focusing on the significance of Mary's maternal and spousal relationship to the mystery of the Incarnation.[31] What is important about Sheen's doctrine is his echoing of the Tradition that Mary's universal mediation of grace is a *consequence* of her unique cooperation with Christ in Redemption. This is evidenced by the words of Pius X when he uses the phrase "*atque ideo*" (see note 28, page 211) to make this explicit connection when introducing Mary's universal distribution of the graces of Redemption. Sheen's reference to Leo XIII also stresses that Mary's mediation of graces pertains not only to the graces of Redemption (e.g. sanctifying grace), which are the most important, but to all other graces (e.g. divine favors).

He concludes his teaching on this subject:

> Christ is the Head of the Mystical Body, but within that Body Mary is the channel between Christ and the members, bringing to them the favours [*sic*] and efficacious powers of Christ (Benedict XV).[32] This does not mean that

---

[31] *MBC*, 327.

[32] Sheen did not provide a specific work from Benedict XV in his citation. However, we have already seen (cf. note 25, page 210) one example of Benedict XV's affirmation of this teaching in his Apostolic Letter *Inter Sodalicia*. Another example is found in his Encyclical Letter *Fausto Appetente Die*: "Dominic realized, on the one hand, that Mary's power of intercession with her Son is so great that she is then in reality the mediatrix and dispensatrix

the Church adores Mary; it does not mean that Mary is
Divine, but it does mean that we could never have Christ
without His Mother; it does mean that as a woman shared
in our fall, so a woman should share in our redemption,
and that as it was through Mary that God came to us, it
is fitting that through Mary we should go back to Him.[33]

This way of expressing Mary's ascending and descending mediation is summarized by the saying, *"Ad Iesum per Mariam."* This
saying was incorporated into the Marian teaching of Popes Leo
XIII and Paul VI. Paul VI stressed the truth of this doctrine on
more than one occasion. He spoke of it in his encyclical *Mense Maio*
of 29 April 1965.[34] However, his best articulation of this teaching
is found in his Encyclical Letter *Signum Magnum* of 13 May 1967:

It is also the duty of all the faithful to pay as tribute to the
most faithful handmaid of the Lord, a veneration of praise,
of gratitude and of love because, by a wise and mild divine
provision, her free consent and her generous cooperation in
the designs of God had, and still have, a great influence in
the attainment of human salvation (*Lumen Gentium* #56).
Therefore *every* Christian must make St. Anselm's prayer
his own: "Oh, glorious Lady, grant that through you we
may deserve to ascend to Jesus, your Son, who through you
deigned to descend among us" (*Orat.* 54, *PL* 158, 961).

---

of all the graces He bestows on men [*quidquid gratiarum hominibus confert,
illa semper administra et arbitra conferat*]. On the other hand, he knew that
so unfailing is her love for even the most miserable of her children, that it is
impossible for her to refuse those who ask her help. Such has always been the
mind of the Church concerning Mary, whom she so frequently addresses as
Mother of Grace and Mother of Mercy. And this is especially the case where
the devotion of the most holy Rosary is concerned. Thus the Roman Pontiffs
have never lost any chance of praising the Rosary and of enriching its use with
numerous indulgences" (Benedict XV, Encyclical Letter *Fausto Appetente Die*
[*AAS* 13 (1921), 334]); cf. "Marian Doctrine of Benedict XV," trans. Richard
Zehnle, S.M., *Marian Reprint* 70 (1959): 11].

[33] *MBC*, 327-328.

[34] *AAS* 57 (1965), 353-354 [*The Pope Speaks*, vol. 10 (1965): 220].

The general norm "Through Mary to Jesus" is therefore valid also for the imitation of Christ....[35]

On one occasion only a few years later in 1970, Paul VI made the same point, but more forcefully during a homily at the shrine of Our Lady of Bonaria in Cagliari, Sardinia, where he stated: "It is, therefore, no negligible, secondary chance circumstance, but an essential part, one that is of the greatest importance, beauty and comfort for us human beings, that Christ came to us through Mary. *We must receive Him from her.*"[36]

Sheen understood that the theological basis of the saying "*Ad Iesum per Mariam*" was the teaching that Mary is the Mediatrix of all graces. In his commentary on the fifth Glorious Mystery of the Rosary, Sheen writes: "Our Lord comes back to us again through Mary as Queen of Heaven, passing his Life and His blessing through her hands as the Mediatrix of all graces. He came through her in Bethlehem; through her, we go back to Him—and through her He comes back again to us."[37] This teaching was explicitly reinforced by the liturgy of the Church until 1970.[38]

---

[35] *AAS* 59 (1967), 470-472 [*St. Paul Editions*, trans. NCWC, 8, 10-11] (emphasis mine).

[36] *Insegnamenti di Paolo VI*, vol. 8 (Vatican City: Libreria Editrice Vaticana, 1970), 361 [*The Pope Speaks*, vol. 15 (1970): 98] (emphasis mine).

[37] *WFL*, 222.

[38] The Missal used until 1970 contained an especially rich theology of Mary's mediation. The most important of these texts is found in the Mass of the "Blessed Virgin Mary, Mediatrix of All Graces" ("*B. Mariae Virginis omnium gratiarum Mediatricis*"), by this point celebrated on May 8. By 1964, the date of this feast had transferred from Cardinal Mercier's selected date of May 31 to May 8, due to Pius XII in 1954 establishing the feast of Mary's universal Queenship on May 31 (a date later moved more appropriately to August 22, at the end of the octave of Mary's Assumption). In the 1964 *Missale Romanum* there are two other feasts which share May 8: The Blessed Virgin Mary, Queen of All Saints and Mother of Fair Love; and The Blessed Virgin Mary, Our Lady of the Sacred Heart.

The liturgical texts prescribed to Mary "Mediatrix of All Graces" are extremely rich and reinforce the primary Scriptural references which the Church uses to express this doctrine: Ecclesiasticus 24:25-26 [Vulgate] and John 19:25-27. It is equally important that we also briefly examine the theological significance of the prayers and antiphons accompanying these Scripture

What did Sheen mean by "all graces"? He never directly treats
that question, but from all that we have learned from his teaching
on Mary's mediation as it relates to the mystery of Christ (the Incarnation and its mystical prolongation), especially Sheen's adherence
to the famous Marian teachings of St. Pius X and Sts. Bernard and
Bernardine on Mary's mediation, it is easy to answer this question.
As we have just seen, St. Bernardine of Siena and St. Bernard of
Clairveaux were clear in their teaching that *every* grace passed from
Christ through Mary. It is reasonable to deduce, therefore, that
if Sheen adopted the Marian teaching of these saints as his own,
then he would have also believed the popular maxim of St. Bernard
that God "wills us to have everything through Mary" [...*est vol-
untas ejus, qui totum nos habere voluit per Mariam*].[39] This popular
maxim of St. Bernard was also incorporated into the teachings of

passages to describe Mary's mediation, especially in the Mass for the Blessed
Virgin Mary [B.V.M.], "Mediatrix of All Graces."
    The Collect of this feast puts forth the order of mediation according to
God's divine plan:
    "Lord Jesus Christ, our mediator before the Father, you have made the
most blessed Virgin, your Mother and ours, a mediatrix before you. May
everyone who comes to you seeking benefits rejoice at receiving all through
her...." [*Domine Iesu Christe, noster apud Patrem mediator, qui beatissimam
Virginem, Matrem tuam, matrem quoque nostram et apud te Mediatricem
constituere dignatus es: concede propitius; ut, quisquis ad te beneficia petiturus
acceserit, cuncta se per eam impetrasse laetetur*] [*The Roman Missal in Latin
and English for Sunday, Feast, Ferial and Votive Masses* (Collegeville, MN:
The Liturgical Press, 1968), 1098].
[39] St. Bernard Clairveaux, *In Nativitate B. Mariae Virginis Sermo*, PL 183, 441;
cf. Elizabeth A. Johnson, C.S.J., "Mary as Mediatrix," in *The One Mediator,
The Saints, and Mary: Lutherans and Catholics in Dialogue VIII*, ed. H. Anderson, J. Francis Stafford, and Joseph A. Burgess (Augsburg: Augsburg Fortress,
1992), 313.

Leo XIII,[40] Pius XI[41] and Pius XII,[42] who undoubtedly influenced
Sheen's consistent teaching on Mary's mediation throughout his
priesthood.

St. Bernard's "everything" ("*totum*") implies more than only the
graces of Redemption. From what we have examined so far, Sheen,
too, does not limit Mary's mediation of graces to redemptive (or
sanctifying) graces, although he would certainly hold that they are
the primary graces which Mary dispenses. As we have seen from
Sheen's commentary on Mary's mediation at Cana, Mary mediates
not only for our salvific needs (sanctifying grace) but also for our
earthly needs (e.g., Mary's intercession also obtained through the
divine power of her Son, a miracle of more wine for the wedding
feast). We will see in the following sections how Mary mediates
even the graces of the sacraments and the grace of conversion to
those who have not received grace.

Sheen, as was saw in Chapter I, was strongly devoted to Mary
and the liturgy, especially on Saturdays. It is plausible that he had a
devotion to the newly created liturgical feast day of "Mary, Mediatrix of All Graces," obtained in 1921 by the efforts of Cardinal
Mercier of whom Sheen was an admitted disciple. It is, therefore,

---

[40] Encyclical Letter *Jucunda Semper* (8 September 1894), *ASS* 27 (1894-1895),
178-80, 182-84. See note 29, page 211, for text cited.

[41] "But rather, as we said in the beginning, shall We beseech God through the
mediation of the Blessed Virgin, so acceptable to Him, since, to use the words
of St. Bernard: 'Such is the will of God who has wished that we should have all
things through Mary' (*Sermo I in Nativ. B.M.V.*)" [Encyclical Letter *Ingravescentibus malis* (29 September 1937), *AAS* 29 (1937), 375; *OL* #338].

[42] "And since, as St. Bernard declares, '*It is the Will of God that we obtain all favors
through Mary*' (*Sermo in Nativ. B.M.V.*), let everyone hasten to have recourse to
Mary. May all mankind bring its petitions, sorrows and anxieties, and lay them
on her altar, beseeching her for aid and comfort. And in this present and most
grave peril, *confidently following the example of our forefathers*, let us not fail to do
that which, *as history testifies*, they did with such gratifying results in their days of
peril and fearful uncertainty.

"So powerful, indeed, is the Blessed Virgin with God and His only-begotten
Son that, as Dante observes, anyone who desires His help and fails to have
recourse to Mary is like one trying to fly without wings (cf. *Paradiso*, 33,
13-15)" [Letter *Superiore Anno* of 15 April 1940 to Cardinal Luigi Maglione,
AAS 32 (1940), 145; *OL* #356-57].

reasonable to assert that Sheen was moved by his piety and by the authority of the feast to embrace the teaching of Mary as "Mediatrix of All Graces."

Mary and Sacramental Grace

Baptism and Sanctifying Grace

All that we have studied of Sheen's teaching on Mary's mediation as it relates to the Incarnation and its mystical prolongation in the Church prepares us to understand how Mary's mediation relates to sacramental grace. In particular, Sheen's teaching on the Annunciation and Calvary provides significant insight into Mary's relationship to the sacraments of Baptism, Confirmation, Holy Orders and the Eucharist. We will now examine Sheen's understanding of Mary's mediation in relation to the graces we receive in the sacraments.

As we saw in Chapter III, the beginning of our recapitulation of the life of Christ is at the moment of our Baptism by which "*all sins* are forgiven, original sin and all personal sins, as well as all punishment for sin."[43] In addition, through Baptism one becomes "an adopted son of God, [...] 'a partaker of the divine nature,' member of Christ and co-heir with him, and a temple of the Holy Spirit."[44] At the same time, St. Thomas reminds us: "As the Apostle says (Rom. vi. 3, 4), *all we who are baptized in Christ Jesus, are baptized in His death: for we are buried together with Him, by Baptism unto death*; which is to say that by Baptism man is incorporated in the very death of Christ."[45] Sheen described the death of Christ as a prolonged *kenosis*, or victimhood, which began at the moment of His Incarnation when He became Priest and Victim. Sheen also stressed that the Annunciation was the beginning of Mary's sharing in the victimhood of Christ through which she would ratify her Redemption.

---

[43] *CCC*, 1263.
[44] Cf. *CCC*, 1265.
[45] *ST*, III, q. 68, a. 5.

We have already seen Sheen explain Baptism as a kind of "Annunciation" and his teaching reveals two important events taking place that are the paradigm of every Baptism. The first is God's dialogue with the soul who has already conceived the Word of God in faith. As He did to Mary, God asks: "Will you give me a human nature?"[46] In other words, "Will you prolong my Incarnation through your human nature by which I will relive My Victimhood, My Passion and My Death in order that you will be glorified as I was glorified?" In other words, our Baptism, as St. Thomas affirms, is the beginning of our participation of Christ's priest-victimhood and the condition of receiving Christ's redemptive grace is uniting ourselves to His Passion, which is the source of His grace, as Sheen already illustrated.[47] This is the meaning of the character we receive at Baptism[48] which is strengthened by another character given at Confirmation, which is oriented toward the same purpose.[49] Participation in the Divine nature requires death to our old nature.

---

[46] Cf. Fulton J. Sheen, "The Cross" (from a series of retreat lectures given at Holy Trinity Seminary, Irving, Texas, 1972, recorded by and in the possession of Mr. Daniel B. Steffen of Plano, Texas), compact disc. Sheen explains how this question is also applied in a unique way to priests where the priest is asked to give his human nature to Christ so that Christ can act more fully as Priest, Teacher (Prophet) and King.

[47] Cf. ST, III, q. 79, a. 1: "...Christ and His Passion are the cause of grace."

[48] "In a sacramental character Christ's faithful have a share in His Priesthood; in the sense that as Christ has the full power of a spiritual priesthood, so His faithful are likened to Him by sharing a certain spiritual power with regard to the sacraments and to things pertaining to the Divine worship" (ST, III, q. 63, a. 5). The baptismal character, therefore, is the "instrumental power" through which we are conformed to the Passion and Death of Christ by participation in Christ's Priesthood, which is the only way we are able to worthily give proper worship to God (cf. ST, III, q. 63, a. 4, ad 1; ST, III, q. 63, a. 5, ad 1; ST, III, q. 63, a. 5, ad 6).

[49] St. Thomas teaches that Confirmation confers a character in that it is unrepeatable and is tied to the Sacrament of Baptism in that it is "a certain spiritual growth bringing man to perfect spiritual age" in which the baptized "receives spiritual combat with the enemies of the Faith (ST, III, q. 72, a. 5). This grace to engage in spiritual combat ties this sacrament to the Cross, where the enemies of the Faith are defeated.

Thus far, we see from Sheen's teaching how Mary serves as the *model* of each Christian's Baptism. How is she involved in mediating the sanctifying grace which the faithful receive? The moment one gives his *fiat* to God, he becomes, as Sheen described, a "conjoined instrument of His Divinity" where the Divine Person of Christ dwells in the soul by grace. Sheen repeatedly emphasized that there is only one Christ and He is always formed from the spousal union between Mary and the Holy Spirit. This was true at the Incarnation in Nazareth and it was repeated at the mystical prolongation of the Incarnation at the birth of the Church at Calvary.

Therefore, whenever the life of Christ is increased in our soul, the nuptial union of Mary and the Holy Spirit takes place in us and Christ is conceived anew, as Sheen puts it: "By her Annunciation she conceives us anew each instant in Christ."[50] This truth is confirmed by such great saints as Louis Marie de Montfort and Maximilian Maria Kolbe, known for their theological insights into Mary's role in salvation history. De Montfort stated: "…The Holy Spirit chose to make use of our Blessed Lady, although he had no absolute need of her, in order to become actively fruitful in producing Jesus Christ and his members in her and by her. This is a mystery of grace unknown even to many of the most learned and spiritual of Christians."[51]

The same teaching is confirmed by St. Maximilian Kolbe who wrote: "The union between the Immaculata and the Holy Spirit is so inexpressible, yet so perfect that the Holy Spirit acts only by the Immaculata, his Spouse. This is why she is the Mediatrix of all graces given by the Holy Spirit."[52]

---

[50] *MBC*, 330.

[51] St. Louis de Montfort, *True Devotion to Mary* in *God Alone: The Collected Writings of St. Louis Marie de Montfort*, 295-296.

[52] St. Maximilian Kolbe, Letter dated 28 July 1935, quoted by H.M. Manteau-Bonamy, O.P., *Immaculate Conception and the Holy Spirit* (Libertyville, IL: Franciscan Marytown Press, 1977), 99.

Mary and the Eucharist

Sheen offers thought-provoking connections between Mary and the Eucharist. First, the Eucharist is directly connected to the Incarnation since it is the Body and Blood of Christ. Sheen writes, "The Body which we receive in the Host is born of Mary."[53] Secondly, Sheen writes that the "Mass is Calvary re-presented. Hence [we have the] universal intercession of Mary at Mass."[54] Third, Sheen recalls that "Mary took part in the breaking of Bread at Pentecost (Acts 2:42-46). Hence, Mary was involved in communion with the Mystical Body."[55]

Next, Sheen explains how "Mary gives us the Eucharist" because she is inseparably bound up in the Incarnation, of which the Eucharist is the sacramental prolongation. Sheen emphasizes that there is "no Body and Blood in Him except hers." He adds:

> "*The Bread that I will give you is My Flesh for the life of the world*" (Jn. 6:51). Who gave that flesh? He was conceived of a woman. St. Ambrose [wrote]: "The Body that we consecrate comes from the Virgin." The Council of Trent [affirms]: "The true Body of Christ contained in the Sacrament is the same which was born of the Virgin Mary and which sits at the right hand of God."[56]

Sheen also stated that Mary's mediation at Cana which brought about the transubstantiation of the water into wine "was a preparation for the Eucharist."[57] Thus, he suggests from that paradigm

---

[53] Sheen, "Mary and Institution of Eucharist," Sheen Archives. Now, Sheen was not saying that Jesus is present as He was present in His earthly life. Sheen knew the distinction between Christ's physical, historical presence, and His sacramental presence in the Holy Eucharist. As a devout student of St. Thomas, he was aware of St. Thomas's teaching which affirmed that "Christ is not moved locally of Himself, but only accidentally, because Christ is not in this sacrament as in a place.…What is not in a place, is not moved of itself locally, but only according to the motion of the subject in which it is" (*ST*, III, q. 76, a. 6).

[54] Ibid.
[55] Ibid.
[56] Ibid.
[57] Ibid.

event that Mary's mediation continues in a mystical sense in relation to the transubstantiation of the water and wine at Mass into the Body, Blood, Soul and Divinity of Christ. He also makes a connection between Mary and the Eucharist because the substance that composed Christ's humanity was taken from Mary. He writes:

> Thus, in forming the Body of Christ though there was an infinite creating power, yet it was made of the substance of the Virgin Mary...The Spirit is the active efficient cause, and the Virgin is the passive material cause, because the Body was formed out of her substance....But from the positive side, there was more than sinlessness but holiness as we read (Isaias 11:1-3), where the Spirit's first sanctifying work is mentioned in the womb of Mary.[58]

Lastly, Sheen makes a connection between Mary giving Christ to the world at the Incarnation when she became Mother of God and the continuation of that giving in the Sacrament of the Eucharist. Sheen simply says regarding Holy Communion, "She gave us Christ, therefore she relates to Communion" because it is the same Christ.[59] This relation to Communion is understood by Sheen's explanation of Mary as mothering Christ (the Christian life of grace) into the souls of all the baptized. Therefore, this relation pertains to Mary distributing the sanctifying grace given through the Eucharist.

Mary's Mediation and the Priesthood

We have already seen that Sheen's main emphasis on Mary's mediation from heaven is that she cooperates with the Holy Spirit to "form Jesus in us *spiritually*" as she cooperated with the Holy Spirit to form Christ physically.[60] This is the meaning of Mary's

---

[58] Sheen, "The Holy Spirit in Relation to the Head and to the Body" (undated typescript from folder labeled "Mystical Body"), Sheen Archives.
[59] Ibid.
[60] Fulton J. Sheen, "Immaculate Conception." What Sheen is conveying when he uses the phrase "form Jesus in us spiritually," is what John Paul later explains as Mary's maternal and loving cooperation "in the birth and development" of those incorporated into the Sonship of Christ (cf. *RM* 6). *LG* 63 uses the

spiritual maternity. Sheen highlights that there is a special relationship in this role of hers in the formation of Christ the Priest-Victim
in the souls of priests as she helped form Jesus, "*Sacerdos-Hostia*,"
in her womb.[61] This suggests, therefore, that "the grace of the Holy
Spirit proper to this sacrament" which more perfectly configures
his soul to Christ the Priest-Victim,[62] is also mediated through
Mary who brings the grace of Christ wherever He is to be formed.[63]
He confirms this when he says that Mary "is the link between the
priest-victim and the One who is always 'making intercession for
us in heaven' (Heb 7:25)."[64]

CONCLUSION

Sheen's placement of Mary's descending mediation within a
renewed ecclesiological understanding of the Church as the mystical prolongation of the Incarnation provides many insights that
make this mystery more intelligible by making it more *personal*. By
emphasizing that the Church is the mystical continuation of the
Incarnation, Sheen's teaching shows that all that we learn about
Mary's mediation as it relates to Christ the Head serves as the blueprint or pattern according to which Mary mediates in relation to
Christ's Mystical Body, the Church—or as Sheen accurately calls
the Church, the Mystical Christ. In this light, Sheen treats ecclesiology as an extension of Christology since both are organically
connected.

With this understanding of the Church as organically connected
to Christ—as the vine is connected to the branches (cf. Jn. 15:5)—

---

phrase, "in whose generation and formation she cooperates with a mother's
love" to describe how Mary *forms* Christ in the souls of the faithful.
[61] *PNHO*, 278.
[62] Cf. *CCC*, 1585-1589.
[63] When Sheen speaks of Christ being "formed" in the baptized, he is speaking about a growth in the soul into the fullness of Christ, which will only be
enjoyed perfectly in heaven. Sheen describes this in another place when he
uses St. Paul's language of the "increase of God" (1 Cor. 1:2-19) to describe
the growth of Christ in the Church (*MBC*, 316).
[64] Ibid., 278.

Sheen emphasized that Mary always mediates as the Mother of the *total* Christ, a mystery virtually present at the Annunciation, but not fully manifested until Calvary where the full scope of Mary's spousal and maternal mediation becomes realized and exercised. In other words, Mary's descending mediation in her role as Spouse of the Holy Spirit and Mother of the Mystical Body of Christ was virtually present at the Annunciation, but not fully exercised until she had fulfilled her ascending mediation at Calvary, enabling her to exercise her spousal and maternal mediation as it related to mystically prolonging the Incarnation of Christ in the souls of those who would be incorporated into His Mystical Body.

Sheen then emphasized that the Church, corporately, and each baptized soul, singularly, enters into the mystery of the Incarnation by which the baptized recapitulate or re-live the life of Christ until each soul can say with St. Paul: "I have been crucified with Christ; it is no longer I who live, but Christ who lives in me; and the life I now live in the flesh I live by faith in the Son of God, who loved me and gave himself for me" (Gal. 2:20). Each Christian, therefore, is incorporated into the Divine Sonship of Christ and thereby inherits His Mother to act as his Mother in the order of grace. For Sheen, the moment of the baptism of a person therefore serves as a type of Annunciation where the soul is asked by God to give him a human nature through which to re-live mystically His priest-victimhood. By recapitulating the redemptive life of Christ the baptized soul enters into the fullness of communion with the glory of Christ. According to Sheen, just as the Incarnation was the fruit of the spousal love and mystical union between Mary and the Holy Spirit, so does that mystical union take place in every soul in which Christ is re-born through sanctifying grace, thus representing the mystery of Christ's *kenosis-pleroma*.

Sheen's teaching then reminds us that Mary's mediation is inextricably bound up in her spousal and maternal relationship to the mystery of the Incarnation. At the Annunciation and at Calvary, Mary mediated by her spousal union with the Holy Spirit to bring forth the Incarnation and henceforth mediated as the faithful spouse of the New Adam and mother of the total Christ. At Calvary, her spousal and maternal mediation as it related to Christ the Head was accomplished. From that point onward, Mary's spousal and maternal mediation would continue as it applied to Christ's Mystical Body, the Mystical Christ. Therefore, the manner in which Mary relates to Christ the Head defines how she relates to Christ's Mystical Body in the order of grace. And it is Mary's relationship to Christ the Head that defines how she mediates in relation to His Mystical Body—she is the faithful and fruitful Spouse of the Holy Spirit who mothers Christ in the souls of the baptized. In this way, according to Sheen, Mary's mediation plays a role in the graces conferred by the sacraments by which souls are conformed more perfectly into Christ.

CHAPTER V

MARY AS MATERNAL MEDIATRIX
IN THE MODERN WORLD

INTRODUCTION

The last 150 years can be characterized as an extraordinary age
of Mary's mediation in the modern world. This is in large part
witnessed by the great Marian shrines which sprung up in honor
of the Marian apparitions which are believed to have taken place
in many areas. Among the most famous are Lourdes and Fatima.
As we explained in the first chapter, Sheen had a deep devotion to
the Blessed Mother and that devotion also rested on a firm faith
and understanding of Mary's ongoing mediation in the world to
expand the Mystical Body of her Son. We will now illuminate
Sheen's understanding of the various ways in which Mary exercises
her maternal mediation in the modern world.

MARY, THE IDEAL FEMININE PRINCIPLE IN
RELIGION

Sheen introduces the question of Mary's role in human anthro-
pology, in particular, the religious nature in every human being.
He asks:

> Can religion do without motherhood? It certainly does not
> do without fatherhood....Since motherhood is as necessary
> as fatherhood in the natural order—perhaps even more

so—shall the devoted religious heart be without a woman to love?[1]

This question is, in a sense, related to the question we have seen Sheen address regarding the fittingness of Mary, the perfect woman, in playing a central role in Redemption from a purely feminine perspective. Developing this teaching from an anthropological view Sheen explains the central role woman has in every culture and how every culture seeks to imitate an ideal of womanhood and motherhood:

> Culture derives from woman—for had she not taught her children to talk, the great spiritual values of the world would not have passed from generation to generation. After nourishing the substance of the body to which she gave birth, she then nourishes the child with the substance of her mind. As guardian of the values of the spirit, as protectress of the morality of the young, she preserves culture, which deals with purposes and ends, while man upholds civilization, which deals only with means....If fatherhood has its prototype in the Heavenly Father, Who is the giver of all gifts, then certainly such a beautiful thing as motherhood shall not be without some original Mother, whose traits of loveliness every mother copies in varying degrees. The respect shown to woman looks to an ideal beyond each woman.[2]

Sheen believed this affinity toward the ideal woman is woven into the religious nature found in every culture. Sheen's approach is similar to that of St. Paul who addressed the Athenians in the Areopagus when he found an altar with the inscription, "To an unknown god."[3] St. Paul acknowledged that while the Athenians did not know who this god was to whom they offered sacrifice,

---

[1] *WFL*, 183-184.

[2] *WFL*, 184.

[3] "Men of Athens, I perceive that in every way you are very religious. For as I passed along, and observed the objects of your worship, I found also an altar with this inscription, 'To an unknown god.' What therefore you worship as unknown, this I proclaim to you" (Acts 17:22-23).

they were responding to an innate affinity to the God who created them and who draws the hearts of all humanity. Sheen understood that Mary's universal motherhood, unknown to many, has a similar attraction for these souls; for all humanity, whether it knows it or not, seeks to know this ideal woman in religion.

Sheen provides an example of how these desires for the ideal woman and mother translate into somewhat iconic figures which portray the ideal feminine principle in world religions. In the Orient, for example, these figures include the Chinese Legend of Kwan-yin, the Chinese goddess of mercy, and the Japanese goddess of mercy, Kwanon.[4] There is one story of particular interest which Sheen used to teach that many who are introduced to Mary often find her as the fulfillment of their ideal feminine principle. He writes:

> It is interesting that the Buddhists, who already know this goddess of mercy and who have come to learn of the Blessed Mother, have seen the first as the preparation for the second. Upon becoming Christian, there is no need for such Buddhists to turn their back on Kwanon as evil; rather, they accept her as the far-off foreshadowing of the woman who was not a goddess but the Mother of Mercy Itself. Very becomingly, the Japanese artist Takahira Toda, who came from a family of Buddhist priests, became a member of Christ's Mystical Body after seeing the similarity between Kwanon and the Virgin Mary.[5]

Sheen thus concludes his thoughts on this interesting subject:

> Thus, whether one studies world history before or after Christ, there is always revealed a yearning in every human breast for ideal motherhood. Reaching out from the past to Mary, through ten thousand vaguely prophetic Judiths and Ruths, and looking back through the mists of the centuries,

---

[4] Ibid., 189, 193.
[5] *WFL*, 193.

all hearts come to rest in her. This is the ideal woman! She
is *the Mother*.[6]

MARY'S UNIVERSAL MEDIATION APPLIES TO NON-CHRISTIANS

The observations of Sheen just presented provoke the theological question of whether Mary's motherhood of grace has influence even on non-Christians. Another way of approaching this
issue is by asking the question of whether Mary's title "Mother
of the Church" or "Mother of the Mystical Body" is too exclusive a term. Sheen's implication that Mary's universal motherhood
influences non-Christians is supported by an important teaching
of St. Thomas in which he explains the significance of membership
in the Mystical Body of Christ, the Church:

> We must therefore consider the members of the mystical
> body not only as they are in act, but as they are in potenti-
> ality. Nevertheless, some are in potentiality who will never
> be reduced at some time to act; and this according to the
> triple class, of which the first is by faith, the second by the
> charity of this life, the third by the fruition of the life to
> come. Hence we must say that that if we take the whole
> time of the world in general, Christ is the Head of all men,
> but diversely. For, first and principally, He is the Head of
> such as are united to Him by glory; secondly, of those who
> are actually united to Him by charity; thirdly, of those
> who are actually united to Him by faith; fourthly, of those
> who are united to Him merely in potentiality, which is not
> yet reduced to act, yet will be reduced to act according to
> Divine predestination; fifthly, of those are united to Him
> in potentiality, which will never be reduced to act; such are
> those men existing in the world, who are not predestined,
> who, however, on their departure from this world, wholly

---

[6] Ibid., 195-196.

cease to be members of Christ, as being no longer in potentiality to be united to Christ.[7]

Applying the teaching of St. Thomas to Mary's role as Mother of the Church, non-Christians would fall under her maternal care because they are members of the Church *in potentia*. This is a very interesting way of looking at non-Christians.

This teaching suggests that Mary is mother in the order of grace even of those who have not yet received sanctifying grace. Sheen believed Mary had a unique role in bringing souls to Christ and Christ to souls. Sheen's anthropological view of mankind as implicitly seeking the ideal feminine is actually an intimation of Mary mediating the grace of conversion to those who do not yet know Christ. Sheen explains this unique role of Mary as being the "Advent" of Christ.

MARY IS ALWAYS THE "ADVENT" OF CHRIST

Sheen's teaching on this is really his application to contemporary life of what Scripture reveals of the earthly lives of Jesus and Mary, which Sheen saw as paradigms for the recapitulation of humanity into Christ. Sheen, therefore, points out from the life of Christ that Mary always precedes Jesus. He explains:

As there would have been no advent of Christ in the flesh in His first coming without Mary, so there can be no coming of Christ in spirit among the Gentiles without Mary's again preparing the way. As she was the instrument for the fulfillment of the hope of Israel, so she is the instrument for the fulfillment of the hope of the pagans. *Her role is to prepare for Jesus.* This she did physically by giving Him a body that could conquer death, by giving Him hands with which He could bless children and feet with which He could seek out the lost sheep. But as she prepared His body, so she now prepares souls for His coming. As she was in Israel before Christ was born, so she is in China, Japan, and Oceania

---

[7] *ST*, III, q. 8, a. 3.

before Christ is born. She *precedes* Jesus—not ontologically but physically—in Israel, as His Mother, and spiritually, among the Gentiles, as the one who readies His tabernacle among men.[8]

Later in the same work, Sheen builds on this point in his customary oratorical style, which is not always expressed with theological precision, but with an intended exaggeration to reinforce his point:

Jesus may not be given an inn, in these lands, but Mary is among their people, preparing hearts for grace. She is grace where there is no grace; she is the Advent where there is no Christmas. In all lands where there is an ideal woman, or where virgins are venerated, or where one lady is set above all ladies, the ground is fertile for accepting the Woman as the prelude to embracing Christ. Where there is the presence of Jesus, there is the presence of His Mother; but where there is the absence of Jesus, through either the ignorance or the wickedness of men, there is still the presence of Mary. As she filled up the gap between the Ascension and Pentecost, so she is filling up the gap between the ethical systems of the East and their incorporation into the Mystical Body of her Divine Son. She is the fertile soil from which, in God's appointed time, the Faith will flourish and bloom in the East. Although there are few tabernacle lamps in India, Japan, and Africa compared to the total population, nevertheless I see, written over the gateways to all these nations, the words of the Gospel at the beginning of the public life of the Savior: "And Mary, the Mother of Jesus, was there."[9]

---

[8] *WFL*, 186-187.
[9] Ibid., 199.

Is Sheen's Teaching on Mary's Role in the Modern World Obscuring the Work of the Holy Spirit?

A fear arises among some that the strong emphasis given by Sheen and others concerning Mary's extraordinary activity in the conversion of souls in the modern world is minimizing—or even replacing—the role of the Holy Spirit. One who expressed such a fear was Yves Congar. He took great exception to the teaching of Pope Leo XIII (which was adopted by Fulton Sheen in his teaching on Mary's mediation), who quoted St. Bernardine of Siena's popular doctrine of the three-fold manner in the distribution of grace. Congar wrote:

> It is, in fact, hardly possible not to react as Elsie Gibson did when we read this text by Bernardino of Siena, quoted in an encyclical letter by Leo XIII, who was, a few years later, to write a fine encyclical on the Holy Spirit, *Divinum illud munus*: "All grace that is communicated to this world comes to us by a threefold movement. It is dispensed according to a very perfect order from God in Christ, from Christ in the Virgin and from the Virgin in us." Bernardino adds to this that Mary has at her disposal "a certain jurisdiction or authority over the temporal procession of the Holy Spirit, to such an extent that no creature has ever received the grace of any virtue from God except through a dispensation of the Virgin herself." This is clearly unacceptable.[10]

Congar's strong disagreement with this doctrine goes so far as to suggest that this teaching of St. Bernardine and Leo XIII could be rejected as an "unacceptable statement."[11] On this subject Congar takes what conciliar historians labeled a "minimalist"[12] approach

---

[10] Yves M. J. Congar, *I Believe in the Holy Spirit*, trans. David Smith, vol. 1, *The Holy Spirit in the 'Economy'—Revelation and Experience of the Spirit* (New York: The Seabury Press, 1983), 163-164.

[11] Ibid., 164.

[12] Cf. Joseph A. Komonchak, "The Struggle for the Council During the Preparation of Vatican II (1960-1962)," *History of Vatican II*, ed. Joseph

to Mary's role in salvation history and in the life of the Church. For example, Congar writes: "Mary has a pre-eminent place in the Christian mystery as the model of the Church and of universal intercession" but has only a "discreet Marian influence" upon the lives of Christians.[13]

One can interpret the evidence differently. For example, millions of people in the twentieth century have attributed profound and lasting conversions to Mary's maternal mediation. Moreover, there is the evidence of the piety and teachings of the popes of the last 150 years who affirmed a strong theological tradition that has consistently taught that Mary is the Mediatrix of *all* graces. For example, the same pope whose doctrine on Mary's mediation Congar deemed "unacceptable," affirmed in his encyclical *Octobri mense adventante* that the doctrine of Mary as the Mediatrix of all graces has been "unanimously" accepted by Christians of every age:

> With equal truth it may be said that of the great treasury of all graces given to us by Our Lord—"for grace and truth came by Jesus Christ" (Jn. 1:17)—nothing comes to us except through the mediation of Mary, for such is the will of God. Thus, as no man goes to the Father but by the Son, so no one goes to Christ except through His Mother. How great are the goodness and mercy revealed in this design of God! What a boon to the frailty of man! We believe in the infinite goodness of the Most High, and we rejoice in it; we believe also in His justice, and we fear it. We adore the beloved Savior who generously gave His blood and His life; but at the same time we dread the inexorable Judge. Thus do those whose actions have disturbed their consciences

---

A. Komonchak, vol. 1, *Announcing and Preparing Vatican II Toward a New Era in Catholicism* (Maryknoll, NY: Orbis Books, 1997), 257; cf. Joseph A. Komonchak, "Toward an Ecclesiology of Communion," *History of Vatican II*, ed. Joseph A. Komonchak, vol. 4, *Church as Communion—Third Period and Intercession: September 1964–September 1965* (Maryknoll, NY: Orbis Books, 2000), 53; cf. Robert Faricy, S.J., "The Blessed Virgin Mary in Vatican II: Twenty Years Later," *The Ecumenical Society of the Blessed Virgin Mary* 29 (1984): 2.

[13] Ibid., 164.

need an intercessor mighty in favor with God, merciful enough to lift up the afflicted and the broken to loving trust in the divine mercy. Mary is this glorious intermediary.

The plan of this most loving mercy, realized by God in Mary and confirmed by the testament of Christ, was understood with the utmost joy by the holy Apostles and the earliest believers. It was the belief and teaching of the venerable Fathers of the Church. Christians of every generation received it with one mind; and even when literature and tradition are silent, there is a voice that breaks from every Christian heart and speaks with eloquence. Nothing is needed other than divine faith....[14]

One also cannot dismiss the theological significance of the liturgical feast day in honor of "Mary, Mediatrix of All Graces" (see note 3 on page 260), even if it was later removed from the liturgical calendar.

What Congar and others who share his opinion perhaps fail to realize, and which is at the heart of Sheen's Mariology, is the full significance of Mary's mediating roles as Spouse of the Spirit of Christ (the Holy Spirit) and Mother of the *totus Christus*. In each of these relationships, Sheen has explained that it is the Holy Spirit which makes Mary fruitful. She was made fruitful at the Incarnation and continues to be fruitful in its mystical prolongation as Mother of the Mystical Body of Christ, the Church. That is why Sheen's teaching on the Church as the mystical prolongation of the Incarnation is critical for a proper Mariology which must include her at the heart of the mystery of the Incarnation, historical and mystical. Moreover, there is nothing theological barring Mary's universal mediation from applying to the intercession and distribution of divine favors that are not salvific in nature. Sheen's explanation of Mary's intercession at Cana supports this point.

In applying Sheen's teaching on Mary's spousal relationship with the Holy Spirit to this argument of Mary replacing the Holy

---

[14] *ASS* 24 (1891-1892), 195-96 [*OL* #113-15].

Spirit, it seems that just the opposite is true. The more Mary's relationship as spouse is brought into relief, the more the Holy Spirit will enter into our reflection because God's providence has determined that the two do not work without each other in the order of grace. Sheen repeatedly emphasized, as we have especially seen in Chapter III, that Mary's nuptial union with the Holy Spirit, while mystical, is *real*. Mary's mediation of all graces is at the heart of this question because all graces come from the Holy Spirit, her inseparable Spouse.

The implications of this teaching are notable. In an ecumenically sensitive climate, where some Catholics and ecclesial communities may minimize discussion on Mary out of fear of division, Sheen's teachings suggest just the opposite is needed.[15] Mary is the Mediatrix between Christ and us. She brings Christ to us and brings us back to Christ. As Sheen has repeatedly pointed out, thanks to Mary, we have Christ. While she waits for us to introduce the truth about her mediation to fellow Christians and non-Christians, she is already preparing the soil for the Seed of her Son to take root in people's souls. On this point, Sheen concludes on this subtle yet powerful influence of Mary's mediation which remains active throughout the world to re-capitulate creation into Christ:

The pagans, who have not yet been baptized either by water or desire, cannot say the Our Father, but they *can* say the Hail Mary. As there is a grace that prepares for grace, so there is in all pagan lands of the world the influence of Mary, preparing for Christ. She is the spiritual "Trojan horse" preparing for the assault of love by her Divine Son, the "Fifth Column" working within the Gentiles, storming their cities from within, even when their Wise Men know

---

[15] It is worth noting that one exception to this statement is the positive dialogue on Mary taking place within the Anglican-Roman Catholic International Commission (ARCIC). Its 2004 statement "Mary: Grace and Hope in Christ," is evidence that Catholics and Anglicans believe Mary plays an important role in achieving ecclesial unity.

it not, and teaching muted tongues to sing her *Magnificat* before they have known her Son.[16]

MARY'S MEDIATION AND THE MOSLEMS

Sheen dedicates a separate section of his Mariological treatise on Mary, *The World's First Love*, to a special application of his teaching that Mary is the "advent of Christ" as it concerns the future conversion of the Moslems. In our time where there is growing concern about the rapid growth of Islam and Islamic violence, the Church continues to ask herself: "How will the followers of Islam embrace the full truth about Jesus as the Christ and Redeemer of the human race?" In this age of inter-religious dialogue, there is growing and justified skepticism that reasonable argument can win over the followers of a religion with critically unreasonable tenets. This was recently brought out by Pope Benedict XVI, in his controversial, but historically accurate speech at the University of Regensburg on 12 September 2006. Using the words of "the erudite Byzantine emperor Manuel II Paleologus" from 1391, he highlights teachings of Islam which are irrational and go against the very nature of God. Benedict said:

In the seventh conversation (διάλεξις - controversy) edited by Professor Khoury, the emperor touches on the theme of the holy war. The emperor must have known that surah 2, 256 reads: "There is no compulsion in religion." According to some of the experts, this is probably one of the suras of the early period, when Mohammed was still powerless and under threat. But naturally the emperor also knew the instructions, developed later and recorded in the Qur'an, concerning holy war. Without descending to details, such as the difference in treatment accorded to those who have the "Book" and the "infidels", he addresses his interlocutor with a startling brusqueness, a brusqueness that we find unacceptable, on the central question about the relationship

---

[16] *WFL*, 187.

between religion and violence in general, saying: "Show
me just what Mohammed brought that was new, and there
you will find things only evil and inhuman, such as his
command to spread by the sword the faith he preached."
The emperor, after having expressed himself so forcefully,
goes on to explain in detail the reasons why spreading the
faith through violence is something unreasonable. Violence
is incompatible with the nature of God and the nature of
the soul. "God", he says, "is not pleased by blood—and not
acting reasonably (σὺν λόγω) is contrary to God's nature.
Faith is born of the soul, not the body. Whoever would
lead someone to faith needs the ability to speak well and
to reason properly, without violence and threats....To con-
vince a reasonable soul, one does not need a strong arm, or
weapons of any kind, or any other means of threatening a
person with death..."

The decisive statement in this argument against violent
conversion is this: not to act in accordance with reason is
contrary to God's nature. The editor, Theodore Khoury,
observes: For the emperor, as a Byzantine shaped by Greek
philosophy, this statement is self-evident. But for Muslim
teaching, God is absolutely transcendent. His will is not
bound up with any of our categories, even that of ratio-
nality.[17]

Fulton Sheen, who was an erudite communicator of the Christian faith, surprisingly does not teach that the conversion of the
Moslems will come through dialogue or persuasive argument
against the tenets of Islam. He believes that Islam shares a close-
ness to Mary that will eventually lead them to embrace the full
truth of Jesus Christ. He writes: "It is our firm belief that the fears

[17] Pope Benedict XVI, "Faith, Reason and the University Memories and
Reflections," (lecture presented during his meeting with the representatives of
science at the University of Regensburg, 12 September 2006, available from
the official website of the Holy See, http://www.vatican.va/holy_father/bene-
dict_xvi/speeches/2006/september/documents/hf_ben-xvi_spe_20060912_
university-regensburg_en.html; Internet).

some entertain concerning the Moslems (a return of the militant spread of Islam in the West) are not to be realized, but that Islam, instead, will eventually be converted to Christianity—and in a way that even some of our missionaries never suspect. It is our belief that this will happen not through the direct teaching of Christianity but through a summoning of the Moslems to a veneration of the Mother of God."[18] We will now examine how Sheen believed the foundations for their conversion are evidenced in their own doctrine on Mary, which is more favorable than their doctrine on Christ; the connection in God's plan between the Moslems and the village of Fatima, Portugal; and how favorably Our Lady of Fatima is generally received by Moslems.

Regarding similarities found in Islam as presented in the Koran of which Sheen was very familiar, Sheen emphasized that Moslems share faith in the Immaculate Conception and the Virgin Birth.[19] He points out: "In the nineteenth chapter of the Koran there are forty-one verses on Jesus and Mary. There is such a strong defense of the virginity of Mary here that the Koran, in the fourth book, attributes the condemnation of the Jews to their monstrous calumny against the Virgin Mary."[20]

Sheen also pointed out that Mary is esteemed with greater veneration than Fatima, the daughter of Mohammed. He writes:

Mary, then, is for the Moslems the true *Sayyida*, or Lady. The only possible serious rival to her in their creed would be Fatima, the daughter of Mohammed himself. But after the death of Fatima, Mohammed wrote: "Thou shalt be the most blessed of all the women in Paradise, after Mary." In a

---

[18] *WFL*, 201.

[19] One finds implicit reference to Moslems' belief in Mary's Immaculate Conception and consecrated life in Sura III, verses 36-48, which describes an original purity of Mary. It is also worth noting that among the sources of Moslem "Mariological" tradition is the *Protoevangelium of James*, which illustrates in great detail the early consecrated life of Mary (Cf. Giancarlo Finazzo, "The Virgin Mary in the Koran," *ORE*, 13 April 1978, 4).

[20] *WFL*, 202.

variant of the text, Fatima is made to say: "I surpass all the women, except Mary."[21]

Sheen believed that these connections with Mary in Moslem teaching were not coincidental and that God Himself confirmed this when He sent Mary to the obscure village of Fatima in 1917, a city which he pointed out has a significant history as it relates to a connection between Islam and Catholicism.[22] Sheen raises an important question when he wonders "why the Blessed Mother, in this twentieth century, should have revealed herself in the insignificant little village of Fatima, so that to all future generations she would be known as Our Lady of Fatima." He adds, "Since nothing ever happens out of Heaven except with a finesse of all details, I believe that the Blessed Virgin chosen to be known as 'Our Lady of Fatima' as a pledge and a sign of hope to the Moslem people and as an assurance that they, who show her so much respect, will one day accept her Divine Son, too."[23]

Sheen remarked how significant it was that Our Lady of Fatima received such an "enthusiastic reception" by Moslems, especially when the pilgrim statue of Our Lady of Fatima traveled to Africa and India. Sheen described this exceptional phenomenon: "Moslems attended the church services in honor of Our Lady; they allowed religious processions and even prayers before their mosques; and in Mozambique the Moslems, who were unconverted, began to be Christian as soon as the statue of Our Lady of Fatima was erected."[24]

---

[21] *WFL*, 202-203.

[22] "The Moslems occupied Portugal for centuries. At the time when they were finally driven out, the last Moslem chief had a beautiful daughter by the name of Fatima. A Catholic boy fell in love with her, and for him she not only stayed behind when the Moslems left but even embraced the Faith. The young husband was so much in love with her that he changed the name of the town where he lived to Fatima. Thus, the very place where Our Lady appeared in 1917 bears a historical connection to Fatima the daughter of Mohammed" (*WFL*, 203).

[23] *WFL*, 203.

[24] *WFL*, 203-204.

Based on this evidence of Mary's powerful influence on
Moslems, Sheen offers some interesting insights into the Marian
dimension of missiology as it relates particularly to converting
Moslems:

> Missionaries in the future will, more and more, see that
> their apostolate among the Moslems will be successful in
> the measure that they preach Our Lady of Fatima. Mary is
> the advent of Christ, bringing Christ to the people before
> Christ Himself is born. In any apologetic endeavor, it is
> always best to start with that which people already accept.
> Because the Moslems have a devotion to Mary, our mis-
> sionaries should be satisfied merely to expand and to
> develop that devotion, with the full realization that Our
> Blessed Lady will carry the Moslems the rest of the way to
> her Divine Son. She is forever a "traitor" in the sense that
> she will not accept any devotion for herself, but will always
> bring anyone who is devoted to her to her Divine Son. As
> those who lose devotion to her lose belief in the Divinity
> of Christ, so those who intensify devotion to her gradually
> acquire that belief.
>
> ...It now remains to use another approach, namely, that
> of taking the forty-first chapter of the Koran, and showing
> them that it was taken out of the Gospel of Luke, that Mary
> could not be, even in their own eyes, the most blessed of
> all the women of Heaven if she had not also borne One
> Who was the Savior of the world. If Judith and Esther of
> the Old Testament were prefigures of Mary, then it may
> very well be that Fatima herself was a postfigure of Mary!
> The Moslems should be prepared to acknowledge that, if
> Fatima must give way in honor to the Blessed Mother, it
> is because she is different from all the other mothers of the
> world and that without Christ she would be nothing.[25]

Considering the perilous times in which we live with growing
tensions between the Moslems and Christianity, Sheen's teaching

---

[25] *WFL*, 204.

on the powerful, yet gentle, influence of Mary's mediation in bringing the Moslems to accept the full truth about Christ, is more necessary than ever to make known. He, like Pope Benedict XV,[26] who guided the Church through the dark years of World War I, saw Mary as having a critical role in the modern world in mediating peace. Sheen believed Mary's apparitions at Fatima two years later were heaven's response to the pope's prayer for peace:

It is particularly interesting that the theology of the Russians, before they were overshadowed by the cold heart of the anti-God, taught that, when the world rejected the Heavenly Father, He sent His Divine Son, Jesus Christ, to illumine the world. Then they went on to predict that, when the world would reject Our Lord as it has done today, on that Dark Night the light of His Mother would arise to illumine the darkness and lead the world to peace. The beautiful revelation of Our Blessed Mother at Fatima in Portugal from April to October 1917 was another proof of the Russian thesis that, when the world would fight against the Savior, He would send His Mother to save us. And her great revelation took place in the very month the Bolshevik Revolution began.[27]

---

[26] "Mother of the Prince of Peace, Mediatrix between rebellious man and the merciful God [Madre del Principe della Pace, mediatrice fra l'uomo ribelle e Iddio commiserante], she is the dawn of peace shining in the darkness of a world out of joint; she never ceases to implore her Son for peace although His hour is not yet come (Jn. 2:4); she always intervenes on behalf of sorrowing humanity in the hour of danger; today she who is the mother of many orphans and our advocate in this tremendous catastrophe will most quickly hear our prayers.

"When man has hardened his heart and hate has overrun the earth, when fire and sword convulse the world and make it resound with clash of arms and wailing, when human plans have proved misleading, and when all social well-being is upset, faith and history point to Mary as the only refuge, the all powerful intercessor, the Mediatrix of all grace [...la fede e la storia Ci additano, come unico scampo, la Onnipotenza supplichevole, la Mediatrice di ogni grazia, Maria...]" (Benedict XV, Allocution to the Consistory of 24 December 1915; La Civiltà Cattolica, Anno 67, vol. 1 [Quaderno 1574–15 gennaio 1916], 213-214 [OL #261]).
[27] WFL, 271.

POWER ENTRUSTED TO MARY OVER THE COSMOS—MARY IS A POWERFUL MEDIATRIX

The apparitions at Fatima had additional significance for Sheen as he was greatly intrigued as to the significance of what he called "the Dance of the Sun" and "Miracle of the Sun," referring to the miraculous solar phenomenon that took place on 13 October 1917. This spectacle was vividly recounted even by atheist reporters present at the event.[28] Among the possible meanings he speculated the miracle has for the modern world, he noted that the event revealed an unfathomable power God has given to Mary over the most powerful forces in the universe. He wrote:

At Fatima, the fact that Mary could take this great center and seat of atomic power and make it her plaything, the fact that she could swing the sun "like a trinket at her wrist," is

---

[28] *WFL*, 271-272. "Those who love the Mother of Our Lord need no further evidence of this event. Since those who unfortunately do not know either would take proof only from those who reject both Our Lord and His Mother, I offer this description of the phenomenon by the atheist editor of the anarchist Portuguese newspaper *O Seculo*, who was among the seventy thousand who witnessed the incident that day. It was

a spectacle unique and credible....One can see the immense crowd turn toward the sun which reveals itself free of the clouds in full noon. The great star of day makes one think of a silver plaque, and it is possible to look straight at it without the least discomfort....The astonished eyes of the people, full of terror, with their heads uncovered, gaze into the blue of the sky. The sun has trembled, and has made some brusque movements, unprecedented, and outside of all cosmic laws. According to the typical expressions of the peasants "the sun danced." The sun turned around on itself like a wheel of fireworks, and it fell almost to the point of burning the earth with its rays....It remains for those competent to pronounce on the *danse macabre* of the sun, which today at Fatima has made Hosannas burst from the breasts of the faithful and has naturally impressed even freethinkers and other persons not at all interested in religious matters.

"Another atheistic and antireligious sheet, *O Ordem*, reported: 'The sun is sometimes surrounded with crimson flames, at other times aureoled with yellow and at still others, red; it seemed to revolve with a very rapid movement of rotation, apparently detaching itself from the sky, and approached the earth while radiating strong heat.'"

a proof that God has given her power over it, not for death, but for light and life and hope. As Scripture foretold: "And now, in heaven, a great portent appeared; a woman that wore the sun for her mantle" (Rev. 12:1).[29]

He concluded, therefore, saying:

Devotion to Our Lady of Fatima is actually a petition to a Woman to save men from nature made destructive through the rebellious intellect of man. At other moments in history, she was a Mediatrix of her Divine Son for man; but here she is a Mediatrix for nature. She seizes the original atomic power, which is the sun, and proves it is hers to use for peace. And yet it is not apart from man that she would save him from nature, as it was not apart from her free consent that God would save humanity from sin. Man must cooperate through penance. At Salette [sic], Our Lady asked for penance. At Lourdes, three times the Blessed Mother said: "Penance, penance, penance." At Fatima, the same penitential antiphon is struck time and time again.[30]

CONCLUSION

We saw in this chapter Sheen's practical application of his understanding of Mary's mediation to its activity in the modern world. He saw Mary's mediation as a vibrant spiritual reality throughout the history of the Church and especially in these modern times. Sheen, once again, based his teaching on Mary's mediation in the modern world on the revelation of Sacred Scripture which always serves as the blueprint for understanding Mary's role in the mysti-

---

[29] Ibid., 273. These words of Sheen are not attributing to Mary a power over nature that she possesses independent from God's power. On the contrary, Mary is exercising the true power of her Queenship over all creation, which includes power over the forces of nature. Because Mary only does the will of the Father, she is not acting independently of God's will when she is associated with miracles like the "miracle of the sun" at Fatima; rather she is acting in accordance with it.

[30] WFL, 274-275.

cal prolongation of the Incarnation in the world. We particularly noted Sheen's application of Mary's role in Sacred Scripture as the Advent of Christ hastening His coming to each and every soul awaiting Him, consciously or unconsciously.

Sheen's teaching also provides unique insights into the universal scope of Mary's mediation in her role as Mother of the Church. By adopting St. Thomas's ecclesiology which treats the whole world as part of the Church either in potentiality or actuality, he states that Mary's mediation as Mother of the Church thus has universal influence. Sheen explained how this is evidenced within many major religions which acknowledge the existence of an ideal woman. As they come to learn of the role of Mary in salvation history, they find their ideal feminine principle fulfilled in her, the world's first love.

Sheen had a profound devotion to Mary and was not ignorant of the "signs of the times." Included among the millions of people around the world who shared profound experiences of Mary's powerful mediation in their own lives at places like Lourdes, Fatima, Knock, and La Sallette, Sheen had total confidence in the loving, maternal and powerful mediation of Mary in the modern world in restoring humanity back to Christ.

CONCLUSION

The genius of Fulton Sheen was always his extraordinary ability to explain seemingly complex theological truths with a logic and language comprehensible to all. This study has demonstrated that Sheen's teaching on the mystery of the mediation of the Blessed Virgin Mary is no exception. Generally speaking, this study provides significant contributions on two levels. First, it serves as the first in-depth study into the heart of the Venerable Servant of God's Mariology.

Second, this study provides a rich and positive response to the debate illustrated in Chapter II in which theologians called for further study of Mary's mediation in a renewed Trinitarian, Christological, pneumatological, ecclesiological and anthropological perspective with a biblical foundation. This study of Sheen's theology of Mary's mediation deserves serious consideration because it reverently approaches the subject according to the manner called for by the Second Vatican Council:

> Following the study of Sacred Scripture, the Holy Fathers, the doctors and liturgy of the Church, and under the guidance of the Church's magisterium, let [theologians] rightly illustrate the duties and privileges of the Blessed Virgin which always look to Christ, the source of all truth, sanctity and piety. Let them assiduously keep away from whatever, either by word or deed, could lead separated brethren or any other into error regarding the true doctrine of the Church. Let the faithful remember moreover that true devotion consists neither in sterile or transitory affection, nor in a certain vain credulity, but proceeds from true faith, by which we are led to know the excellence of the Mother

of God, and we are moved to a filial love toward our mother and to the imitation of her virtues (*LG*, 67).

Following this approach, Sheen presents a theology of Mary as the New Eve that provides penetrating insights into each of the dimensions of Mary's mediation. This approach explains Mary's mediation in terms of her relation to the New Adam as Spouse and Mother. Sheen's teaching, therefore, emphasizes the inherently *personal* nature of Mary's mediation. His teaching does not treat the relationships between the New Adam and the New Eve as mere figures of speech. On the contrary, Sheen understood them as being as real as the relationship between the first Adam and the first Eve, and the key to understanding how each mediates in relation to the other. Therefore, what we learn of Eve's mediation as spouse and mother in the natural order provides great insight into Mary's mediation as Spouse and Mother in the supernatural order of grace—a truth with great implications on the spiritual life of every Christian.

1. TRINITARIAN

Sheen's theology of Mary's mediation illustrates that in the order of Redemption, Mary can relate to the mystery of the Trinity in different ways. First, she is God's Immaculate Conception—His masterpiece—filled with the fullness of graces from the rich treasury of Redemption. As such, she is the highly favored daughter of the Father predestined by Him to become the fruitful Spouse of the Holy Spirit and, consequently, to become the Virgin Mother of the Son by consenting to God's plan of Redemption by means of the Incarnation. Therefore, while in every relationship with the Trinity, Mary, as a member of humanity, is infinitely less than God, her unique roles in salvation history as the Immaculate Conception, Spouse of the Spirit, the New Eve to the New Adam, and Mother of the *totus Christus* place Mary in a unique category all her own within God's plan of Redemption.

2. SOTERIOLOGICAL—CHRISTOLOGICAL

Sheen's presentation of the Christological perspective of Mary's mediation from a renewed soteriological approach is his greatest contribution. He masterfully does this by re-presenting the mystery of Mary's mediation as it relates to the Incarnation in her role as the New Eve. However, Sheen's approach to a proper understanding of Mary's mediation as the New Eve rightly flows from a proper understanding of the soteriological nature of Christ's mediation as the New Adam because "there is only one Mediator between God and man, the man Jesus Christ" (1 Tm. 2:5). Mary's mediation, therefore, is rightly called a mediation only to the extent it participates in the one mediation of Christ. It draws all of its power and significance from its relation to Christ's mediation; for just as the nature and purpose of Eve's mediation as spouse and mother in the order of creation derived from and was oriented to Adam, so also in the order of Redemption is the nature and purpose of the New Eve's mediation as Spouse and Mother derived from and oriented to the one mediation of the New Adam.

Based upon that logic, Sheen's teaching distinguishes between the two dimensions of Christ's mediation—ascending and descending—which correspond to the ascending and descending dimensions of Redemption, the latter being a consequence of the former. Likewise, if we are to explain properly Mary's mediation as a participation in the one mediation of Christ, then it, too, must be understood according to its ascending and descending dimensions.

Sheen then explains Christ's ascending mediation as it relates to His role as the New Adam. In order to be worthy of that title, the New Adam must have the power and the means to make a complete expiation for the sins of mankind and thus establish Himself as the Head of redeemed humanity. Therefore, the New Adam would have to be both God and man and both Priest and Victim because "without the shedding of blood there is no remission of sin" (Heb. 9:22). At the heart of Christ's ascending mediation, therefore, is the soteriological nature and purpose of the Incarnation to make God both Priest and Victim.

Secondly, Christ's ascending mediation via his priest-victimhood (which Sheen explained is at the heart of His *kenosis*) was the means by which the New Adam would redeem the image of man particularly disfigured by Adam's sin. Through His priest-victimhood Christ the New Adam "learned obedience through what he suffered" (Heb. 5:8) and ultimately offered His life for His Bride, the New Eve (Mary—the Church). Hence, the ascending mediation (priest-victimhood) of Christ particularly concerns the mediatory role of the New Adam as faithful Spouse of the New Eve. As the faithful Spouse of the New Eve, Christ worthily establishes His universal Headship over the new humanity and restores the image of man. Only after the New Adam accomplished all that the ascending mediation necessitated to redeem humanity did He make possible the communication of the fruits of Redemption which consisted in the remission of sin and the beginning of the restoration of humanity to communion with God, which He accomplished through His descending mediation.

In her role as the New Eve, Mary's ascending mediation consisted in her giving God the human nature through which He could become Priest and Victim as well as fulfill her role in Redemption as Spouse of the New Adam. As Spouse of the New Adam, Mary had the unique role of restoring the image of woman, which was shattered by Eve's disobedience and seduction of her spouse, Adam, to sin. This untying of "the knot of Eve's disobedience" necessitated the New Eve uniting herself to the priest-victimhood (ascending mediation) of her Spouse, the New Adam. Like the New Adam, the New Eve would learn obedience through suffering (victimhood) and thus accomplish the restoration of the image of woman as Christ did the image of man. Only through Mary's union with the priest-victimhood of Christ was she made a worthy and fitting Mother of the new humanity in the order of grace, which characterizes her descending mediation.

Sheen's teaching on the New Eve's [Mary's] participation as spouse in the priest-victimhood (ascending mediation) of the New Adam [Christ] is significant in that it essentially explains the mystery of Mary's role as "Coredemptrix" in the language of Mary's role as Mediatrix. Moreover, he presents this mystery according to its biblical foundations, thus giving it a more universal appeal to all Christians. Therefore, this insightful perspective of Sheen's theology of Mary's mediation provides a helpful commentary on Articles 55-59 of *Lumen Gentium* which summarize this role of Mary.

Since the Second Vatican Council, Mary's mediation has been identified primarily with her spiritual maternity. This, indeed, is an important emphasis for our times as it explains how Mary's mediation directly relates to the spiritual life of the Church. Sheen's teaching, however, illustrates that Mary's spiritual maternity represents only half of the picture of Mary's mediation. Sheen's theology of Mary's mediation rediscovers the most important and often ignored theological aspect of Mary's mediation which made her spiritual maternity possible, namely Mary's mediation as Spouse of the New Adam in God's plan of Redemption. His theology thus presents the complete picture of Mary's mediation.

3. ECCLESIOLOGICAL

Another significant contribution of Sheen's theology of Mary's mediation is his presentation of Mary's descending mediation from a renewed ecclesiological perspective which gives new insights into what it means to say that Mary is the Mother of Christ. Sheen presents ecclesiology as an extension of Christology, in which the Church is the mystical prolongation of the Incarnation. His teaching therefore explains that all that we learn about Mary's mediation as it relates to the Incarnation (the historical life of Christ) applies to its mystical prolongation in His Mystical Body, the Church (the mystical life of Christ). In this light, the Church is seen as the Mystical Christ which recapitulates, or re-lives, the mysteries of the Incarnation beginning with the spiritual rebirth of those baptized into the death of Christ. In other words, the mystery of the Incarnation as it began at the Annunciation and culminated at Calvary is relived in the souls of Christians, individually, and in the Church, corporately. This is why Sheen's teaching focuses on a proper understanding of Mary's role in the mystery of the Incarnation as revealed in Sacred Scripture. It provides the blueprint for her role in the mystery of the mystical prolongation of the Incarnation in the life of the Church.

This renewed approach to the classical recapitulation theology of St. Irenaeus presents an interior logic which is summarized by the saying, "What applies to the Head applies to the Body." In other words, the mystery of the New Adam and the New Eve *continues* as they continue their cooperation in the application of the fruits of Redemption to all those incorporated into Christ's Mystical Body. Mary, therefore, mediates as Spouse of the Holy Spirit with Whom and by Whom she continues her motherhood of Christ in the order of grace, thus mystically prolonging the Incarnation in the world.

Another way Sheen's teaching helps us understand this mystery is by explaining the Church according to Augustine's theology of the *totus Christus* which presents the complete Christ as the organic unity between Christ the Head and His Mystical Body. In other words, there is only one Christ—composed of the historical Christ and the mystical Christ, His Church. Therefore, as Mary mediated in relation to Christ the Head, so will she mediate in relation to His Mystical Body; for there is only one Christ and only one Mother of Christ.

4. PNEUMATOLOGICAL

Sheen's theology of Mary's mediation shows that the Holy Spirit plays an inseparable role in Mary's ascending and descending mediation because both mediations are made possible only by Mary's spousal union with the Holy Spirit. This mystical union and cooperative mediation brought about the means of Redemption, the Incarnation—the Holy Spirit mediating the Divine nature and Mary mediating the human nature of Christ. It also allowed for Mary's subsequent active participation in the ascending mediation (priest-victimhood) of Christ. Only by the power and mediation of the Holy Spirit—by Whom Mary was redeemed in advance and completely filled with redemptive grace at the moment of her Immaculate Conception—was Mary able to participate in Christ's priest-victimhood.

Since Sheen's theology of Christ's descending mediation is explained in terms of the mystical prolongation of the Incarnation in the Church, he explains that what is true concerning Mary's relationship with the Holy Spirit in relation to the Incarnation is true also in relation to its mystical prolongation. Thus, Mary's descending mediation consists in her continued fruitfulness by her spousal union with the Holy Spirit, by Whose power Mary is able bear and mother the mystical life of Christ in the souls of the baptized.

5. ANTHROPOLOGICAL

Sheen's presentation of Mary's mediation according to her role as the New Eve in the plan of Redemption offers unique insights into the anthropological dimension of Mary's mediation. Sheen's teaching explains how the New Eve, Mary, had a special role in untying the "knot of Eve's disobedience" as it specifically concerned the restoration of the image of woman which was shattered by the sin of Eve, who failed in her role as spouse of Adam. It is interesting to note, therefore, that Eve was termed a "cruel Mediatrix" because of her failure in her *spousal* role with Adam. The consequences of that sin affected Eve's motherhood, which would mediate the Original Sin transmitted by Adam to all humanity.

Mary's mediatory role as the New Eve, therefore, would first be according to her role as spouse by which Mary united herself to the priest-victimhood of Christ, the New Adam. By this union with the ascending mediation of Christ from Nazareth to Calvary, Mary accomplished her part in the Redemption which fittingly necessitated a New Eve, whose obedience and spousal fidelity to the New Adam would restore the image of woman shattered by Eve's disobedience. The consequences of her faithful mediation as Spouse of the New Adam would flow into her descending mediation as spiritual mother of the new humanity, who would mediate the Divine life of Christ in the order of grace.

ECUMENICAL AND MISSIOLOGICAL IMPLICATIONS OF SHEEN'S TEACHING

Sheen was the first to acknowledge that a renewed approach to Mary's mediation within the mystery of the Incarnation and the *totus Christus* has "tremendous implications"[1] for missiology and ecumenism. His teaching reminds us that there is only one Church because there is only one Body and because Christ has only one Spouse. Sheen reinforces this in his teaching that Mary, representing the Church, is the New Eve who is espoused to Christ, the New Adam.

Therefore, Sheen's teaching strongly emphasizes that at the heart of understanding the Church is her oneness with Christ the Head. Consequently, the Head and Body have the same mother, Mary. This is at the heart of Sheen's teaching on the mystery of the Incarnation which expresses the unity of Christ and His Mystical Body. We learn from Sheen's teaching, therefore, that there can be no true ecumenism that diminishes or neglects Mary's inseparable role in the Incarnation.

One issue which greatly divides Christians is a proper understanding of the nature of sanctifying grace. Sheen's teaching affirms that a proper understanding will come about only when it sees Mary's relation to grace, which is at the heart of her mediation. If Christians come to understand that sanctifying grace is the life of Christ mystically prolonged in their souls, then they will see how Mary's role, too, is *prolonged* as the Mother of Christ in their lives of sanctifying grace, for Mary is Mother of the *whole* Christ, Head and Body. This is why Sheen believed the title "Mother of the Church" given by Paul VI was an extremely important event in the history of the Church:

> ...The bishops of the Second Vatican Council] saw the need of this title today—the Mother of the Church. They recalled that that was what she [Mary] was at the Cross, the Church. Then John was the beginning of it. And finally at Pentecost she's in the midst of the Apostles abiding in

---

[1] *MBC*, 224.

prayer. And now Mary is just as it were identified and dissolved almost with the Church itself. And, hence, whenever you have in the world a decline of devotion to Our Lady you also have a decline of love of the Church. That is why in order to restore the [sic] love of the Church we will have to restore love of Our Lady.[2]

Sheen reinforces this last point when he says: "It is impossible to love Christ adequately without also loving the Mother who gave Him to us. Those who begin by ignoring her soon end by ignoring Him, for the two are inseparable in the great drama of redemption."[3] That is why the Second Vatican Council reminds us that true love of Our Lady must proceed from true faith about Our Lady (cf. *LG,* 67). True Christian unity, therefore, will necessarily involve Christians understanding Mary's mediation as it relates to the mystery of the *totus Christus.* Sheen's ecclesiology shows that Mary as our loving Mother will have an active role in bringing about this unity.

Sheen applied his teaching on the inseparability of Christ and Mary in the mystery of the Incarnation to Mary's role in holding the truths of Christianity together. Using the analogy of a kite, he writes:

Mary holds all the great Truths of Christianity together, as a piece of wood holds a kite. Children wrap the string of a kite around a stick and release the string as the kite climbs to the heavens. Mary is like that piece of wood. Around her we wrap all the precious strings of the great Truths of our holy Faith—for example, the Incarnation, the Eucharist, the Church. No matter how far we get above the earth, as the kite may be, we always have need of Mary to hold the doctrines of the Creed together. If we threw away the stick, we would no longer have the kite; if we threw away Mary, we would never have Our Lord. He would be lost in the

[2] Sheen, "Our Blessed Mother" (from a series of retreat lectures given at Holy Trinity Seminary, Irving, Texas, 1972, recorded by and in the possession of Mr. Daniel B. Steffen of Plano, Texas), compact disc.
[3] *MBC,* 328.

Heavens, like our runaway kite, and that would be terrible, indeed, for us on earth.[4]

Lastly, in light of Sheen's Marian ecclesiology, there are also missiological contributions which flow from Sheen's teaching on Mary's mediation. Since Sheen adopts St. Thomas's presentation of the Church as relating to everyone in the world either potentially or actually, Mary's maternal mediation will play a critical role in bringing all humanity to her Son as the universal mother of humanity.

In closing, Sheen taught that Mary is always the Advent of Christ. It is the hope of this writer that this in-depth study into the heart of Sheen's Mariology will hasten the advent of similar studies into his Christology and Ecclesiology and bring his theological contributions to the forefront of the Church's reflection as this study hopefully will do concerning his theology of Mary's mediation. Thus, having thoroughly presented Sheen's profound insights into the theology of Mary's mediation in the mystery of Christ, we give the final words to this wise Servant of God and of Mary, "loyal son of the Church" and prophet for our times, who understood how important it is that we never dissolve the link between Mary and her Son, especially in our difficult times when Mary is most active in mediating to a world surrounded by darkness the Light of her Son:

> The key to understanding Mary is this: We do not start with Mary. We start with Christ, the Son of the Living God! The less we think of Him, the less we think of her; the more we think of Him, the more we think of her; the more we adore His Divinity, the more we venerate her Motherhood; the less we adore His Divinity, the less reason we have for respecting her....
>
> ...There is never any danger that men will think too much of Mary; the danger is that they will think too little of Christ. Coldness toward Mary is a consequence of indifference to Christ....

---

[4] *WFL*, 75-76.

...God, Who made the sun, also made the moon. The moon does not take away from the brilliance of the sun. The moon would be only a burnt-out cinder floating in the immensity of space were it not for the sun. All its light is reflected from the sun. The Blessed Mother reflects her Divine Son; without Him, she is nothing. With Him, she is the Mother of Men. On dark nights we are grateful for the moon; when we see it shining, we know there must be a sun. So in this dark night of the world when men turn their backs on Him Who is the Light of the World, we look to Mary to guide their feet while we await the sunrise.[5]

[5] *WFL*, 63, 70, 77.

APPENDIX

"STATUS QUAESTIONIS" OF THE CHURCH'S TEACHING ON MARY'S MEDIATION

CURRENT THEOLOGICAL DEBATE ON MARY'S MEDIATION

It would be very difficult to appreciate fully the theological insights and contributions of Fulton Sheen concerning Mary's universal, maternal mediation without placing it within its proper historical and theological context. Presently, there is no single subject of Mariology which generates more debate than the proper understanding of Mary as Mediatrix and how this relates to her role in Redemption. The Christological, soteriological, ecclesiological, pneumatological and ecumenical ramifications which are connected to this notion are critical. It is therefore important that we place this study within the context of the present theological debate surrounding Mary's mediation, which developed over the question of whether Mary's mediation should be dogmatically defined—a question that has its roots in the first half of the twentieth century.

The subject of Mary's mediation was a popular theological topic leading up to Vatican II, with, according to Michael O'Carroll, C.S.Sp., 313 bishops requesting that a dogma be defined concerning Mary as "Mediatrix of All Graces."[6] The strong inclination of

---

[6] Cf. Michael O'Carroll, C.S.Sp., "Mediation, Mary Mediatress," in *Theotokos: A Theological Encyclopedia of the Blessed Virgin Mary* (Wilmington: Michael Glazier, 1982), 242 (hereafter cited as *Theotokos*).

these bishops toward a dogmatic definition had its origins in the dogmatic movement initiated by Désirée Cardinal Mercier (1851-1926), which began toward the end of the pontificate of Pope Benedict XV (1914-1922) and continued until the Second Vatican Council.[1] While Mercier's efforts did not achieve their ultimate goal of a dogmatic definition of Mary's universal mediation, he was able to obtain a liturgical feast of Mary under the title "Mediatrix of All Graces." The entrance of this doctrine into the liturgical *lex orandi* of the Church remains the weightiest authority to date of the Church's belief in Mary's universal mediation of graces—an authority that should not be ignored or minimized.[2] The Collect

---

[1] Cf. Ibid., 242.

[2] The doctrine of Mary as Mediatrix of all graces increased in popularity during the pontificate of Benedict XV (1914-1922), so much that at the end of his pontificate, there was a movement led by Désiré Cardinal Mercier (1851-1926) which sought a dogmatic definition of Mary as the "intercessory Mediatress of all graces" (*"médiatrice universelle d'intercession"*) (Manfred Hauke, *Mary, "Mediatress of Grace": Mary's Universal Mediation of Grace in the Theological and Pastoral Works of Cardinal Mercier* [New Bedford, MA: Academy of the Immaculate, 2004], 8 [hereafter cited as *Mediatress of Grace*]). This title included Mary's distribution of all graces. Benedict XV, however, did not take a position on the request. A pious and erudite study into this movement led by Cardinal Mercier was recently conducted by Father Manfred Hauke, who illuminates a fascinating history surrounding this subject. Currently, his study represents the only of its kind on Cardinal Mercier and the "worldwide movement for a dogmatic definition" which he initiated and thus provides penetrating insight into this subject (cf. Manfred Hauke, *Mediatress of Grace*, 56).

The neutral position of Benedict XV toward a new Marian dogma remained with his successors until Pope Pius XII when the emphasis turned to defining solemnly Mary's Assumption. However, in 1921 (only two years after Fulton Sheen's ordination to the priesthood) Cardinal Mercier did succeed in obtaining from the Sacred Congregation of Rites a liturgical feast of "Mary, Mediatrix of All Graces" (Cf. John D. Miller, *Marian Mediation: Is It True to Say that Mary Is Coredemptrix, Mediatrix of All Graces and Advocate?* [New Bedford, MA: Academy of the Immaculate, 2004], 51). The liturgical feast was originally celebrated on the 31st of May, which marked the end of the Marian month and served as the bridge to the month of June consecrated to the Most Sacred Heart of Jesus. Hauke states, "This detail shows the already noticed close bond between Sacred Heart devotion and veneration of Mary as Mediatress of all graces" (Manfred Hauke, *Mediatress of Grace*, 56).

of the Mass of "The Blessed Virgin Mary, Mediatrix of All Graces" highlights this truth about Mary: "Lord Jesus Christ, our mediator before the Father, you have made the most blessed Virgin, your Mother and ours, a mediator before you. May everyone who comes to you seeking benefits rejoice at receiving all through her: You who live and reign."[3]

The momentum of the movement carried right into Vatican II, despite Pius XII's solemn proclamation of the dogma of Mary's

---

The readings selected for the feast are rich in theological content regarding Mary's universal mediation. The original Latin text can be found in the *Missale Romanum 4th Editio Juxta Typicam Vaticanam* (New York: Benziger Brothers, Inc., 1942), page 161. The Gradual attributes to Mary the following passage taken from *Ecclesiasticus* 24:25, "In me is all grace of the way and of the truth, in me is all hope of life and of virtue." After Lent, the following is said in place of the *Alleluia*, taken from chapter 22 of the Book of Revelation: *I am the root and the offspring of David, the bright morning star. The Spirit and the Bride say, "Come." And let him who hears say, "Come." And let him who is thirsty come, let him who desires take the water of life without price.*

The most important text is the Gospel reading, which is taken from the nineteenth chapter of St. John, verses 25-27:

Standing by the cross of Jesus were his mother, and his mother's sister, Mary the wife of Clopas, and Mary Magdalene. When Jesus saw his mother, and the disciple whom he loved standing near, he said, "Woman, behold your son!" Then he said to the disciple, "Behold your mother!" And from that hour the disciple took her to his own home.

This passage, central also in Sheen's teaching on Mary's mediation, thus represents the primary biblical text which from the Church draws its understanding and teaching of Mary's universal mediation. Another text which was considered, but not selected for the Gospel, was the wedding feast at Cana in John 2. Cardinal Mercier insisted, however, that Mary at the foot of the Cross served as a better biblical foundation for Mary's universal mediation (Manfred Hauke, *Mediatress of Grace*, 56).

[3] *Domine, Jesu, Christe, noster apud Patrem mediator, qui beatissimam Virginem matrem tuam, matrem quoque nostram et apud te Mediatricem constituere dignatus es: concede propitious; ut quisquis ad te beneficia petiturus accesserit, cuncta se per eam impetrasse laetetur: Qui vivis et regnas cum eodem Deo Patre (Missale Romanum 4th Editio Juxta Typicam Vaticanam* [New York: Benziger Brothers, Inc., 1942], 160). The English translation of the same Latin text is provided by the International Committee on English in the Liturgy, Inc., as found in *The Roman Missal in Latin and English For Sunday, Feast, Ferial and Votive Masses* (Collegeville, MN: The Liturgical Press, 1968), page 1098.

Assumption. Accompanying that momentum, however, was a growing debate over the pre-conciliar theological expression of Mary's mediation as well as the suitability of such a doctrine for a dogmatic definition. John XXIII, however, resolved that the Council would not make any dogmatic definitions. After a lively history revolving around the theology and textual development of the Council's treatise on Mary, the final text, *Lumen Gentium* VIII, satisfactorily adhered to and expressed the Church's theological tradition on Mary's mediation, while giving a renewed emphasis on its particularly maternal nature. This satisfaction was expressed by the virtually unanimous vote in favor of the final text which is now *Lumen Gentium* VIII.

During the first two decades following the Second Vatican Council, the subject of Marian mediation was not given the significant attention it received during the first half of the twentieth century. It was not until Pope St. John Paul II's 1987 encyclical *Redemptoris Mater* that a reinvigorated interest surfaced on the subject of Mary's mediation. In fact, John Paul II's pontificate was characterized by significant teaching on Mary's mediatory role in salvation history as seen in his lengthy catechesis on Mary during his general audience addresses from 25 October 1995 to 9 April 1997. That topic, however, is beyond the scope of this book, but there are striking similarities in the doctrine of Mary's mediation which Fulton Sheen shares with John Paul II that will be referenced throughout this study, primarily in the footnotes.

At present, there is no Mariological topic which draws as much attention and debate as the doctrine of Mary's mediation and its relationship with Jesus Christ and His unique mediation. During the last decade, this debate came to a head because of the efforts of the *Vox Populi Mariae Mediatrici* movement, which was founded to coordinate efforts among the Catholic hierarchy and lay faithful to petition the Holy Father to define dogmatically "the Marian roles of Coredemptrix, Mediatrix of all grace, and Advocate for the people of God."[4]

---

[4] Mark I. Miravalle, ed., *Mary Coredemptrix, Mediatrix, Advocate: Theological Foundations: Towards a Papal Definition?* (Santa Barbara, CA: Queenship

The efforts of *Vox Populi Mariae Mediatrici* have obtained the support of millions of Catholics around the world. *Vox Populi Mariae Mediatrici* reports to have "about seven million petitions from over 150 countries...along with the endorsements of 550 bishops and over 40 cardinals."[5] Dr. Mark Miravalle, President of *Vox Populi Mariae Mediatrici*, notes that this effort "constitutes the largest petition drive per annum in the history of the Church."[6] Among *Vox Populi Mariae Mediatrici*'s earliest supporters was Blessed Mother Teresa who wrote a brief letter to Dr. Miravalle on 14 August 1993, expressing her thoughts about the proposed titles and the significance of the dogma:

Mary is our Co-redemptrix with Jesus. She gave Jesus his body and suffered with him at the foot of the Cross.

Mary is the Mediatrix of all grace. She gave Jesus to us, and as our Mother she obtains for us all his graces.

Mary is our Advocate who prays to Jesus for us. It is only through the Heart of Mary that we come to the Eucharistic Heart of Jesus.

The papal definition of Mary as Co-redemptrix, Mediatrix, and Advocate will bring great graces to the Church.

All for Jesus through Mary.

God bless you,

M. Teresa, M.C.[7]

Publishing, 1995), xxiii.

[5] Mark I. Miravalle, "Why Now Is the Time For a Dogma of Mary Co-redemptrix," interview by ZENIT (31 October 2002, accessed 10 June 2006); available from http://www.voxpopuli.org/zenit.php; Internet.

[6] Ibid.

[7] Mother Teresa of Calcutta, "Letter of Endorsement for the Papal Definition of Mary Co-redemptrix, Mediatrix, Advocate" (14 August 1993), quoted in Mark I. Miravalle, "In Continued Dialogue with Czestochowa," (address presented at the International Symposium on Marian coredemption "*Maria Mater Unitatis*," Downside Abbey, Stratton-on-the-Fosse, England, 24 August 2002, accessed 10 June 2006); available from http://www.voxpopuli.org/cze-stochowa.pdf; Internet.

The final line of Mother Teresa's letter is worth noting because she implies a causal connection between a papal proclamation defining Mary's mediatory role in salvation history and its greater exercise and manifestation in the Church. Pope St. Pius X implied a similar connection in 1904 in his Encyclical Letter *Ad diem illum* on the 50th anniversary of the proclamation of the dogma of the Immaculate Conception. Pius X stated in the opening of this encyclical that the pronouncement of the dogma of the Immaculate Conception brought with it a time of special graces to the Church through the intercession of Mary, many of which he believed were overlooked. He wrote:

> ...No sooner had Pius IX proclaimed as a dogma of Catholic faith the exemption of Mary from the original stain, than the Virgin herself began in Lourdes those wonderful manifestations, followed by the vast and magnificent movements which have produced those two temples dedicated to the Immaculate Mother, where the prodigies which still continue to take place through her intercession furnish splendid arguments against the incredulity of our days.

> Witnesses, then, as we are of all these great benefits which God has granted through the benign influence of the Virgin in those fifty years now about to be completed, why should we not believe that our salvation is nearer than we thought; all the more since we know from experience that, in the dispensation of Divine Providence, when evils reach their limit, deliverance is not far distant. "Her time is near at hand, and her days shall not be prolonged. For the Lord will have mercy on Jacob and will choose one out of Israel" (*Isaias* xiv., 1).[8]

---

[8] "Ad haec, vix fere Pius Mariam ab origine labis nesciam fide catholica credendam indixerat, cum in oppido Lourdes mira ab ipsa Virgine ostenta fieri coepta: exinde, molitione ingenti et opere magnifico Deiparae Immaculatae excitatae aedes; ad quas, quae quotidie, divina exorante Matre, patrantur prodigia, illustria sunt argumenta ad praesentium hominum incredibilitataem profligandam.

Vox Populi Mariae Mediatrici was met with stiff opposition during the meeting of The 12th International Mariological Congress at Czestochowa in 1996. A group of Catholic theologians, later called "The Theological Commission of the Pontifical Marian Academy," gathered to discuss whether such a dogmatic definition was opportune. The Czestochowa Commission was unanimously against the proposed dogmatic definition. Its conclusion was published in the Italian 4 June 1997 *L'Osservatore Romano* and other language editions, including English. The conclusion was printed under the title, "Declaration of the Theological Commission of the Pontifical Marian Academy." In its Declaration, the Czestochowa Commission not only objected to the suitability of the proposed Marian dogma, but also raised theological objections to the proposed titles themselves. Moreover, the Czestochowa Commission implicitly accused the *Vox Populi Mariae Mediatrici* movement of acting contrary to the theological direction taken by the Second Vatican Council. *Vox Populi Mariae Mediatrici* disagreed with the Czestochowa Commission, stating that the titles of its proposed dogma are consistent with the theology of Vatican II. Their response, written by Dr. Miravalle, was published and the theological debate intensified.

Therefore, the *status quaestionis* concerning the Church's teaching on Mary's mediation is best demonstrated by an examination of the ongoing debate between *Vox Populi Mariae Mediatrici* and its supporters and those who support the 1997 Declaration of The Theological Commission of the Pontifical Marian Academy. The debate revolves around one critical question: What was the theological direction of Mariology set by Vatican II concerning Mary's

---

"Tot igitur tantorumque beneficiorum testes, quae, Virgine benigne implorante, contulit Deus quinquagenis annis mox elabendis; quidni speremus *propiorem esse salutem nostram quam cum credimus?* eo vel magis, quod divinae Providentiae hoc esse experiendo novimus ut extrema malorum a liberatione non admodum dissocientur. *Prope est ut veniat tempus eius, et dies eius non elongabuntur. Miserebitur enim Dominus Iacob, et eliget adhuc de Israel* (Isai. XIV, 1)." (*ASS* [1903-1904], 450; English trans. from http://www.vatican.va/holy_father/pius_x/encyclicals/documents/hf_p-x_enc_02021904_ad-diem-illum-laetissimum_en.html [accessed 10 July 2007]; Internet).

role in salvation history? The answer to this question necessitates a separate study.[9]

Our analysis will focus on the objections presented by the Declaration of the Czestochowa Commission in 1997 and the ensuing debate until its dissipation at the end of 2002 when both parties had basically exhausted their opposing arguments. The two sides of the debate are represented by the supporters of the negative decision of the 1997 Declaration and the supporters of the theological positions of the *Vox Populi Mariae Mediatrici* movement. We will begin by presenting the full text of the 1997 Declaration followed by an examination of its authority, and then provide a summary of its main points of objection to the proposed Marian dogma by *Vox Populi Mariae Mediatrici*. We will then present each objection with the arguments of those who support the theological position of the Czestochowa Commission juxtaposed by the counterarguments.

Those who expressed support of the negative decision of the 1997 Declaration include the unsigned commentary[10] appended to the Declaration in the 4 June 1997 *L'Osservatore Romano*; Father Salvatore M. Perrella, O.S.M., of the Pontifical Faculty Marianum; Canon René Laurentin, member of the Pontifical Marian Academy and member of the Theological Commission of the Pontifical International Marian Academy at Czestochowa in 1997; the negative position on the proposed dogma of the Pontifical Faculty Marianum in 1999; Father Stefano de Fiores, S.M.M., faculty member of the Pontifical Faculty Marianum; and Father Angelo Amato, S.D.B., now Secretary to the Congregation for the Doctrine of the Faith.

The arguments objecting to the position of the 1997 Declaration are represented by Mark Miravalle, S.T.D., and Monsignor Arthur Calkins, Ph.D., who is a member of the Pontifical Marian Academy and the Pontifical Roman Theological Academy.

---

[9] The four-volume study of Vatican II, *History of Vatican II*, edited by Joseph A. Komonchak (Maryknoll, NY: Orbis Books, 1995–2000), provides an excellent historical context for this subject.

[10] When unsigned articles in *L'Osservatore Romano* are marked with three asterisks, the article is considered more authoritative than usual. This particular commentary was neither signed nor starred.

DECLARATION OF THE THEOLOGICAL COMMISSION OF THE PONTIFICAL MARIAN ACADEMY

Throughout this chapter we will refer to the Czestochowa Commission's Declaration as "the Declaration." Due to the brevity of the Declaration and its importance as the central point of controversy surrounding the debate which followed, its content (with exception to the list of members) is presented here in full for reference throughout this chapter:

The 12th International Mariological Congress, held at Czestochowa (Poland) in August 1996, was asked by the Holy See to study the possibility and the opportuneness of a definition of the Marian titles of Mediatrix, Coredemptrix and Advocate, as is being requested of the Holy See by certain circles. A commission was established, composed of 15 theologians chosen for their specific preparation in this area, so that together they could discuss and analyze the question through mature reflection. In addition to their theological competence, care was also taken to ensure the greatest possible geographical diversity among the members, so that any possible consensus would become especially significant. It was also sought to enrich the study group by adding, as external members, some non-Catholic theologians who were present at the Congress. The commission arrived at a twofold conclusion.

1. The titles, as proposed, are ambiguous, as they can be understood in very different ways. Furthermore, the theological direction taken by the Second Vatican Council, which did not wish to define any of these titles, should not be abandoned. The Second Vatican Council did not use the title "Coredemptrix," and uses "Mediatrix" and "Advocate" in a very moderate way (cf. *Lumen Gentium* 62). In fact, from the time of Pope Pius XII, the term "Coredemptrix" has not been used by the papal Magisterium in its significant documents. There is evidence that Pope Pius XII himself intentionally avoided using it. With respect to the

title "Mediatrix", the history of the question should not be forgotten: in the first decades of this century the Holy See entrusted the study of the possibility of its definition to three different commissions, the result of which was that the Holy See decided to set the question aside.[11]

---

[11] This statement by the Commission is misleading as it insinuates that Pius XII "set the question aside" because he received negative responses from the three commissions. A recent scholarly study by Manfred Hauke on the history of Cardinal Mercier and the dogmatic movement he initiated reveals a different picture.

Following the brief papacy of Benedict XV, who issued the liturgical feast day of the "Blessed Virgin Mary, Mediatrix of All Graces" in 1921, Pius XI was committed to teaching on the Blessed Virgin's mediation. During his pontificate Cardinal Mercier's dogmatic movement grew in momentum. Pius XI, therefore, in 1922 set up three commissions—Belgian, Spanish, and Roman—to investigate the possibility of a dogma on Mary's universal mediation (cf. "Mediation, Mary Mediatress," *Theotokos*, 242). In fact, according to Manfred Hauke, on the day of his election to the papacy, Pius XI spoke with Cardinal Mercier about the proposals for a solemn definition of Mary's universal mediation (cf. Manfred Hauke, *Mediatress of Grace*, 75).

Each of the commissions examined the dogmatic question of Mary's universal mediation from three theological perspectives: biblical foundations, the witness of Tradition, and speculative presentation. Of particular significance are the conclusions from the Belgian commission, which was comprised of Camille van Crombruggle (biblical foundations), Joseph Lebon (witness of Tradition), and Benoît Henri Merkelback, O.P. (speculative presentation). The results of their study reaffirmed the unique mediation of Christ while allowing for secondary and subordinate mediators (Merkelback rooted his position in that of St. Thomas Aquinas [*ST*, III, q. 26, a.1]); that Mary's mediation has strong biblical foundations with the Annunciation and Incarnation, the Visitation, the wedding feast at Cana, and Mary at the foot of the Cross serving as the primary texts. Lastly, the study affirmed that Mary's universal mediation was commonly accepted by the Tradition of the Church (Ibid., 80-84).

All three members of the Belgian commission concluded their report, which was submitted in 1923, recommending that Mary's mediation be solemnly defined. They concluded: "It is certain that Mary not only personally cooperated in the redemption for the forgiveness of sins and the acquisition of the means of sanctification; not only really intercedes for all and is in the distribution of graces a very powerful Mediatress – which without doubt is a matter of faith (*quae extra dubium ad fidem pertinent*) – *but also in this way is active in the bestowal of all assistance*" (Ibid., 85). The conclusion of the Spanish report agreed with that of the Belgian commission (Ibid, 86-87).

2. Even if the titles were assigned a content which could

The difficulty with this study is knowing exactly the position of the Roman commission, whose work took place between 1924-1925. Scholarly research has not been able to assess with certainty who comprised the membership of the Roman commission. Hauke reported that a directive from Pius XI stated that the members of the commission were to be "professors of theology taken from the then four existing theological faculties in Rome: the Gregorian University, the Lateran Major Seminary, the Propaganda Fide (today, the Urbaniana) and the Angelicum;" and that "care [was] to be taken not to fill the commission exclusively with known defenders of the thesis" (Ibid., 98).

From an examination of the correspondence of Cardinal Mercier, Hauke has strong evidence to suggest that the representative from the Angelicum was none other than the great Dominican theologian, Réginald Garrigou-Lagrange, who Hauke asserts "exercised a substantive influence in the counsels of the Roman Commission and on the position of Pius XI" concerning Mary's mediation (cf. Ibid., 98-103). We will give due attention to his observations on this subject shortly when we examine more closely the theological problems the commissions attempted to resolve.

To date, the conclusions of the Roman commission have yet to be published, making it impossible to know with certainty whether or not they favored a dogmatic definition of Mary's mediation. Hauke's research in his study of Cardinal Mercier revealed that there is evidence to support Rome's favorable position on the matter. His primary source comes from a statement made in 1927 by one of the redactors of the Spanish commission's report, José Maria Bover, at a Spanish Mariological Congress in Covadonga. Bover claimed that all three papal commissions were in agreement that Mary's mediation includes her cooperation both in the acquisition of graces and in their distribution:

The Spanish Commission of theologians established by His Holiness treated the universal mediation under all its aspects and in so doing ascribed a preeminent importance to its first moment [i.e., to her cooperation in the acquisition of grace]. When I informed His Eminence, Cardinal Mercier, of our criterion, he replied that our approach was in essentials in agreement with that of the Belgian Commission. And according to what Fr. Garrigou-Lagrange wrote me, there can be no doubt, but that this is also the position of the Roman Commission (Ibid., 87).

Pope Pius XI never proclaimed the dogma of Mary's universal mediation and his successor, Pope Pius XII inherited the unanswered *votum* of Cardinal Mercier and the dogmatic movement. In 1950, at the midpoint of his pontificate, the first international Mariological Congress, held in Rome, approved the *votum* of Pius XI's committee regarding the desire of the faithful for a dogmatic definition of Mary's universal mediation. This *votum* was subsequently submitted to Pius XII and read as follows:

Since the principal, personal attributes of the Blessed Virgin Mary, Divine Maternity, Perpetual Virginity, Immaculate Conception, bodily Assumption, have been already dogmatically defined, it is the wish of the faithful that it should also be dogmatically defined that the Blessed Virgin Mary was intimately associated with Christ the Saviour in effecting human salvation, and, accordingly, she is a true collaborator in the work of redemption, spiritual Mother of all men, intercessor and dispenser of all graces, *in a word universal Mediatrix of God and men.*

Cum personalia B. V. Mariae attributa praecipua, divina maternitas, perpetua virginitas, immaculata conceptio, corporalis assumptio, sint iam dogmatice definita, restat in fidelium votis, ut dogmatice quoque definiatur: B. V. Mariam Christo Servatori in operanda humana salute esse intime sociatam, ideoque veram existere in redemptionis opere cooperatricem, spiritualem hominum matrem, omnium gratiarum deprecatricem et administram, uno verbo, universalem Dei hominumque mediatricem [Alma Socia Christi: Acta Congressus Mariologici-Mariani Romae Anno Sancto MCML Celebrati, vol. 1 (Roma: Academia Mariana, 1951), 234 (emphasis mine)].

This *votum* is an accurate summary of what is meant by "Mediatrix of all graces" because it illustrates the three elements comprised in the single office—namely, 1) Mary's direct cooperation in Christ's work of Redemption making her spiritual Mother of all mankind; 2) Mary's intercession to obtain every grace; and 3) Mary's role as the dispensatrix of these graces.

Pope Pius XII eventually chose not to define dogmatically Mary's universal mediation. Instead, he turned his attention to what became the dogma of Mary's Assumption into heaven, which he proclaimed on 1 November 1950. This leads to the question: "Why did the *votum* die?"

Unfortunately, at this time, there does not seem to be a published response to this question, since the findings of the Roman Commission remain in the secret archives of the Holy See. There is the assertion of Laurentin that the reason the *votum* died was because of unanswered objections to theological problems posed by the Roman Commission to which Pius XI yielded (cf. Manfred Hauke, *Mediatress of Grace,* 112-113). Hauke, convinced of Laurentin's personal opposition and efforts to hinder a new dogma defining Mary's universal mediation, is suspicious of his claim because they are from "unidentified oral sources" (cf. Ibid., 112-113). In Hauke's work on Mercier he listed what Laurentin wrote were the objections of the Roman Commission as follows:

The objections of the Roman Commission were judged to be unanswerable. The Pope, who was personally prefect of this Dicasterium [the Holy Office], yielded in the face of considerations, which according to the hints entrusted to me were the following:

– on the one hand Mary cannot formally be Mediatress of the graces of the Old Testament, which preceded her existence;

– on the other hand she cannot be the Mediatress of sanctifying grace, which entails an *immediate* bestowal of divine life.

On these grounds Pius XII, an enthusiastic devotee of Mary, definitely dropped the project and turned his efforts to honor Mary with the new definition of the Assumption (Ibid., 113).

In light of our examination of Pius XII's teaching on Mary's mediation, especially his vigorous endorsement of St. Bernard's maxim, his references to Mary as the "generous and wise treasurer of God's favors [*"la munifica e sapiente tesoriera dei divini favori"*] (Bertetto, *Il Magistero Mariano di Pio XII*, no. 47 [*OL* #365])," and "Mediatrix and Dispenser of graces" [*"Maria è mediatrice e distributrice di grazie"*] (Pius XII, Radio Message to Italian Catholic Action (8 December 1953), *AAS* 45 (1953), 850-851; *OL* #624-625), it seems difficult to hold that Pius XII changed his position on the teaching. Hauke is also doubtful that Laurentin accurately represents the conclusions of such a scholarly commission. He responds:

> Had the Commission, for example, held the first argument "unanswerable", then it would also have had to regard the universal mediation of Christ as questionable. The mediation of Christ is as man, as the First Letter to Timothy affirms (1 Tim 2, 5 f.) and Thomas Aquinas explains [*ST*, III, q. 26, a. 2]. As man Jesus Christ no more existed in the Old Testament than did the All Holy Virgin Mary. The mediation of all graces by Jesus Christ as man in that period must consist in an orientation to the Redeemer of the grace bestowed by God (Ibid., 113).

Hauke remained critical of the accuracy of Laurentin's account also because of observations made in February 1925 by Garrigou-Lagrange, who seems to have been associated with the Roman Commission either by direct membership or by providing observations for the Commission's consideration. These observations, reproduced by Hauke both in their original Latin and in English translation, had satisfactorily and "without great difficulty" addressed what Laurentin claims are the two main objections against Mary's universal mediation: Mary's mediation of the graces of the Old Testament and of sacramental graces.

Concerning Mary's mediation of the graces of the Old Testament, Garrigou-Lagrange wrote thus:

> 1. On grounds of the foregoing arguments [theological objections of the Roman Commission alleged by Laurentin] it is certain that the Blessed Virgin Mary is the spiritual Mother of all men, in so far as she in union with Christ cooperated in their redemption. As in the case of Christ, so with her a distinction is to be drawn between the way in which this mediation affected the men who lived under the old and new covenants. *On behalf of all fallen men who preceded the coming of Christ Mary exercised together with Christ a certain satisfactory and meritorious causality; in relation to those who*

be accepted as belonging to the deposit of the faith, the

---

live under the new covenant she exercises a special intercession for each and dispenses to them the means of salvation.

This influence began at the moment of Christ's conception; *she exercises this unto the fullest after her assumption [into heaven] [sic].*

It is inconceivable that her intervention (*interventus*) [*sic*] on any grounds might be restricted only to some men or to some graces. That would be in contradiction of the common teaching of the blessed in heaven, of the documents of tradition already cited, and against the liturgy, which accommodates the following words of Scripture to Mary: "In me is every grace of life and truth, in me every hope of life and virtue" (Sir 24, 25 [Vulg]) [*sic*].

Whence, Mary has uninterruptedly been called throughout the Church *Gate of heaven, our Life, our Hope, Mother of divine grace or graces, Mother of mercy, Health of the sick, Refuge of sinners, Consolatrix of the afflicted, Help of Christians, Queen of the Apostles, of Martyrs, of Confessors, of Virgins, of all Saints.*

1. *Ex praedictis argumentis constat B. M. Virginem esse Matrem spiritualem omnium hominum, prout cooperata est cum Christo ad eorum redemptionem. Attamen, sicut pro Christo, notanda differentia activitatis mediatricis relate ad homines Veteris Testamenti et relate ad eos qui in N.T. vivunt. Erga omnes homines lapsos qui Christum praecesserunt, una cum Christo, Maria exercet causalitatem cujusdam satisfactionis et meriti: relate ad eos qui in N.T. vivumt, insuper pro singulis specialiter intercedit et eis omnia salutis auxilia distribuit.*

Hunc influxum incepit a tempore Conceptionis Christi, et perfecte exercet post Assumptionem.

Nullo modo intelligi potest quare interventus ejus ad aliquos tantum homines aut ad speciales gratias limitaretur. Hoc esset, contra communem sententiam de cognitione beatorum, et contra traditionis documenta supra citata, contra liturgiam quae Mariae applicat haec S. Scripturae verba: 'In me omnis gratia viae et veritatis, in me omnis spes vitae et virtutis' (Eccli. XXIV, 25). Item quasi sine intermissione in tota Ecclesia, Maria vocatur Janua coeli, Vita nostra, Spes nostra, Mater divinae gratiae vel gratiarum, Mater misericordiae, Salus infirmorum, Refugium peccatorum, Consolatrix afflictorum, Auxilium Christianorum, Regina Apostolorum, Martyrum, Confessorum, Virginum, Sanctorum omnium" [Réginald Garrigou-Lagrange, "De Definibilitate Mediationis Universalis B.M.V." (note 502), 15-17; Cf. Hauke, *Mediatress of Grace*, 114-115, 151-152 (italics represent emphases by Garrigou-Lagrange)].

The observations of Garrigou-Lagrange also reveal the fruit of his speculative reflection on the question of Mary's mediation of graces as they concern those effected *ex opere operato*, such as those of the sacraments:

2. From the abovementioned universal influence is *not to be exempted the operation of the Sacraments of the new law*, which *ex opere operato* produce their fruit; the Blessed Virgin in fact merits for us *de congruo* or fittingly, what Christ merits for us *de condigno* or out of justice, and in addition she indirectly works in them in so far as she prepares for us a valid administration of the Sacraments and bestows on us the actual grace whereby we are prepared to receive the Sacraments fruitfully....

3. ...Some object: the mother of the king has no right to dispose of those goods proper to the king. Answer: the difference to be noted is this, the Blessed Virgin in the acquisition of the blessings of salvation had an active part together with Christ, in so far as she assented to the Incarnation and Redemption through the sacrifice of the Cross; together with Him she suffered in satisfaction and merited, with a merit grounded in the *rights of friendship*; were God to overlook such a right, it would be to treat a right as inconsequential, something contrary to his gentle Providence. Consequently, he has recognized the rights of Mary, like those of Christ, as holy, just as the whole of tradition and prayer of the Church demonstrate.

Still others object: the Blessed Virgin did not merit *de congruo* for *all*, what Christ out of justice merited *de condigno*. For she did not merit in this way her own graces, since the principle of merit cannot be the object of merit. This objection simply makes it clear that the Blessed Virgin as Mediatress is subordinated to Christ and was redeemed by Him. She could hardly have merited her own redemption itself, which is the principle of all merit. But the influence of Mary is indeed present in the bestowal of the fruits of redemption on all because and in so far as she is spiritual Mother of all men.

From all this it is certain that the *universal* mediation of the Blessed Virgin is not only moral [involving the will], but *absolute*; not only collective, but also distributive and *for each singly* (*singillatim*) [*sic*]; universal not only as fact, but also by right; i.e., God bestows on all [men] all graces in such wise, that he has determined to give none without the intercession of the Blessed Virgin, since she has been associated (*consociata est*) [*sic*] with Christ in the work of Redemption and distribution of grace.

2. *Imo a praedictis universalis influxu* <u>*non excludendus est effectus sacramentorum Novae Legis*</u>, *ex opere operato productus; nam B. Virgo nobis meruit do congruo quae Christus de condigno, et insuper indirecte influit ad effectum sacramentorum prout nobis obtinet validam sacramentorum administrationem et nobis elargitur gratiam actualem qua recte disponamur ad gratiam sacramentalem fructuose recipiendam....*

3. *...Objiciunt quidam dicentes: Mater regis non habet jus disponendi de bonis ipsius regis. Respondetur: Disparitas est quod B. M. V. in acquisitione bonorum salutis simul cum Christo partes activta habuit, consentiendo*

definition of these titles, however, in the present situation would be lacking in theological clarity, as such titles and the doctrines inherent in them still require further study in a renewed Trinitarian, ecclesiological and anthropological perspective. Finally, the theologians, especially the non-Catholics, were sensitive to the ecumenical difficulties which would be involved in such a definition.[12]

DEBATE OVER THE AUTHORITY OF THE DECLARATION

Before we examine each of the objections stated in the Declaration, it is important that we first examine the question of the authority which this Declaration possesses. One of the appended

---

Incarnationi et Redemptioni per sacrificium Crucis; cum illo satisfecit et meruit, merito fundato in jure amicabili; quod si Deus tale jus negligeret, id merito aestimari posset inconveniens, suavi Providentiae oppositum. Et ideo jura Mariae sicut Christi sancivit, ut manifestat tota traditio et modus orandi in Ecclesia.

Alii objiciunt: Beata Maria Virgo non meruit de congruo omnia quae Christus de condigno, quia non potuit suam propriam gratiam sic mereri, cum principium meriti non cadat sub merito.

Sed ex hoc probatur solum quod B. M. V. fuit mediatrix Christo subordinata, ab ipso redempta. Nequivit quidem propriam redemptionem et gratiam mereri, nec a fortiori ipsum Redemptoris opus, quod est principium totius meriti: sed in distribuendis effectibus Redemptionis, causalitas Mariae ad omnes se extendit, prout est spiritualis Mater omnium hominum.

Ex his omnibus constat mediationem B. M. V. esse universalem non solum moraliter, sed abolute; neque solum collective sed etiam distributive et singillatim; imo non facti tantum, sed etiam juris universalitate; id est Deus ita omnes gratias omnibus largitur, ut nullam dare statuerit nisi mediante B. Virginis deprecatione, prout Christo consociata est in opere redemptionis et gratiarum distributionis (Réginald Garrigou-Lagrange, "De definibilitate" [note 502], 15-17; Cf. Hauke, *Mediatress of Grace*, 115-116, 152-153).

[12] Theological Commission of the Pontifical International Marian Academy, "Declaration of the Theological Commission of the Pontifical International Marian Academy," *L'Osservatore Romano English Edition* (hereafter cited as *ORE*), 25 June 1997, 10.

commentaries to the Declaration was written by Salvatore Perrella, O.S.M. He stated: "the *Declaration of the Theological Commission of the Pontifical Marian Academy* at Czestochowa in August 1996, **intends to present an authoritative response** to the multiplication of such requests [of a dogma defining Mary as "Coredemptrix, Mediatrix, and Advocate"]."[13] Canon René Laurentin went on record to state that, although not expressly stated in *L'Osservatore Romano*:

> The Congregation for the Doctrine of the Faith does not support this initiative [*Vox Populi Mariae Mediatrici's* petitioning for a final Marian dogma]. In the Vatican newspaper, *L'Osservatore Romano*, it published the negative response of the Pontifical Mariological Academy (to which I belong) during its Mariological Congress in Czestochowa, Poland, in August 1996.[14]

Both Miravalle and Calkins respectfully disagreed. In Miravalle's 13 June 1997 response to the Czestochowa Commission, he stated: "…This statement of the commission, while providing a valuable contribution to the theological dialogue concerning Maternal Mediation [*sic*] and its potential solemn definition, contains no authoritative or official prohibition of the activities [right to gather petitions and submit them to the Holy Father] of *Vox Populi Mariae Mediatrici* [which Miravalle reminded his readers was in accord with its canonical rights as stated in Canon 212, §2, 3][15] which will continue to work in obedience and solidarity to

---

[13] Salvatore M. Perrella, O.S.M., "Mary's Co-operation in work of Redemption," *ORE*, 2 July 1997, 9 (emphasis mine).

[14] René Laurentin, "Proposed Dogma: 'Mary: Co-Redemptrix, Mediatrix, and Advocate.' Something to Consider before You Sign," *The Tablet*, (31 January 1998, accessed 10 June 2006); available from http://www.udayton.edu/Mary/respub/summer98.html; Internet.

[15] Canon 212, §2 The Christian faithful are free to make known to the pastors of the Church their needs, especially spiritual ones, and their desires. §3 According to the knowledge, competence, and prestige which they possess, they have the right and even at times the duty to manifest to the sacred pastors their opinion on matters which pertain to the good of the Church and to make their opinion known to the rest of the Christian faithful, without

[*sic*] the Papal Magisterium of Pope St. John Paul II[16] in seeking to bring about the necessary theological and ecclesial maturity for the solemn definition of Maternal Mediation, [...] the final and definitive judgment of which, of course, remains with the present Pontiff."[17] Miravalle then reminded his readers that there are other historical precedents in the Church when "advisory theological commissions requested by the Holy See have come to conclusions which ultimately were not adopted by the Holy See; the most radical example within recent Church precedence was the theological commission requested by the Holy See to examine the question of artificial birth control, the conclusion of which was overridden by Pope Paul VI, when he reaffirmed the constant Church teaching against artificial birth control in his 1968 Encyclical, *Humanae Vitae*."[18]

Calkins also expressed his opinion concerning the authoritative nature of the Declaration:

The first and most important fact to be kept in mind about these two documents is that they are not official documents of the Holy See, even though they were published in the daily Vatican newspaper, *L'Osservatore Romano*, as well as in the weekly English and other language editions of that paper. They do not represent a broad spectrum of the opinion of the members of the Pontifical International Marian Academy, of which I also am a member, nor, insofar as I am aware, was there an open, fair and honest consideration of the issues involved. The initial polling was

---

prejudice to the integrity of faith and morals, with reverence toward their pastors, and attentive to common advantage and the dignity of persons.

[16] This statement by *Vox Populi* is not exclusive to Pope St. John Paul II. They had hopes that John Paul II would be the Pope to proclaim their proposed dogma, but their proposal is equally directed to his successors. This is reflected on the home page of their website: http://www.voxpopuli.org.

[17] Mark I. Miravalle, "Response to a Statement of an International Theological Commission of the Pontifical International Marian Academy" (13 June 1997, accessed 10 June 2006); available from http://www.voxpopuli.org/response_4.php; Internet.

[18] Ibid.

taken without any representation by those who are in favor of the definition or any serious debate.[19]

The best articulation of *Vox Populi's* response to the problems it found in the 1997 Declaration came in an address which Dr. Miravalle delivered at the International Symposium on Marian coredemption in Stratton-on-the-Fosse, England, on 24 August 2002. The symposium was entitled *"Maria Mater Unitatis."* The address was called "In Continued Dialogue with the Czestochowa Commission." In the beginning of his address he revisited the question of the authoritative nature of the 1997 Declaration and revealed details about what he believes are the questionable origins of the "Theological Commission of the Pontifical International Marian Academy" at Czestochowa.

Miravalle began his address by explaining the nature of the Marian congresses such as the one held in Czestochowa in 1997. He stated that "a typical component of the Mariological-Marian Congresses since the Second Vatican Council has been an ecumenical discussion group, consisting of members from different countries, with participation by several non-Catholic theologians with interest in Mariology." He added, "The purpose of the ecumenical group is to provide the opportunity to discuss the dimensions of the congress theme or other relevant Mariological issues from a specifically ecumenical perspective."[20]

After listing the members of the Czestochowa Commission Miravalle stated: "During the meeting of the ecumenical discussion group, and without any prior knowledge on the part of the members themselves (as some later indicate in response to questions from the press and colleagues as well) the issue of the opportuneness of the definition of the Marian doctrine of Co-redemptrix, Mediatrix of all graces and Advocate was brought before the group,

---

[19] Arthur B. Calkins, "A Response to the Declaration of the Commission of the Pontifical International Marian Academy," in Mark I. Miravalle, S.T.D., ed., *Contemporary Insights on a Fifth Marian Dogma–Mary Coredemptrix, Mediatrix, Advocate: Theological Foundations III* (Santa Barbara, CA: Queenship Publishing Company, 2000), 125-126.
[20] Mark I. Miravalle, "In Continued Dialogue with Czestochowa," available from http://www.voxpopuli.org/czestochowa.pdf; Internet.

with the request for an opinion by some authority from within the
Holy See." He continued:

> After one discussion period, estimated by group members
> to have lasted approximately thirty minutes and which
> essentially consisted of comments by a few theologians
> decidedly against the definition, a request was made for
> anyone who wished to speak in favor of the definition to
> comment. After a brief silence, the discussion was brought
> to a close, and a unanimous 21 to 0 vote was recorded as
> its conclusion. According to the members themselves, no
> specific study was made, no working paper was presented
> to the committee, no opportunity for research was given,
> no draft of the conclusion was submitted to the ecumenical
> group for final approval, and no presentation of any posi-
> tion in favor of the definition was offered an examination.

Approximately ten months later, on June 4, 1997,
L'Osservatore Romano published the conclusion of the Czestochowa ecumenical group, but under the new designation of a "commission established by the Holy See." The
Commission was reportedly made up of members who
were "chosen for their specific preparation in this area,"
and a written document was released as a "Declaration of
the Theological Commission of the Congress of Czestochowa." Once again to the surprise of the members, who
report they were never informed that they were acting as a
"commission established by the Holy See," but only on the
request by some authority within the Holy See to offer their
opinion on the question of the definition, the results of the
Czestochowa ecumenical ad hoc group and their negative
conclusion concerning the proposed definition of Mary
Co-redemptrix, Mediatrix and Advocate, was promulgated
by the Catholic and secular press as a definitive magisterial
rejection of the petitions of some six million faithful and
over 500 cardinals and bishops for the proclamation of the

proposed fifth Marian dogma, with headlines of "No New Marian Dogma," circulated worldwide.[21]

In light of the procedural abnormalities alleged by Dr. Miravalle, it is worth noting that the *Marian Library Newsletter* of 28 January 1997, published through the International Marian Research Institute in Dayton, Ohio, does not use the word "commission" at any point in its article to describe the gathering of theologians who met at the Mariological Congress in Czestochowa. As this article is perhaps the first written on the Czestochowa Congress prior to the Declaration printed in the 4 June 1997 *L'Osservatore Romano*, it may validate the insinuation of Miravalle that the new designation of the ecumenical group as a "Theological Commission" may have been created at a time after the Mariological Congress without the prior knowledge of some or all of the theologians listed on the commission.[22]

Miravalle also found the timing of the release of the statement of what he referred to as "the Czestochowa ecumenical group... under its new designation [The Theological Commission of the Pontifical Marian Academy]" deliberate. He stated: "The release of the conclusion...happened to coincide with the timing of the close of the international *Vox Populi Mariae Mediatrici* Conference held...in Rome" where "over 70 bishops and 100 theologians and leaders from five continents...ended their theological symposium and unified prayer with a petition to Pope St. John Paul II in filial request for the solemn definition of Mary Co-Redemptrix, Mediatrix of all graces and Advocate."[23]

While the nature and history of the Czestochowa Commission's Declaration remain among some theologians as points of question and intrigue, the articles of debate between the supporters and opponents of the Czestochowa Commission's Declaration

---

[21] Ibid.

[22] Cf. *The Marian Library/International Marian Research Institute,* "Dialogue on Coredemptrix, Mediatrix, Advocate," *Marian Library Newsletter* (28 January 1997, accessed 11 June 2006); available from http://www.udayton.edu/mary/news97/0128.html#Poland; Internet.

[23] Miravalle, "In Continued Dialogue with Czestochowa," available from http://www.voxpopuli.org/czestochowa.pdf; Internet.

revolve around the central question of what *really* is the theological direction taken by Vatican II concerning Mary's role in salvation history? The Czestochowa Commission held that Vatican II was not only against pronouncing a new Marian dogma at the Council, but also insinuates that a dogma defining Mary as "Coredemptrix, Mediatrix, and Advocate" is and always will be contrary to the direction of the Council because it will cause grave impediments to Christian unity. Moreover, the Declaration of the Czestochowa Commission insinuates that pre-conciliar Mariological terms such as "Coredemptrix, Mediatrix and Advocate" are no longer in vogue (as well as the pre-conciliar theology upon which those terms were used).

OBJECTIONS OF THE DECLARATION AND ITS SUPPORTERS, AND THE RESPONSE BY *VOX POPULI MARIAE MEDIATRICI* AND MONSIGNOR CALKINS

The Declaration's objections can be summarized into four main points: 1) "The titles ['Coredemptrix, Mediatrix, and Advocate'], as proposed, are ambiguous;" 2) Defining these titles would be contrary to the theological direction of Vatican II; 3) the titles are presently "lacking in theological clarity" and "the doctrines in them require further study in a renewed Trinitarian, ecclesiological, and anthropological perspective;" and 4) A definition of these titles would cause "ecumenical difficulties."

1. "The titles [*Coredemptrix, Mediatrix*, and *Advocate*], as proposed, are ambiguous"

The unsigned commentary stated: "This is a serious observation, for, in a doctrinal pronouncement of such weight as a dogmatic definition, it is necessary that the terms should not lend themselves to ambiguous interpretations and that they be understood in a substantially univocal way."[24] The author asserted that if one were to examine "recent books [1987–1997] on Mariology," one would find that theologians present the title "Mediatrix" "in contrasting ways—in terms of its doctrinal evaluation, the determination of the area in which it is exercised and in comparison with the mediation of Christ and the Holy Spirit."[25]

In his commentary on the Declaration, Salvatore Perrella stated that the proposed titles "do not clearly, suitably or in a uniform manner express the doctrine that the drafters of the petition wish to maintain."[26] Father Perrella did not clarify what he believed that doctrine to be. While agreeing with Perrella, René Laurentin posited that the ambiguities which he believes are present in the titles could be "a cause of confusion to the faithful and of scandal to Protestants."[27]

The official position of the Pontifical Faculty Marianum also believed that the titles lack a univocal meaning which they assert is crucial for any solemn definition. Their difficulty lies in the nature of the titles causing them to raise the questions: "Are they ontological, that is, do they refer to an action on Mary's part that was determining and necessary for the redemptive event, as was her *fiat* for the Word's becoming man? Or are they functional titles that make clear the role entrusted to Mary, namely, that through her cooperation, redemption comes to all people?"[28] The Marianum stated that a biblical examination of the terms would demonstrate that "these three titles refer properly to Christ."[29] They add: "In the New Testament, none of these three titles—Coredemptrix, Mediatrix, Advocate—is attributed to Mary. On the contrary, the New Testament texts describing Christ as the Redeemer, Mediator and Advocate *seem*—and we repeat, *seem*—not to support the idea of

---

[24] Anon., "A new Marian dogma?", *ORE*, 25 June 1997, 10.

[25] Ibid.

[26] René Laurentin, "Proposed Dogma: 'Mary: Co-Redemptrix, Mediatrix, and Advocate.' Something to Consider before You Sign."

[27] Ibid.

[28] Pontifical Faculty Marianum, "The Marianum's Position on the Dogmatic Definition," *Marian Library Newsletter* 38 (1999): 4.

[29] Ibid., 4.

a creature alongside him acting as Coredemptrix, Mediatrix and Advocate in an ontological sense."[30] The Marianum also believed the title "Mediatrix" does not share the same meaning in Eastern theology as it does it Western theology.[31]

The Marianum's position is not entirely clear. On the one hand, they emphasize that the proposed titles are in need of further theological clarification. On the other hand, they admit that the essential underlying doctrine of the proposed titles [Mary's cooperation in the work of salvation] is already firmly rooted in all the fonts that are necessary to move a doctrine toward a dogmatic definition. The following is their list of reasons explaining why they do not support the request for a dogmatic definition:

- The doctrine on Mary's cooperation in the work of salvation has been formally, repeatedly, and authoritatively taught by both the extraordinary (Vatican II) and the ordinary (papal and episcopal) magisterium of the Church.

- The doctrine is not contested or denied in any essential element by Catholic theologians.

- In both the sacred liturgy and popular devotions, Mary's cooperation in the work of salvation, her constant intercession, and her spiritual motherhood are widely confessed. [32]

While these reasons clearly affirm the theological foundations which strongly support the proposed dogma, it seems that the Marianum was suggesting that a *new* dogma is unnecessary, the extant doctrine being sufficient.

In response, Dr. Mark Miravalle suggests: "Perhaps it would be best to analyze how the Church uses the three titles and their inherent roles as manifested in papal and conciliar documents, and then to proceed in evaluating whether or not the Church's uses of the titles lack the theological specificity appropriate for a solemn

---

[30] Ibid., 4.
[31] Ibid., 4.
[32] Ibid., 4.

definition."[33] This task continues to be the work of *Vox Populi Mariae Mediatrici*.

2. Defining these titles would be contrary to the theological direction of the Second Vatican Council

This objection of the Czestochowa Commission is not entirely clear. As we shall see, its supporters seemingly contradict what this objection seems to imply. The Czestochowa Commission does not qualify whether the theological direction of the Council means that there is never to be a definition on Mary's mediation according to these titles or under any other. This is a significant distinction because it is one thing to object to the timing of a solemn definition or to the proposed terms—hence, one would use the word "inopportune" to describe one's hesitation. It is another thing to say that the Council's decision not to proclaim a new Marian dogma sets a deliberate precedent for preventing any new dogma from ever being proclaimed if, for example, it seems to be an obstacle to Christian unity. In short, it seems that the words used in this objection imply that there is *never* an opportune time to define Mary's mediation, even if all the clarifications were made, on the premise that Vatican II chose not to define Mary's mediation and we should not deviate from its decision.

The unsigned commentary seems to support a literal reading of the Declaration implying that there is no need for a dogma of Mary's coredemption and mediation. This seems evident from the serious charge it implicitly made against the *Vox Populi Mariae Mediatrici* movement:

> From whatever perspective it is considered, the movement that is petitioning for a dogmatic definition of the Marian titles of *Coredemptrix, Mediatrix* and *Advocate* is

---

[33] Miravalle, "In Continued Dialogue with Czestochowa," available from http://www.voxpopuli.org/czestochowa.pdf; Internet.

not in line with the direction of the great Mariological text of the Second Vatican Council, chapter eight of *Lumen Gentium*, which, in the judgment of Paul VI, constitutes the most extensive synthesis "of the Catholic doctrine on the place that the Blessed Virgin Mary occupies in the mystery of Christ and the Church" ever traced by an Ecumenical Council (*Closing Allocution of the Third Session of the Council*, 21 November 1964, n. 7). One should not undervalue the importance of the Mariological teaching of Vatican II.[34]

Since there was and remains only one movement petitioning the Holy Father for a dogmatic definition of Mary's universal motherhood, it is not difficult to deduce that the primary audience of the Declaration and its appended commentaries is the *Vox Populi Mariae Mediatrici* movement. The commentary later reiterated its point stating that the dogmatic movement [*Vox Populi Mariae Mediatrici*] "is not manifestly in line with the direction of Vatican II, both with respect to the request for a new Mariological dogma, and the content that is proposed for such a hypothetical dogmatic definition."[35] The commentary, however, did not explain how the dogmatic proposal of *Vox Populi Mariae Mediatrici* is not in line with the Council's teaching. Later, Laurentin takes an even stronger position against *Vox Populi* labeling it a "pressure group" that "[does] not make for health and peace in the life of the Church."[36]

Salvatore Perrella seemed to imply that the Mariology of Vatican II closed the door to pre-conciliar Mariological terms, unless they were explicitly used by the Council. He stated: "The request [for a new Marian dogma] makes use of terminology belonging to pre-conciliar theological manuals....It shows, therefore, a certain under-appreciation of the Council's teaching."[37]

---

[34] Anon., "A new Marian dogma?", *ORE*, 25 June 1997, 10.

[35] Ibid., 10.

[36] René Laurentin, "Proposed Dogma: 'Mary: Co-Redemptrix, Mediatrix, and Advocate.' Something to Consider before You Sign."

[37] Salvatore M. Perrella, O.S.M., "Mary's Co-operation in work of Redemption," *ORE*, 2 July 1997, 9.

Stefano De Fiores stated that Vatican II's teaching on Mary marked "the historic-salvific-conciliar change of direction" emphasizing "Mary in the mystery of Christ and of the Church."[38] He added, "Mary is not a separate chapter." Moreover, Angelo Amato went as far as to imply that the doctrine of Marian coredemption is not to be found in the teachings of Vatican II. He stated, "In its first document, Vatican Council II does not see in Mary a co-redemptrix, but rather 'the most sublime fruit of the Redemption' [*Sacrosanctum Concilium*, 103]."[39] Amato did not define what he meant by "co-redemptrix," but since his comments were made in relation to the proposed dogma, it seems that he was making a point to say that the theology of coredemption is not found in the teachings of Vatican II.

Calkins objected to these comments of Amato. First, regarding his statement about *Sacrosanctum Concilium* just quoted, Calkins responded:

The assertion that Mary is the object of the Redemption is not denied by anyone who seriously upholds Mary's role as Coredemptrix. As a creature, Mary needed to be redeemed and her redemption was accomplished "in a more sublime way" from the first moment of her conception precisely in view of the role that she would play in the Redemption. Indeed, the very same text that Father Amato cites also states that Mary "is inseparably linked with her Son's saving work" [*Sacrosanctum Concilium*, 103]. This is an assertion that is consistently made in the magisterium about no one except Mary and it is a statement precisely about her role as Coredemptrix!

---

[38] Stefano De Fiores, S.M.M., "Why It's Not the Right Time for a Dogma on Mary as Co-redemptrix," interview by ZENIT (31 October 2002, accessed 10 June 2006); available from http://www.zenit.org/english/visualizza.phtml?sid=26714; Internet.

[39] Archbishop Angelo Amato, S.D.B., "Christ Is Humanity's Only Savior," interview by ZENIT (24 November 2002, accessed 10 June 2006); available from the archive section of http://www.zenit.org/english/; Internet.

Calkins then reminded the Czestochowa Commission and its supporters that the Council never intended to provide a definitive and complete doctrine on Mary. He cited *Lumen Gentium* 54, where the Council Fathers explicitly stated that the Council

does not intend to give a complete doctrine on Mary, nor does it wish to decide those questions which the work of theologians has not yet fully clarified. Those opinions therefore may be lawfully retained which are propounded in Catholic schools concerning her, who occupies a place in the Church which is the highest after Christ and also closest to us.

Calkins then comments on this teaching of *Lumen Gentium* in light of the statement quoted above by the unsigned commentary:

Interestingly, up until the very vigil of the Council the intimately related questions about Mary's active role in the work of our redemption as Coredemptrix and Mediatrix were reaching an ever higher level of clarity and maturity among both theologians and members of the faithful. At the same time, however, opposition was beginning to emerge. We have already noted that "ecumenical sensitivity" would be presented as a prime reason for avoiding this topic or dealing with it obliquely and there was also emerging among various influential Bishops and their *periti* (experts) distaste for the general language of mediation as it had been traditionally applied to Mary.

Given this conflict which came out into the open on the Council floor, the above declaration [*Lumen Gentium* 54] is particularly significant.

It makes clear, beyond any doubt, that the Council Fathers went on record as not wishing to close any doors on the free discussion of Marian theology, even if they were not ready to make explicit declarations on some matters which had been largely "in possession" and then subsequently became contested, such as Mary's active collaboration in the work of redemption.[40]

3. The titles are presently "lacking in theological clarity" and "the doctrines in them require further study in a renewed Trinitarian, ecclesiological, and anthropological perspective"

This objection is connected to the previous two objections of the Declaration in that it suggests that the theological direction of Vatican II introduced a new context in which to study the subject of Mary's role in salvation history. Supporters of the Declaration hold that the proposed titles "Coredemptrix, Mediatrix, and Advocate" do not satisfactorily express this new theological context set forth by Vatican II.

This objection is also a complex one. We will, therefore, analyze each of the terms according to what the opponents of the dogma assert is lacking in theological clarity in them. We will begin with the title "Coredemptrix" because the opponents to the dogma believe that this title poses greater problems than "Mediatrix" and "Advocate."

"Coredemptrix"

We have already seen that Angelo Amato made the strong assertion that Vatican II "does not see in Mary a Coredemptrix, but rather 'the most sublime fruit of the Redemption.'" The other opponents to the dogma did not go as far as Amato. They

---

[40] Arthur B. Calkins, "A Response to the Declaration of the Commission of the Pontifical International Marian Academy," in Mark I. Miravalle, S.T.D., ed., *Contemporary Insights on a Fifth Marian Dogma–Mary Coredemptrix, Mediatrix, Advocate: Theological Foundations III* (Santa Barbara, CA: Queenship Publishing Company, 2000), 131.

concentrated more on the historical development of the doctrine of Marian coredemption and came to their own conclusions, which they believe are supported by the teaching of Vatican II.

The first objection, as stated in the Declaration, concerns an assertion that the title "Coredemptrix" fell out of usage during the pontificate of Pope Pius XII and "has not been used by the papal Magisterium *in its significant documents.*"[41] The unsigned commentary stated that this statement of the Declaration highlights "an important qualification, because here and there, in papal writings which are marginal and therefore devoid of doctrinal weight, one can find such a title, be it very rarely."

Salvatore Perrella commented further on the significance of Pius XII's omission of the term "Coredemptrix" and its effect on the approach taken at Vatican II. He stated that Pope Pius XII, "by his choice and conviction, never used this title ["Coredemptrix"] in his magisterial teaching, preferring to have recourse to a less binding and controversial vocabulary, more in keeping with expressing, even in a formal way, the association of the Blessed Virgin in the mystery of Redemption."[42] He continued to explain that the Council adopted Pius XII's way of thinking on this matter, which explains its emphasis on Mary's "*cooperatio*" rather than "*coredemptio*." The purpose of this was not to detract from, but rather highlight the unique mediation of Jesus Christ, the one Mediator [cf. 1 Tim 2:5]. Therefore, the Council expressed Mary's role in the work of Redemption as the "New Eve" and "the Associate of the Redeemer."[43] Perrella went as far as to say that the Council not only refused to define Mary as "Coredemptrix," but that this refusal also served as a "rejection of a certain terminology" in association to Mary's cooperation in the work of Redemption.[44]

René Laurentin was one of the *periti* at the Second Vatican Council. He stated:

---

[41] Anon., "A new Marian dogma?", *ORE*, 25 June 1997, 10 (emphasis mine).
[42] Salvatore M. Perrella, O.S.M., "Mary's Co-operation in work of Redemption," 9.
[43] Ibid., 9.
[44] Ibid., 9.

It was whispered in the doctrinal commission that the authorities thought it inopportune to use the title, which was ambiguous and needed to be discussed. The mariologists of the commission always kept in line with this discreetly expressed wish. There was no question of such a title being sanctioned. But Vatican II did not neglect the problem. Its main document, the Constitution on the Church, *Lumen Gentium*, deals with it, in a profoundly biblical way (in sections 58 and 62), which, in a remarkable fashion, sets out all that is essential.[45]

This description appears to contradict the assertion of Amato that the Council did not see in Mary a "co-redemptrix" because Laurentin is affirming that the Council *did*, but articulated this truth in a language that was "profoundly biblical." It is this renewed biblical approach that the Marianum encouraged for future study on this subject as it relates to Mary's mediation.[46]

While Stefano De Fiores also does not prefer the title "Coredemptrix" he acknowledged: "Indeed, co-redemption is not something new. Already, Irenaeus, the Church Father, referred to Mary as '*causa salutis*' [cause of our salvation] given her '*fiat*.'"[47] This was the language adopted by the Council when expressing this truth about Mary.[48]

Laurentin preferred using St. Paul's terminology that we are all "co-operators with God" (1 Cor 3:9). He did not neglect to note, however:

Mary was the first, and has a better claim than anyone else to a unique title, since she was the foundation of the Incarnation itself, was united through her exemplary faith

---

[45] René Laurentin, "Proposed Dogma: 'Mary: Co-Redemptrix, Mediatrix, and Advocate.' Something to Consider before You Sign."

[46] Cf. Pontifical Faculty Marianum, "The Marianum's Position on the Dogmatic Definition," 5.

[47] Stefano De Fiores, S.M.M., "Why It's Not the Right Time for a Dogma on Mary as Co-redemptrix," available from http://www.zenit.org/english/visual-izza.phtml?sid=26714; Internet.

[48] Cf. *Lumen Gentium* (*LG*), 56.

(Lk. 1:45) to Christ's whole mission, and was present, standing on Calvary, when Christ confirmed her role as mother in his last testament (Jn. 19:25-27). But let us not forget that Christ, the only mediator, is also the only Redeemer.[49]

While appropriately emphasizing Christ's unique mediation, Laurentin later noted: "Mary's co-operation is the first—foundational and unique. She is the closest to Christ and the most perfectly involved with him." The Marianum confirmed Laurentin's position when it stated: "...Mary is 'preeminent' (*Lumen Gentium* 53) among the members of the Body of Christ. There is no doubt that, in her faith and obedience, she cooperated in a more intense way in the realization of God's saving project and in a unique way in the redemptive incarnation of the Word."[50]

Laurentin objects to the title "Coredemptrix" [Laurentin uses "Co-Redeemer"[51]] because he believes it "makes us forget that Mary was raised up to heaven, and, through that redemption, arrived at supreme co-operation." Moreover, for Laurentin the title "Co-Redeemer" is problematic because "at the divine level the Holy Spirit is the Co-Redeemer."[52]

---

[49] René Laurentin, "Proposed Dogma: 'Mary: Co-Redemptrix, Mediatrix, and Advocate.' Something to Consider before You Sign."

[50] Pontifical Faculty Marianum, "The Marianum's Position on the Dogmatic Definition," 4.

[51] Laurentin uses this term instead of "Co-Redemptrix" without explanation. One can reasonably speculate that he is trying to persuade the reader into thinking that the term "Co-Redemptrix" is synonymous in meaning to the term "Co-Redeemer." However, it is the opinion of this writer that the terms "Co-Redeemer" and "Co-Redemptrix" are not synonymous and should not be substituted loosely as Laurentin appears to do. The argument can be made, using the words of Cardinal Julet, "we are all co-redeemers" (cf. René Laurentin, "Proposed Dogma: 'Mary: Co-Redemptrix, Mediatrix, and Advocate.' Something to Consider before You Sign") does not apply to the Mother of God in the same way or degree than it does to the rest of the baptized. No other person is considered "causa salutis" for the human race (cf. *LG*, 56). Hence, the title "Co-Redemptrix" refers not only to one who co-redeems with Christ the Redeemer, but "the woman" (cf. Gn. 3:15) who holds a singular and indispensable role in Redemption.

[52] Ibid.

Both Miravalle and Calkins object to the Czestochowa Commission's declaration that "from the time of Pope Pius XII, the term 'Coredemptrix' has not been used by the papal Magisterium *in its significant documents*."[53] First, the Declaration never specifies the criteria by which documents of the papal Magisterium are considered significant or insignificant. Moreover, the unsigned commentary, addressing this phrase of the Declaration, stated that it is "an important qualification, because here and there, in papal writings *which are marginal and therefore devoid of doctrinal weight*, one can find such a title, be it very rarely."[54]

Both Calkins and Miravalle believe that such a statement is contrary to the teaching of *Lumen Gentium* 25, which stresses that a doctrine frequently taught by the pope should not be considered "devoid of doctrinal weight" even if it is not taught at the authoritative level as an encyclical. The Council states:

This loyal submission of the will and intellect must be given, in a special way, to the authentic teaching authority [magisterium] of the Roman Pontiff, even when he does not speak ex cathedra in such wise, indeed, that his supreme teaching authority be acknowledged with respect, and that one sincerely adhere to decisions made by him, conformably with his manifest mind and intention, which is made known principally either (1) by the character of the documents in question, or (2) by the frequency with which a certain doctrine is proposed, or (3) by the manner in which the doctrine is formulated.[55]

Regarding this teaching of *Lumen Gentium*, Miravalle stated: "While granting a legitimate hierarchy of expressions of the Papal Magisterium, if nonetheless the Commission seeks to infer that they do not regard papal addresses below the level of encyclicals or apostolic letters as 'significant,' then they themselves seem to

---

[53] Anon., "A new Marian dogma?", *ORE*, 25 June 1997, 10.
[54] Ibid., (emphasis mine).
[55] Arthur B. Calkins, "A Response to the Declaration of the Commission of the Pontifical International Marian Academy," 133-134.

be straying from the Council, both in thought and in practice."[56] Miravalle later countered the Czestochowa Commission's statement further when he stated: "The Second Vatican Council makes reference to papal allocutions on numerous occasions as doctrinal support for its conciliar conclusions. As papal addresses were recognized by the council as legitimate doctrinal sources, so John Paul's Marian Magisterium should be recognized in the same way in this post-conciliar period. [Here Miravalle is referring to at least five times when John Paul II used the term 'Coredemptrix']."[57]

Perhaps the best example to demonstrate Pope St. John Paul II's usage and theological understanding of Mary as "Coredemptrix" is found in his address which he gave at the Marian shrine of Alborada in Ecuador in 1985. Miravalle believes this homily "provides a clearly articulate theological framework and identifies Mary's unique cooperation in the Redemption":

> The silent journey that begins with her Immaculate Conception and passes through the "yes" of Nazareth, which makes her the Mother of God, finds on Calvary a particularly important moment. There also, accepting and assisting at the sacrifice of her Son, Mary is the dawn of Redemption....Crucified spiritually with her crucified son (cf. Gal. 2:20), she contemplated with heroic love the death of her God, she "lovingly consented to the immolation of this Victim which she herself had brought forth" (*Lumen Gentium* 58).

> In fact, at Calvary she united herself with the sacrifice of her Son that led to the foundation of the Church; her maternal heart shared to the very depths the will of Christ "to gather

---

[56] Miravalle, "In Continued Dialogue with Czestochowa," available from http://www.voxpopuli.org/czestochowa.pdf; Internet.

[57] Mark I. Miravalle, S.T.D., interview by ZENIT (31 October 2002, accessed 10 June 2006); available from http://www.voxpopuli.org/zenit.php; Internet; cf. "Palm Sunday Address at Alborada, Guayaquil, Ecuador," *ORE*, 11 March 1985, 7; Angelus address to Arona (Novara), *OR*, 4 November 1984, 1; Palm Sunday and World Youth Day, *OR*, 31 March 1985, 12; "Address Commemorating Sixth Centenary of Canonization of St. Bridget of Sweden," *OR*, 6 October 1991, 4.

into one all the dispersed children to become the Mother of all the disciples of her Son, the Mother of their unity...."

...As she was in a special way close to the Cross of her Son, she also had to have a privileged experience of his Resurrection. In fact, Mary's role as Co-redemptrix did not cease with the glorification of her Son.[58]

"Mediatrix" and "Advocate"

The titles "Mediatrix" and "Advocate" are less problematic than "Coredemptrix" because they were terms explicitly used at Vatican II in *Lumen Gentium* 62: "By her maternal charity, she cares for the brethren of her Son, who still journey on earth surrounded by dangers and difficulties, until they are led into their blessed home. Therefore, the Blessed Virgin is invoked in the Church under the titles of Advocate, Helper, Benefactress, and Mediatrix."

The only opponent of the dogma who addressed the title "Advocate" was René Laurentin. He believes this title carries the same problem as the title "Co-Redeemer" does when applied to Mary because "it is to the Holy Spirit and to him alone that Jesus Christ gives this title."[59] Laurentin asserts that, "If Mary can also be said to be our advocate, it is in Christ and the Holy Spirit." He believes "it would unbalance things to define this title solemnly for her when that of the Holy Spirit is misunderstood or ignored by the faithful."[60]

Laurentin raises a good point in that the Church's doctrinal development on the Holy Spirit is one area of theology that needs more attention. Miravalle, however, does not agree that such a title would cause confusion because it is a title which has been used throughout the Church's tradition to refer to Mary.[61] He asserts

---

[58] John Paul II, "Palm Sunday Address at Alborada, Guayaquil, Ecuador," *ORE*, 11 March 1985, 7.
[59] René Laurentin, "Proposed Dogma: 'Mary: Co-Redemptrix, Mediatrix, and Advocate.' Something to Consider before You Sign."
[60] Ibid.
[61] The multi-volume work *Mary Coredemptrix, Mediatrix, Advocate: Theological Foundations* I-III (Santa Barabara, CA: Queenship Publishing) demonstrates

that Mary's title and role as "Advocate" underscores Mary's "pre-eminent intercessory role within the communion of saints."[62] It is worth noting that Mary as "Advocate" is part of the *lex orandi* of the Church. As part of the Divine Office, the Church frequently chants the *Salve Regina* where Mary is clearly referred to as "*advocata nostra.*"

The main argument used by the supporters of the Declaration in objection to the title "Mediatrix" is the historical precedent set by the popes of the twentieth century as well as the Fathers of Vatican II who, despite the positive conclusions of the investigative commissions (see footnote 12, pages 268-274) into the matter and dogmatic movements promoting it, chose not to define Mary's mediation. Laurentin stated:

> Pope Pius XII planned to define Mary as Mediatrix of All Graces, following an initial wave of petitions, supported by Cardinal Mercier and many bishops. But, for many reasons, the theologians of the Holy Office dissuaded him from doing so. Was Mary truly the mediatrix of all graces? What about those in the Old Testament, before she existed? What about sanctifying grace, which is the immediate communication of God's life in us? Pius XII gave up the idea.[63]

The research of Manfred Hauke on this subject which we presented earlier (see footnote 12, pages 268-274) demonstrates that not only did Pius XII's personal teaching on Mary's universal mediation of grace confirm his belief in the doctrine, but that the conclusions from the theological commissions and the response by Garrigou-Lagrange regarding the theological questions presented here by Laurentin illustrate that there were no theological obstacles preventing a solemn definition. It therefore seems plausible that

Mary's role as Advocate throughout the Church's tradition.
[62] Miravalle, "In Continued Dialogue with Czestochowa," available from http://www.voxpopuli.org/czestochowa.pdf; Internet.
[63] René Laurentin, "Proposed Dogma: 'Mary: Co-Redemptrix, Mediatrix, and Advocate.' Something to Consider before You Sign."

there were other reasons, non-theological in nature, why Pius XII "gave up the idea."

Angelo Amato, in an interview he granted to ZENIT on 24 November 2002, used strong language describing how Vatican II considered the "hypothesis" for a dogma on Mary's mediation "but discarded it."[64] This leaves one to think that the dogmatic proposal was permanently rejected, whereas the Declaration's expression "the Holy See decided to set the question aside" suggests that a change is possible at a later time.

The unsigned commentary took a position similar to Amato's which seemed to imply that Vatican II's decision not to define Mary's mediation was meant to represent a definitive and permanent decision of the Magisterium on the question. The commentary posited that since the popes of Vatican II chose not to make any dogmatic definitions at the Council and since the vote over the final text of *Lumen Gentium* was virtually unanimous, contemporary Mariology should not depart from the Council's position. A departure would be tantamount to undervaluing the Council's Marian teaching.[65]

In an interview granted to KATH.NET on 11 December 2002, Calkins clarified Amato's statements of November 24. Regarding Vatican II "discarding" the possibility of a Marian dogma, Calkins said: "There was never a vote on the Council floor which dealt specifically and only with Mary as Coredemptrix. So the idea that this concept was discarded is clearly contrary to fact."[66] He added: "The fact is that the Council did deal with the reality of Mary as Coredemptrix without using the title," citing the following passages from *Lumen Gentium*:

> The Father of mercies willed that the incarnation should be preceded by the acceptance of her who was predestined

---

[64] Interview of Archbishop Angelo Amato, S.D.B., "Christ Is Humanity's Only Savior" with ZENIT, 24 November 2002.

[65] Anon., "A new Marian dogma?", *ORE*, 25 June 1997, 10.

[66] Arthur B. Calkins, "Mary Coredemptrix and the Second Vatican Council," interview by KATH.NET (11 December 2002, accessed 10 June 2006); available from http://www.voxpopuli.org/calkins2.php; Internet.

to be the mother of His Son, so that just as a woman contributed to death, so also a woman should contribute to
life (*Lumen Gentium* 56). This union of the Mother with
the Son in the work of salvation is made manifest from
the time of Christ's virginal conception up to His death
(*Lumen Gentium* 57). The Blessed Virgin…faithfully persevered in her union with her Son unto the cross, where
she stood…uniting herself with a maternal heart with His
sacrifice….(*Lumen Gentium* 58).[67]

Calkins also emphasized that the first draft of the document
which would become *Lumen Gentium* VIII "explicitly acknowledged the legitimacy of the term Coredemptrix as applied to Our
Lady, but refrained from using it as not to cause undue problems
with our Protestant brothers and sisters."[68] One English translation of that text reads:

Certain expressions and words used by Supreme Pontiffs
have been omitted, which, in themselves are absolutely
true, but which may only be understood with difficulty by
separated brethren [in this case Protestants]. Among such
words may be numbered the following: "Coredemptrix of
the human race [Pius X, Pius XI]…."[69]

---

[67] Excerpts from *LG* 56, 57, 58, quoted in Arthur B. Calkins, "Mary Coredemptrix and the Second Vatican Council," available from http://www.voxpo-
puli.org/calkins2.php; Internet.

[68] Arthur B. Calkins, "Mary Coredemptrix and the Second Vatican Council," available from http://www.voxpopuli.org/calkins2.php; Internet. The
full Latin text reads: *Omissae sunt expressiones et vocabula quaedam a Summis
Pontificibus adhibita, quae, licet in se verissima, possent difficilius intelligi a frat-
ribus separatis (in casu a protestantibus). Inter alia vocabula adnumerari queunt
sequentia: "Corredemtprix [sic] humani generis"* [S. Pius X, Pius XI]; *"Reparatrix totius orbis"* [Leo XIII]; *"materna in Filium iura pro hominum salute
abdicavit"* [Benedictus XV, Pius XII], *"merito dici queat Ipsam cum Christo
humanum genus redemisse"* [Benedictus XV], *etc.;"* (*Acta Synodalia Sacrosancti
Concilii Oecumenici Vaticani II*, vol. 1, part IV, *Congregationis Generales* XXXI
(1 December 1962), 99.

[69] Arthur B. Calkins, "A Response to the Declaration of the Commission of
the Pontifical International Marian Academy," 129.

We now return to Laurentin's questions about the difficulty surrounding Mary's mediation of "all graces" which was a central teaching in the Mariology of St. Bernard of Clairveaux and St. Bernard of Siena whose teachings were later incorporated into the Marian papal Magisterium of the nineteenth and twentieth centuries.[70] Miravalle stated that proper distinctions must be made when analyzing the *"omnium gratiarum"* component of Mary's mediation: "1. An appropriate limitation within the general genus of grace; 2. An understanding of the title in light of Mary's own Immaculate Conception; 3. The universality of her mediation of graces regardless of historical and temporal limitations." He continued:

> In light of the multiform schools and categorizations of grace, from uncreated grace to the graces of creation, it is appropriate to limit the grace mediated by Mary to humanity to the category of the *graces of redemption*, merited by Christ the Redeemer at Calvary. This specification allows the beauty of diversity in respect to the different schools and classifications of grace, while at the same time expressing the universal nature of Mary's mediation of all graces derived from Calvary for fallen humanity's salvation.[71]

However, we will see in the following chapters of this study that Sheen did not believe that Sts. Bernard and Bernardine, as well as the papal Magisterium of his time, intended to place limitations on the universality of Mary's mediation of grace. He believed and taught that Mary's mediation includes not only the salvific graces which flow from Redemption, but also those secondary graces which pertain to the temporal order.

---

[70] Blessed Pope Pius IX, Encyclical Letter *Ubi Primum*, in Amletto Tondini, ed., *Le Encicliche Mariane*, 2d. ed. (Roma: Angelo Belardetti Editore, 1954), 4-5; Pope Leo XIII, Encyclical Letter *Jucunda Semper*, ASS 27 (1894-1895), 178-80, 182-84; Pope St. Pius X, Encyclical Letter, *Ad diem illum*, ASS 36 (1903-1904), 454; Pope Pius XI, *Ingravescentibus malis*, AAS 29 (1937), 375; Venerable Pius XII, *Superiore Anno*, AAS 32 (1940), 145; *Doctor Mellifluus*, AAS 45 (1953), 369.

[71] Miravalle, "In Continued Dialogue with Czestochowa," available from http://www.voxpopuli.org/czestochowa.pdf; Internet.

Mary's Mediation Needs Further Study

The supporters of the Declaration agree that based on their arguments just presented, the question of Mary's mediation and cooperation in Redemption needs further study. The unsigned commentary stressed that such studies should concentrate on "a renewed Trinitarian, ecclesiological, and anthropological perspective."[72] Salvatore Perrella added that it is to this kind of study that the Fathers of Vatican II invited theologians. He asserted: "In fact, the question of the salvific co-operation...is to be considered of extreme relevance for its undeniable consequences, which still need to be completely investigated, as well as for its implications of a Trinitarian, Christological, pneumatological, ecclesiological and anthropological nature."[73] In addition to these approaches, the Marianum emphasized that future studies on this subject should involve presenting the underlying theology of the terms "from a biblical viewpoint."[74]

Angelo Amato did not hold entirely to the same position as the Declaration regarding Mary's role as "Mediatrix." He believes Pope St. John Paul II provided the Church with the additional reflection it needed on Mary's mediation. He went so far as to state that John Paul II, "in [his] encyclical Redemptoris Mater...fully developed the title of mediator [Amato used the title "mediator" to represent "Mediatrix" throughout the interview]."[75]

Calkins disagreed with this last comment by Amato. He stated: "I do not believe...that there is any evidence that the Pope [John Paul II] would maintain that he has fully developed all that can be said about Mary's mediation. The great tour de force which he achieved in Redemptoris Mater was to begin to reverse the minimiz-

---

[72] Ibid.
[73] Salvatore M. Perrella, O.S.M., "Mary's Co-operation in work of Redemption," ORE, 2 July 1997, 9.
[74] Pontifical Faculty Marianum, "The Marianum's Position on the Dogmatic Definition," 5.
[75] Archbishop Angelo Amato, S.D.B., "Christ Is Humanity's Only Savior," interview by ZENIT (24 November 2002, accessed 10 June 2006); available from the archive section of http://www.zenit.org/english/; Internet (emphasis mine).

ing tendency in interpreting Marian mediation and thus to open the door anew to the magisterial teaching of his predecessors on Mary as Mediatrix of all graces."

Theologians have already provided a serious and scholarly response to the Czestochowa Commission's call for further study of the Trinitarian, anthropological and ecclesiological dimensions of Mary's universal motherhood. Monsignor Arthur Calkins, during his 26 October 2002 interview with KATH.NET, elaborated on studies underway to help clarify the doctrinal issues surrounding the present debate on Marian mediation and coredemption. He stated:

[The dogmatic definition of Mary's universal motherhood] was obviously a topic of interest at the Second Vatican Council and, as in the case of so many other conciliar themes, we are only now beginning to grasp the richness of what was said, especially with the help of Pope John Paul II's teaching. Of course the ground needs to be prepared for such a definition and in recent years there have been excellent studies which have been devoted to this topic, especially in English and Italian. Dr. Mark Miravalle has already published four volumes of studies (cf. www.queen-ship.org) as have the Franciscan Friars of the Immaculate in Frigento [Italy] along with numerous monographs, while the American Friars of the Immaculate have published two volumes of scholarly studies with a third on the way (cf. www.marymediatrix.com). Studies of Mary's collaboration in the work of redemption have also begun to appear in other places such as in the theological faculty of Lugano, Switzerland.[76]

Such scholarship on this subject is best demonstrated by the contributions of the theologians and philosophers who, beginning in 2000, have continued to meet annually for this purpose. The

---

[76] Arthur B. Calkins, "Why it's the right time for a dogma on Mary as Core-demptrix," interview by KATH.NET (26 October 2002, accessed 10 June 2006); available from http://www.kath.net/detail.php?id=3949&&print=yes; Internet.

fruits of these symposia reflect the most comprehensive collection of contemporary scholarly works on Mary's unique and inseparable cooperation in Christ's work of Redemption. These works are found in the now seven published volumes of *Mary at the Foot of the Cross: Acts of the International Marian Symposium on Marian Coredemption* (New Bedford, MA: Academy of the Immaculate). While the numerous articles contained in each of these volumes are not the only response to the Czestochowa Commission's invitation, the now more than 2000 pages of articles on the various dimensions of Marian mediation and coredemption written throughout the five volumes of *Mary at the Foot of the Cross* represent the greatest concerted effort to clarify these doctrines in preparation for a possible fifth Marian dogma.

4. A definition of these titles would cause "ecumenical difficulties"

This last objection of the Declaration and its supporters is perhaps their greatest. It has certainly been a difficult obstacle to overcome for *Vox Populi Mariae Mediatrici*. As we already have seen from a few brief examples in this chapter, ecumenical sensitivities surrounding this subject during Vatican II ultimately dissuaded the Council fathers from solemnly defining Mary's mediation. This is a serious point of debate. Strong statements have been made by opponents of the dogma concerning the ecumenical fallout which they believe could happen if this dogma is proclaimed. For example, the unsigned commentary wrote that the Czestochowa Declaration understates the "grave negative consequences which a definition of these titles would have on the ecumenical level."[77] René Laurentin goes so far as to say that a dogma using what he and others consider ambiguous titles ["Coredemptrix, Mediatrix, and Advocate"] could be a source of "scandal to Protestants."[78]

---

[77] Anon., "A new Marian dogma?", *ORE*, 25 June 1997, 10 (emphasis mine).
[78] René Laurentin, "Proposed Dogma: 'Mary: Co-Redemptrix, Mediatrix, and Advocate.' Something to Consider before You Sign."

The Marianum stated in its official position on the dogma: "The proposed dogmatic definition could inflict a serious wound, difficult to heal, on the ecumenical movement, something that would be counter to a Church commitment aroused and guided by the Spirit."[79]

Laurentin believes that the theological imbalance and "display of exaggeration" of the dogma proposal as it is presently formulated will "quite properly shock Protestants."[80] He also emphasized the difficulties the Orthodox churches would have concerning the manner of proclamation of a new Marian dogma, if it were made by a pope, since they believe that only an ecumenical council has the authority to make definitions. He recalled their aversion to previous dogmatic proclamations exclusively made by popes such as the Immaculate Conception (1854) and the Assumption (1950)—two doctrines which the Orthodox do not deny. In addition to the problem of the manner of proclamation, Laurentin added, "There will be greater dissention [sic] if Mary were defined as Co-Redeemer, a title foreign to the Orthodox tradition."[81] He added that the complexities surrounding the doctrinal positions of the Orthodox in relation to the Catholic Church explain why "the Council for Christian Unity…does not favor the definition."[82]

Stefano De Fiores takes a more moderate approach to the ecumenical sensitivities surrounding the dogma. Interestingly, De Fiores does not entirely discard a future need for this dogma on Mary. In an interview he granted to ZENIT on 21 October 2002, he stated: "From the conciliar and ecumenical point of view, it is certainly not opportune to proclaim this dogma at this time. The separated brethren, Protestants and Orthodox, reproach us for not consulting them in regard to the last dogmas on Mary. This is why I think a dogma of this type would have to include their participation….Let us first move toward union or toward a

---

[79] Pontifical Faculty Marianum, "The Marianum's Position on the Dogmatic Definition," 5.
[80] René Laurentin, "Proposed Dogma: 'Mary: Co-Redemptrix, Mediatrix, and Advocate.' Something to Consider before You Sign."
[81] Ibid.
[82] Ibid.

certain convergence among Christians; we will then examine if it is pertinent to proclaim Mary Co-Redemptrix." [83] De Fiores believes the key to presenting the underlying doctrines of this proposed dogma is to present Mary's mediation as Vatican II did, namely, that "Mary's mediation is *in* Christ, not next to Christ." De Fiores added, "It is shown that not only does she save but that she makes salvation possible. This way she is acceptable to all."[84]

Shortly after these statements were made by De Fiores, Calkins was asked to comment on them during an interview he granted with KATH.NET on 26 October 2002. In particular, Calkins was asked to comment on the statements of De Fiores that the separated brethren should be consulted about such a definition, implying that a future definition depends on reaching a consensus of theological opinion between the Catholic Church and separated brethren. He responded rather strongly:

My first comment is that genuine Catholic ecumenism should never be seen as a simple matter of consensus or compromise even though that impression often seems to be given today. While we Catholics should have genuine Christian love for our separated brethren and respect for their positions, we must have no less love and respect for "the Catholic faith that comes to us from the Apostles." Hence I do not believe that we must allow either our separated brethren or "political correctness" to dictate Catholic doctrine or when it is opportune to proclaim it.

If Mary's coredemptive role raises objections inside the Church, I believe it is because there has often been an unconscious tendency on the part of Catholics in recent times to accept the fundamental Lutheran dogma of *Christus solus* without recognizing that Catholic doctrine has always maintained the absolute centrality and primacy of Christ but without denying the necessity of man's collabo-

[83] Stefano De Fiores, S.M.M., "Why It's Not the Right Time for a Dogma on Mary as Co-redemptrix," available from http://www.zenit.org/english/visual-izza.phtml?sid=26714; Internet.
[84] Ibid.

rating with him in the work of salvation. Further, Catholic teaching from the time of the post-Apostolic Fathers has clearly upheld that no one has collaborated as fully as Mary, the "New Eve," in the work of our salvation. This is a "saving truth" that says a great deal about Mary's role in the economy of salvation and in our lives, about us, about the nature of salvation and the value of salvific suffering.[85]

While the Czestochowa Commission sees a dogmatic definition of Mary's spiritual maternity under the titles "Coredemptrix, Mediatrix and Advocate" as acting contrary to the ecumenical initiatives of Vatican II, Miravalle believes just the opposite. He believes that a dogmatic definition will more effectively bring about Christian unity. In his 31 October 2002 interview with ZENIT he stated: "It is time to be more straightforward with other Christian ecclesial bodies about Catholic doctrine on Marian co-redemption and mediation, and to articulate this truth with the greatest possible theological integrity and precision, while at the same time manifesting great sensibility to those who do not share our Catholic vision. This would be the significant ecumenical benefit of a definition of Mary Co-redemptrix."[86] He added, "The late Cardinal O'Connor of New York stated that a definition would greatly assist in ecumenism because its precise articulation would assure other Christians that we do distinguish adequately between Mary's unique association with Christ and the redemptive power exercised by Christ alone."[87]

Miravalle further supported his position in his address *In Continued Dialogue with the Czestochowa Commission* by referring to the words of John Paul II in his 1995 encyclical on ecumenism, *Ut Unum Sint* 36:

---

[85] Arthur B. Calkins, "Why it's the right time for a dogma on Mary as Coredemptrix," available from http://www.kath.net/detail.php?id=3949&&print=yes; Internet.
[86] Mark I. Miravalle, "In Continued Dialogue with Czestochowa," available from http://www.voxpopuli.org/czestochowa.pdf; Internet.
[87] Ibid.

Full communion of course will have to come about through the acceptance of the whole truth into which the Holy Spirit guides Christ's disciples. Hence all forms of reductionism or facile "agreement" must be absolutely avoided.[88]

Miravalle believed that this teaching of John Paul II is consistent with the teaching of *Unitatis Redintegratio* 11, which states: "It is, of course, essential that the doctrine be clearly presented in its entirety. Nothing is so foreign to the spirit of ecumenism as a false irenicism which harms the purity of Catholic doctrine and obscures its genuine and certain meeting."[89]

CONCLUSIONS FROM THIS DEBATE

Since the Declaration and its supporters believe that the theology of Mary's mediation and cooperation in God's plan of Redemption must steer clear of pre-conciliar terminology, which they view as ambiguous and inappropriate to an ecumenically oriented Church, what direction do they suggest we take? The two commentaries to the Declaration map out what they believe is the clear theological direction of the post-Vatican II Church. The unsigned commentary explained that the theological issues underlying Mary's role in Redemption and her mediation are best expressed by putting the emphasis on Mary's spiritual maternity "with respect to the disciples of Christ and all people (cf. *Lumen Gentium* 53, 54, 55, 56, 58, 61, 63, 65, 67, 69) whether through her historical co-operation in the event of the Redemption or as permanent intercessor on behalf of all people, from the moment of her glorious Assumption until the coronation of all the elect (cf. *Lumen Gentium* 62)."[90]

---

[88] *Ut Unum Sint* 36, quoted in Mark I. Miravalle, "In Continued Dialogue with Czestochowa," available from http://www.voxpopuli.org/czestochowa.pdf; Internet.
[89] Cf. Mark I. Miravalle, "In Continued Dialogue with Czestochowa," available from http://www.voxpopuli.org/czestochowa.pdf; Internet.
[90] Anon., "A new Marian dogma?", *ORE*, 25 June 1997, 10 (emphasis mine).

Salvatore Perrella summarized what he believes is at the heart of Vatican II's teaching on Mary's role in salvation history. He highlighted the Council's emphasis of Mary's "unique…*maternal* cooperation in the life and messianic ministry of the Saviour, directed '*ad vitam animarum supernaturalem restaurandam. Quam ob causam mater nobis in ordine gratiae exstitit*'" (*Lumen Gentium* 61).[91] He then concluded: "…Thus it follows that the comprehensive celebration of the saving work of the Lord Jesus implies the proper celebration of the participation of Mary in that work, to which she, by the disposition of divine Providence (cf. *Lumen Gentium* 61) was indissolubly joined (cf. *Sacrosanctum Concilium* 103; *Lumen Gentium* 53, 56, 58, 61, 63, 66)."[92] Perrella added that this was the theological direction emphasized by John Paul II whose teaching on Mary's spiritual maternity deepened Vatican II's doctrine on this subject "in a Christological, theological, and anthropological sense."[93]

The unsigned commentary recalled our attention to the fact that Paul VI "held that the doctrine of Mary's spiritual motherhood was a truth of faith: the Blessed Virgin 'continues now from heaven to exercise her motherly function of co-operation in the birth and development of divine life in the individual souls of the redeemed. This is a most consoling truth, which by the free design of the most wise God, is an integrating part of the mystery of human salvation: therefore, *it must be held by faith by all Christians*' (*Signum magnum*, 1)."[94]

So far, it is safe to say that both sides of the debate would agree with these statements just taken from Perrella and the unsigned commentary. However, *Vox Populi Mariae Mediatrici* would still hold that their proposed titles best express the three essential dimensions of Mary's spiritual maternity. The titles "Coredemptrix, Mediatrix and Advocate" have been used by both the pre-conciliar and post-conciliar papal Magisterium to express Mary's spiritual

[91] Salvatore M. Perrella, O.S.M., "Mary's Co-operation in work of Redemption," *ORE*, 2 July 1997, 9.

[92] Ibid., 9.

[93] Ibid., 9.

[94] Anon., "A new Marian dogma?", *ORE*, 25 June 1997, 10.

maternity. However, that does not mean that further study cannot be made concerning the underlying theology of the titles.

Thus, we return to our initial question surrounding this debate: What was the theological direction of Mariology set by the Second Vatican concerning Mary's role in salvation history? The unsigned commentary provided a response which summarizes the direction the Czestochowa Commission and its supporters believe theologians need to direct their studies:

> The Declaration of Czestochowa indicates the path to follow: deepen the study of the questions relative to Mary's mediation and to her function as advocate within the context of her spiritual motherhood, as significant moments of its exercise. The *sensus fidelium* is clearly oriented in this direction. To move in the opposite direction could turn out to be misleading or leading toward dead ends.[95]

Vox Populi Mariae Mediatrici would most likely not have any objections to the first part of that statement. However, it would continue to hold its position that the theological expression of Mary's spiritual motherhood is best articulated by a precise understanding of Mary's roles as Coredemptrix, Mediatrix and Advocate. They believe that the *sensus fidelium* shares this direction as is evidenced by the seven million petitions they have gathered, which include the endorsements of over 40 cardinals and 550 bishops.

There still remain questions concerning the suitability of the titles "Coredemptrix, Mediatrix, and Advocate." Are these really outdated and ambiguous terms? The papal Magisterium of Pope St. John Paul II is evidence enough to demonstrate that these titles are still relevant in post-conciliar Mariology. The teaching of John Paul II seemed to serve as a reawakening of pre-conciliar terminology. He explained the mystery of Mary combining pre-conciliar terminology with language and themes expressed in the Marian teachings of Vatican II. The ecumenically minded John Paul II intentionally used all three titles during his pontificate, which suggests that he possessed a clear understanding of the underlying doctrines

---

[95] Ibid., 10.

that allowed him to articulate the meaning of these titles. Salvatore Perrella, for example, also observed this phenomenon. He noted that Pope John Paul intentionally reintroduced the term "mediation" into post-conciliar theological language concerning Mary as an effort to highlight the unity between the pre-conciliar and post-conciliar Marian doctrine. He stated: "It has to be said that the Holy Father [John Paul II]...prefers to recover the term *mediation*, to which from time to time he adds the adjectives *maternal* and *participated*, thus, in a certain way, restoring the pre-conciliar vocabulary or theological reflection, liturgy and the papal Magisterium....Furthermore, the Encyclical *Redemptoris Mater* has linked the mediation of Mary with her messianic motherhood."[96]

An exposition of John Paul II on Mary's mediation is clearly beyond the scope of this study. However, it is sufficient to highlight that his teaching on Mary, reviving the pre-conciliar language of his predecessors, clearly demonstrates that the theological direction of Vatican II, to which John Paul II dedicated his pontificate, includes these titles of Mary to articulate her spiritual maternity. Is there a way to reconcile the two theological positions, so that the organic unity of the Church's teaching on Mary's mediation before and after Vatican II can be expressed and integrated in a language that accurately articulates the Church's teaching on this important subject? Do the terms "Coredemptrix, Mediatrix, and Advocate" best articulate Mary's spiritual maternity?

Whether or not the Church moves to define the Blessed Mother's mediation with these terms, the theological, liturgical and historical foundations for such a dogma are indisputable. This thesis exposing Archbishop Fulton Sheen's teaching on this critical subject confirms this fact further; illustrating that Mary's co-redemptive and mediatory role in the salvific mission of Christ and His Church are undeniable and well-grounded truths of our holy Catholic Faith. It is the opinion of this author, along with that of Venerable Fulton Sheen, St. Maximilian Maria Kolbe and millions of Catholics around the world, that defining these truths about

---

[96] Salvatore M. Perrella, O.S.M., "Mary's Co-operation in work of Redemption," *ORE*, 2 July 1997, 9.

Mary in her inseparable role in obtaining our redemption and distributing its merits will bring nothing less than great graces and blessings upon the Church and the world—at a time when they are desperately needed.

BIBLIOGRAPHY

WORKS CITED

Published Works of Venerable Fulton J. Sheen (Alphabetical Order)

Sheen, Fulton J. "The Blessed Mother." *Renewal and Reconciliation: Retreat Conferences by Archbishop Fulton J. Sheen.* Ministr-O-Media Inc., 1976. Compact disc.

_____. "Crucifixion and Seven Last Words." *Called and Chosen: The Never Ending Face of the Priesthood.* Santa Barbara, CA: St. Joseph Communications, 1992. Compact disc.

_____. *The Eternal Galilean.* New York: D. Appleton-Century Company, 1934. Reprint, Garden City, New York: Garden City Books, 1950.

_____. *Life of Christ.* New York: McGraw-Hill Book Company, 1958.

_____. *The Mystical Body of Christ.* New York: Sheed and Ward, 1935.

_____. *The Priest Is Not His Own.* New York: McGraw-Hill Book Company, 1963. Reprint, San Francisco: Ignatius Press, 2005.

_____. *Those Mysterious Priests.* New York: Doubleday & Company, 1974. Reprint, Staten Island: Society of St. Paul, 2005.

_____. *Treasure in Clay*. New York: Doubleday & Company, 1980.

_____. *The World's First Love*. New York: McGraw-Hill Book Company, 1952. Reprint, San Francisco: Ignatius Press, 1996.

Unpublished Works of Venerable Fulton J. Sheen (Alphabetical Order)

Sheen, Fulton J. "Christ the First Born Among the Brethren." Undated manuscript (photocopy) within folder labeled "Mystical Body." Archbishop Fulton J. Sheen Archives, Box 8, Catholic Diocese of Rochester, Rochester, New York.

_____. "Christ the Head of the Church." Undated typescript (photocopy) within folder labeled "Mystical Body." Archbishop Fulton J. Sheen Archives, Box 8, Catholic Diocese of Rochester, Rochester, New York.

_____. "Church." Undated manuscript (photocopy). Archbishop Fulton J. Sheen Archives, Box 1, Catholic Diocese of Rochester, Rochester, New York.

_____. "The Church as a Bride of the Bridegroom Christ." Undated typescript (photocopy) within folder labeled "Mystical Body." Archbishop Fulton J. Sheen Archives, Box 8, Catholic Diocese of Rochester, Rochester, New York.

_____. "The Church as Spouse." Undated typescript (photocopy) within folder labeled "Mystical Body." Archbishop Fulton J. Sheen Archives, Box 8, Catholic Diocese of Rochester, Rochester, New York.

_____. "The Church Both Temporal and Eternal." Undated typescript (photocopy) within folder labeled "Mystical Body." Archbishop Fulton J. Sheen Archives, Box 8, Catholic Diocese of Rochester, Rochester, New York.

_____. "The Church and Christ or the Head and Body Are One Person." Undated typescript (photocopy) within folder labeled "Mystical Body." Archbishop Fulton J. Sheen Archives, Box 8, Catholic Diocese of Rochester, Rochester, New York.

_____. "The Church and the Side of Christ." Undated typescript (photocopy) within folder labeled "Mystical Body." Archbishop Fulton J. Sheen Archives, Box 8, Catholic Diocese of Rochester, Rochester, New York.

_____. "The Cross." Recorded by and in the possession of Mr. Daniel B. Steffen. From a series of retreat lectures given at Holy Trinity Seminary, Irving, TX, 1972. Compact disc.

_____. "The Holy Spirit in Relation to the Head and to the Body." Undated typescript (photocopy) within folder labeled "Mystical Body." Archbishop Fulton J. Sheen Archives, Box 8, Catholic Diocese of Rochester, Rochester, New York.

_____. "Immaculate Conception." Manuscript (photocopy) from spiral notebook marked "Vol. 1: Notes for Sermons in Novena at Dublin, Ireland, July 16–25 (no year)." Archbishop Fulton J. Sheen Archives, Box 6, Catholic Diocese of Rochester, Rochester, New York.

_____. "The Marriage Feast of Cana and Christ the Bridegroom." Undated typescript (photocopy) within folder labeled "Mystical Body." Archbishop Fulton J. Sheen Archives, Box 8, Catholic Diocese of Rochester, Rochester, New York.

_____. "Mary and Institution of Eucharist." Undated manuscript (photocopy) of outline and notes for sermon in green notebook. Archbishop Fulton J. Sheen Archives, Box 7, Catholic Diocese of Rochester, Rochester, New York.

_____. "Mary and the Tabernacle." Corrected copy of typescript (photocopy) of address given at the Eucharistic Congress, Philadelphia, Pennsylvania, 6 August 1976. Archbishop Fulton J. Sheen Archives, Box 7, Catholic Diocese of Rochester, Rochester, New York.

_____. "Our Blessed Mother." Recorded by and in the possession of Mr. Daniel B. Steffen. From a series of retreat lectures given at Holy Trinity Seminary, Irving, TX, 1972. Compact disc.

_____. "Priest Prophet and King." Undated typescript (photocopy) within folder labeled "Mystical Body." Archbishop Fulton J. Sheen Archives, Box 8, Catholic Diocese of Rochester, Rochester, New York.

_____. "The Priesthood of Christ in Heaven." Undated typescript (photocopy) within folder labeled "Mystical Body." Archbishop Fulton J. Sheen Archives, Box 8, Catholic Diocese of Rochester, Rochester, New York.

_____. "Priests and the Blood of Christ." Undated manuscript (photocopy) of outline and notes for sermon in green notebook. Archbishop Fulton J. Sheen Archives, Box 9, Catholic Diocese of Rochester, Rochester, New York.

_____. "The Remission of Sin." Recorded by and in the possession of Mr. Daniel B. Steffen. From a series of retreat lectures given at Holy Trinity Seminary, Irving, TX, 1972. Compact disc.

_____. "Spirituality." Recorded by and in the possession of Mr. Daniel B. Steffen. From a series of retreat lectures given at Holy Trinity Seminary, Irving, TX, 1972. Compact disc.

_____. "Theandric Actions in Christ." Undated typescript (photocopy) within folder labeled "Mystical Body." Archbishop Fulton J. Sheen Archives, Box 8, Catholic Diocese of Rochester, Rochester, New York.

Studies on Venerable Fulton J. Sheen (Alphabetical Order)

Apostoli, Andrew, CFR. *Fulton J. Sheen: A Prophet for Our Time.* San Diego, CA: St. Joseph Communications, 2004. Compact disc.

Conniff, James C. G. *The Bishop Sheen Story.* New York: Fawcett Publications, 1953.

Murphy, Miles P. *The Life and Times of Archbishop Fulton J. Sheen.* New York: Alba House, 2000.

Noonan, D.P. *The Passion of Fulton Sheen.* New York: Dodd, Mead & Company, 1972.

Reeves, Thomas C. *America's Bishop: The Life and Times of Fulton J. Sheen.* San Francisco: Encounter Books, 2001.

Riley, Kathleen L. *Fulton Sheen: An American Catholic Response to the Twentieth Century.* New York: Alba House, 2004.

Other Studies (Alphabetical Order)

Cooney, John. *The American Pope: The Life and Times of Francis Cardinal Spellman.* New York: Times Books, 1984.

Gade, John A. *The Life of Cardinal Mercier.* New York: Charles Scribner's Sons, 1935.

Sacred Scripture

The Holy Bible: Revised Standard Version—Catholic Edition. San Francisco: Ignatius Press, 1966.

Works of the Magisterium (Alphabetical Order)

Acta et Documenta Concilio Oecumenico Vaticano II Apparando, Series 2 Praeparatoria III: 1. Rome: Typis Polyglottis Vaticanis, 1969.

Bertetto, Domenico, S.D.B. *Il Magistero Mariano di Pio XII.* Roma: Edizione Paoline, 1956.

Catechism of the Catholic Church: Second Edition. English translation of the *Catechism of the Catholic Church: Modifications from the Editio Typica.* Vatican City: Libreria Editrice Vaticana, 1997.

Flannery, Austin, O.P., ed. *Vatican Council II: The Conciliar and Post Conciliar Documents*. Grand Rapids, Michigan: William B. Eerdsmans Publishing, Co., 1988.

Insegnamenti di Paolo VI (1963–1978). 15 Vols. Vatican City: Libreria Editrice Vaticana, 1965–1979.

"Marian Doctrine of Benedict XV." Translated by Richard Zehnle, S.M. *Marian Reprint* 70 (1959).

The Pope Speaks (1954—). 50 Vols. Huntington, Indiana: Our Sunday Visitor, 1955—.

Benedict XV. Allocution to the Consistory (24 December 1915). In *La Civiltà Cattolica*, Anno 67, Vol. 1 [Quaderno 1574–15 gennaio 1916], 213-214.

_____. Apostolic Letter *Fausto Appetente* (29 June 1921). In *Acta Apostolicæ Sedis* 9 (1917), 329-335.

_____. Apostolic Letter *Inter Sodalicia* (22 May 1918). In *Acta Apostolicæ Sedis* 10 (1918), 181-184.

John Paul II. Apostolic Exhortation *Familiaris Consortio* (22 November 1981). Boston: Daughters of Saint Paul, 1981.

_____. Apostolic Letter *Mulieris Dignitatem* (15 August 1988). Official Vatican translation. In *Mother of Christ, Mother of the Church: Documents on the Blessed Virgin Mary*. Edited by Marianne Lorraine Trouvé. Boston: Pauline Books & Media, 2001.

_____. Encyclical *Redemptoris Mater* (25 March 1987). Official Vatican translation. In *Mother of Christ, Mother of the Church: Documents on the Blessed Virgin Mary*. Edited by Marianne Lorraine Trouvé. Boston: Pauline Books & Media, 2001.

_____."Mary is Outstanding Figure of Church." *L'Osservatore Romano*, weekly edition in English, *ORE*, 13 August 1997, 11.

_____. "Palm Sunday Address at Alborada, Guayaquil, Ecuador." *L'Osservatore Romano*, weekly edition in English, 11 March 1985, 7.

Leo XIII. Encyclical *Fidentem Piumque* (20 September 1896). In *Acta Sanctæ Sedis* 29 (1896–1897), 204-209.

_____. Encyclical *Jucunda Semper* (8 September 1894). In *Acta Sanctæ Sedis* 27 (1896-1897), 177-184.

Paul VI. Apostolic Exhortation *Marialis Cultus* (2 February 1974). Official Vatican translation. In *Mother of Christ, Mother of the Church: Documents on the Blessed Virgin Mary.* Edited by Marianne Lorraine Trouvé. Boston: Pauline Books & Media, 2001.

_____. Encyclical *Mense Maio* (29 April 1965). In *Acta Apostolicæ Sedis* 57 (1965), 353-358.

_____. Encyclical *Signum Magnum* (13 May 1967). In *Acta Apostolicæ Sedis* 59 (1967), 465-475.

Pius IX. Encyclical *Ubi Primum* (2 February 1849). In *Le Encicliche Mariane*, 2d. ed. Edited by Amleto Tondini. Roma: Angelo Belardetti Editore, 1954, 1-7.

Pius X. Encyclical *Ad Diem Illum* (2 February 1904). In *Acta Sanctae Sedis* 36 (1903–1904), 449-462.

Pius XI. Encyclical *Ingravescentibus Malis* (29 September 1937). In *Acta Apostolicæ Sedis* 29 (1937), 373-380.

_____. Encyclical *Miserentissimus Redemptor* (8 May 1928). In *Acta Apostolicæ Sedis* 20 (1928), 165-178.

Pius XII. Apostolic Letter *Per Christi Matrem* (5 May 1947). In *Acta Apostolicæ Sedis* 40 (1948), 536-538.

_____. Encyclical *Doctor Mellifluus* (24 May 1953). In *Acta Apostolicæ Sedis* 45 (1953), 369-384.

_____. Encyclical *Mystici Corporis Christi* (29 June 1943). London: Catholic Truth Society, 1952.

_____. Letter *Superiore Anno* (15 April 1940). In *Acta Apostolicæ Sedis* 32 (1940), 144-146.

_____. Radio Message to Italian Catholic Action (8 December 1953). In *Acta Apostolicæ Sedis* 45 (1953), 848-855.

Solesmes, Benedictine Monks of, eds. *Our Lady: Papal Teachings.* Translated by Daughters of St. Paul. Boston: St. Paul Editions, 1961.

Liturgical Texts (Alphabetical Order)

Missale Romanum 4ᵗʰ Editio Juxta Typicam Vaticanam. New York: Benziger Brothers, 1942.

The Roman Missal in Latin and English for Sunday, Feast, Ferial and Votive Masses. Collegeville, MN: The Liturgical Press, 1968.

Fonts (Alphabetical Order)

Augustine, Saint. *De Sancta Virginitate. PL* 40, 396-428.

_____. *The Fathers of the Church: St. Augustine—Treatises on Marriage and Other Subjects.* Edited by Roy J. Deferrari. Translated by Charles T. Wilcox et. al. New York: Fathers of the Church, Inc., 1955.

_____. "Tractate 120." In *The Fathers of the Church.* Translated by John W. Rettig. Vol. 92, *Tractates on the Gospel of John.* Washington, D.C.: The Catholic University of America Press, 1995.

Bernard of Clairveaux, Saint. *Dominica Infra Octavam Assumptionis B. V. Mariae. PL* 183, 429-438.

_____. *In Nativitate B. Mariae Virginis Sermo. PL* 183, 437-448.

_____. *St. Bernard's Sermons for the Seasons & Principal Festivals of the Year.* Translated by "A Priest of Mount Melleray." Vol. 3. Westminster, MD: Carroll Press, 1950.

Irenaeus, Saint. *Contra Haereses III. PG* 7, 843-972.

Jerome, Saint. *Epistola 2. PL* 22, 394-425.

Justin Martyr, Saint. *Dialogus cum Tryphone Judaeo. PG* 6, 471-800.

Thomas Aquinas, Saint. *Summa Theologica*. Translated by Fathers of the English Dominican Province. New York: Benziger Brothers, 1948.

Theological Works (Alphabetical Order)

Alma Socia Christi: Acta Congressus Mariologici–Mariani Romae Anno Sancto MCML Celebrati. Vol. 1. Roma: Academia Mariana, 1951.

Alonso, Joaquin Maria, C.M.F. *The Secret of Fatima*. Translated by Dominican Nuns of the Perpetual Rosary. Cambridge: The Ravengate Press, 1979.

Amato, Angelo, S.D.B. "Christ is Humanity's Only Savior." Interview by ZENIT, 24 November 2002. Available from the archive section of http://www.zenit.org/english/. Internet.

Anderson, H., Joseph A. Burgess, J. Francis Stafford, eds. *The One Mediator, The Saints, and Mary: Lutherans and Catholics in Dialogue VIII*. Augsburg: Augsburg Fortress, 1992.

Benedict XVI, Pope. "Faith, Reason and the University Memories and Reflections." Lecture presented during his meeting with the representatives of science at the University of Regensburg, 12 September 2006. Available from http://www.vatican.va/holy_father/benedict_xvi/speeches/2006/september/documents/hf_ben-xvi_spe_20060912_university-regensburg_en.html. Internet.

Calkins, Arthur B. "Mary Coredemptrix and the Second Vatican Council." Interview by KATH.NET, 11 December 2002. Available from http://www.voxpopuli.org/calkins2.php. Internet.

_____. "Why it's the right time for a dogma on Mary as Coredemptrix." Interview by KATH.NET, 26 October 2002. Available from http://www.kath.net/detail.php?id=3949&&print=yes. Internet.

Cano, R.D. Melchior, O.P. *Opera Theologica—Nova editio emendatissima*. Roma, 1900.

Congar, Yves M. J. *I Believe in the Holy Spirit.* Translated by David Smith. Vol. 1, *The Holy Spirit in the 'Economy'— Revelation and Experience of the Spirit.* New York: The Seabury Press, 1983.

De Fiores, Stefano, S.M.M. "Why It's Not the Right Time for a Dogma on Mary as Co-redemptrix." Interview by ZENIT, 31 October 2002. Available from http://www.zenit.org/english/visualizza.phtml?sid=26714. Internet.

Faricy, Robert, S.J. "The Blessed Virgin Mary in Vatican II: Twenty Years Later." *The Ecumenical Society of the Blessed Virgin Mary* 29 (1984).

Fries, Albert, C.Ss.R. *Die unter dem Namen des Albertus Magnus überlieferten mariologischen Schriften.* Beiträge zur Geschichte der Philosophie und Theologie des Mittelalters, Band XXXVII, Heft 4. Münster: Aschendorff, 1954.

Gambero, Luigi. *Mary and the Fathers of the Church: The Blessed Virgin Mary in Patristic Thought.* Translated by Thomas Buffer. San Francisco: Ignatius Press, 1999.

Hauke, Manfred. *Mary, "Mediatress of Grace"—Mary's Universal Mediation of Grace in the Theological and Pastoral Works of Cardinal Mercier.* New Bedford, MA: Academy of the Immaculate, 2004.

Komonchak, Joseph A., ed. *History of Vatican II.* Vol. 1, *Announcing and Preparing Vatican II—Toward a New Era in Catholicism.* Maryknoll, New York: Orbis Books, 1995, 167-356.

_____, ed. *History of Vatican II.* Vol. 2, *The Formation of the Council's Identity—First Period of Intercession: October 1962–1963.* Maryknoll, NY: Orbis Books, 1997.

_____, ed. *History of Vatican II.* Vol. 3, *The Mature Council—Second Period and Intercession: September 1963–September 1964.* Maryknoll, NY: Orbis Books, 2000.

_____, ed. *History of Vatican II.* Vol. 4, *Church as Communion—Third Period and Intercession: September 1964–September 1965.* Maryknoll, NY: Orbis Books, 2000.

_____. "Proposed Dogma: 'Mary: Co-Redemptrix, Media-trix, and Advocate.' Something to Consider Before You Sign." *The Tablet* (January 1998): Available from http://www.udayton. edu/Mary/respub/summer98.html. Internet.

_____. *A Short Treatise on the Blessed Virgin Mary*. Trans-lated by Charles Neumann, S.M. Washington, New Jersey: Ami Press, 1991.

L'Osservatore Romano English Edition (Rome). 25 June–2 July 1997.

Louis de Montfort, Saint. *True Devotion to Mary*. In *God Alone: The Collected Writings of St. Louis Marie de Montfort*. Bay Shore, NY: Montfort Publications, 1995, 289-397.

Manteau-Bonamy, H.M., O.P. *Immaculate Conception and the Holy Spirit*. Libertyville, IL: Franciscan Marytown Press, 1977.

The Marian Library/International Marian Research Institute. "Dia-logue on Coredemptrix, Mediatrix, Advocate." *Marian Library Newsletter* (28 January 1997): Available from http://www.uday-ton.edu/mary/news97/0128.html#Poland. Internet.

Messori, Vittorio with Joseph Ratzinger. *The Ratzinger Report*. Translated by Salvator Attanasio and Graham Harrison. San Francisco: Ignatius Press, 1985.

Miller, John D. *Marian Mediation: Is It True to Say that Mary Is Coredemptrix, Mediatrix of All Graces and Advocate?* New Bed-ford, MA: Academy of the Immaculate, 2004.

Miravalle, Mark I., ed. *"Contemporary Insights on a Fifth Marian Dogma—Mary Coredemptrix, Mediatrix, Advocate: Theologi-cal Foundations III*. Santa Barbara, CA: Queenship Publishing Company, 2000.

_____. "In Continued Dialogue With Czestochowa." Address presented at the International Symposium on Mar-ian coredemption *"Maria Mater Unitatis,"* Downside Abbey, Stratton-on-the-Fosse, England, 24 August 2002. Available from http://www.voxpopuli.org/czestochowa.pdf. Internet.

_____, ed. *Mary—Coredemptrix, Mediatrix, Advocate—Theological Foundations—Towards a Papal Definition?* Santa Barbara, CA: Queenship Publishing, 1995.

_____. "Response to a Statement of an International Theological Commission of the Pontifical International Marian Academy." 13 June 1997. Available from http://www.voxpopuli.org/response.php. Internet.

_____. "Why Now Is the Time For a Dogma of Mary Coredemptrix." Interview by ZENIT, 31 October 2002. Available from http://www.voxpopuli.org/zenit.php. Internet.

O'Carroll, Michael, C.S.Sp. *Theotokos: A Theological Encyclopedia of the Blessed Virgin Mary.* Wilmington: Michael Glazier, 1982.

Pontifical Faculty Marianum. "The Marianum's Position on the Dogmatic Definition." *Marian Library Newsletter* 38 (1999): 4.

The Raccolta. Edited by Joseph P. Christopher, Charles E. Spence, and John F. Rown. New York: Benziger Brothers, Inc., 1952.

Ratzinger, Joseph. Address to the Bishops of Chile Regarding the Lefebvre Schism. 13 July 1988. Available from http://www.unavoce.org/cardinal_ratzinger_chile.htm. Internet.

_____. "Communio: A Program." *Communio: International Catholic Review* 19 (Fall, 1992): 436-449.

Tavard, George H. *Council Daybook.* Washington D.C.: National Catholic Welfare Conference, 1965.

Tracey, Martin J. "St. Albert the Great and the Conception of Mary." Date unknown. Available from http://www.catholic.net/RCC/Periodicals/Dossier/0506- 96/Article5.html. Internet.

Other Works

The Holy Qur'ān: Arabic Text and English Translation. Translated by Maulawi Sher Ali. Tilford, Surrey: Islam International Publications Limited, 1997.

Works Consulted

Published Works of Venerable Fulton J. Sheen (Alphabetical Order)

Sheen, Fulton J. *Cor ad Cor Loquitur: Heart Speaks to Heart*. Dublin Retreat at All Hallows College Chapel, Drumcondra, Dublin, Ireland. Ministr-O-Media Inc., 1979. Audio cassette.

_____. *Life Is Worth Living*. New York: McGraw-Hill Book Company, 1953. Reprint, San Francisco: Ignatius Press, 1999.

Unpublished Works of Venerable Fulton J. Sheen (Alphabetical Order)

Sheen, Fulton J. "The Action of the Spirit on Men." Undated typescript (photocopy) within folder labeled "Holy Spirit." Archbishop Fulton J. Sheen Archives, Box 6, Catholic Diocese of Rochester, Rochester, New York.

_____. "The Acts of the Apostles and the Quahal." Undated typescript (photocopy) within folder labeled "Mystical Body." Archbishop Fulton J. Sheen Archives, Box 8, Catholic Diocese of Rochester, Rochester, New York.

_____. "All Merit Related to the Cross." Undated typescript (photocopy) within folder labeled "Mystical Body." Archbishop Fulton J. Sheen Archives, Box 8, Catholic Diocese of Rochester, Rochester, New York.

_____. "The Anointing of the Priest, Prophet and King in the Old Testament." Undated typescript (photocopy) within folder labeled "Mystical Body." Archbishop Fulton J. Sheen Archives, Box 8, Catholic Diocese of Rochester, Rochester, New York.

_____. "The Ascension." Undated typescript (photocopy) within folder labeled "Mystical Body." Archbishop Fulton J. Sheen Archives, Box 8, Catholic Diocese of Rochester, Rochester, New York.

_____. "The Ascension in Ephesians 4/8,9." Undated typescript (photocopy) within folder labeled "Mystical Body." Archbishop Fulton J. Sheen Archives, Box 8, Catholic Diocese of Rochester, Rochester, New York.

_____. "The Ascension in Relationship to the Threefold Office of Christ." Undated typescript (photocopy) within folder labeled "Mystical Body." Archbishop Fulton J. Sheen Archives, Box 8, Catholic Diocese of Rochester, Rochester, New York.

_____. "The Body of the Church." Undated typescript (photocopy) within folder labeled "Mystical Body." Archbishop Fulton J. Sheen Archives, Box 8, Catholic Diocese of Rochester, Rochester, New York.

_____. "The Body of the Physical Christ." Undated typescript (photocopy) within folder labeled "Mystical Body." Archbishop Fulton J. Sheen Archives, Box 8, Catholic Diocese of Rochester, Rochester, New York.

_____. "Breathing of the Holy Spirit." Undated typescript (photocopy) within folder labeled "Holy Spirit." Archbishop Fulton J. Sheen Archives, Box 6, Catholic Diocese of Rochester, Rochester, New York.

_____. "The Bride—the Church." Undated typescript (photocopy) within folder labeled "Mystical Body." Archbishop Fulton J. Sheen Archives, Box 8, Catholic Diocese of Rochester, Rochester, New York.

_____. "Bridegroom." Undated typescript (photocopy) within folder labeled "Mystical Body." Archbishop Fulton J. Sheen Archives, Box 8, Catholic Diocese of Rochester, Rochester, New York.

_____. "The Bridegroom." Undated typescript (photocopy) within folder labeled "Mystical Body." Archbishop Fulton J. Sheen Archives, Box 8, Catholic Diocese of Rochester, Rochester, New York.

_____. "Calvary and Pentecost." Undated typescript (photocopy) within folder labeled "Holy Spirit." Archbishop Fulton J. Sheen Archives, Box 6, Catholic Diocese of Rochester, Rochester, New York.

_____. "Cana and the Holy Spirit." Undated typescript (photocopy) within folder labeled "Holy Spirit." Archbishop Fulton J. Sheen Archives, Box 6, Catholic Diocese of Rochester, Rochester, New York.

_____. "The Catholicity of the Church." Undated typescript (photocopy) within folder labeled "Mystical Body." Archbishop Fulton J. Sheen Archives, Box 8, Catholic Diocese of Rochester, Rochester, New York.

_____. "Christ as Mediator." Undated typescript (photocopy) within folder labeled "Mystical Body." Archbishop Fulton J. Sheen Archives, Box 8, Catholic Diocese of Rochester, Rochester, New York.

_____. "Christ as Priest." Undated typescript (photocopy) within folder labeled "Mystical Body." Archbishop Fulton J. Sheen Archives, Box 8, Catholic Diocese of Rochester, Rochester, New York.

_____. "Christ Emptying Himself." Undated typescript (photocopy) within folder labeled "Mystical Body." Archbishop Fulton J. Sheen Archives, Box 8, Catholic Diocese of Rochester, Rochester, New York.

_____. "Christ the First-Born." Undated typescript (photocopy) within folder labeled "Mystical Body." Archbishop Fulton J. Sheen Archives, Box 8, Catholic Diocese of Rochester, Rochester, New York.

_____. "Christ the First Born of All Creatures." Undated typescript (photocopy) within folder labeled "Mystical Body." Archbishop Fulton J. Sheen Archives, Box 8, Catholic Diocese of Rochester, Rochester, New York.

_____. "Christ the Head of the Church." Undated typescript (photocopy) within folder labeled "Mystical Body." Archbishop Fulton J. Sheen Archives, Box 8, Catholic Diocese of Rochester, Rochester, New York.

_____. "Christ the Head of the Mystical Body." Undated typescript (photocopy) within folder labeled "Mystical Body." Archbishop Fulton J. Sheen Archives, Box 8, Catholic Diocese of Rochester, Rochester, New York.

_____. "Christ the Head of the Mystical Body (Colossians 2/19)." Undated typescript (photocopy) within folder labeled "Mystical Body." Archbishop Fulton J. Sheen Archives, Box 8, Catholic Diocese of Rochester, Rochester, New York.

_____. "Christ and the Holy Spirit." Undated typescript (photocopy) within folder labeled "Holy Spirit." Archbishop Fulton J. Sheen Archives, Box 6, Catholic Diocese of Rochester, Rochester, New York.

_____. "Christ's Human Pedigree in Relationship to the Old Quahal." Undated typescript (photocopy) within folder labeled "Mystical Body." Archbishop Fulton J. Sheen Archives, Box 8, Catholic Diocese of Rochester, Rochester, New York.

_____. "Christ Is the Head of the Church." Undated typescript (photocopy) within folder labeled "Mystical Body." Archbishop Fulton J. Sheen Archives, Box 8, Catholic Diocese of Rochester, Rochester, New York.

_____. "Christ the King." Undated typescript (photocopy) within folder labeled "Mystical Body." Archbishop Fulton J. Sheen Archives, Box 8, Catholic Diocese of Rochester, Rochester, New York.

_____. "Christ the King in Power." Undated typescript (photocopy) within folder labeled "Mystical Body." Archbishop Fulton J. Sheen Archives, Box 8, Catholic Diocese of Rochester, Rochester, New York.

_____. "Christ the Priest." Undated typescript (photocopy) within folder labeled "Mystical Body." Archbishop Fulton J. Sheen Archives, Box 8, Catholic Diocese of Rochester, Rochester, New York.

_____. "Christ the Priest (Journet)." Undated typescript (photocopy) within folder labeled "Mystical Body." Archbishop Fulton J. Sheen Archives, Box 8, Catholic Diocese of Rochester, Rochester, New York.

_____. "Christ the Priest, Prophet, and King." Undated typescript (photocopy) within folder labeled "Mystical Body." Archbishop Fulton J. Sheen Archives, Box 8, Catholic Diocese of Rochester, Rochester, New York.

_____. "Christ and the Quahal." Undated typescript (photocopy) within folder labeled "Mystical Body." Archbishop Fulton J. Sheen Archives, Box 8, Catholic Diocese of Rochester, Rochester, New York.

_____. "Christ the Rock (1 Corinthians 10/4)." Undated typescript (photocopy) within folder labeled "Mystical Body." Archbishop Fulton J. Sheen Archives, Box 8, Catholic Diocese of Rochester, Rochester, New York.

_____. "Christ the Spouse of Humanity." Undated typescript (photocopy) within folder labeled "Mystical Body." Archbishop Fulton J. Sheen Archives, Box 8, Catholic Diocese of Rochester, Rochester, New York.

_____. "Christ the Teacher." Undated typescript (photocopy) within folder labeled "Mystical Body." Archbishop Fulton J. Sheen Archives, Box 8, Catholic Diocese of Rochester, Rochester, New York.

_____. "Christ the Teacher or Prophet." Undated typescript (photocopy) within folder labeled "Mystical Body." Archbishop Fulton J. Sheen Archives, Box 8, Catholic Diocese of Rochester, Rochester, New York.

_____. "The Church and the Acts of the Apostles." Undated typescript (photocopy) within folder labeled "Mystical Body." Archbishop Fulton J. Sheen Archives, Box 8, Catholic Diocese of Rochester, Rochester, New York.

_____. "The Church and the Ascension." Undated typescript (photocopy) within folder labeled "Mystical Body." Archbishop Fulton J. Sheen Archives, Box 8, Catholic Diocese of Rochester, Rochester, New York.

_____. "The Church as Body and Spouse." Undated typescript (photocopy) within folder labeled "Mystical Body." Archbishop Fulton J. Sheen Archives, Box 8, Catholic Diocese of Rochester, Rochester, New York.

_____. "The Church as a City." Undated typescript (photocopy) within folder labeled "Mystical Body." Archbishop Fulton J. Sheen Archives, Box 8, Catholic Diocese of Rochester, Rochester, New York.

_____. "The Church Before Christ." Undated typescript (photocopy) within folder labeled "Mystical Body." Archbishop Fulton J. Sheen Archives, Box 8, Catholic Diocese of Rochester, Rochester, New York.

_____. "The Church the Bride of Christ." Undated typescript (photocopy) within folder labeled "Mystical Body." Archbishop Fulton J. Sheen Archives, Box 8, Catholic Diocese of Rochester, Rochester, New York.

_____. "The Church the Fulness of Christ (Journet)." Undated typescript (photocopy) within folder labeled "Mystical Body." Archbishop Fulton J. Sheen Archives, Box 8, Catholic Diocese of Rochester, Rochester, New York.

_____. "The Church Has the Fullness of Christ." Undated typescript (photocopy) within folder labeled "Mystical Body." Archbishop Fulton J. Sheen Archives, Box 8, Catholic Diocese of Rochester, Rochester, New York.

_____. "The Church Is the Body of Christ." Undated typescript (photocopy) within folder labeled "Mystical Body." Archbishop Fulton J. Sheen Archives, Box 8, Catholic Diocese of Rochester, Rochester, New York.

_____. "The Church's Kingdom." Undated typescript (photocopy) within folder labeled "Mystical Body." Archbishop Fulton J. Sheen Archives, Box 8, Catholic Diocese of Rochester, Rochester, New York.

_____. "The Church the Mystical Body (Christ, the Christian and the Church, Mascall)." Undated typescript (photocopy) within folder labeled "Mystical Body." Archbishop Fulton J. Sheen Archives, Box 8, Catholic Diocese of Rochester, Rochester, New York.

_____. "The Church and Other Religions." Undated typescript (photocopy) within folder labeled "Mystical Body." Archbishop Fulton J. Sheen Archives, Box 8, Catholic Diocese of Rochester, Rochester, New York.

_____. "The Church Teaches." Undated typescript (photocopy) within folder labeled "Mystical Body." Archbishop Fulton J. Sheen Archives, Box 8, Catholic Diocese of Rochester, Rochester, New York.

_____. "The Communication of Idioms." Undated typescript (photocopy) within folder labeled "Mystical Body." Archbishop Fulton J. Sheen Archives, Box 8, Catholic Diocese of Rochester, Rochester, New York.

_____. "The Correct Theology of the Mystical Body." Undated typescript (photocopy) within folder labeled "Mystical Body." Archbishop Fulton J. Sheen Archives, Box 8, Catholic Diocese of Rochester, Rochester, New York.

_____. "The Cross Summarizes the Earthly Life of Christ." Undated typescript (photocopy) within folder labeled "Mystical Body." Archbishop Fulton J. Sheen Archives, Box 8, Catholic Diocese of Rochester, Rochester, New York.

_____. "The Desire of the Spirit." Undated typescript (photocopy) within folder labeled "Mystical Body." Archbishop Fulton J. Sheen Archives, Box 8, Catholic Diocese of Rochester, Rochester, New York.

_____. "Did Our Lord Look Forward to the Continuation of the Quahal After His Death?" Undated typescript (photocopy) within folder labeled "Mystical Body." Archbishop Fulton J. Sheen Archives, Box 8, Catholic Diocese of Rochester, Rochester, New York.

_____. "Did the Power of Peter Extend After His Time?" Undated typescript (photocopy) within folder labeled "Mystical Body." Archbishop Fulton J. Sheen Archives, Box 8, Catholic Diocese of Rochester, Rochester, New York.

_____. "Did the Prophets of the Old Quahal Expect the Conversion of the Gentiles?" Undated typescript (photocopy) within folder labeled "Mystical Body." Archbishop Fulton J. Sheen Archives, Box 8, Catholic Diocese of Rochester, Rochester, New York.

_____. "Ecclesia and the Septuagint." Undated typescript (photocopy) within folder labeled "Mystical Body." Archbishop Fulton J. Sheen Archives, Box 8, Catholic Diocese of Rochester, Rochester, New York.

_____. "The Eucharist and the Mystical Body." Undated typescript (photocopy) within folder labeled "Mystical Body." Archbishop Fulton J. Sheen Archives, Box 8, Catholic Diocese of Rochester, Rochester, New York.

_____. "The Foundation of the Church." Undated typescript (photocopy) within folder labeled "Mystical Body." Archbishop Fulton J. Sheen Archives, Box 8, Catholic Diocese of Rochester, Rochester, New York.

_____. "The Fullness of the Holy Spirit." Undated typescript (photocopy) within folder labeled "Holy Spirit." Archbishop Fulton J. Sheen Archives, Box 6, Catholic Diocese of Rochester, Rochester, New York.

_____. "The Function of the Spirit in the Gospel of John." Undated typescript (photocopy) within folder labeled "Holy Spirit." Archbishop Fulton J. Sheen Archives, Box 6, Catholic Diocese of Rochester, Rochester, New York.

_____. "Good Friday—St. Aidans—Mass and the Mystical Body." Undated manuscript (photocopy). Archbishop Fulton J. Sheen Archives, Box 5, Catholic Diocese of Rochester, Rochester, New York.

_____. "Growth in Holiness." Undated typescript (photocopy) within folder labeled "Holy Spirit." Archbishop Fulton J. Sheen Archives, Box 6, Catholic Diocese of Rochester, Rochester, New York.

_____. "The Holy Spirit." Undated typescript (photocopy) within folder labeled "Holy Spirit." Archbishop Fulton J. Sheen Archives, Box 6, Catholic Diocese of Rochester, Rochester, New York.

_____. "The Holy Spirit and the Body of Christ." Undated typescript (photocopy) within folder labeled "Mystical Body." Archbishop Fulton J. Sheen Archives, Box 8, Catholic Diocese of Rochester, Rochester, New York.

_____. "The Holy Spirit and Conversion." Undated manuscript (photocopy) within folder labeled "Holy Spirit." Archbishop Fulton J. Sheen Archives, Box 6, Catholic Diocese of Rochester, Rochester, New York.

_____. "Holy Spirit Forming the Body of Christ." Undated manuscript (photocopy) within folder labeled "Holy Spirit." Archbishop Fulton J. Sheen Archives, Box 6, Catholic Diocese of Rochester, Rochester, New York.

_____. "The Holy Spirit Forming the Body of Christ in the Church." Undated typescript (photocopy) within folder labeled "Mystical Body." Archbishop Fulton J. Sheen Archives, Box 8, Catholic Diocese of Rochester, Rochester, New York.

_____. "The Holy Spirit and the Head of the Church." Undated typescript (photocopy) within folder labeled "Holy Spirit." Archbishop Fulton J. Sheen Archives, Box 6, Catholic Diocese of Rochester, Rochester, New York.

_____. "The Holy Spirit in the Church." Undated typescript (photocopy) within folder labeled "Holy Spirit." Archbishop Fulton J. Sheen Archives, Box 6, Catholic Diocese of Rochester, Rochester, New York.

_____. "The Holy Spirit in Relation to the Head and the Body." Undated typescript (photocopy) within folder labeled "Holy Spirit." Archbishop Fulton J. Sheen Archives, Box 6, Catholic Diocese of Rochester, Rochester, New York.

_____. "The Holy Spirit in Relation to Redemption." Undated typescript (photocopy) within folder labeled "Holy Spirit." Archbishop Fulton J. Sheen Archives, Box 6, Catholic Diocese of Rochester, Rochester, New York.

_____. "The Holy Spirit in the Son." Undated typescript (photocopy) within folder labeled "Holy Spirit." Archbishop Fulton J. Sheen Archives, Box 6, Catholic Diocese of Rochester, Rochester, New York.

_____. "The Holy Spirit and the Mass." Undated typescript (photocopy) within folder labeled "Mystical Body." Archbishop Fulton J. Sheen Archives, Box 8, Catholic Diocese of Rochester, Rochester, New York.

_____. "The 'Hour' in the Gospels." Undated typescript (photocopy) within folder labeled "Mystical Body." Archbishop Fulton J. Sheen Archives, Box 8, Catholic Diocese of Rochester, Rochester, New York.

_____. "How Christ is the Head of the Church." Undated typescript (photocopy) within folder labeled "Mystical Body." Archbishop Fulton J. Sheen Archives, Box 8, Catholic Diocese of Rochester, Rochester, New York.

_____. "How the Church Continues the Incarnation." Undated typescript (photocopy) within folder labeled "Mystical Body." Archbishop Fulton J. Sheen Archives, Box 8, Catholic Diocese of Rochester, Rochester, New York.

_____. "How Our Blessed Lord Was the Fulfillment in the Time of the Old Quahal." Undated typescript (photocopy) within folder labeled "Mystical Body." Archbishop Fulton J. Sheen Archives, Box 8, Catholic Diocese of Rochester, Rochester, New York.

_____. "How St. Paul Connects Up the Old and New Quahal." Undated typescript (photocopy) within folder labeled "Mystical Body." Archbishop Fulton J. Sheen Archives, Box 8, Catholic Diocese of Rochester, Rochester, New York.

_____. "The Human Nature the Instrument of the Divine." Undated typescript (photocopy) within folder labeled "Mystical Body." Archbishop Fulton J. Sheen Archives, Box 8, Catholic Diocese of Rochester, Rochester, New York.

_____. "The Imitation of Christ Through the Holy Spirit." Undated typescript (photocopy) within folder labeled "Holy Spirit." Archbishop Fulton J. Sheen Archives, Box 6, Catholic Diocese of Rochester, Rochester, New York.

_____. "Immaculate Conception." Undated manuscript (photocopy). Archbishop Fulton J. Sheen Archives, Box 7, Catholic Diocese of Rochester, Rochester, New York.

_____. "The Importance of the Spirit in the Church." Undated typescript (photocopy) within folder labeled "Holy Spirit." Archbishop Fulton J. Sheen Archives, Box 6, Catholic Diocese of Rochester, Rochester, New York.

_____. "Instrumentum Conjunctum." Undated typescript (photocopy) within folder labeled "Mystical Body." Archbishop Fulton J. Sheen Archives, Box 8, Catholic Diocese of Rochester, Rochester, New York.

_____. "Irish Retreat Conference." Undated manuscript (photocopy) of notes for Irish Retreat Conference. Archbishop Fulton J. Sheen Archives, Box 6, Catholic Diocese of Rochester, Rochester, New York.

_____. "The Manifestation of Glory Through the Spirit." Undated typescript (photocopy) within folder labeled "Holy Spirit." Archbishop Fulton J. Sheen Archives, Box 6, Catholic Diocese of Rochester, Rochester, New York.

_____. "The Marriage Feast of Cana." Undated typescript (photocopy) with some written notes within folder labeled "Mystical Body." Archbishop Fulton J. Sheen Archives, Box 8, Catholic Diocese of Rochester, Rochester, New York.

_____. "Mary and the Tabernacle." Undated typescript (photocopy) within folder labeled "Holy Spirit." Archbishop Fulton J. Sheen Archives, Box 7, Catholic Diocese of Rochester, Rochester, New York.

_____. "The Meaning of the Church." Undated typescript (photocopy) within folder labeled "Mystical Body." Archbishop Fulton J. Sheen Archives, Box 8, Catholic Diocese of Rochester, Rochester, New York.

_____. "The Missions of the Holy Spirit." Undated typescript (photocopy) within folder labeled "Mystical Body." Archbishop Fulton J. Sheen Archives, Box 8, Catholic Diocese of Rochester, Rochester, New York.

_____. "The Necessity of the Holy Spirit." Undated typescript (photocopy) within folder labeled "Holy Spirit." Archbishop Fulton J. Sheen Archives, Box 6, Catholic Diocese of Rochester, Rochester, New York.

_____. "New Quahal and the Old Quahal." Undated typescript (photocopy) within folder labeled "Mystical Body." Archbishop Fulton J. Sheen Archives, Box 8, Catholic Diocese of Rochester, Rochester, New York.

_____. "The Old and the New Covenant." Undated typescript (photocopy) within folder labeled "Mystical Body." Archbishop Fulton J. Sheen Archives, Box 8, Catholic Diocese of Rochester, Rochester, New York.

_____. "The Old Testament Quahal." Undated typescript (photocopy) within folder labeled "Mystical Body." Archbishop Fulton J. Sheen Archives, Box 8, Catholic Diocese of Rochester, Rochester, New York.

_____. "Our Blessed Lord and the Quahal of Israel." Undated typescript (photocopy) within folder labeled "Mystical Body." Archbishop Fulton J. Sheen Archives, Box 8, Catholic Diocese of Rochester, Rochester, New York.

_____. "Our Lord Expected the Quahal to Continue After His Death." Undated typescript (photocopy) within folder labeled "Mystical Body." Archbishop Fulton J. Sheen Archives, Box 8, Catholic Diocese of Rochester, Rochester, New York.

_____. "Our Lord's Teaching in the Synoptics About the Spirit." Undated typescript (photocopy) within folder labeled "Holy Spirit." Archbishop Fulton J. Sheen Archives, Box 6, Catholic Diocese of Rochester, Rochester, New York.

_____. "The Passion of Our Lord in Relation to the Holy Spirit." Undated typescript (photocopy) within folder labeled "Holy Spirit." Archbishop Fulton J. Sheen Archives, Box 6, Catholic Diocese of Rochester, Rochester, New York.

_____. "Pentecost." Undated typescript (photocopy) within folder labeled "Mystical Body." Archbishop Fulton J. Sheen Archives, Box 8, Catholic Diocese of Rochester, Rochester, New York.

_____. "Pentecost, Koinonia and Ecclesia." Undated typescript (photocopy) within folder labeled "Holy Spirit." Archbishop Fulton J. Sheen Archives, Box 6, Catholic Diocese of Rochester, Rochester, New York.

_____. "Peter After the Resurrection Returns to Fishing." Undated typescript (photocopy) within folder labeled "Mystical Body." Archbishop Fulton J. Sheen Archives, Box 8, Catholic Diocese of Rochester, Rochester, New York.

_____. "The Piercing with the Lance (John 19/34)." Undated typescript (photocopy) within folder labeled "Mystical Body." Archbishop Fulton J. Sheen Archives, Box 8, Catholic Diocese of Rochester, Rochester, New York.

_____. "Pleroma (Hastings Bible)." Undated typescript (photocopy) within folder labeled "Mystical Body." Archbishop Fulton J. Sheen Archives, Box 8, Catholic Diocese of Rochester, Rochester, New York.

_____. "The Priesthood of Christ Continued in Worship." Undated typescript (photocopy) within folder labeled "Mystical Body." Archbishop Fulton J. Sheen Archives, Box 8, Catholic Diocese of Rochester, Rochester, New York.

_____. "The Priesthood of the Church or Christ the Priest in the Church." Undated typescript (photocopy) within folder labeled "Mystical Body." Archbishop Fulton J. Sheen Archives, Box 8, Catholic Diocese of Rochester, Rochester, New York.

_____. "Priest's Retreat." Undated typescript (photocopy) within folder containing carbon copies of notes and dictation records for Retreat given at Los Angeles in June, 1965. Archbishop Fulton J. Sheen Archives, Box 9, Catholic Diocese of Rochester, Rochester, New York.

_____. "The Quahal of the Old Testament." Undated typescript (photocopy) within folder labeled "Mystical Body." Archbishop Fulton J. Sheen Archives, Box 8, Catholic Diocese of Rochester, Rochester, New York.

_____. "References to the Old Quahal in the Gospel." Undated typescript (photocopy) within folder labeled "Mystical Body." Archbishop Fulton J. Sheen Archives, Box 8, Catholic Diocese of Rochester, Rochester, New York.

_____. "The Relationship Between Sciences." Undated typescript (photocopy). Archbishop Fulton J. Sheen Archives, Box 9, Catholic Diocese of Rochester, Rochester, New York.

_____. "The Relationship Between the Two Covenants." Undated typescript (photocopy) within folder labeled "Mystical Body." Archbishop Fulton J. Sheen Archives, Box 8, Catholic Diocese of Rochester, Rochester, New York.

_____. "The Relationship of the Blessed Mother in the Church." Undated typescript (photocopy) within folder labeled "Mystical Body." Archbishop Fulton J. Sheen Archives, Box 8, Catholic Diocese of Rochester, Rochester, New York.

_____. "The Relationship of the Body to the Head." Undated typescript (photocopy) within folder labeled "Mystical Body." Archbishop Fulton J. Sheen Archives, Box 8, Catholic Diocese of Rochester, Rochester, New York.

_____. "The Relationship of Christ to the Spirit." Undated typescript (photocopy) within folder labeled "Mystical Body." Archbishop Fulton J. Sheen Archives, Box 8, Catholic Diocese of Rochester, Rochester, New York.

_____. "The Relationship of the Holy Spirit to Christ." Undated typescript (photocopy) within folder labeled "Mystical Body." Archbishop Fulton J. Sheen Archives, Box 8, Catholic Diocese of Rochester, Rochester, New York.

_____. "Remnant of Israel or Quahal." Undated typescript (photocopy) within folder labeled "Mystical Body." Archbishop Fulton J. Sheen Archives, Box 8, Catholic Diocese of Rochester, Rochester, New York.

_____. "The Restoration of Israel after the First Five Chapters of the Acts." Undated typescript (photocopy) within folder labeled "Mystical Body." Archbishop Fulton J. Sheen Archives, Box 8, Catholic Diocese of Rochester, Rochester, New York.

_____. "The Resurrection and the Church." Undated typescript (photocopy) within folder labeled "Mystical Body." Archbishop Fulton J. Sheen Archives, Box 8, Catholic Diocese of Rochester, Rochester, New York.

_____. "Sanctification by the Holy Spirit." Undated typescript (photocopy) within folder labeled "Mystical Body." Archbishop Fulton J. Sheen Archives, Box 8, Catholic Diocese of Rochester, Rochester, New York.

_____. "The Shepherd and the Flock." Undated typescript (photocopy) within folder labeled "Mystical Body." Archbishop Fulton J. Sheen Archives, Box 8, Catholic Diocese of Rochester, Rochester, New York.

_____. "The Spirit and the Paraclete." Undated typescript (photocopy) within folder labeled "Holy Spirit." Archbishop Fulton J. Sheen Archives, Box 6, Catholic Diocese of Rochester, Rochester, New York.

_____. "The Spirit of Truth." Undated typescript (photocopy) within folder labeled "Mystical Body." Archbishop Fulton J. Sheen Archives, Box 8, Catholic Diocese of Rochester, Rochester, New York.

_____. "The Teaching Office of the Church." Undated typescript (photocopy) within folder labeled "Mystical Body." Archbishop Fulton J. Sheen Archives, Box 8, Catholic Diocese of Rochester, Rochester, New York.

_____. "Theandric Actions or Instrumentum Conjunctum." Undated typescript (photocopy) within folder labeled "Mystical Body." Archbishop Fulton J. Sheen Archives, Box 8, Catholic Diocese of Rochester, Rochester, New York.

_____. "The Three Anointings in the Old Testament." Undated typescript (photocopy) within folder labeled "Mystical Body." Archbishop Fulton J. Sheen Archives, Box 8, Catholic Diocese of Rochester, Rochester, New York.

_____. "The Three Gifts—Gold, Frankincense and Myrrh." Undated typescript (photocopy) within folder labeled "Mystical Body." Archbishop Fulton J. Sheen Archives, Box 8, Catholic Diocese of Rochester, Rochester, New York.

_____. "Three Ways of Knowing Christ and the Church." Undated typescript (photocopy) within folder labeled "Mystical Body." Archbishop Fulton J. Sheen Archives, Box 8, Catholic Diocese of Rochester, Rochester, New York.

_____. "The Threefold Body of Christ." Undated typescript (photocopy) within folder labeled "Mystical Body." Archbishop Fulton J. Sheen Archives, Box 8, Catholic Diocese of Rochester, Rochester, New York.

_____. "The True Feminine Mystique." Undated typescript (photocopy) within folder labeled "Scattered Notes 1964–1965." Archbishop Fulton J. Sheen Archives, Box 10, Catholic Diocese of Rochester, Rochester, New York.

_____. "Two Kinds of Sanctification by the Holy Spirit." Undated typescript (photocopy) within folder labeled "Holy Spirit." Archbishop Fulton J. Sheen Archives, Box 6, Catholic Diocese of Rochester, Rochester, New York.

_____. "Two Missions of the Spirit." Undated typescript (photocopy) within folder labeled "Holy Spirit." Archbishop Fulton J. Sheen Archives, Box 6, Catholic Diocese of Rochester, Rochester, New York.

_____. "The Unity of Christ and His Church As Revealed in the Gospel of John." Undated typescript (photocopy) within folder labeled "Mystical Body." Archbishop Fulton J. Sheen Archives, Box 8, Catholic Diocese of Rochester, Rochester, New York.

_____. Untitled and undated manuscript (photocopy) on the subject of the Church. Archbishop Fulton J. Sheen Archives, Box 1, Catholic Diocese of Rochester, Rochester, New York.

_____. "Vine and Branches." Undated typescript (photocopy) within folder labeled "Mystical Body." Archbishop Fulton J. Sheen Archives, Box 8, Catholic Diocese of Rochester, Rochester, New York.

_____. "Vine and Branches (Journet)." Undated typescript (photocopy) within folder labeled "Mystical Body." Archbishop Fulton J. Sheen Archives, Box 8, Catholic Diocese of Rochester, Rochester, New York.

_____. "The Visit of the Magi." Undated typescript (photocopy) within folder labeled "Mystical Body." Archbishop Fulton J. Sheen Archives, Box 8, Catholic Diocese of Rochester, Rochester, New York.

_____. "The Visit of Pope John Paul II." Undated typescript (photocopy). Archbishop Fulton J. Sheen Archives, Box 11, Catholic Diocese of Rochester, Rochester, New York.

_____. "The Way the Holy Spirit Is Used." Undated typescript (photocopy) within folder labeled "Holy Spirit." Archbishop Fulton J. Sheen Archives, Box 6, Catholic Diocese of Rochester, Rochester, New York.

_____. "Were the Apostles Members of the Ecclesia?" Undated typescript (photocopy) within folder labeled "Mystical Body." Archbishop Fulton J. Sheen Archives, Box 8, Catholic Diocese of Rochester, Rochester, New York.

_____. "What Grace Does When It Enters the Soul." Undated typescript (photocopy) within folder labeled "Mystical Body." Archbishop Fulton J. Sheen Archives, Box 8, Catholic Diocese of Rochester, Rochester, New York.

_____. "What Happened at Pentecost." Undated typescript (photocopy) within folder labeled "Holy Spirit." Archbishop Fulton J. Sheen Archives, Box 6, Catholic Diocese of Rochester, Rochester, New York.

_____. "Who Are Members of the Church?" Undated typescript (photocopy) within folder labeled "Mystical Body." Archbishop Fulton J. Sheen Archives, Box 8, Catholic Diocese of Rochester, Rochester, New York.

_____. "Woman." Undated typescript (photocopy) sent to preparatory commission of Vatican II. Archbishop Fulton J. Sheen Archives, Box 11, Catholic Diocese of Rochester, Rochester, New York.

_____. "Womanhood." Typescript (photocopy) for article apparently prepared for Loretta Young to submit to "Womanhood" magazine dated 28 February 1966 and 17 August 1966. Archbishop Fulton J. Sheen Archives, Box 11, Catholic Diocese of Rochester, Rochester, New York.

_____. "The Word Church." Undated typescript (photocopy) within folder labeled "Mystical Body." Archbishop Fulton J. Sheen Archives, Box 8, Catholic Diocese of Rochester, Rochester, New York.

_____. "The Word Was Made Flesh (John 1/14)." Undated typescript (photocopy) within folder labeled "Mystical Body." Archbishop Fulton J. Sheen Archives, Box 8, Catholic Diocese of Rochester, Rochester, New York.

Works of the Magisterium (Alphabetical Order)

Leo XIII. Encyclical *Adiutricem Populi* (5 September 1895). In *Acta Sanctæ Sedis* 28 (1895–1896), 129-136.

_____. Encyclical *Octobri Mense Adventante* (22 September 1891). In *Acta Sanctæ Sedis* (1891–1892), 193-203.

_____. Encyclical *Superiore Anno* (30 August 1884). In *Acta Sanctæ Sedis* 17 (1884), 49-51.

_____. Encyclical *Supremi Apostolatus* (1 September 1883). In *Acta Sanctæ Sedis* 16 (1883), 113-118.

Pius IX. Apostolic Constitution *Ineffabilis Deus* (8 December 1854). In *Pii IX Pontificis Maximi Acta*. Graz, Austria: Akademische Druck- u. Verlagsanstalt, 1971, 610-618.

Pius XI. Apostolic Letter *Cognitum Sane* (2 March 1922). In *Acta Apostolicæ Sedis* 24 (1932), 213-214.

_____. Apostolic Letter *Galliam Ecclesiae Filiam* (2 March 1922). In *Acta Apostolicæ Sedis* 14 (1922), 185-187.

_____. Encyclical *Caritate Christi Compulsi* (3 May 1932). In *Acta Apostolicæ Sedis* 24 (1932), 177-194.

Pius XII. Encyclical *Ad Caeli Reginam* (11 October 1954). In *Acta Apostolicæ Sedis* 46 (1954), 625-640.

_____. Radio Message "Bendito Seja O Senhor" (13 May 1946). In *Acta Apostolicæ Sedis* 38 (1946), 264-267.

Liturgical Texts

Collection of Masses of the Blessed Virgin Mary. 2 Vols. New York: Catholic Book Publishing Co., 1988.

Theological Works (Alphabetical Order)

Arellano, Joaquín Ferrer. "Marian Coredemption in the Light of Christian Philosophy." In *Mary at the Foot of the Cross–II: Acts of the Second International Symposium on Marian Coredemption*. New Bedford, Massachusetts: Franciscans of the Immaculate, 2002, 113-149.

Aumann, Jordan. *Christian Spirituality in the Catholic Tradition*. San Francisco: Ignatius Press, 1985.

Calkins, Arthur B. "Mary as Coredemptrix, Mediatrix and Advocate in the Contemporary, Roman Liturgy." In *Mary—Coredemptrix, Mediatrix, Advocate—Theological Foundations—Towards a Papal Definition?* Edited by Mark I. Miravalle. Santa Barbara, CA: Queenship Publishing, 1995, 45-118.

_____. *Totus Tuus: John Paul II's Program of Marian Consecration and Entrustment*. Libertyville, Illinois: Academy of the Immaculate, 1992.

_____. *Totus Tuus: Il Magistero Mariano di Giovanni Paolo II*. Siena: Edizioni Cantagalli, 2006.

Cole, William J., S.M. "Mary at the Council and Reunion." *Marian Reprint* 101-102 (1963): 9-14.

Congar, Yves M.J. *Christ, Our Lady and the Church—A Study in Eirenic Theology*. Translated by Henry St. John, O.P. Westminster, Maryland: The Newman Press, 1957.

De Lastic, Alan. *Mary and the Church According to Pope Leo XIII*. New Delhi: Mayur Enterprises, 1992.

Friethoff, C.X.J.M., O.P. *A Complete Mariology*. Westminster, Maryland: Newman Press, 1958.

Fumagalli, Vittorio, I.M.C. *I Fondamenti della dispensazione mariana di tutte le grazie nell' insegnamento di San Pio X*. Alexandria: Rosignano Monf., 1966.

Garrigou-Lagrange, Reginald, O.P. *The Mother of the Saviour and Our Interior Life*. Translated by Bernard J. Kelly, C.S.Sp. Rockford, Illinois: Tan Books and Publishers, Inc., 1993.

Graef, Hilda. *Mary: A History of Doctrine and Devotion, Volume I: From the Beginnings to the Eve of the Reformation*. New York: Sheed and Ward, 1963.

_____. "Our Lady and the Church." In *Vatican II: The Church Constitution: Texts and Commentaries*. Edited by Austin Flannery, O.P. Dublin: Scepter Books, 1966, 177-184.

Haffert, John M. *Meet the Witnesses of the Miracle of the Sun*. Spring Grove, PA: The American Society for the Defense of Tradition, Family and Property, 2006.

John Damascene, Saint. *Homilia II in Dormitionem B.V. Mariae*. PG 96, 721-754.

Journet, Charles. *The Theology of the Church*. San Francisco: Ignatius Press, 2004.

Kelleher, James R., S.O.L.T. *Pope John Paul II's Theology of the Virgin Mary's Maternal Mediation.* S.T.D. diss., Pontifical University of St. Thomas Aquinas, 1998.

Laurentin, René. "The Blessed Virgin at the Council." *Marian Reprint* 109 (1964).

Livius, Thomas. *The Blessed Virgin of the First Six Centuries.* London: Burns and Oates, 1893.

Manelli, Stefano Maria, F.I. "Pope St. Pius X and Marian Coredemption." Available from http://motherofallpeoples.com/index.php?option=com_content&task=view&id=438&Itemid=40. Internet.

Meo, Salvatore, O.S.M. "Mediatrice." In *Nuovo Dizionario di Mariologia.* Edited by Stefano De Fiores, S.M.M., and Salvatore Meo, O.S.M. Milan: Edizione San Paulo, 1986, 827-841.

Mersch, Emil, S.J. *The Theology of the Mystical Body.* New York: B. Herder Book Co., 1951.

Miravalle, Mark I. *Introduction to Mary.* Santa Barbara, California: Queenship Publishing Company, 1993.

Mitchell, Valentine Albert, S.M. *The Mariology of St. John Damascene.* Kirkwood, Missouri: Maryhurst Normal Press, 1930.

Most, William G. *Vatican II—Marian Council.* Athlone, Ireland: St. Paul Publications, 1972.

Nau, Louis J. *Mary, Mediatrix of All Graces For All Men.* New York: Frederick Pustet Co., Inc., 1928.

Neubert, Emil, S.M. *Mary in Doctrine.* Milwaukee: The Bruce Publishing Company, 1954.

Neumann, Charles W., S.M. "Mary and the Church: *Lumen Gentium*, Articles 60 to 65." *Marian Studies* 37 (1986): 96-142.

O'Connell, Raphael V., S.J. *Our Lady: Mediatrix of all Graces.* Baltimore: Metropolitan Press of John Murphy Company, 1926.

Palmer, Paul F., S.J. *Mary in the Documents of the Church.* Westminster, Maryland: The Newman Press, 1952.

Pelikan, Jaroslav. *The Christian Tradition, Volume 3: The Growth of Medieval Theology (600–1300)*. Chicago: University of Chicago Press, 1978.

_____. *Mary Through the Centuries: Her Place in the History of Culture*. New Haven: Yale University Press, 1996.

Phan Nam, Joseph M., C.M.C. *The Biblical Sources of Pope John Paul II's Teaching on Mary's Mediation*. S.T.D. diss., Pontifical Urban University, 1995.

Philippe, Marie-Dominique, O.P. *Mystery of Mary: Mary, Model of the Growth of Christian Life*. Translated by André Faure-Beaulieu. Laredo, Texas: Congregation of St. John, 1958.

Rahner, Hugo, S.J. *Our Lady and the Church*. Translated by Sebastian Bullough, O.P. Bethesda, Maryland: Zaccheus Press, 2004.

Robichaud, Armand J., S.M. "Mary, Dispensatrix of All Graces." In *Mariology*. Edited by Juniper B. Carol, O.F.M. Vol. 2. Milwaukee: The Bruce Publishing Company, 1957, 426-460.

Thomas Aquinas, Saint. *Commentary on the Gospel of St. John*. Translated by James A. Weisheipl, O.P. Albany, New York: Magi Books, 1980.

ABOUT THE AUTHOR

Dr. Peter Howard is married to his wife, Chantal, and has four children. He is a national speaker and currently serves as a pro- fessor of Theology at the Avila Institute for Spiritual Formation Graduate Program and School of Spiritual Formation. He served on the advisory board for the Archbishop Fulton Sheen Foundation, and he is the founder and president of The Fulton Sheen Society and director of The Catholic Hour grassroots movement (**TheCatholicHour.org**). Through The Catholic Hour, Peter founded a media apostolate dedicated to the New Evangelization called **MEDIAtrix.tv**.

In addition to hosting a Catholic television program "The Catholic Hour" in Aspen, Colorado, Peter has served the Church in various capacities from working for a Metropolitan Tribunal to serving as the director of communications, theological consultant, and executive assistant to Bishop Michael Sheridan in Colorado Springs. Peter also worked as Director of Evangelization and Adult Faith formation at St. Mary Catholic Church in Aspen, Colorado, during which time he completed his Doctorate in Sacred Theology (S.T.D.) from the Pontifical University of St. Thomas Aquinas [Angelicum] in Rome, Italy. Dr. Howard's theological expertise lies in Mariology—especially that of Venerable Fulton J. Sheen.

Peter is passionate about communicating the truth and beauty of the Catholic faith as the answer to the challenges and errors of the world. If you would like Dr. Howard to speak at your event, you can contact him at invite@thecatholichour.org.

About Leonine Publishers

Leonine Publishers LLC makes fine Catholic literature available to Catholics throughout the English-speaking world. Leonine Publishers offers an innovative "hybrid" approach to book publication that helps authors as well as readers. Please visit our web site at www.leoninepublishers.com to learn more about us. Browse our online bookstore to find more solid Catholic titles to uplift, challenge, and inspire.

Our patron and namesake is Pope Leo XIII, a prudent, yet uncompromising pope during the stormy years at the close of the 19th century. Please join us as we ask his intercession for our family of readers and authors.

Do you have a book inside you? Visit our web site today. Leonine Publishers accepts manuscripts from Catholic authors like you. If your book is selected for publication, you will have an active part in the production process. This book is an example of our growing selection of literature for the busy Catholic reader of the 21st century.

www.leoninepublishers.com

CPSIA information can be obtained
at www.ICGtesting.com
Printed in the USA
FFHW02n1726111018
48775692-52880FF